A Historical Commentary on Thucydides

# A Historical Commentary on Thucydides

## *A Companion to Rex Warner's Penguin Translation*

David Cartwright

*Ann Arbor*

THE UNIVERSITY OF MICHIGAN PRESS

Published in the United States of America by
The University of Michigan Press
Manufactured in the United States of America
⊗ Printed on acid-free paper

2011 2010 2009 2008 6 5 4 3



*A CIP catalog record for this book is available from the British Library.*

Library of Congress Cataloging-in-Publication Data

Cartwright, David, 1950–
A historical commentary on Thucydides : a companion to Rex Warner's Penguin translation / David Cartwright.
p. cm.
Includes bibliographical references and index.
ISBN 0-472-10695-3 (alk. paper) — ISBN 0-472-08419-4 (pbk.)
1. Thucydides. History of the Peloponnesian War. I. Warner, Rex, 1905– . II. Title.
DF229.T6C37 1997
938'.05—dc20 96-45789
CIP



ISBN 978-0-472-10695-0 (alk. paper)
ISBN 978-0-472-08419-7 (pbk.)

# Preface

This book is designed, first, for those coming to Thucydides for the first time, to help them find their way around his complex narrative, and, second, to offer at least a starting point for students who wish to pursue in greater depth issues raised in his work. Readers already familiar with Thucydides will immediately recognize my debt to the major English commentaries by Gomme, Andrewes, Dover, and, more recently, Simon Hornblower and P.J. Rhodes. On a more personal level I owe much to pupils and colleagues at four schools at which I have taught: Repton School, Ascham and Cranbrook Schools in Sydney, and Dulwich College. I am also indebted to friends at Dulwich who have struggled to teach me the rudiments of word processing. Had it not been for their generous assistance this volume would never have seen the light of day. Finally, I must thank my wife for her support and patience and my parents, who did me the great service of urging me in the direction of Greek when I, with the naïveté of youth, had other ideas in mind.

# Contents


| | |
|---|---|
| Abbreviations | *ix* |
| Introduction | *1* |
| Book One | *9* |
| Book Two | *91* |
| Book Three | *133* |
| Book Four | *169* |
| Book Five | *199* |
| Book Six | *227* |
| Book Seven | *253* |
| Book Eight | *271* |
| Glossary | *305* |
| Select Bibliography | *307* |
| Index of Places and People | *309* |
| Maps | *following page 148* |

# Abbreviations

## Modern Articles and Books

| | |
|---|---|
| *A.E.* | Hornblower, S. and M.C. Greenstock, eds. *The Athenian Empire.* 3d ed. LACTOR (London Association of Classical Teachers Original Records) No. 1. London: London Association of Classical Teachers, 1984. |
| Bury and Meiggs 1975 | Bury, J.B., and R. Meiggs. *A History of Greece to the Death of Alexander.* 4th ed. London: Macmillan; New York: St. Martin's Press, 1975. |
| *C.A.* | Sabben-Clare, J.P., and M.S. Warman, eds. *The Culture of Athens.* LACTOR (London Association of Classical Teachers Original Records) No. 12. London: London Association of Classical Teachers, 1978. |
| Connor 1971 | Connor, W.R. *The New Politicians of Fifth-Century Athens.* Princeton: Princeton University Press, 1971. Reprint, Indianapolis: Hackett, 1992. |
| Connor 1984 | Connor, W.R. *Thucydides.* Princeton: Princeton University Press, 1984. |
| de Ste. Croix 1954/55 | de Ste. Croix, G.E.M. "The Character of the Athenian Empire." *Historia* 3 (1954/55): 1–41. |
| de Ste. Croix 1972 | de Ste. Croix, G.E.M. *The Origins of the Peloponnesian War.* London: Duckworth, 1972. |

| | |
|---|---|
| Dover 1978 | Dover, K.J. *Greek Homosexuality.* London: Duckworth, 1978. |
| Edmunds 1975 | Edmunds, L. *Chance and Intelligence in Thucydides.* Cambridge: Harvard University Press, 1975. |
| Forrest 1980 | Forrest, W.G. *A History of Sparta 950–192 B.C.* 2d ed. London: Duckworth, 1980. |
| Graham 1964 | Graham, A.J. *Colony and Mother-City in Ancient Greece.* Manchester: Manchester University Press, 1964. |
| Griffin 1982 | Griffin, A. *Sikyon.* Oxford: Oxford University Press, 1982. |
| Grundy 1948 | Grundy, G.B. *Thucydides and the History of His Age.* Oxford: Blackwell, 1948. |
| Hammond 1967 | Hammond, N.G.L. *Epirus.* Oxford: Oxford University Press, 1967. |
| Hammond and Griffith 1972–79 | Hammond, N.G.L., and G.T. Griffith. *A History of Macedonia.* Oxford: Oxford University Press, 1972–79. |
| Hansen 1981 | Hansen, M.H. "The Number of Athenian Hoplites in 431 B.C." *Symbolae Osloenses* 56 (1981): 19ff. |
| *H.C.T.* | Gomme, A.W., A. Andrewes, and K.J. Dover. *A Historical Commentary on Thucydides.* 5 vols. Oxford: Oxford University Press. 1945–81. |
| Hornblower 1987 | Hornblower, S. *Thucydides.* London: Duckworth, 1987. |
| Hornblower 1991 | Hornblower, S. *A Commentary on Thucydides.* Vol. 1, *Books I–III.* Oxford: Oxford University Press, 1991. |
| Kagan 1969 | Kagan, D. *The Outbreak of the Peloponnesian War.* Ithaca: Cornell University Press, 1969. |
| Kagan 1987 | Kagan, D. *The Fall of the Athenian Empire.* Ithaca: Cornell University Press, 1987. |
| Kerferd 1981 | Kerferd, G.B. *The Sophistic Movement.* Cambridge: Cambridge University Press, 1981. |

| | |
|---|---|
| Macleod 1983 | Macleod, C.W. *Collected Essays.* Oxford: Oxford University Press, 1983. |
| Meiggs 1972 | Meiggs, R. *The Athenian Empire.* Oxford: Oxford University Press, 1972. |
| M.L. | Meiggs, R., and D.M. Lewis. *A Selection of Greek Historical Inscriptions to the End of the Fifth Century* B.C. Oxford: Oxford University Press, 1969. |
| Morrison and Coates 1986 | Morrison, J.S., and J.F. Coates. *The Athenian Trireme: The History and Reconstruction of an Ancient Greek Warship.* Cambridge: Cambridge University Press, 1986. |
| North 1966 | North, H. *Sophrosyne: Self- Knowledge and Self-Restraint in Greek Literature.* Ithaca: Cornell University Press, 1966. |
| Parry 1981 | Parry, A.M. *Logos and Ergon in Thucydides.* New York: Ayer, 1981. |
| Powell 1988 | Powell, A. *Athens and Sparta: Constructing Greek Political and Social History from 478* B.C. London: Routledge, 1988. |
| Rhodes 1972 | Rhodes, P.J. *The Athenian Boule.* Oxford: Oxford University Press, 1972. |
| Rhodes 1981 | Rhodes, P.J. *A Commentary on the Aristotelian* Athenaion Politeia. Oxford: Oxford University Press, 1981. |
| Rhodes 1985 | Rhodes, P.J. *The Athenian Empire.* Greece and Rome: New Surveys in the Classics, no. 17. Oxford: Oxford University Press, 1985. |
| Rhodes 1988 | Rhodes, P.J. *Thucydides, History II.* Warminster: Aris and Phillips, 1988. |
| *T.D.G.R.* | Fornara, C.W., ed. *Translated Documents of Greece and Rome.* Vol. 1, *Archaic Times to the End of the Peloponnesian War.* 2d ed. Cambridge: Cambridge University Press, 1983. |
| Tod 1946 | Tod, M.N. *A Selection of Greek Historical Inscriptions.* Vol. 1. *To the End of the Fifth Century* B.C. 2d ed. Oxford: Oxford University Press 1946. |

| | |
|---|---|
| Westlake 1969 | Westlake, H.D. *Essays on the Greek Historians and Greek History.* Manchester: Manchester University Press, 1969. |
| Wilson 1979 | Wilson, J. *Pylos 425 B.C.: A Historical and Topographical Study of Thucydides' Account of the Campaign.* Warminster: Aris and Phillips, 1979. |
| Ziolkowski 1981 | Ziolkowski, J.E. *Thucydides and the Tradition of Funeral Speeches at Athens.* New York: Arno, 1981. |

## Classical Authors and Their Works

| | |
|---|---|
| Aristophanes | |
| *Lysis.* | *Lysistrata* |
| Aristotle | |
| *Ath. Pol.* | *Athenaion Politeia* (Constitution of the Athenians) |
| Hdt. | Herodotus |
| Plut. | Plutarch |
| *Arist.* | *Aristides* |
| *Per.* | *Pericles* |
| *Them.* | *Themistocles* |
| Th. | Thucydides |

All unidentified references are to Thucydides. All dates are B.C. unless otherwise stated.

# Introduction

## The Life of Thucydides

Thucydides, the Athenian historian, records that he lived through the whole of the Peloponnesian War and was "of an age to understand what was happening" (V.26). How old do these words suggest he might have been in 431? Twenty? Twenty-five? He could not have been too much older than that if, as this claim suggests, he is defending himself against a charge of immaturity. The same chapter also tells us that he was *strategos* (general) in 424. This position was important, more important than that of juryman or councillor, offices for which the minimum age was thirty. If the same age qualification applied to the generalship, then Thucydides was perhaps a little over thirty in 424 and thus was born in the early to mid-450s.

References to himself are rare in Thucydides' work. In IV.104–7 we learn that his father was called Olorus, a unusual Thracian name, favored by the Thracian royal family, and that Thucydides had the right to work gold mines in Thrace and had great influence with the inhabitants of that area. These chapters also recount his only known participation in the Peloponnesian War—a failure, which resulted in his banishment from Athens for twenty years (V.26). Of his political career we know no more; indeed, apart from the fact that he suffered from the great plague that fell on Athens in 430, this is all we can glean about Thucydides' life from his writings.

For further information on his life we must turn to Plutarch's *Life of Cimon* (chap. 4) and the ancient biography of Thucydides written by one Marcellinus, probably in the fourth century A.D. Here we discover that Thucydides was linked by blood with the family of the Athenian general Cimon, whose mother was the daughter of a Thracian king, another Olorus. It was common practice in those times to name grandsons after grandfathers, and it is thus possible that this Thracian king was the grandfather of Thucydides' father. Whatever the precise family connections, it is certain that Thucydides' background was affluent and aristocratic.

Where he spent his exile we do not know, though there are hints in his work that he traveled widely. His banishment came to an end in 404/3. Marcellinus states that he was in his fifties when he died. As he lived through the whole of the war, we must put his death at about 400.

Thucydides lived, then, in a period that saw the peak of Athenian military might, political self-confidence, and cultural development. Above all, the 440s and the 430s were the heyday of the Athenian empire, an exercise in power unprecedented in Greek history. The war that brought this empire to an end was the subject of Thucydides' lifework.

## The Intellectual Background of Thucydides

Greek literature begins with the great epic poems of Homer, and for centuries the *Iliad,* a tale of human courage and suffering centered on a great war, was the nearest thing the Greeks had to history. Even the skeptical Thucydides accepted without question the historicity of Homer's major characters and the essentials of the story of the *Iliad.* Indeed he himself chose a great war as his subject and defined its greatness in terms of the suffering it caused.

But another essential feature of Homer's poems finds no counterpart in the writings of Thucydides: the divine powers who exercised such a great influence on human affairs. Thucydides was not the first to reject this vision of a world controlled by gods. In the sixth century intellectuals who lived in Greek states of Ionia (the eastern seaboard of the Aegean) had started to question traditional religious beliefs and to look for explanations of the world around them that were based on empirical evidence rather than on superstition or faith. They were the first Western philosophers and scientists; among them too were the earliest prose writers.

The writing of "history" (we have little choice but to use modern terminology, but we must be conscious that our standards and aims—in themselves far from universally agreed—are very different from those of the ancients) was still some way off. The Greek word *historia* predates Thucydides, but it meant no more than "inquiries" or "researches"; its scope was virtually unlimited. Early writers who showed an interest in the past included in their work material that we might put in such categories as geography, anthropology, ethnography, folklore, or myth. The fifth century saw the rise of local "historians" who, in researching the past of individual cities, attempted to apply more rational methods and to establish a basis of chronology, but they often failed to distinguish fact from fiction.

The great leap forward seems to have come with the Ionian Herodotus, who was born in the early years of the fifth century and probably died in the 420s. Homer's influence on him is clear enough: he chose a grand theme, the

Persian Wars and the Greek struggle for freedom, and acknowledged the possibility of divine intervention in human affairs. But there are signs of historiographical progress: he showed an awareness of the importance of causation in historical explanation and an alertness to the need for evidence that he personally was in a position to evaluate. His opening sentence declares that his scope was broad, "the astonishing achievements both of our own and of other peoples," but he added a qualification, "more particularly, to show how they came into conflict," imposing a structure, a chronological framework, and an overall purpose on his wide-ranging early books. His focus narrows in the latter part of his work, which is devoted to the Persian Wars themselves. The result is a rounded picture of the Greek and barbarian worlds, a skillfully organized work of vast intellectual curiosity and some moral fervor, informative, entertaining, and instructive. For Thucydides it may still have lacked sharpness of focus, and the intrusion of gods into human affairs would have been unacceptable to him, but he knew his Herodotus well, and there is anecdotal evidence that he was impressed by it. He would have seen Herodotus' achievement as a huge step in the right direction.

Thucydides was the product not only of a long literary tradition but also of a highly intellectual age, in which writers and thinkers in science, medicine, philosophy, and the dramatic arts were engaged in a radical reexamination of traditional beliefs, the climax of the Ionian movement already mentioned. Attempts have been made to establish Thucydides' relationships with contemporary thinkers, in particular with the tragedians, with whom he shared a tragic view of life, and the Sophists, those men of ideas who made Athens the intellectual center of Greece in the late fifth century. In the case of the latter our understanding is limited by the fragmentary nature of the sources, but we can discern connections: for instance, they share with Thucydides an interest in the nature of power politics and in rhetoric. Unfortunately the obscurity in which Thucydides' relationships with these fellow intellectuals are shrouded prevents us from assessing his originality as a thinker. Let us turn to his contribution to the writing of history.

## The Aims and Methods of Thucydides

Thucydides' opening chapters demonstrate an appreciation of the importance of factual accuracy based on verifiable evidence. This concern for truth and the occurrence in his lifetime of a suitable theme, a war of unprecedented magnitude, combined to suggest a departure from previous practice: the choice of a contemporary subject.

As for his researches, Thucydides tells us little about his sources and methods. Where possible he relied on his own observations and made some use of original documents. He was aware that "different eyewitnesses give different accounts of the same event" and that information transmitted by word of mouth easily becomes distorted through prejudice, carelessness, or forgetfulness. Thus, he tells us, he always checked secondhand information as thoroughly as possible (I.22). He was on occasions critical of the accuracy of fellow writers (I.21; cf. I.97) and of those who casually accepted tradition (I.20). On occasion he reports that his evidence is incomplete (e.g., I.1), and if he has been unable to verify something to his satisfaction he will sometimes add "it is said" or "as is said" (e.g., II.48, 98).

But factual accuracy was a means to an end. A historian's belief in his or her particular interpretation of events is what prompts him or her to write, and Thucydides was an interpreter as well as a reporter of information. He did not see "history" as straightforward record of fact, a source of amusement, a medium for moralizing, or an instrument of propaganda. He wrote to offer his reader an opportunity to come to understand something permanent and profound.

He states his position in I.22: "It will be enough for me . . . if these words of mine are judged useful by those who want to understand clearly the events which happened in the past and which (human nature being what it is) will, at some time or other and in much the same ways be repeated in the future. My work is not a piece of writing designed to meet the taste of an immediate public but was done to last forever."

Thucydides is asserting that his work has a lasting intellectual and, we may perhaps infer, practical value. Such a claim is based on the conviction that only through a full understanding of the past can one have at least a general idea of the way events are likely to turn out in the future; such an understanding is the only proper basis for action.

Thus Thucydides gave new purpose to the business of recording human activity. How did he hope to fulfill this ambitious claim? First, let me make some points about his approach. To achieve depth, Thucydides abandoned breadth. In particular, he limited his scope to war and politics. Following the practice of earlier literature, he acknowledged the part played in events by particular individuals who were dominant in political life and who could influence their fellow citizens in debate. But because in the complex society of Athens decisions were made and action was undertaken by the whole citizen body, Thucydides gave no less attention to the forces that shape collective thought and action. In his efforts to give a complete picture of political and military activity, he sometimes introduced related issues—social, cultural, demographic, financial, and (inadequately for some modern tastes) economic—but only as and when relevant, and not, one is tempted to add, always then; what did not contribute to his carefully defined theme was excluded. Then, in a significant departure from the practice of Herodotus as already noted, Thucydides analyzed human events in strictly human terms; he never fell back on the gods as a convenient means of explaining phenomena whose causes are obscure. He ascribed some power of predetermination to human nature and recognized the role of chance in human affairs (see I.120n.), but he believed that within this framework humans exercise freedom of choice and are responsible for their actions.

Then Thucydides sought to identify and elucidate some of the deeper issues that underlie the political behavior of powerful states, such as the essential nature of power and the conflict between justice and self-interest. His work is, ultimately, concerned with human nature as reflected in human political and social behavior, with, in short, the human condition, what Thucydides calls "the human thing" (I.22). His aim was to delve beneath the outward, visible action to explore the inner, invisible motivation. Externally, things may appear to be in a state of flux, but human nature is unchanging, Thucydides believed, and, as the ultimate causative factor in human affairs, it provides an element of continuity and constancy in them. Thus the progress of human affairs is subject to certain basic—and to some degree predictable—influences, and historical events, while they will vary enormously in detail, will tend to share some fundamental similarities. An understanding of such influences is the key to an appreciation of why, in broad terms, things happen as they do. Armed with this knowledge, the reader will be able to respond more wisely to his or her own circumstances.

His method was necessarily selective. Episodes were chosen for inclusion not so much on the basis of their contribution to the outcome of the war (indeed some, e.g., the Melian Dialogue at the end of book V, treated at considerable length, contributed little or nothing) as for their broader significance, the issues they raised. Presentation had to elicit these issues without oversimplifying them. Thucydides did not set out to offer easy answers or simple formulas for action. His subject matter is complex, and the reader must wrestle with it, as it is clear Thucydides did, and come to an understanding by his or her own efforts. It is from this rigorous intellectual process that the reader has the most to gain.

In fact, passages of direct analysis or interpretation by the author are rare in Thucydides. The underlying issues that interested him are generally aired in speeches, and a large proportion of his work is devoted to discussions and debates in assemblies or elsewhere, where the various possible courses of action are considered in depth—a process that reveals motives, ambitions, fears, and character—before a decision is taken and acted on.

Speech making was a long-established element of Greek verse literature, as it was of Greek life. The study of rhetoric, which was the natural concomitant of the development of radical democracy in the fifth century, lent it even greater prominence. Herodotus had included some direct discourse in his work. Thucydides took matters to their logical conclusion and interwove formal speeches into his narrative. They often appear in pairs, presenting two sides of a debate, and tend to occur at crucial moments when an important decision is being made. Thucydides realized that the forces at work on such occasions were complex and varied, and he used speeches to explore the "psychology" of both speakers and audience and to analyze the relationship between the two. Further, since many of the policy speeches are delivered by prominent individuals, they sometimes (e.g., Sthenelaidas, Pericles, Alcibiades), act as a medium for presenting characterizations of influential statesmen and generals. They also have a dramatic or artistic function that is twofold. First, they bring to events a certain vitality that a dry listing of the arguments for and against a particular course of action would lack. Second, they introduce an element of irony into the work, since words, in the form of argument, promises, predictions, or claims, are often at odds with actions and events, illustrating the ultimate failure of mankind to control their destiny: mankind's best chance of solving practical problems is through rational analysis in discussion and argument, although even then success is not guaranteed.

The speeches, then, are an essential ingredient of Thucydides' method. There is, however, a serious and difficult problem regarding their composition. Thucydides sets forth his policy on this matter as follows: "I have found it difficult to remember the precise words used in the speeches which I listened to myself and my informants have experienced the same difficulty; so my method has been, while keeping as closely as possible to the general sense of the words that were actually used, to make the speakers say what, in my opinion, was called for by each situation" (I.22). What exactly is Thucydides saying? On the one hand, he claims he is reporting what was said; on the other hand, he acknowledges that he is putting into the mouths of his speakers things that he believes they should have said in view of the circumstances in which the speech was delivered. Both parts of this process were presumably intended to complement one another, but they are often deemed to conflict with each other. Moreover, given that Thucydides did not have the means to record speeches verbatim, that on many occasions he was not in a position to hear a speech himself or even at times to speak to a member of the audience, and given also the abstract character of some of his speeches, the recurrence of particular themes within them, and the sheer difficulty and impenetrability of the Greek in which they are cast, many commentators have concluded that, far from being trustworthy summaries or paraphrases of the original words, the speeches are Thucydides' main vehicle for the development of his own ideas and are, in effect, his own compositions.

There is no need to go this far. That Thucydides refashioned his speeches and supplied some material for them is put beyond doubt by his own words, but those words do not entitle us to accuse him of wholesale invention or self-contradiction. A better approach is to remind ourselves that Thucydides himself in the passage just quoted refers to the general sense (or the main argument) of the words that were actually used—we should not neglect this clear reference to the original speech on the grounds that it appears in a participial clause: it deserves our attention no less than Thucydides' admission of invention. Thus each speech has a genuine core. The remainder of it, which will vary in quantity from speech to speech according to the information Thucydides was able to acquire, has been invented in the light of that genuine element and to fit in with it. That certain ideas crop up repeatedly in the speeches, that it is possible to trace some philosophical consistency linking certain speeches, may mean no more than that such ideas were current in intellectual circles in Athens in Thucydides' time and that he is keen to reflect (and, perhaps, expand on) these preoccupations.

It should be clear from this discussion that it is at best risky, and perhaps quite misguided, to attempt to draw conclusions about Thucydides' own beliefs from material found in the speeches (after all, speeches often contradict each other, and Thucydides cannot have held opposing opinions).

## Conclusion

Above all Thucydides was an intellectual, but that is not the whole story. Like his predecessor, he displays an engaging curiosity and could not entirely resist the temptation to introduce irrelevant material, especially on topics that interested him, such as natural phenomena, geography, antiquities, or points of historical detail that he believed required correction. As a citizen and a soldier he participated in or witnessed some of the events he describes. He had firsthand experience of the tragedy of war and was sympathetic to its victims. He was conscious of the drama of history: he was capable of irony and pathos and could involve his reader in scenes of great emotional intensity. He could excite the feelings and stir the intellect of the reader simultaneously. Consider, for instance, his description of the plague at Athens in 429, which is based on thorough and objective observation of the sufferings of the victims; its language is very precise, even technical at times. Yet, paradoxically, it is intensely moving, somehow revealing rather than obscuring the author's sympathy for the sick and the dying. Likewise the reader's response is twofold, emotional and intellectual—a complete and balanced reaction.

Perhaps, then, there is more variety in Thucydides than immediately meets the eye, but his main focus, war and politics, remains too narrow for some modern tastes, and he offers a distorted vision of the fifth century by ignoring social, economic, and cultural matters. Moreover, there were occasions when the search for truth appears to have been subordinate to artistic and other considerations.

For example, one feature of his technique that prompts disquiet is his ascription of motives to characters for their actions. We find ourselves asking, How could he have known? Then his inclusion of speeches that were not word-for-word transcripts of the originals (however we may attempt to explain and justify his practice) worries the modern reader. But most disturbing is the fact that he made no attempt to conceal his own political beliefs and prejudices: the reader must be ever conscious that Thucydides' portrait of the Athenian democracy and some of its politicians is colored by his antidemocratic convictions.

These are serious criticisms of an author who espoused high principles and laid claim to intellectual integrity. But in the final analysis Thucydides' work has great authority and his failings are not sufficient to deny him a unique place among ancient historians, as an astute, ambitious innovator who set new goals for history and new standards for the writing of it.

# Book One

## I.1. Introduction

The traditional book and chapter divisions to be found in modern texts and translations of Th. are not the historian's own but the work of later editors. Th. did not separate his work into what a modern reader would consider manageable portions or use any system of reference. The subheadings in the Penguin translation are the device of that translator.

**Thucydides the Athenian:** Th. opens in the conventional manner (cf. Hdt.'s opening words) by introducing himself and his subject—the ancient equivalent of the title page. Of himself he tells us only his name and the identity of his state (he is writing for all Greeks, not only for Athenians—and, of course, for later generations: see I.22). He has a little more to say about his approach to his task in the so-called second introduction at V.26, but no more than what is required to confirm his credentials and explain a change in the conditions under which he worked. See my introduction, under "The Life of Thucydides."

**wrote the history:** the word *history* does not appear in the Gk. and, indeed, did not exist in our sense in Th.'s time. See my introduction, under "The Intellectual Background of Thucydides." The Gk. verb means simply "wrote" or "wrote an account of."

**the war:** there is no doubt in this context that Th. means the entire Peloponnesian War but elsewhere it is not always clear whether these words refer to the whole war of 431–404 or to the period 431–421 only, the phase of the war that finished with the Peace of Nicias and is generally referred to by modern commentators as the Archidamian War (unfairly so: Archidamus was consistently against fighting). The explanation of this inconsistency probably lies in the fact that Th. wrote his history over a considerable period of time during which his perspective of the war will have changed with events, in particular with the renewal of war in 415. In his later books he talks of the period 431–421 variously as "the first war" (V.24, VII.18), "the ten years' war" (V.25, 26), "the Attic war" (V.28, 31), and "the years of continuous war" (VI.26).

**the war fought between Athens and Sparta:** the work's title, as it were. The Gk. actually means "the war of the Peloponnesians and the Athenians," which is still not absolutely accurate: by "the Peloponnesians" Th. means the Peloponnesian League, which had some non-Peloponnesian members (II.9) and excluded a few Peloponnesian states, e.g., Argos (V.28); "the Athenians" were assisted by their independent allies and subject-allies in the empire. Th.'s "title" is, however, less prejudicial than the modern name for the conflict, "the Peloponnesian War" (not found in Th.), which embodies a pro-Athenian bias; cf. II.1n. Th. is establishing his parameters at the outset: the scope of his work is to be limited to the war itself. He will not digress into contemporary affairs unrelated to the conduct of the war or into ethnographical and other matters favored by some earlier writers, though he will consider the effects of the war on Greek society.

**a great war:** the first and most restrained of several claims concerning the greatness of the Peloponnesian War. See n. later in this chapter, **the greatest disturbance.**

**more worth writing about than any of those [wars] which had taken place in the past:** a bold and confident claim, designed to establish the supreme importance of Th.'s theme at the opening of his work. Also a piece of one-upmanship directed against fellow "historians"?

**the two sides were at the very height of their power and preparedness:** such a statement would seem to be more obviously true of Athens, with its empire and financial resources, than of Sparta. Th. explains more fully at I.18–19.

**the greatest disturbance in the history of the Hellenes:** this point, already made in this chapter, is repeated at I.21, by which time Th. has argued for the small scale of earlier conflicts. The greatness of the Peloponnesian War lies in its duration and the suffering it caused; see I.23.

**a large part of the non-Hellenic world:** e.g., non-Greek Sicilians and, of course, the Persians.

**the whole of mankind:** an exaggeration, as Th. recognized ("I might almost say"). He certainly knew of peoples who did not participate in the war, e.g., Italians and Carthaginians.

**impossible . . . to acquire a really precise knowledge:** Th. knows the importance of getting the facts right; cf. I.21–22. Hence he has decided to write contemporary history (I.21n.).

**the history preceding our own period:** it is unclear to what period Th. is referring. Certainly he was familiar with many of the events in the years between the Persian and Peloponnesian Wars: see the Pentecontaetia, I.89–117.

**all the evidence leads me to conclude:** cf. I.21 and see my introduction, under "The Aims and Methods of Thucydides."

## I.2–19. The Archaeology

Before embarking on his subject proper, Th. puts the Peloponnesian War in its long-term context. At the same time he is at pains to explain and justify his choice of subject and to support his claim that the Peloponnesian War is greater than any earlier Greek war. Hence he offers this difficult and complex introduction, commonly known as the Archaeology, literally "an account of ancient history."

The reconstruction of the past was of interest to Th.'s contemporaries (cf. Plato *Protagoras* 320c–323a and *Hippias Major* 285d), and more was known than Th. suggests here. Even so, he will have had little in the way of material evidence: the Homeric epics, the unreliable prose chroniclers (I.21), the ruins of buildings (e.g., I.10), and even archaeological evidence (e.g., I.8). Otherwise he is dependent on anecdote and oral tradition (cf. I.20) and, for recent events, the cross-questioning of eyewitnesses (I.21–22). Th. found traditional accounts of the distant past intellectually unacceptable: they were too remote from the world in which he lived. He sought a form of history that linked past and present instead of creating a gulf between them. He had few details but believed he could define the broader patterns. Thus, relying on a cautious and critical evaluation of the evidence and some intelligent extrapolation, he elicits the essential themes and long-term developments underlying early Greek history, concentrating on process and playing down the romantic deeds of traditional heroic individuals. In this way he traces the broad sweep of Greek history for over a millennium, demonstrating that from the time of Minos (I.4n.) onward the sources of power and prosperity in Greece had been political stability and unification (usually enforced by a centralized authority), financial resources, and a navy. He proceeds to argue that by the time of the Peloponnesian War the Athenians had established an Aegean empire, which brought them unprecedented levels of prosperity and naval power, while the Spartans, though they had neither the income nor the navy of Athens, enjoyed a political stability unique in Greece and were leaders of a powerful league whose combined forces made it invincible on land. Both sides had vast experience of warfare and by 431 were in a position to make war on a scale greater than ever before. Thus Th. not only justifies his choice of subject but also establishes at the beginning of his work a sense of continuity in Greek history, a link, in terms of power politics, between the distant, semimythological past and the realities of human experience and behavior in his own time.

**I.2. the country now called Hellas:** after Hellen (I.3n.). This was the Gk. name in the fifth century for Greece (which is derived from the Latin *Graecia,* the name of the Roman province). Mainland Greece may be defined as the area between the southern tip of the Peloponnese and the borders of Epirus and Macedonia. The single name, *Hellas,* should not be taken to imply political unity: Greece in Th.'s time was made up of separate, independent communities called *poleis* (sing. = *polis,* usually translated as "city-state," but this obscures the fact that it included surrounding rural areas). Each polis had its own distinct laws, customs and mythology (in particular, a belief in a common kinship), government, armed forces, and, of course, community of citizens and others ("men are the polis," says Nicias, end of VII.77). Not only were these communities quite separate, they were frequently at war with each other (cf. I.15n.).

**ancient times:** the period before the Trojan War (I.9n.).

**no surplus left over for capital:** financial considerations loom large in bk. I as the two sides prepare for war; see the words of Archidamus at I.83 and of Pericles at I.141; see also I.19, II.13.

**the protection of fortifications:** Th.'s narrative makes it clear that at the time of the Peloponnesian War most Greek towns had walls. The prime example is, of course, Athens (cf. the story of the rebuilding of the Athenian walls after the Persian Wars, I.89–93), and the most notable exception is Sparta (I.10n.). For compulsory defortification as a means of control see I.101, 117; III.33n.

**disunity:** Gk. *stasis,* literally "a standing," i.e., a standing apart or separation into factions. The weakness of many Greek states in Th.'s time was the result of internal political dissension that frequently resulted in civil war, usually between oligarchs (often pro-Spartan) and democrats (often pro-Athenian). Athens itself fell prey to stasis in 411 (VIII.45ff.). Stasis, in the words of the Sicilian Hermocrates, was "the main reason for the decline of cities" (IV.61), while Herodotus wrote, "internal stasis is a greater evil than a war fought by the whole state against an external enemy in the same proportion as war is a greater evil than peace" (VIII.3). Th. comments on the huge amount of bloodshed caused by stasis during the Peloponnesian War at I.23 and analyzes its nature in a justly famous passage, III.82–84. Cf. Athenagoras' analysis of stasis, VI.38–39. On Sparta's immunity from stasis see I.18.

**because of the poverty of her soil:** parts of Attica, e.g., the plains of Marathon, have quite rich soil, but Attica was not fertile enough to support a large population. In particular, Athens had long depended on imported grain: cf. I.89n., 120n., and Nicias' words at VI.20. Th.'s argument that poor soil prevented stasis is compressed: he is assuming his previous point that fertility led to prosperity that in turn resulted in power struggles.

**my theory that it was because of migrations that there was uneven development elsewhere:** by "elsewhere" Th. must mean other parts of Greece, but the Gk. is difficult and probably corrupt; the translation is suitably vague. Other Greek states developed unevenly, i.e., not as smoothly as Athens, because they were less stable and suffered losses of citizens while Athens grew in size.

**colonies were sent out to Ionia:** see I.12n.

**I.3. Trojan War:** see I.9n.

**Hellen:** the son of Deucalion, the mythological ancestor of the human race. The first Hellenes, i.e., speakers of Gk., may have arrived in Greece as early as 2000. Th. accepts without question the historicity of several figures, pre-Homeric and Homeric, whom we would regard as mythological. If this surprises us, we must remember that Th. is writing here about events long before his own time (cf. I.21n.) and that, even if he had doubts, he had no evidence by which he could distinguish fact from fiction.

**with the name 'Pelasgian' predominating:** the Pelasgians were, in all probability, a pre-Hellenic northern tribe, whose exact original homeland is unknown but who spread throughout the northern Aegean as well as to Crete and possibly Attica (cf. II.17). The name *Pelasgian* was extended to cover primitive peoples throughout Greece but denoted not so much racial identity as an early stage in the development of the peoples inhabiting the area that came to be known as Hellas. The term in effect denotes "pre-Greeks."

**his sons:** Xuthos, Doros, and Aeolus. The latter two, along with Ion, stepson of Xuthos, were the eponymous originators of the Gk. dialects, Dorian, Aeolic, and Ionian.

**The best evidence for this can be found in Homer, who . . . nowhere uses the name 'Hellenic' for the whole force:** note Th.'s insistence on the use of evidence when it is available and his respect for and familiarity with Homer's poems.

**Homer:** despite his fame, we know almost nothing about him, not even his precise contribution to our *Iliad* and *Odyssey*. According to tradition, he came from Chios and was blind (III.104). Heroic poetry, composed orally by unknown bards, had existed for centuries by the time the *Iliad* and the *Odyssey*, traditionally attributed to Homer, were written down in something like their present form. This would have been no earlier than ca. 750, when the Greeks adopted a new alphabet from the east (Hdt. V.58). Th. owes much to Homer in these chapters, though he is occasionally skeptical of his reliability; see e.g., I.9, 10.

**Achilles:** the leading warrior on the Greek side at Troy and the hero of Homer's *Iliad.* His homeland, **Phthiotis,** was in the southeast corner of Thessaly.

**foreigners:** Gk. *barbaroi,* the name (an onomatopoeia from the unintelligible sound of their speech) applied by Greeks to all who did not speak Gk.

**I.4. Minos:** legendary king and eponymous founder of a flourishing civilization in Crete in the middle of the second millennium. The Minoans traded widely in the eastern Mediterranean and established a thalassocracy (control of the sea) and a naval empire in the Cyclades, a group of islands in the southern Aegean (**Hellenic Sea**). Some of these islands would have paid tribute to their Cretan rulers. At the root of this growth of Cretan influence and prosperity were a navy and financial resources, the bases of power throughout the period covered by Th. The story of Minos' campaign against piracy in the Aegean is resumed in I.8.

**Carians:** from the southwest corner of Asia Minor. See I.8n.

### *I.5–8. An Excursus on Piracy, Containing Further Digressions on Trends in Fashion (Chapter 6) and the Siting of Cities (Chapter 7)*

Th. demonstrates that brigandage once flourished all over Greece, and he seeks to bolster the validity of his account by reference to long-surviving practices (still followed in distant parts) that, he believes, provide a link with the past he is trying to recreate.

**I.5. the old poets:** the question occurs in Homer, e.g., *Odyssey* III.72–74.

**Ozolian Locrians . . . Aetolians . . . Acarnanians:** these peoples of northwest Greece were considered somewhat primitive by other Greeks. Being at a distance from the mainstream of Greek life, they had developed slowly and still lived in unfortified villages. Cf. III.94 on Aetolia. More distant non-Greek nations also aroused contempt among Greeks: cf. Th.'s remarks on the Scythians at II.97 and the Thracians at VII.29 and Brasidas' speech on the Illyrians at IV.126. On racial prejudice as a factor in the Peloponnesian War see I.124n.

**I.6. The fact that the peoples I have mentioned still live in this way is evidence that once this was the general rule among all the Hellenes:** Th.'s logic is not immediately apparent. He points out that some less civilized western Greek tribes still carry arms, a relic from the old days of brigandage, and argues that if such conditions once prevailed throughout all Greece, then it is a reasonable assumption that all Greeks carried arms at that time.

**their kinsmen in Ionia:** cf. I.12n.

**the Olympic Games:** an athletic contest, part of a larger religious festival, held every four years in honor of Zeus at Olympia in Elis in the Peloponnese. The games began, according to Greek tradition, in 776 (*T.D.G.R.* 3). Lists of victors were drawn up and published ca. 400.

**the manners of the ancient Hellenic world are very similar to the manners of foreigners [barbarians] today:** Th. emphasizes the cultural superiority of Greece (as within Greece Pericles will claim Athens is the most advanced polis: II.35ff.). During the war Greece will descend into savagery.

**I.7. Cities were sited differently:** Th. distinguishes between cities built on the coast **in the later periods,** e.g., colonies such as Syracuse (733), and **the ancient cities** built inland, such as Athens and Argos.

**I.8. Delos:** the Cycladic island that was the mythological birthplace of Apollo and the headquarters of the Delian League (I.96). On its purification in 424 see III.104. Purification involved the removal of all the graves on the island and the prevention of births and deaths there in the future. Modern archaeological research has cast doubt on Th.'s statement that the graves on Delos were Carian.

**wealth and . . . a more settled life:** Th. resumes from I.4 the theme of the growth of economic prosperity in the Aegean and the consequent polarization of political power. He is interested not only in the behavior of strong powers but also in the way in which weaker states react when pressure is put on them. At this period, it seems, the weak regarded it as in their interest to give in to the strong. Later, during the war, he will give an example of a state, Melos, that refused to surrender and was exterminated as a result (V.84–116).

**I.9. Agamemnon, it seems to me, must have been the most powerful of the rulers of his day; and it was for this reason that he raised the force against Troy, not because . . . :** Th. rationalizes myth, applying the rules of power politics. Cf. n. later in this chapter, **fear played a greater part than loyalty.**

**Agamemnon:** king of **Mycenae,** the source of his power and wealth. His father, **Atreus,** had taken over Mycenae from the descendants of **Perseus,** the last of whom was **Eurystheus.** The father of Atreus was **Pelops,** who gave his name to the Peloponnese. Agamemnon led the Greek forces against Troy in the Trojan War in order to recover **Helen,** the wife of Menelaus, who had been abducted by Paris, son of King Priam of Troy. Before her marriage Helen's father, **Tyndareus,** had obliged her suitors to take an oath to abide by her decision and to uphold her honor in the future. Archaeology has verified the existence of a town believed to be Troy and its destruction ca. 1200 but cannot prove the historicity of the Trojan War as we know it.

**empire . . . a stronger navy than any other:** further economic progress and concentration of power meant that war could be conducted on a larger scale than before. For the Trojan War Th. makes it clear that he is dependent on tradition but rejects elements of it that seem to him unsatisfactory, reinterpreting myth in accordance with his more pragmatic, less romantic theory of early Greek history. Needless to say, the gods do not figure in his version of the war. Cf. I.3n. for Th.'s respect for the authority of Homer.

**fear played a greater part than loyalty:** Th. is asserting that the motives of the Greek participants in the war have been misunderstood and the role of fear underestimated; on fear cf. I.75n.

**I.10. the city of Sparta:** described by Th. as a cluster of unwalled villages, but we should not imagine anything too primitive. Th. himself mentions temples (e.g., the temple of the Goddess of the Brazen House with precinct at I.134 and a temple of Zeus at V.16) and Herodotus a theater (Hdt. VI.67). On Th.'s knowledge of Sparta see V.26n.

**two-fifths of the Peloponnese:** an inevitably approximate fraction, referring to Laconia and Messenia; much of this region was occupied by helot serfs under the control of Sparta (I.101n.).

**the whole Peloponnese:** Th. exaggerates the extent of the Peloponnesian League; see I.1n. On the league see I.18–19, 141, and the Penguin translation, app. 1, p. 607.

**numerous allies beyond its frontiers:** see II.9 for a list of such allies in 431.

**a collection of villages, in the ancient Hellenic way:** i.e., it did not undergo the process of synoecism, the coming together of communities that in early Greece was a preliminary to the development of walled cities (which were the norm: see I.2n.). Synoecism naturally had political implications: cf. the case of Attica, discussed at II.15, and see also I.58n., III.2n.

**We have no right . . . to judge cities by their appearances rather than by their actual power . . . It is questionable whether we can have complete confidence in Homer's figures:** note again Th.'s critical approach to the available evidence.

**it was not on the scale of what is done in modern warfare:** in terms of numbers (1,200 x 85, the mean of 120 and 50, equaling 102,000), the expedition to Troy was much greater than any of the Peloponnesian War.

**the crew . . . numbered 120:** much smaller than the later triremes, which had a crew of some two hundred; cf. I.14n.

**Philoctetes:** a famous archer who was abandoned on the way to Troy by his fellow Greeks because they could not stand the stench of his wound that resulted from a snakebite.

**his catalogue of the ships:** in *Iliad* II.494ff.

**The men not only rowed in the ships but also served in the army:** in Th.'s time this would happen only in an emergency (e.g., III.18, VI.91); otherwise these two functions are associated with two different groups (though in practice there was some overlap; see, e.g., III.16). Ships were rowed by professional oarsmen who generally came from the lowest of the Solonian wealth-based classes (III.16n.), Thetes (for the use of foreign mercenaries see I.121n.); the army consisted largely of hoplites (I.49n.), usually from the next class up, Zeugitae. In addition each vessel carried a small complement (usually ten: cf. III.95n.) of marines (Gk. *epibatae*), probably also Thetes (VI.43, VIII.24n., but cf. III.98n.) but equipped as hoplites. On the use of slaves as rowers see I.55n., VII.13n.

**they had to cross the open sea . . . ships that had no decks:** cf. I.14n.

**I.11. . . . shortage of money. Lack of supplies . . . :** Th.'s second argument for the smaller scale of the Trojan expedition is that the Greeks could not have used all their forces continuously for warfare because of their need for supplies.

**I.12. There was party strife in nearly all the cities:** in the period following the Trojan War widespread stasis (I.2n.) caused many shifts of populations. The instability was increased with the invasion of **the Dorians.** According to tradition (e.g., Hdt. I.56) these invaders came from the north, probably at some time in the twelfth century, and eventually occupied much of the Peloponnese (cf. I.18). The evidence for this invasion is archaeological: towns and cities were destroyed over a wide area and their civilization vanished. Thus Greece entered the period traditionally known as the Dark Ages, in which the strength and unity it had exhibited in the Trojan War went into decline.

**Arne:** in central, southern Thessaly.

**the descendants of Heracles:** the Heraclids, a group of families who claimed that they were descended from the great hero and had led the Dorian invasion. Cf. I.24.

**Thus many years passed by:** after some artificially precise dates, Th.'s chronology suddenly becomes very loose. He is passing over the period from ca. 1100 to perhaps the end of the tenth century.

**colonization:** the sending out of citizens to new homes overseas, the result of overpopulation, land hunger, and commercial enterprise. The process may have begun as early as the ninth century, while a few colonies were founded as late as the fifth, but the main phase was in the eighth and seventh centuries. The Athenians tended to colonize Ionia on the eastern shores of the Aegean (cf. VII.57). Peloponnesians, Euboeans, and others went westward to Sicily and southern Italy and to the shores of the Black Sea. Cf. I.2, VI.2–5. On another type of Athenian overseas settlement, the cleruchy, see III.50n. and *A.E.* p. 118. For an introduction to the subject of colonization see Graham 1964.

**I.13. hereditary monarchy:** the form of government found in Homer and at Sparta throughout its history.

**limitations:** the Spartan kings, for instance, were by no means omnipotent: see, e.g., V.63 (though they had absolute power when in command of an army: see V.60n.).

**as Hellas became more powerful . . . tyrannies were established:** Th. moves on to the seventh century, when many monarchies (Sparta was a notable exception: I.18n.) gave way, usually via an intermediate aristocratic stage, to tyrannies as the new rich, men previously excluded from government, demanded a share in political power and promoted new leaders who lacked a legal and hereditary claim to rule. The Gk. word *tyrannos* did not originally have the same connotations of oppressiveness as the English *tyrant.* The Greek tyrant was a sole ruler who would probably have seized power by force, but far from being oppressive, some tyrants were mild and enlightened in their rule. See, e.g., VI.54 for Th.'s account of the Pisistratids at Athens. In due course the word took on its modern meaning (e.g., I.95, 122). In 427 Cleon could openly acknowledge that the Athenian empire was a tyranny (III.37; cf. Pericles' words, "like a tyranny," II.63).

**Corinth:** its wealth came from its unique position on the Isthmus of Corinth, which enabled it to control land traffic moving between northern and southern Greece and, with ports on both the Corinthian and Saronic Gulfs, to trade both to the east and to the west. Thus we are introduced to the state that will play an important role in fomenting war and will dominate much of the narrative of bk. I.

**Ameinocles:** otherwise unknown.

**(this present war):** the Archidamian War of 431–421 or the Peloponnesian War of 431–404? See I.1n.

**the first naval battle on record:** the rivalry between Corinth and its colony Corcyra, which played a part in the outbreak of the Peloponnesian War, was of long standing.

**Cyrus:** the first king of Persia (following his defeat of the Medes, who had previously dominated the Persians), 559–529. He defeated Croesus and annexed Lydia in ca. 546. He was succeeded by **Cambyses** (529–522).

**Polycrates, the tyrant of Samos:** Herodotus (III.39) gives further details of his navy. Th. notes that his reign overlapped roughly with that of Cambyses, but these words are omitted from the Penguin translation. See *T.D.G.R.* 32.

**Delian Apollo:** according to legend Delos (cf. I.8n.) was the birthplace of

Apollo (and Artemis). Games and a festival in honor of Apollo were held there at least as early as the eighth century.

**Phocaeans:** from Phocaea in Ionia; founders of **Marseilles** ca. 600, but the Gk. says "Massalia," and the identity with Marseilles is not certain.

**I.14. triremes:** the trireme was the standard Greek warship in the time of the Peloponnesian War. It was some 120 feet long, it was equipped with two masts, and the prow was fitted at the water line with a bronze beak, used for ramming. It had a total crew of some 200, of whom 170 were rowers sitting in three rows, one roughly above the other, each man with his own oar. Its crew included a small complement of hoplites (I.10n.; cf. VI.31n.). Because it was lighter and had a larger crew, the trireme was much swifter than the old **long boats** and the **boats of fifty oars** (*penteconters,* as used by Philoctetes at I.10 and still in use in the fifth century: see VI.43). An important practical difference between a trireme and a merchant vessel was that while the latter could cross open seas (cf. I.44n.), the warship had to stay close to land so that it could be beached each night: it was built for speed and maneuverability (I.49n.), and there were no sleeping quarters or other facilities on board. The development of the trireme gave further impetus to the growth of naval power in Greece. See Morrison and Coates 1986.

**Sicilian tyrants:** Sicilian cities were ruled by tyrants in the early fifth century. In particular they were involved in wars with the Carthaginians and the Etruscans. Most notable were Gelon of Syracuse (491–478) and his successor, Hieron (478–467), under whom Syracuse became the most powerful city in Sicily.

**the Corcyraeans:** see I.13n. on their early naval prowess.

**Darius:** king of Persia 521–486, succeeded by his son **Xerxes** (486–465). The expedition referred to is Xerxes' great invasion of Greece (480/79), recorded by Herodotus. The turning point of the war was the Greek naval victory in the battle of **Salamis** (an island in the Saronic Gulf), engineered by **Themistocles,** the architect of Athens' naval power and one of Th.'s heroes (I.89–93, 93n., 135–38). For an Athenian view of the war see I.73–74.

**Aegina:** an island in the Saronic Gulf, some fifteen miles southwest of Piraeus. Athens conducted an intermittent war with it in the early years of the fifth century. Herodotus (VI.49–50, 85–93) gives some details, but the cause is obscure. As far as we can tell from our limited information (I.67, 105, 108; II.27), relations between the two were poor for the remainder of the century.

**not yet constructed with complete decks:** after the Persian Wars decks were added to triremes to protect the rowers and provide greater freedom of movement on board (cf. I.10).

**I.15. navies . . . were the foundation of empire:** Th. continues his argument that a navy was the source of power in the Greek world, providing opportunities for enrichment and conquest, while warfare on land was limited to unproductive local squabbles. The implication is that Athens ought to be the stronger party in a war with Peloponnesian states.

**simply frontier skirmishes:** disputes over frontiers were a common cause of war in Greece at all periods. Cf. text later in this chapter, **local affairs between neighbours**; I.122 ("boundary disputes"); IV.92 (where Pagondas, the Boeotian, says, "others fight battles with their neighbours for one frontier or another"). Athens' quarrel with Megara, which resulted in the Megarian Decree, arose in part from a dispute over border territory (I.139); for other instances see I.103, V.41, VI.6. According to Pericles, wars between Peloponnesian states were "short affairs" because of their poverty (I.141). The tyrants likewise had been concerned with only "immediate local interests" (I.17).

**the ancient war between Chalcis and Eretria:** the Lelantine War, of uncertain date, duration, and outcome, in which some far-flung allies of either side seem to have participated. It is named after the Lelantine Plain, which lay between the two cities and was one cause of the conflict. See Hdt. V.99; *T.D.G.R.* 7.

**I.16. Cyrus:** see I.13n. After defeating **Croesus** of Lydia in 546, the Persians gradually moved westward, putting down the Ionian revolt in 494 and spreading their power into the Aegean islands.

**Darius:** see I.14n.

**the Phoenician navy:** the Phoenicians were great sailors from early times, and the Persians were heavily dependent on their fleet in the Mediterranean. Cf., for instance, I.100, 110, 116; VIII.46. The Persians also used Cyprian and Cilician vessels; see, e.g., I.112.

**I.17. no great action:** Th. is not so much belittling the achievements of tyrants such as the Pisistratids at Athens (which he acknowledges at VI.54) as explaining why the wars they undertook were on a small scale.

**the tyrants in Sicily:** see I.14n.

**So for a long time:** the period Th. is referring to is, very approximately, the eighth and seventh centuries.

**I.18. the Spartans put down tyranny:** why they did so is nowhere adequately explained, though the fact that many tyrants were replaced with pro-Spartan oligarchies speaks for itself; cf. I.19. Th. adds, "these were, with the exception of the Sicilian tyrants, the last," but these words are omitted from the Penguin translation.

**most of which had been governed by tyrants for much longer than Athens:** the tyranny of Pisistratus and his sons at Athens was relatively short lived (546–510). Cf. VI.53–59 and Hdt. V.65.

**the Dorians:** see I.12n.

**the country [Sparta] has never been ruled by tyrants:** tyranny was avoided by a switch to "good laws" (says the Gk.), traditionally associated with the name of Lycurgus. Sparta created a unique system of government based on a dual kingship (two kings, from two different royal houses, the Agiad and the Eurypontid, reigning simultaneously); a body of five senior magistrates (ephors), elected annually, who had considerable influence and power (cf. I.58n., 87, 131; V.36); a council of elders, which had thirty members including the two kings; and an assembly of citizens, the Spartiates.

**For rather more than 400 years, dating from the end of the late war:** i.e., presumably, the Peloponnesian War (cf. I.1n.); this would put the origin of the Spartan constitution at ca. 800. Cf. *T.D.G.R.* 2. For allied criticism of Spartan conservatism see I.70.

**a source of internal strength:** Sparta was free of the stasis that proved so destructive in other Greek cities, including Athens (I.2n.); it was thus able to expand its power. Th. admired Spartan stability: see VIII.24.

**enabled them to interfere in the affairs of other states:** see I.19.

**Not many years after:** in 490.

**the battle of Marathon was fought between the Persians and the Athenians:** the first Persian assault on Greece was repulsed at Marathon on the north coast of Attica by the Athenians and their allies, the Plataeans (ignored here by Th.; cf. I.73n.). The Persians returned under Xerxes in 480: see I.14n.

**the Athenians decided to abandon their city . . . and became a people of sailors:** the policy of Themistocles. See I.14, 89–90, 93 with nn., 144; *T.D.G.R.* 55.

**those who later revolted from the King of Persia:** the Greeks on the eastern seaboard of the Aegean who had been under Persian domination but rebelled from Persia during the Mycale campaign of 479 (I.89).

**split into two divisions, one group following Athens:** the origins of the Delian League; see I.95–97.

**one being supreme on land, the other on the sea:** an essential difference between Sparta and Athens, which did much to determine the course (and length) of the Peloponnesian War. Cf. IV.12.

**the wartime alliance:** the Greek union established in 481 before the arrival of the Persians (Hdt. VII.145ff., 172). It remained in force, technically, until ca. 461 (I.102).

**it was not long before . . . Athens and Sparta . . . were at war with each other:** the so-called First Peloponnesian War of 460–446 (I.105–15).

**from the end of the Persian War till the beginning of the Peloponnesian War:** i.e., 479–431, the period loosely called the Pentecontaetia (the Fifty Years). It is dealt with by Th. in I.89–117, though events of the late 430s are treated separately and in much greater detail (I.24–88, 118–25, 139–46).

**putting down revolts among their allies:** this may seem odd language to use of Sparta, since the Peloponnesian League (another modern name; Th. speaks more correctly of "the Spartans and their allies") was a series of separate bilateral agreements between Sparta and its allies. The allies were formed into a league at some time toward the end of the sixth century, though they remained (technically) free and autonomous. In practice, however, it was sometimes necessary for Sparta to use force to maintain its supremacy and hold the league together. Athens had, of course, reduced its allies to the status of subjects and frequently had to suppress revolts (I.98–99, 100–101, 114–15). On the structure and character of the Peloponnesian League see de Ste. Croix (1972), 101–24.

**I.19. The Spartans did not make their allies pay tribute:** Th. has stressed in the Archaeology (I.2–19) the importance of financial reserves and now draws an important distinction between Athens and Sparta. Sparta had a network of independent allies (but see I.18n.) and no common fund; the members of the Delian League had paid tribute from the beginning cf. Archidamus' words at 1.80, 83. Thus Pericles argued that Athens was in a much stronger position than Sparta to fight the war: see I.141. For a list of each side's allies and subjects in 431 see II.9.

**but saw to it that they were governed by oligarchies:** often after the deposition of a tyrant; see I.18n. This was one of the means by which Sparta held the Peloponnesian League together. Cf. Pericles' comment at I.144, claiming that Sparta imposes on its allies "the kind of government that suits Spartan interests," and III.82.1 for Sparta's support of oligarchy in general; see also Aristotle's generalized statement at *Politics* 1307b22 (= *A.E.* 104): "For the Athenians everywhere destroyed oligarchies, the Spartans democracies." On Athenian support of democracy see *A.E.* 100–107.

**Athens . . . had made them pay contributions of money instead:** see I.96, 99.

**Chios and Lesbos:** see I.96n.

**the forces available to Athens:** see II.13.

## I.20–23. Thucydides on His Aims, Methods, and Choice of Subject

**I.20. which has come down to us by way of tradition:** see I.2–19, introductory n.

**People are inclined to accept all stories of ancient times in an uncritical way:** Th. is dissatisfied with the methods of earlier writers and is determined to set higher standards (I.22). Cf. the final sentence of this chapter and VI.54.

**Hipparchus, who was killed by Harmodius and Aristogiton:** in 514. For the full story see VI.53–59.

**the Panathenaic procession:** a festival held in honor of the patron goddess of the city, Athena, conducted in midsummer each year and with particular magnificence every fourth year (the Great Panathenaea).

**many incorrect assumptions:** Th. appears to be referring to mistakes in Herodotus (VI.57, IX.53).

**whereas in fact they have only one . . . Such a company has never existed:** Th. has no doubt about his facts; cf. V.26n. on his knowledge of Spartan affairs.

**I.21. prose chroniclers:** Gk. *logographoi,* who wrote about the past (often of their own city) in prose (much early writing, including what we would consider material quite unsuited to poetry, was in verse); see my introduction, under "The Intellectual Background of Thucydides." Connor (1984, 66 n. 37), however, takes *logographoi* to be "a sneer at speech writers and orators rather than a technical term for Th.'s predecessors in the writing of history."

**less interested in telling the truth than in catching the attention of their public:** cf. Th.'s criticism of Hellanicus at I.97. His own purpose is more serious and ambitious: above all, he sought the truth (I.22).

**evidence . . . conclusions:** see my introduction, under "The Aims and Methods of Thucydides"; I.2–19, introductory n.

**we have been dealing with ancient history:** an important point, easily forgotten by the modern reader who might tend to telescope the vast period covered by Th.

**As for this present war:** i.e., Th. is writing contemporary history, a departure from previous practice, in the belief that he thus stands the best chance of establishing the truth. The lack of a long-term perspective entails risks—**people are apt to think that the war in which they are fighting is the greatest of all wars**—but the truth will be achieved by examining **the facts themselves.** His procedure for getting at the facts is explained in the following chapter.

**this was the greatest war of all:** cf. I.1n., 23n.

**I.22.** See my introduction, under "The Aims and Methods of Thucydides."

**In this history I have made use of set speeches . . . And with regard to my factual reporting of the events of the war:** history consists of words (Gk. sing. *logos*) and deeds (Gk. sing. *ergon*), the former no less important than the latter and a form of action themselves. For Th. (as for many of his speakers, e.g., Pericles at II.40, Diodotus at III.42) words and deeds complement each other: action is preceded by debate in which opposing arguments are confronted and compared; a decision is taken that is the basis of the action that follows. On other occasions words were opposed to deeds and compared unfavorably with them. This happens particularly when a speaker is attempting to prompt his audience to action, as is, e.g., Sthenelaidas at I.86, Cleon at II.37–40, and the Theban speaker at III.67. The distinction between words and deed is one of several antitheses that are fundamental to Th.'s thinking (I.32n.). For a full treatment of it see Parry 1981. It will be clear that in Th. words generally take the form of argument and persuasion (Gk. *peitho*). The ability to persuade was fundamental to the democratic process, and dependence on persuasion (rather than force) for the making of decisions was seen as one of the hallmarks of a civilized society. Training in the art of persuasion, rhetoric, was provided by the Sophists (I.32n.) in late fifth-century Athens. Pericles (on whose rhetorical powers see I.139n.) speaks on the importance of rhetorical ability in Greek society at II.60: "A man who has the knowledge but lacks the power clearly to express it is no better off than if he never had any ideas at all."

**I have found it difficult to remember the precise words used in the speeches:** but he recognizes the importance of doing so, and (he goes on to say) the speeches in his work will reflect the originals as closely as possible.

**what . . . was called for by each situation:** the Gk. (*ta deonta,* literally "the necessary things") is, in fact, precisely what teachers of rhetoric claimed to teach. Its meaning is twofold: first, it refers to content, the material that is needed to supply the argument in any given case; second, it refers to the construction and presentation of the speech, elements of technique that bestow persuasiveness on a speech whether its argument is valid or not. In his recasting of the speeches, then, Th. is doing something very close to what an orator would do.

**My work is not a piece of writing designed to meet the taste of an immediate public:** the translation "piece of writing" is feeble; the Gk. means "showpiece" or "prize composition" to be entered in a competition such as that described by Cleon at III.38; see n. there. Cf. Pericles' comment on Homer at II.41.

**I.23. The greatest war in the past was the Persian War:** see I.14n., 18n. The **two naval battles** were presumably Artemisium and Salamis (480) (or possibly Salamis and Mycale, the latter fought in Ionia in 479) and the **two battles on land** Thermopylae (480) and Plataea (479). The Persian Wars involved vast numbers and vital issues but are quickly dismissed by Th. because they do not meet his definition of greatness.

**The Peloponnesian War . . . not only lasted for a long time but . . . brought with it unprecedented suffering:** Th.'s narrative comes full circle and he concludes with the point he made in I.1, that the Peloponnesian War was the greatest war of all. He now defines his criteria for greatness and elaborates on the suffering caused by the war and the horrors that accompanied it: internal conflict (see I.2n. and especially III.82ff.), superstition (e.g., II.8n., 54), even disease (II.47ff.); human life was thrown into confusion and the forces of nature seemed to add to the chaos (e.g., II.8n.).

**more frequent eclipses of the sun:** modern astronomy supports Th.'s assertion; cf. II.8n.

**the Thirty Years' Truce:** concluded at the end of the First Peloponnesian War in 446/5 (I.115), following the revolt of Euboea (I.114).

**As to the reasons why they broke the truce, I propose first to give an account of the causes of complaint . . . and . . . specific instances where their interests clashed . . . But the real reason for the war . . . What made war inevitable . . . :** Th. distinguishes simultaneously between two causes (or, to be more precise, one group of causes and one cause) and two levels of causation. First are what he calls **aitiai,** recent events that resulted in complaints and disputes between Athens and some of Sparta's allies; these led to breaches of the treaty and finally to war. Second is what he describes as the "real reason" (Gk. **alethestate prophasis,** literally "truest cause/reason"), the growth of Athenian power and the increasing fear this caused in Sparta; this, he claims, actually drove the Spartans to go to war. See also I.88, 118. These two causes, then, though distinct and unequal in their effects, are part of the same process. The disputes of Corcyra, Potidaea, and Megara are immediate causes that, through their ramifications, contribute to and are part of the longer-term and more profound cause of the war, Spartan fear of Athens. The distinction is crucial, and recognition of it was a vital historiographical development.

**But the real reason . . . is . . . most likely to be disguised by such an argument:** i.e., the "truest" cause of the war is obscured by emphasis on events immediately preceding its outbreak, as if they were its sole cause. This makes sense, but the Gk. is difficult and could equally mean that the "real reason" was "not openly expressed" or was "most unclear in discussion." Such an interpretation is supported by Th.'s remark that the reasons for breaking the truce ***[aitiai]*** **. . . were openly expressed.** A context for the suppression of such a real reason could be the negotiations between Sparta and Athens: if the Spartans' fear were the real reason for the war, they might well have kept quiet about it because it provided them with no valid justification for declaring war. Or Th. could be attempting to combat a general unawareness of the real reason in Athens: it seems (e.g., from Aristophanes: see I.67n.; cf. the charge leveled by Athens at Aegina in 431, II.27) that at the outbreak of war and in its early years the Megarian Decree and other incidents of the late 430s were generally regarded as its causes, though Th. himself came to realize that the real cause of the war was deeper and of longer standing than the incidents that sparked it off (cf. V.26n.). Th. uses the expression *truest cause* on one other occasion, when he is giving the real, underlying motive for Athens' expedition to Sicily as opposed to pretexts publicly expressed (VI.6, where it is translated by Warner as "In fact").

**What made war inevitable was the growth of Athenian power and the fear which this caused in Sparta:** the Gk. is better translated as "fear of Athens' growing power compelled the Spartans to go to war." In theory the Spartans could have chosen not to go to war; in practice, because they believed their survival was threatened, they felt they had no choice. See I.36n., 118n. on the question of whether Th. does enough to establish the links between the growth of Athenian power, Spartan fear, and the outbreak of war.

Herodotus (I.1) had established the importance of determining the causes of events, but his scope was too wide-ranging for Th., who focused on interstate politics and war (cf. I.1n.). We may feel that he went too far: we would like to know more, for instance, about internal Athenian politics or about economic matters. But such matters are outside his parameters: Th. is presenting us with what he has decided we need to know about the causes of the war. The remainder of bk. I is devoted to an account of these causes. It falls into three major sections: the Corcyraean and Potidaean and other episodes that angered certain of Sparta's allies and caused them to urge Sparta to declare war on Athens (I.24–88); the somewhat inaccurately named Pentecontaetia (Fifty Years), covering the period from the end of the Persian Wars to the early 430s and describing the growth of Athenian power that, Th. asserts, ultimately frightened the Spartans into declaring war (I.89–118); and the period immediately preceding the outbreak of hostilities, during which negotiations were conducted between Athens and Sparta (I.118–46, with a digression in I.126–38). Thus the first and third of these sections give an account of events from the Epidamnus episode and the Corcyraean War to the outbreak of the Peloponnesian War. This narrative is interrupted by the Pentecontaetia at the point where the Spartans take their first step toward war because of their fear of the further growth of Athenian power. This leads Th., naturally enough, to describe the origins and growth of that power.

## I.24–30. The Dispute over Epidamnus

**I.24. Epidamnus:** called Dyrrachium by the Romans, now Durres in Albania. It was located on the eastern side of the approach to the **Ionic Gulf** (or Adriatic), about 150 miles to the north of **Corcyra,** modern Corfu. It was a colony (cf. I.12n.) of Corcyra, founded about 625.

**Heraclids:** cf. I.12n.

**political unrest . . . the democratic party . . . The aristocratic party:** the usual form of stasis, between democrats and oligarchs; see I.2n.

**the temple of Hera:** for the use of altars and temples as sanctuary see I.126, 128, 134; III.28, 70, 75, 79–81—all cases in which the right of asylum was abused. Cf. the discussions recounted in IV.97–98.

**I.25. Delphi:** site of the oracle of Apollo. The oracle would have been consulted before any major undertaking such as the foundation of a colony (cf. the case of Heraclea, III.92) and was perhaps considered to have some interest in its development: see Graham 1964, 25–27. The Delphic oracle remained even at this period an important factor in Greek politics, and Greek states were anxious both to have influence there (shown, e.g., by the Sacred War, I.112) and to have its support for major enterprises (for its pro-Peloponnesian leanings at the beginning of the war see I.118, II.54). There was also the possibility of borrowing from its treasuries (I.121, 143). For Th.'s views on oracles see II.8n.

**colony . . . mother city:** a colony would be self-governing but would normally retain sentimental and religious ties with its mother city, though Corinth had a hand in the government of some of its colonies (e.g., Potidaea, I.56). Ill feeling between Corinth and Corcyra went back a long way, and Corcyra asserted its independence from its mother city at a very early date: see I.13.

**their naval superiority:** there were three great naval powers in Greece at this time, Athens, Corinth, and Corcyra; cf. I.33, 36.

**Phaeacians:** for their reputation as sailors see Homer *Odyssey* VI.270–72, VII.34–36.

**I.26. Ambraciots, Leucadians:** Corinthian colonies and pro-Peloponnesian in the war; cf. II.9.

**Apollonia, a Corinthian colony:** in fact, it was founded jointly by Corinth and Corcyra.

**the Illyrian army:** Illyria was north of Epirus and west of Macedonia.

**I.27. fifty Corinthian drachmae:** each state minted its own coins, which varied in weight and thus in value (dependent entirely on weight at the time). The Corinthian drachma was about two-thirds the value of its Attic equivalent, for which see the Penguin translation, app. 2, p. 612.

**I.28. envoys from Sparta:** the affair was now being taken seriously in high places and was regarded as a threat to peace and potentially damaging to Peloponnesian unity.

**arbitration:** the appointment, by mutual agreement, of impartial mediators to settle the matter. It was often provided for in treaties (e.g., the Thirty Years' Truce of 446/5) in case of disputes. It was an important issue in the period before the outbreak of war: see I.78n.

**the colony should go to whichever side the arbitrators awarded it:** as this episode develops Th. gradually loses sight of the interests and rights of the Epidamnians, who, following the intervention (ironically at Epidamnian request) of greater powers, are now too weak and strife-ridden to assert their independence. Further, the purpose of the arbitration proposed by Corcyra is to decide whether possession and control of Epidamnus should go to Corinth or Corcyra, as if the Epidamnians' own wishes were irrelevant and Corinth and Corcyra had the right to assume control over them and settle their fate. This behavior is, of course, typical of imperialist states, as we shall see in the case of Athens, and illustrates one of Th.'s main interests: the abuse of superior military power and the exploitation and oppression of the weak by the strong. The Archaeology (I.2–19) has already prepared us for this theme (e.g., I.8n.).

**in quarters where they had no wish to make friends:** Athens presumably. The Corinthians made a similar threat to the Spartans in 432 (I.71).

**I.29. They sent . . . a herald to declare war:** the usual procedure before hostilities were commenced. The herald enjoyed a kind of diplomatic immunity, so that even in wartime interstate communication could be safely conducted. Cf. I.146, II.1.

**2,000 hoplites:** though three thousand (from Corinth alone) were equipped at I.27; either there has been a copyist's error or, for some reason not explained by Th., the full force was not sent out.

**I.30. the Corcyraeans put up a trophy:** armor captured from the enemy was dedicated in gratitude by the victorious side.

**Leucas:** for its earlier assistance to Corinth see I.26.

**Cyllene:** a Peloponnesian naval base on the coast of Elis. Cf. II.84. For Elean assistance to Corinth see I.27.

**Chimerium in Thesprotis:** Thesprotis was the southern, coastal region of Epirus; Chimerium was approximately east of the island of Paxos; cf. I.46.

## I.31–44. The Dispute over Corcyra: (i) The Debate at Athens

The Athenian response to Corcyra's request will have serious repercussions, and Th. gives the episode the full treatment. The arguments of the participants, the forces that act on the Athenians' thinking, and the motives underlying their decision are investigated in what is to be Th.'s standard technique, a pair of antithetical speeches. See I.22 and my introduction, under "The Aims and Methods of Thucydides." Like most of Th.'s debates this one goes beyond the immediate circumstances to raise wider, more abstract issues that, it will be seen, are relevant to other episodes and thus provide a thread of continuity through the war. In this case the Athenians are faced with a choice between securing an advantage and fulfilling what the Corinthians claim to be obligations the Athenians owe them, a choice, to put it simply, between expediency and justice. It is possible that Th. was present at this meeting of the assembly and heard what was said.

**I.31. good terms were offered to bring them also from the rest of Hellas:** cf. I.35n.

**to join the Athenian alliance:** not the Delian League. Athens had alliances on equal terms with a number of states (II.9); this is what Corcyra now sought.

**An assembly:** Gk. *ekklesia.* Meetings were held regularly and all citizens (free Athenian males over the age of eighteen) could participate. Speeches for various courses of action would be followed by a vote, as in the following debate.

**spoke as follows:** Warner's translation of the formula with which most of Th.'s speeches are introduced. The Gk. literally means "said such things as these," which makes it clear that Th. is not claiming to give a verbatim record of the speech (for his method see I.22). Warner's translation thus suggests a precision that is not present in the Gk. Perhaps "along these lines" would be better.

### *I.32–36. The Corcyraean Speech at Athens*

**I.32. a wise thing . . . lack of foresight:** the Gk. language lends itself particularly well to making contrasts between opposing ideas, and such verbal antitheses figure frequently in Th.'s speeches. The phenomenon reflects the interest in the analysis of individual words and the search for ever more precise meanings that were widespread in intellectual circles in the Athens of Th.'s time. Sharpness of definition was often achieved by opposing contrasting ideas, e.g., justice and expediency (as in this speech), words and deeds (I.22n.), calculation and chance (I.120n.), reason and passion (I.86n.), and law and nature (V.105n.; *C.A.* 410–22). This interest was seen by some as a form of overcleverness. It was particularly associated with the Sophists (see my introduction, under "The Intellectual Background of Thucydides"; I.22n.), who gave instruction in the art of public speaking and whose subtle use of the techniques of persuasion aroused some mistrust—the theme of

Aristophanes' *Clouds;* cf. I.84n., III.38n. For source material on the Sophists a good place to start is *C.A.* 209–18, and on rhetoric in particular see *C.A.* 394–405. A useful modern account is Kerferd 1981.

**a wise thing:** an inadequate translation of the Gk. *sophrosyne,* a combination of decency, good sense, and moderation, described by Archidamus as "prudent," Gk. *emphron* (I.84). *Sophrosyne* is an important concept in Th. and is contrasted with both "lack of counsel" (Gk. *aboulia,* as here) and "arrogance" or "excess" (Gk. *hybris*). It acquired oligarchic overtones and is used by Th. as a mark of approval (e.g., VIII.24), though occasionally he seems to use it ironically (III.82, VIII.64). For a full study see North 1966.

**keeping ourselves to ourselves:** the pursuit of a quiet life or inactive neutrality (Gk. *hesychia* or *apragmosyne:* cf. I.70–71, II.40, VI.18, with nn.), the opposite of the continual activity and interventionism (Gk. *polypragmosyne,* VI.87n.) that were hallmarks of the Athenian character and empire.

**I.33. we are, after you, the greatest naval power in Hellas:** cf. I.25n.

**In case of war we should obviously be useful to you:** but in fact Corcyra remained detached from the mainstream of Greek events and was racked by stasis in 427 (III.70–85). It was of little assistance to Athens during the war (II.25; III.94–95; VI.30, 42; VII.31).

**Sparta is frightened of you and wants war:** Spartan fear of Athens was, in Th.'s view, the true cause of the war (I.23, 88, 118). The Corcyraeans play on Athenian concern for their security (for evidence of which see I.36n.).

**Corinth has attacked us first in order to attack you afterwards:** no proof is—or could be—offered.

**I.34. If the Corinthians say that you have no right:** the Corcyraeans are perhaps anticipating a Corinthian argument that the Corcyraeans have "rebelled" from them (cf. I.38, 40) and that Athens thus has no right, according to the terms of the Thirty Years' Truce (I.115), to receive them as allies.

**arbitration:** see I.28n.

**I.35. it is expressly written down in your treaty:** the Thirty Years' Truce again. The Corcyraeans appear to be summarizing from it and the Corinthians later (I.40) repeat the relevant clause in much the same words.

**to stop them from engaging troops:** it is interesting to note that members of states subject to Athens could serve as mercenaries in the forces of another state (as long as, presumably, that state was not at war with Athens); at the same time it looks as if Athens was able to put a stop to such service if it wished. Cf. I.31 and I.121n. on mercenaries in general.

**I.36. a war . . . which has almost broken out already:** the Corcyraeans are, naturally enough, anxious to persuade the assembly that a war is inevitable.

Their point is supported by Th. himself in I.44 and by two pieces of independent evidence: (1) the Decrees of Callias of 434/3 (M.L. 58 = *T.D.G.R.* 119), which arrange for the careful conservation of Athenian resources, implying that there is a serious danger of a Peloponnesian invasion of Attica; (2) the renewal of alliances, originally made in the 440s, between Athens and Rhegium (in southern Italy) and Athens and Leontini (in Sicily) in 433/2 (M.L. 63, 64 = *T.D.G.R.* 124, 125), which suggests that Rhegium and Leontini, foreseeing a war after the Corcyraean dispute, were anxious to confirm their link with Athens, in case they should need its help in a war against a pro-Peloponnesian Syracuse. It looks, therefore, as if war was widely regarded as a probability at the time when the Corcyraean ambassadors were in Athens. Why this should be has not been adequately explained: no sufficient grounds for Spartan fear, which is claimed to be the real cause of the war (I.23), have been advanced by this stage. See I.118n.

**is thus able to prevent naval reinforcements coming to the Peloponnese from there [Sicily and southern Italy]:** certainly an exaggeration; see I.44n. The Spartans hoped for assistance from the west (II.7), though they received virtually none.

**you will enter upon the war with our ships as well as your own:** the essence of the Corcyraean case. Corcyra had a fleet of 120 triremes (I.25). It was to be of little use to Athens in practice (I.33n.); it was more important that it should not fall into the hands of the Corinthians (see I.44, and cf. Corinthian irritation at their failure to acquire the Corcyraean navy, I.68).

**After this speech:** the Gk. says "such things did the Corcyraeans say," and Th. uses a similar formula to round off most of his speeches; see I.31n.

### *I.37–43. The Corinthian Reply*

**I.37. "Wisdom" and "Moderation" . . . entirely evil:** see I.32n. on the contrast and on moderation *(sophrosyne).*

**The ships of other states are forced to put into their harbours:** because of Corcyra's position en route to Sicily; but see I.44n.

**showing their good qualities in the relations of common justice:** the Gk., in fact, is a phrase normally translated as "submit their differences to arbitration"—which the Corcyraeans had offered to do (I.28).

**I.38. It is obvious, then, that, if the majority are pleased with us, Corcyra can have no good reason for being the only one that is dissatisfied:** the logic of this assertion is not immediately apparent.

**Epidamnus, which belongs to us:** a claim that speaks volumes about Corinthian attitudes. Epidamnus had been a Corcyraean colony with a Corinthian founder (I.24).

**I.39. arbitration:** the Corinthians now acknowledge the Corcyraean offer (I.28n., 34, 37n.).

**I.40. a clause in the treaty:** the Corinthians cannot deny the presence of the "neutrals clause" in the treaty of 446/5. This presents them with an awkward problem.

**Samos:** for its revolt in 440–439 see I.115–17. We have no other reference to this debate, which is part of the story of Spartan hostility toward Athens during the Pentecontaetia (I.69n.). Since only the Spartans could summon a meeting of the Peloponnesian League, presumably they took this initiative in support of Samos. Corinth's relations with Athens during this period were generally good, except during the First Peloponnesian War. There is no comparison between the Samians' withdrawal from the Delian League and Corcyra's request to join the Athenian alliance: Samos was an ally of Athens and the league and owed them certain obligations; Corcyra was quite independent of Corinth and had been for over two hundred years (I.13).

**I.41. Corinth then gave you twenty ships:** for Corinth's assistance to Athens in the latter's war with Aegina (date uncertain, but probably in the 490s), see Hdt. VI.89.

**I.42. we should like your young men to ask their elders about them:** cf. II.8n.

**Megara:** the reference is unclear, especially as we do not know the date of the so-called Megarian Decrees (I.67, 139, with nn.). There was clearly some ill feeling between Athens and Megara; relations between the two would have been strained since Megara's defection to the Peloponnesian side (I.114).

**I.43. the discussions at Sparta:** see I.40.

**I.44. The Athenians . . . discussed the matter at two assemblies:** in view of the temptations offered by the Corcyraeans and the weakness of many of the Corinthian counterarguments, it is perhaps surprising to discover that the Athenians were not wholeheartedly in favor of accepting Corcyra's offer—even more so when we read in Plutarch (*Per.* 29) that Pericles himself would have supported Corcyra. There must have been at Athens an influential body of opinion that saw a Corcyraean alliance as dangerously provocative. How did they present their case and why was there a change of mood at the second meeting? Th., always highly selective, chooses not to say.

**the alliance was to be of a defensive character:** i.e., the alliance operated only for purposes of defense against a third party; cf. V.48. It was changed to a full offensive/defensive alliance in 427 (III.75).

**The general belief was that . . . war . . . was bound to come:** as the Corcyraeans claimed; see I.33, 36n.

**Athens had no wish to see the strong navy of Corcyra pass into the hands of Corinth:** this seems a satisfactory explanation of the Athenian decision (cf. I.36n.), but some scholars have sought to improve on Th.—a bold move since he is very confident about Athenian motives (he could well have attended this meeting of the assembly). It has been suggested, for instance, that Athens wanted to extend its empire to the west and that Corcyra was a stepping stone to Sicily (cf. VI.30). It is difficult to establish the extent of Athenian interests in the west at this time. They had had allies in Sicily since, perhaps, the 450s (Egesta: M.L. 37 = *T.D.G.R.* 81; Leontini, early 440s: I.36n.) and in southern Italy (Rhegium, early 440s: I.36n.; cf. Thurii, a Panhellenic foundation of 444/3: *T.D.G.R.* 108). In 427 a small force set out from Athens to Sicily to examine the possibility of conquering the island (III.86), and later in the war, in addition to the planned conquest of Sicily in 415, there were some vague and highly ambitious ideas in the air at Athens (e.g., VI.90; Plut. *Nicias* 12, *Alcibiades* 17). But there is no evidence to suggest that Athens had any serious imperialist ambitions in the west in the late 430s. Another theory popular at one time, though it is quite unsupported by Th., was that Athens' interest in the west was essentially commercial. It is true that Athens, because of its poor soil (I.2), depended largely on imported grain (cf. I.120n.), some of which, along with other commodities, came from Sicily and southern Italy. But it is difficult to see how an alliance with Corcyra could have been of much value to Athens in this connection. The convenience of its position is noted by Th. at the end of this chapter, but its importance is easily exaggerated (I.36n.). Corcyra was not the only staging post on the route to Italy and Sicily, and merchant ships often sailed across the open sea between Sicily and Greece (e.g., VI.88, VII.31). Certainly control of Corcyra would not give Athens the power to close the route to the west or even restrict commercial intercourse between Greece and the west to any great degree.

**Then, too, it was a fact that Corcyra lay very conveniently on the coastal route to Italy and Sicily:** see previous n. and I.36n. This factor was clearly subsidiary in Athenian thinking.

### I.45–55. The Dispute over Corcyra: (ii) The Battle of Sybota

**I.45. Athens sent ten ships:** little more than a token contribution: Athens is keeping its involvement to a minimum (though Plut. *Per.* 29 offers a different, and less convincing, explanation). This and the second expedition are dated by an inscription (M.L. 61 = *T.D.G.R.* 126), detailing their finances, to the thirteenth and final days of the first prytany (a period of thirty-six days, beginning in mid-June) of 433/2.

**Lacedaimonius, son of Cimon:** so named because of his father's Spartan sympathies (I.102n.). He would thus be likely to show moderation in his command and would perhaps be a trusted and acceptable (to the Corinthians) mediator, should the need for negotiations arise.

**to avoid breaking the existing treaty:** all very well, and further evidence of Athens' desire not to be (or to be seen as) the aggressor, but Lacedaemonius is put in an almost impossible position—as the Athenians themselves later realized (hence the reinforcements of twenty ships: I.50).

**I.46. a fleet of 150 ships:** note that Epidaurus, Hermione, Troizen, and Cephallenia, which had participated in the first campaign (I.27), are now absent—perhaps under pressure from Sparta: see I.28.

**Acheron:** according to Greek mythology, the entrance to the Underworld.

**I.47. Sybota:** about five miles due east of the southern tip of Corcyra. The battle took place in (late) August 433.

**I.48. admirals:** the Gk. word, *strategoi* (sing. *strategos*), is the same as that for "generals," since the Athenians did not distinguish between leaders of naval forces and generals of armies. Ten generals were elected annually, one from each Attic tribe (though it seems that in special circumstances more than one general could be selected from the same tribe: *A.E.* p. 100, n. ii). This was the only remaining office of importance at Athens filled by voting (as opposed to the use of the lot, which was the means used in the latter part of the fifth century for the selection of most officials). The Spartans had a special office of naval commander, also translated by Warner as "admiral."

**I.49. The fighting was of a somewhat old-fashioned kind:** the development of the trireme (I.14n.) had resulted in a change in the nature of naval battles. The older types of ships were heavy and slow and thus difficult to maneuver; consequently naval battles often turned into land battles at sea, as the ships became jammed against each other and the troops boarded enemy vessels and fought hand to hand. The swiftness of the trireme meant that a skillful commander could outmaneuver his opponents, breaking through their line, perhaps shearing off enemy oars in the process, turning, ramming them amidships, and sinking them ("the maneuver of encirclement," Gk. *diekplous,* literally "a sailing through and out"). See, e.g., the victories of Phormio, 429/8 (II.83ff.). The great naval battle in the harbor of Syracuse in 413 turned into a land battle at sea because the large number of ships fighting in a confined space inhibited mobility: see VII.36 (where Th. mentions another maneuver, the *periplous*, which involved wheeling round and ramming), 62, 67, 70.

**hoplites:** heavily armed Greek infantrymen, the backbone of Greek armies since the seventh century. Hoplites fought in the phalanx, a roughly square formation that, if it maintained order, was able to "steamroller" the enemy. In fifth-century Athens the hoplite had to be wealthy enough to provide his own armor (which consisted of a metal helmet, a corselet, greaves, a spear, and a sword) and tended to belong to the **middle classes** (or Zeugitae, III.16n.), a cut above the Thetes who manned the fleet (I.10n.).

**who were on the decks:** see I.14n.

**Corinthians and Athenians were openly fighting with each other:** the crucial moment, the climax of Th.'s story. The Athenian intervention tips the balance against the Corinthians.

**I.50. the biggest battle:** the scale of the battle, the confusion, and the slaughter are a taste of things to come. Th. has chosen the Peloponnesian War as his subject because of the unique degree of suffering it caused (I.23).

**paean:** a battle hymn sung by Greek troops as they entered the fight.

**I.51. Andocides:** presumably a mistake made by a copyist; the name does not appear in *T.D.G.R.* 126; cf. I.45n.

**I.53. a herald's wand:** used to indicate a desire for a truce, thus presupposing a state of war.

**Peloponnesians . . . we are not breaking the treaty . . . we shall do our best to prevent you:** the generals of the second squadron had clearly been given the same instructions as those of the first.

**I.54. They also put up a trophy:** see I.30n.

**The reasons that each side had for claiming the victory:** i.e., victory in the battle, but, of course, the campaign belonged to Corcyra, as Th. recognizes with something of an understatement ("remained undefeated") in I.55.

**on the day after the battle:** a translator's error; the Gk. says "on the previous day," i.e., the day of the battle.

**I.55. Anactorium:** a Corinthian colony that may have included Corcyraean settlers. It had assisted Corinth but with only one ship (I.46).

**800 . . . slaves:** an unusual case, but cf. VIII.15 (Chios), VIII.84 (Syracuse and Thurii), and the battle of Arginusae in 406 (Xenophon *Hellenica* I.6.24); see also VII.13n. Otherwise it seems to have been Athenian and general Greek practice to use free men as rowers; cf. I.10n. For the return of the 250 to Corcyra see III.70.

**But this gave Corinth her first cause for war:** see I.23. Th. makes no judgment; he merely records a Corinthian grievance. Note the emphasis on Corinth; Sparta's role up to this point has been limited to an early embassy supporting negotiations (I.28), and interest elsewhere seems to have declined (cf. I.46n.).

## I.56–65. The Dispute over Potidaea

**I.56. Potidaea . . . Pallene:** in the northwest corner of the Aegean, a key strategic position (cf. the Corinthians' words at I.68). Potidaea was a Corinthian colony, founded in the late seventh century, but also at this time a tribute-paying member of the Athenian empire. This presumably means that in the Thirty Years' Truce the name of Potidaea would have been listed among the allies of Athens. This relationship should have taken precedence over its association with Corinth.

Possibly connected with Potidaea's revolt is the matter of its tribute payment to Athens. At some stage in the early 430s Potidaea's payment was raised from six to fifteen talents. The reason for the increase is unknown, but it was probably resented and may have been a factor in the revolt. Potidaea may also have felt intimidated by the Athenian foundation of Amphipolis in 437 (IV.102). Thus there is more to this than meets the eye: Potidaea seems to have been under pressure from Athens for some time.

**Corinth was searching for means of retaliation:** Th. offers little support for this claim, merely citing Athenian anxiety.

**Corinthian magistrates:** their exact functions are unknown. It was not customary for a mother city to intervene in the government of its colony; see I.25n.

**Perdiccas:** king of Macedonia. For the erratic course of his relations with Athens see II.29 (Perdiccas is an ally); II.80, 95 (Perdiccas is an enemy); IV.79 (Perdiccas is still an enemy, supporting Brasidas); IV.128, 132 (Perdiccas falls out with Brasidas and goes over to Athens); V.80 (Perdiccas breaks with Athens and in V.83 is at war with it); VII.9 (by this time, 414, Athens and Perdiccas are again allies). This catalog of caprice speaks for itself. Grundy (1948, 371) refers to Perdiccas as "the Mr. Mikawber of the Peloponnesian War—always waiting for something to turn up and always making singularly ineffective use of whatever came to hand . . . He changed often, but he changed nothing so far as the issue of the war was concerned." On earlier Macedonian history see II.99.

**the Thracian area:** on the importance to Athens of this northern region (with special reference to Amphipolis) see IV.108.

**I.57. his brother Philip and . . . Derdas:** little is known about either, though the latter was also probably a member of the Macedonian royal household, perhaps a cousin of Philip and Perdiccas.

**the Chalcidians in Thrace . . . the Bottiaeans:** inhabitants of the three peninsulas in the northwest Aegean and the region beyond them toward Macedonia.

**I.58. The Spartan authorities:** Th. presumably means the ephors, five senior Spartan magistrates (I.18n.). It is clear that there had been a drastic change of opinion in this body since the Corcyra episode (cf. I.69n.). Th. seems to have had an intimate knowledge of Spartan politics: see V.26n.

**making that into one big city:** the process of synoecism; see I.10n.

**Mygdonia . . . Lake Bolbe:** in northern Chalcidice.

**I.60. a force of volunteers . . . and of mercenaries:** i.e., not conscripted Corinthian troops (war has not yet been declared). But were they still part of an official Corinthian expedition? See I.66n.

**Aristeus, the son of Adeimantus:** Adeimantus had commanded the Corinthian contingent at the battle of Salamis in 480. Th. seems keen here to emphasize his son's popularity.

**I.61. Callias:** probably the Callias who moved the so-called Decrees of Callias (M.L. 58 = *T.D.G.R.* 119; cf. I.36n.).

**Therme:** at the site of modern Thessalonica. **Pydna** was on the western shore of the Thermaic Gulf, south of Methone.

**Leaving Macedonia, then, they came to Beroea:** there is probably a textual problem here, since the only Beroea we know of is inland in Macedonia.

**Strepsa:** its exact site is uncertain, but it was probably northwest of Therme on the Pella road.

**Pausanias:** not mentioned before.

**Gigonus:** on the coast, northwest of Potidaea.

**I.62. the isthmus facing Olynthus:** about a mile north of Potidaea. Cf. I.63.

**I.64. Phormio:** a prominent Athenian general; see III.7n. For some of his earlier activity see II.68, and for his important victories in the Corinthian Gulf in 429/8 see II.83–92.

**Potidaea was firmly invested:** for the date of the battle see II.2. For the Athenian capture of Potidaea, after a long and costly siege, see II.70. The

Athenians continued to keep a close eye on the Chalcidice area: see, e.g., II.79. The episode illustrates (if we need further illustration) Athens' determination to keep the empire intact at all costs.

**Aphytis:** on the eastern side of Pallene, southeast of Potidaea.

## I.66. Survey of the Consequences of the Corcyra and Potidaea Episodes

**on the private initiative of Corinth:** it is unclear whether the Gk. means that the Corinthians acted on their own, i.e., without the authority and cooperation of the Peloponnesian League, or unofficially, i.e., without the formal sanction of the Corinthian government. The former is more natural and would mean that Corinth, by its assistance to the rebel Potidaea, an ally of Athens, had broken the Thirty Years' Truce.

## 1.67–88. The Debate at Sparta

This crucial stage in the progress toward war, in which the Spartans decide that the Athenians have acted aggressively and have broken the treaty, is marked by a unique quartet of speeches, the longest debate in Th.'s work and perhaps the most complex.

The first pair of speeches, delivered anonymously, focuses on the growth of Athenian power: first, a Corinthian speaker examines certain key national characteristics and attitudes of both the Athenians and the Spartans that he claims underlie the rise of Athens, and then an Athenian advances the Athenian case (in historical and philosophical terms) for their empire. It is often pointed out that the Athenian speech sits uncomfortably in its surroundings: the speaker is unidentified, his presence and authority are unexplained, and his speech bears little relation to that of the Corinthian delegate before it or that of Archidamus after it. The speech is, in effect, a general justification of Athenian behavior, set in the context of an analysis of power in terms found elsewhere in Th.'s history. Only in his final words does the Athenian speaker refer to immediate issues. Is Th., then, using this important occasion to raise the essential questions of imperialism that will be fundamental to his work? Did he compose the bulk of the speech himself? Possibly, but the abstractness of the Athenian speech is not in itself an argument for such a view and, if it is the delegate's purpose to convince his audience that the Athenians will do all they can to cling to power, then the speech is by no means irrelevant to the situation. Nor must we overlook the impression given in I.72 that Th. had spoken to the Athenian delegates and knew their intentions.

The second pair of speeches, delivered in the privacy of the Spartan assembly, addresses the immediate situation, revealing the extremes of attitude to be found among the Spartans at this time and concluding with a demand for war. At the same time Archidamus' speech corresponds to that of the Corinthians, defending the Spartan character and way of life against Corinthian criticism, while Sthenelaidas' brief outburst is a response to the self-justification of the Athenians. Finally, the second and third speeches, though delivered by parties from opposing sides, share the same overall purpose—to prevent or at least postpone the outbreak of war—and have a number of arguments in common.

**I.67. Corinth . . . Aegina . . . Megara:** thus the three major naval powers of the Peloponnese are particularly keen to incite the Spartans to war. They would suffer more than their continental allies at the hands of the Athenians, as the Corinthians say later (I.120). Cf. I.69n.

**She . . . urged the allies to send delegates to Sparta:** though it was the Spartans who summoned the meeting, as the Corinthians acknowledge in the following chapter. This was clearly not a meeting of the Peloponnesian League but a Spartan assembly (cf. text later in this chapter, **their usual assembly**) to which allies were invited, to be followed by a meeting of the league proper (I.87, 119–25).

**Aegina:** see I.14n. The island had been besieged and captured by Athens in 457 (I.105, 108) and was a member of the Delian League. The Athenians later accuse the Aeginetans of "having been largely responsible for the war" (II.27).

**independence:** the Gk. is a cognate of the noun *autonomia*, "autonomy." This is an imprecise and flexible term that is regularly used of states within the empire that are paying tribute (e.g., I.97, V.18), even, as in the present case, of a state that has lost its walls and navy. Literally the word means "freedom to live under one's own laws" or, in the words of Gomme (*H.C.T.* 1:384), "the freedom of a state to conduct its own internal affairs," the true mark of which was a state's "complete control over her magistrates" (*H.C.T.* 1:342). Autonomy is often associated with full freedom (Gk. *eleutheria*), which is, of course, a broader concept.

**the independence promised to them by the treaty:** the treaty referred to is either the treaty of 457 between Athens and Aegina, by which Aegina joined the Delian League and began to pay tribute (I.108), or the Thirty Years' Truce of 446/5, which must thus have contained a special clause relating to Aegina of which we hear nothing elsewhere. The latter seems more likely, since the Peloponnesians were in a much stronger position in 446/5 than in 457 to secure concessions from Athens. We do not know how Aegina's autonomy was infringed: perhaps it was by the installation of an Athenian garrison on the island, a position of considerable strategic importance to Athens. It need hardly be added that we are in no position to judge the claim that a treaty has been broken.

**Megara:** the sources are much fuller than for the case of Aegina, though they do not lead us to any more positive conclusions. They are I.67, 139, 140, 144; Plut. *Per.* 29–31; Aristophanes *Acharnians* 515–39 and *Peace* 605–18; see also *T.D.G.R.* 122, 123. Of these, Th. is our most trustworthy source, though he mentions the Megarian Decree only a few times and then very briefly. Aristophanes was, of course, also contemporary with the events he is describing, but as a writer of comedies he employed a degree of license in his references to politicians and political events: we cannot take what he says at face value. Plutarch was a biographer, writing ca. A.D. 100; his reliability varies according to the quality of his sources and his clearheadedness at the time of writing.

The original offense of the Megarians was that they had cultivated some consecrated ground and had harbored runaway slaves (I.139, elaborated on by Plutarch). Th. mentions only one decree, of which the gist is that the Megarians were excluded from all the ports in the Athenian empire and from the agora of Athens itself (I.67, 139). The agora was the social and civic center of Athens as well as a marketplace. The Megarians asserted that this decree contravened the Thirty Years' Truce (I.67).

A widely accepted interpretation of the decree is that its immediate purpose was economic, to destroy the commerce of Megara, but that the ultimate motive was political, to weaken Megara and to reduce its value (cf. I.103n. on its position) to the Peloponnesians. The Athenians would thus be the aggressors, abusing their control of the Aegean to destroy a neighbor dependent on trade in that region, and, perhaps, breaking the terms of the 446/5 truce. This interpretation is to some extent based on material to be found in the plays of Aristophanes, where the decree is claimed to be a major cause of the war, presumably reflecting (or exaggerating) talk current in the mid-420s (cf. I.139n.). Otherwise it is a modern invention, going far beyond anything Th. has to say on the subject. De Ste. Croix (1972) offered a radically different interpretation of the decree, arguing that its purpose was neither economic nor imperialist but religious and that the behavior of Athens in this affair was both justified and moderate.

## *I.68–71. The Corinthian Speech*

**I.68. the great trust and confidence which you have in your own constitution and in your own way of life:** the Spartans were well known for being conservative and inward-looking. The Spartan constitution was some four hundred years old. Cf. I.18n.

**moderate . . . ignorance:** see I.32nn. on *sophrosyne* (moderation) and on the contrast.

**insolent aggression:** the Corinthians' opening remarks set an emotive tone for the debate.

**Corcyra might have contributed a very large fleet to the Peloponnesian League:** 120 triremes, according to the Corcyraeans themselves (I.25).

**I.69. It was you who . . . allowed the Athenians to fortify their city:** for the story of the rebuilding of the Athenian walls after the Persian Wars of 480/79 see I.89–93.

**you have withheld freedom:** on a number of occasions since the early 470s Sparta had considered taking aggressive action against the growing power of Athens: ca. 477, soon after Athens had taken over the leadership of the Greek fleet (Diodorus XI.50; cf. I.95n.); in the 460s when the Spartans promised Thasos that they would invade Attica (I.101); in 440 when they summoned a meeting of the Peloponnesian League to discuss intervention on behalf of Samos in its revolt against Athens but could not secure a majority in favor (I.40); in 432 when "the authorities" in Sparta promised to support Potidaea (I.58); and at an unknown date before the outbreak of war when Sparta declined to support a revolt of Lesbos (III.2, 13). If the Spartans rendered assistance to Athenian oligarchs who were working to destroy the democracy in the 450s (I.107), their help was ineffectual. Indeed, all promises of military intervention came to nothing. Even in the First Peloponnesian War (460–46), where again the initiative was taken by Corinth, the Spartans' contribution appears to have been less than wholehearted, and when they had an opportunity to strike a truly damaging blow at Athens they passed it up (I.114). There was in Sparta an anti-Athenian faction that was stronger at some times than at others. We should not be surprised at this inconsistency: a change in the ephorate could produce a swing in foreign policy in Sparta (V.36). But the fact is that no action was taken against Athens. Cf. I.118: "The Spartans . . . did little or nothing to prevent it [the growth of Athenian power] . . . being traditionally slow to go to war, unless they were forced into it." Promises were made and broken. Intervention was prevented either by circumstance or by those elements that wished to limit Spartan activity to within the Peloponnese, concentrating on internal security and avoiding foreign commitments, preferring an uneasy friendship with the Athenians to war with them.

But as far as some of the Spartans' allies were concerned, Sparta's cautious awareness of its limitations had developed into a powerful negative influence that had strangled its initiative. It had blinded Sparta to the threat presented by the growth of Athenian power to those states that were not self-sufficient (Sparta was much more self-sufficient than most), those states whose influence in the Aegean or elsewhere had been eroded by Athenian encroachment, or those who were simply too close to Athens for comfort—and in the late 430s Corinth, Aegina, and Megara fell into all three categories.

**those who have been enslaved by Athens:** not to be taken literally; see I.98n.

**the liberator of Hellas:** a reference to the Spartan policy of deposing tyrants (I.18) and the Spartan leadership of the Greek forces against the Persians in 480–479. In the Peloponnesian War too Sparta undertook to bring freedom to the Greeks (II.8).

**You Spartans are the only people in Hellas who wait calmly on events . . . You alone do nothing in the early stages:** Th. concurs; cf. again I.118, "The Spartans . . . did little or nothing to prevent it . . . " Cf. I.70n.

**the chief reason for the failure of the Persian invasion was the mistaken policy of the Persians themselves:** hardly fair to Themistocles and the Athenians, but the Corinthians are unlikely to be objective on an occasion such as this. Cf. Hermocrates at VI.33.

**I.70. the enormous difference between you and the Athenians:** this speech is perhaps best known for its lengthy analysis of the Spartan and Athenian characters, in which the speaker, in a string of rhetorical contrasts, highlights some fundamental differences between the two states and the consequences these had in terms of their attitudes and political development. His main point is that it was Athenian enterprise, ambition, and speed of action that built an empire and that the process was encouraged by the excessive caution and indifference of the Spartans. The speech thus gives us another angle on the growth of Athenian power that is, in Th.'s view, the main cause of the war. Energy and restlessness (Gk. *polypragmosyne;* see I.32n.), both corporate and individual, are essential characteristics of the Athenian way of life and the basis of Athenian imperialism. They are recurrent themes in Th.: see especially the words of Pericles at II.41, Nicias at VI.9, Alcibiades at VI.18, and Euphemus at VI.87; see also the endorsement of Th. himself at IV.55 and VIII.96; cf. Pericles' attacks on individual political apathy at II.40, 63. But the possession of power and the need to exercise and expand it (and to be seen to be doing so) impose an increasing strain on Athens. Power is a trap: see I.75nn., VI.18n.

Sparta, in contrast, never went to war unless compelled to do so (I.118, quoted at I.69n.). During the war the Spartans were slow to act (cf. V.75n.), even lethargic (IV.108), and this worked in Athens' favor (VIII.96). Their caution sprang in part from concern for security (cf. VIII.24), especially in relation to the helots (I.101n., IV.80), but was also a matter of national character (cf. V.63). Brasidas was an interesting exception (IV.81), and the response of his fellow Spartans to his success is enlightening (IV.108).

**You, on the other hand, are good at keeping things as they are:** cf. I.71, "your whole way of life is out of date when compared with theirs . . . Athens . . . is a far more modern state than you are." See I.18n. on Sparta's famed political conservatism, which, however, served it well during the war—unlike Athens, Sparta did not fall prey to stasis. As Th. himself saw things, the Spartans "kept their heads in prosperity" (VIII.24).

**peace and quiet:** the Gk. is the adjective from *apragmosyne,* the opposite of *polypragmosyne;* see n. earlier in this chapter.

**I.71. Your inactivity:** Gk. *apragmosyne* again; see previous n.

**the help you promised:** see I.58.

**to join a different alliance:** possibly with Argos, possibly even with Athens, perhaps a new alliance altogether.

**the gods who witnessed our oaths:** the oaths sworn by states entering the Peloponnesian League. They swore to have the same friends and enemies as the Spartans and to follow wheresoever the Spartans should lead. Thus the oath enshrined the principle of Sparta's military leadership. Cf. V.30.

### *I.72–78. The Athenian Speech*

**I.72. some Athenian representatives who had come there on other business:** Th. must have known more about them but chooses not to tell us. Perhaps the speech, which is a justification of Athenian policy over nearly half a century, is too important to be linked with any particular individual. This is Athens itself speaking.

**to inform the younger ones of matters in which they were ignorant:** cf. II.8n.

**I.73. even though you may be tired of constantly hearing the story:** the Athenians seem to have found it difficult to resist the temptation to recall their contribution to Greek success in the Persian Wars. Pericles acknowledged that the story was a familiar one (II.36).

**In our actions at that time we ventured everything for the common good:** thus the Athenians justify their empire. Such "fine phrases" are later eschewed by the Athenian delegate at Melos (V.89) and by Euphemus at Camarina (VI.83).

**At Marathon we stood out against the Persians . . . single-handed:** in 490, during the first Persian invasion of Greece. Athens had been one of the Persians' prime objectives because of the assistance it had given to the Ionians in their revolt against Persia. This claim ignores the Plataean support of Athens on this occasion (Hdt. VI.108); cf. I.18n.

**we and all our people took to our ships:** see I.89n.

**Salamis:** see I.14n.

**I.74. the most unflinching courage:** acknowledged even by Sparta; see I.90, 92.

**Out of the 400 ships:** there is some uncertainty over the figure. The ancient sources are far from consistent. Herodotus (VIII.48) gives 378 as the total and Athens' contribution as 200, which can hardly be described as **nearly two-thirds.** Other sources (Aeschylus *Persae* 338; Demosthenes XVIII.238; Nepos *Themistocles* 3) give 300 as the total, and 300 has been suggested as a possible emendation for the 400 in Th.'s text.

**Themistocles:** cf. I.14, 90–93, 135–38.

**You . . . treated him with more distinction than you have ever treated any visitor from abroad:** Themistocles was feted at Sparta after the war was over; see Hdt. VIII.124. Cf. I.91 for the Spartans' respect for Themistocles and the use he made of it in the affair of the walls.

**all the states up to our frontier already enslaved:** see I.90n. On "enslaved" see I.98n.

**a city that had ceased to exist:** a city without its citizens is a city no longer. Cf. Pericles' statement, "What we should lament is not the loss of houses or of land, but the loss of men's lives. Men come first; the rest is the fruit of their labor" (I.143), and Nicias' statement, "It is men who make the city, and not walls or ships with no men inside them" (VII.77). See also VI.23n.

**I.75. we did not gain this empire by force . . . you were unwilling to fight on to the end against the Persians:** see I.95n.

**our allies came to us of their own accord and begged us:** confirmed by Th. at I.95; cf. Euphemus at VI.82.

**It was the actual course of events which first compelled us . . . :** the Athenians are not in complete control of their power: cf. next n. and n. later in this chapter, **it was clearly no longer safe. . .**

**fear . . . honour . . . interest:** the motives that originally led the Athenians to create their empire and now compel them to cling to it. Similar motives (but fear in particular) drove the Spartans to destroy it (I.23, 88, 118). Fear too had driven the Greeks to support the expedition against Troy, Th. believed (I.9), and later compelled the Athenians to attack Melos (V.99) and Sicily (VI.18, 82–87). Fear prompted the Greeks to support Sparta against Athens at the beginning of the war (II.8). According to the Athenian

Euphemus fear lay at the root of Athens' search for power: "we rule in order not to be ruled" (VI.87). See I.70n.

The Athenian pursuit of honor, respect, and admiration is referred to a number of times in speeches, e.g., I.76, 144; II.41 ("Future ages will wonder at us . . ."), 64 ("Athens has the greatest name in all the world"). Other states too acted from this motive, e.g., Corinth (I.38), Sparta (IV.18, VI.11; cf. III.57), and Syracuse (VII.56).

**we were surrounded by enemies:** the Athenians clearly considered themselves unpopular among their subjects; cf. I.77n.

**it was clearly no longer safe for us to risk letting our empire go:** cf. Pericles' words at II.63, "it may have been wrong to take it; it is certainly dangerous to let it go," and Alcibiades' speech in 415, "we are . . . forced to hold on to what we have got" (VI.18). Pericles says that some Athenians talked of abandoning the empire, but it seems unlikely, and there is no evidence that the idea was seriously entertained at this (or any other) time. For consideration of it as a last resort by oligarchic extremists in 411 see VIII.91.

**I.76. if . . . you had gone on taking an active part in the war:** see I.75n.

**Three very powerful motives:** cf. I.75n.

**the weak should be subject to the strong:** cf. IV.61 and the Melian Dialogue (V.84–113, especially 105n.).

**I.77. contracts:** Gk. *symbola,* agreements between two states that determined judicial procedures to be followed in cases arising between members of those two states, ensuring reciprocal rights. See *A.E.* 166–72. The Athenians are claiming that despite their reasonableness on this matter they suffer a double disadvantage: first, when cases are tried by allied courts the Athenians have to face local prejudice; second, when the allies bring cases to Athens (as they were compelled to do in certain circumstances: see Old Oligarch I.16) the Athenians are criticized for litigiousness (**overfond of going to law:** cf. Aristophanes' *Wasps*). On Athens' general beneficence and restraint see Pericles' words at II.40. On the economic benefits for ordinary Athenians of bringing allies cases to Athens for trial see Old Oligarch I.16–18.

**Our subjects, on the other hand, are used to being treated as equals:** the speaker declines to give further examples. Cf. Th.'s own words at I.99, and for an allied point of view see III.10.

**indeed they feel more bitterly:** this example of allied ill feeling toward Athens raises the vexed question of the popularity of the Athenian empire among its subjects. The evidence is one-sided (i.e., Athenian)—we must therefore allow for the possibility of distortion—and inconsistent. It is often assumed, from the testimony of Th. and the epigraphic evidence of revolts, that Athens' rule was unpopular among its subjects: cf. I.99, II.8, VI.69 (final sentence), VIII.2. Athens' unpopularity is also mentioned a number of times in speeches (e.g., II.11, III.10, V.99) and is openly acknowledged by Athenian politicians (at II.63 by Pericles, at III.37 by Cleon). However, de Ste. Croix (1954/55, 1ff.) argues, from evidence supplied by Th. himself, that generally the masses in allied states were happy with Athenian rule (see in particular the words of Diodotus at III.47; cf. opening of III.82, IV.84); de Ste. Croix suggests that Th., whose political outlook was oligarchic (see my introduction), looked at Athens' relations with its allies from the point of view of the oligarchs in the subject states who resented Athenian domination since they often lost power as a result of it. See *A.E.* pp. 19–21.

**in the short time when you led Hellas against the Persians:** for the unpopularity of Spartan leadership in the period immediately following the Persian Wars see I.94–96.

**when one of you goes abroad:** the speaker was perhaps thinking of Pausanias (I.95, 128–35). For examples of individual Spartan tactlessness and brutality abroad during the war see III.32, 93. For an exception see IV.81 on Brasidas.

**I.78. the unpredictable in war:** Archidamus makes the same point at I.82, 84; see also I.120n.

**Action comes first, and it is only when they have already suffered that they begin to think:** this is what Archidamus also fears (I.85n.). The speaker is in fact drawing the distinction between deeds and words: see I.22n., 32n. Cf. Pericles' words at II.40, "the worst thing . . . "

**arbitration:** the Thirty Years' Truce of 446/5 required that differences should be settled by arbitration (I.28n.); this should be the next step. This point is picked up by Archidamus at the end of his speech (I.85), and the Spartans later (VII.18) acknowledge their failure to follow proper procedure. See also Pericles' words at I.140, 144, and the repeat of the Athenian offer at I.145.

**I.79. King Archidamus:** king of the Eurypontid house, one of the two Spartan royal families (I.18n.); he reigned ca. 469–ca. 427.

**intelligence:** Gk. *synesis* (noun), *synetos* (adj.), an accolade given to a number of men admired by Th. for their intellect, e.g., Themistocles (I.138), Theseus (II.15), Brasidas (IV.81), the Pisistratids (VI.54), Hermocrates (VI.72), and Phrynicus (VIII.27), but not Pericles, who is accorded another quality, Gk. *gnome,* also translated by Warner as intelligence (II.65n.).

**moderation:** Gk. *sophrosyne* again; cf. I.32n.

Archidamus remained cautious till the very outbreak of war: cf. the tone of his speech at II.11 and II.12n., 18n.

**I.80. Spartans, in the course of my life:** Archidamus' opening reference to his age and experience is intended to establish his credentials as an elder statesman. Age in Th. is often equated with wisdom and caution; cf. II.8n.

**general enthusiasm:** the Athenians had warned against haste at the end of their speech, and Archidamus picks up the point. On the influence of emotion as opposed to reason in Th. see I.86, introductory n.

**When we are engaged with Peloponnesians and neighbors:** the Greeks had always found it difficult to live peaceably together. Cf. I.2n. and I.15n. on a common cause of friction between neighbors.

**a population bigger than that of any other place in Hellas:** see Th.'s figures at II.13; see also Rhodes 1988, 271–77. But the Peloponnesian total was greater: see I.81n.

**Our navy:** the Peloponnesian navy was much inferior to the Athenian, especially now that Athens could call on assistance from Corcyra (I.44). Peloponnesian hopes of securing naval help from Sicily (II.7) came to nothing.

**we have no public funds:** members of the Peloponnesian League did not pay tribute; thus there was no common fund on which they could now draw (cf. I.19n.). For some attempts at fund-raising in the early years of the war see II.7 and *T.D.G.R.* 132. Archidamus returns to the subject of money in I.83. The Corinthians were also aware of the problem but were, of course, more optimistic (I.121). Th. had recognized the importance of finance in connection with naval expeditions in the Archaeology (I.11–12). Pericles notes this Peloponnesian weakness (I.142).

**I.81. the superiority which we have in heavy infantry and in actual numbers:** the Corinthians make the same claim at I.121, and the point is acknowledged by Pericles at I.143. On the total numbers of troops available to the Peloponnesians see II.10n.

**devastate their land:** the primary weapon of the Peloponnesians in the opening years of the war was the annual invasion of Attica, undertaken to destroy crops and property; see II.10n.

**Athens . . . can import what she wants by sea:** cf. Pericles' words at II.38, with n.; also I.120n.

**to make her allies revolt from her:** eventually, with Persian help, the Peloponnesians brought down Athens in this way, but earlier attempts to encourage and support rebellion were sometimes worse than useless (e.g., III.32).

**especially if it is thought that it was we who began the quarrel:** as will prove to be the case, because they reject Athenian offers of arbitration; cf. VII.18n.

**false hope:** cf. I.121n. The Peloponnesians did indeed enter the war with this hope: see V.14, VII.28.

**I.82. What I do suggest is that we should not take up arms at the present moment:** Archidamus gets his way on this point (I.125).

**instead we should send to them and put our grievances before them . . . In the meantime we should be making our own preparations:** thus Archidamus' response to the present crisis consists of a mixture of words and action (cf. I.22n.); his opponent Sthenelaidas advocates action alone (I.86).

**new allies:** e.g., the Greeks in the west (II.7) and Persia (II.67, IV.50).

**I warn you . . . still more shame and still greater difficulties:** Archidamus has little sympathy with the plight of the Corinthians. He does not see why the Spartans and other Peloponnesian states should get embroiled in a long and destructive war on their account. However, with a majority clearly in favor of war, the best Archidamus can do is propose a course of action that will postpone its outbreak and thus give Sparta a chance to prepare.

**it is impossible to foresee the course that the war will take:** Archidamus is reinforcing a point made by the Athenian speaker at I.78. See also I.120n.

**I.83. money:** cf. I.80n.

**I.84. the usual criticism made against us:** there follows a defense of the traditional Spartan virtues attacked by the Corinthians (I.68–69).

**"wise" and "sensible":** in the Gk. *sophrosyne,* reinforced by the adjective *emphron* (prudent); see I.32n.

**being too clever:** Gk. *synetos,* intelligent, generally a term of praise in Th.; see I.79n. Archidamus is implicitly criticizing Athens, the home at this period of intellectual experimentation—dangerous nonsense, perhaps, in the eyes of the conservative Archidamus, who preferred Spartan rigor and unquestioning acceptance (though he himself is capable of a sophistic approach to argument if this chapter is anything to go by). Suspicion of these new ideas was not unknown in Athens: cf. I.32n. and the case of Cleon at III.37, who echoes some of Archidamus' ideas. Pericles denied that intellectual pursuits had a deleterious effect on the Athenian character (II.40).

**being able to produce an excellent theoretical criticism of one's ene-**

**mies, and then failing in practice:** the distinction in the Gk. is again that between word and deed, the antithesis employed by the Athenian speaker at I.78

**impossible to calculate accurately events that are determined by chance:** another point made by the previous speaker (I.78; cf. I.82n.).

**to put our hopes in the reliability of our own precautions:** see I.81n.

**I.85. We ought to take time over such a decision:** the advice of the Athenian delegate; see I.78n.

**arbitration:** cf. I.78n.

## *I.86. The Speech of Sthenelaidas*

An idea fundamental to Th.'s thinking is the antithesis between passion (Gk. *orge*) and rational forethought or calculation (Gk. *gnome* or *logismos*), and a feature of some Thucydidean debates is the power of emotive rhetoric to overwhelm reasoned argument. Sthenelaidas' speech is the most emotional in this debate; it is also the most influential. This is not the last time we shall see in Th. an important decision being made in an atmosphere unsuited to calm and rational consideration, in which men's minds (particularly those of the young; see, e.g., II.8, 21) are governed by emotion rather than by reason (see especially the Sicilian debate, VI.9–23, with Th.'s comments in VI.24). Cleon actually advocated making decisions in the heat of passion (III.38). This for Th. was a major weakness of the Athenian democratic system. On a similar contrast, between the gratification of immediate pleasure and rational planning to satisfy long-term needs, see II.65n.; cf. also I.121n. on wishful thinking, another enemy of calculation.

**I do not understand these long speeches:** like Cleon at III.37–38, Sthenelaidas presents himself as the down-to-earth anti-intellectual who will not allow his clear and simple view of the situation to be obscured by lengthy discussion. On Spartan brevity cf. IV.17.

**they make no attempt to contradict the fact that they are acting aggressively:** true, but the Athenians had argued that this was not the occasion for discussion of this issue (I.73).

**they had a good record in the past against the Persians:** cf. I.69n., 73–74.

**they deserve to pay double:** cf. the Theban argument about the Plataeans, III.67.

**We are the same then and now:** cf. Cleon again at III.38, but also Pericles at I.140, II.61.

**if we are sensible:** the verb from *sophrosyne;* cf. I.32n. Sthenelaidas claims this important virtue, of which Archidamus has made much, in support of his own case.

**this is not a matter to be settled by law-suits and by words . . . let no one try to tell us that . . . we should sit down and discuss matters:** Sthenelaidas rejects words (as advocated by the Athenian delegate and Archidamus) and demands action; cf. I.22n.

**Do not allow the Athenians to grow still stronger!:** the essence of Sthenelaidas' argument and, as Th. shows in I.88, the point that particularly appealed to his audience. Cf. I.23n.

*I.87–88. The Vote for War*

**I.87. voting:** usually done by the raising of hands or by written ballot (on pebbles or potsherds).

**make them all the more enthusiastic for war:** cf. I.80n.

**The great majority were of the opinion that the treaty had been broken:** the policy division represented by the speeches of Archidamus and Sthenelaidas had existed in Sparta since the early days of the Delian League (I.69n.), but by 432 anti-Athenian sentiment in Sparta had reached unprecedented levels. In due course the Spartans were able to take a more objective view (VII.28).

**a unanimous resolution:** it was decided to call a full meeting of the league so that Sparta could secure the commitment of all its allies. In fact, support for war was not unanimous (I.125).

**the allied delegates, having got their own way:** cf. I.67.

**the thirty years' truce . . . the affair of Euboea:** see I.114–15.

**I.88. The Spartans voted that . . . war should be declared:** it seems unlikely that the Spartans went this far at this early stage. So far they have voted only that Athens has broken the treaty (I.87). They have yet to consult their allies and try negotiation as a means of settling their differences with Athens; see I.125n.

**not so much because they were influenced by the speeches . . . as because they were afraid:** Th. is conscious of the possibility that his readers may see this Spartan hostility as a new phenomenon, a response to the speech just delivered by the Corinthian delegate and to further allied pressure (cf. I.67). Thus, at the end of his account of the disputes and grounds of complaint, aware that his reader is in danger of overestimating their significance and may now be under the impression that a reluctant Sparta is being cajoled into war by Corinthian persistence and intimidation, he puts the situation in its true perspective again. He is not, of course, denying that the speeches had an effect on Spartan opinion; he is saying that, in making up their minds, the Spartans were influenced more by their own fear (for their position as leaders of the Peloponnesian League and therefore for their own power) than for the concerns of their allies. Thus the Spartans are acting from the same motives as the Athenians (I.76). Cf. I.23, 118. On the expression "not so much . . . as" cf. II.65n.

### I.89–117. The Pentecontaetia, or the Fifty Years

Within the structure of bk. I, the Corcyra and Potidaea episodes put the outbreak of war in its immediate context; they are followed by the debate at Sparta, which both completes the account of "the causes of complaint . . . and the specific instances where their interests clashed" and begins the process of putting the war in its long-term context by examining aspects of Athenian and Spartan society that were ultimately responsible for the growth of Athenian power and thus the outbreak of war. This process is completed by the Pentecontaetia, a historical record of the events that marked the growth of Athenian power.

This passage is our main source for the period of Greek history from the end of the Persian Wars to the early 430s (a period, in fact, of about forty years, the remainder of the 430s having been already dealt with in greater detail). It is one of two surviving continuous accounts of the period and the only one written by a contemporary (the other being Diodorus XI.38ff., written in the first century B.C.). But the Pentecontaetia is not intended to be a full history of the years between the Persian and the Peloponnesian Wars. Its purpose is more limited: to provide the background to what Th. has stated is the truest cause of the Peloponnesian War, the growth of Athenian power and the fear caused by this in Sparta (I.23, 88, 118). At the same time it illustrates some of the general points made in the preceding debate, in particular the energy and resourcefulness of Athens.

Th. was always highly selective, but this will not account for the patchy and somewhat haphazard nature of this excursus. Its limited purpose explains the omission of many events and developments of this period with which Th. was probably thoroughly familiar, e.g., Athens' cultural activities and internal politics. But it makes all the more puzzling his neglect of important milestones in the development of Athens' empire, such as the transference of the league treasury to Athens and (assuming it is historical) the Peace of Callias. His description of the workings of the Delian League is also tantalizingly brief. (For a full list of omissions see *H.C.T.* 1:365–89.) Moreover, Th. is inconsistent in his treatment of those events that he does cover. Some episodes, such as the rebuilding of the Athenian walls at the beginning of the excursus and the Samian revolt at its end, are described in great detail, while others, of, one would think, similar significance, are accorded no more than a few lines. Finally the Pentecontaetia provides us with no dates. Frequent signposts (e.g., at I.98, "The first action . . . Then . . . Next . . . After this") suggest that Th. is putting events in chronological order, though even this is disputed by some modern scholars; cf. I.98n. The character of the excursus can best be explained, perhaps, by assuming that at the time of writing Th. had only very inadequate information to hand (it may well have been written in exile: see my introduction, under "The Life of Thucydides") and that the document we have is an initial draft that he planned to write up more fully later.

**I.89. on sea and land . . . Mycale:** cf. I.23n.

**Leotychides:** one of the two Spartan kings, he reigned ca. 490–476; see I.79n. for the other.

**returned home:** the Spartans were clearly unwilling to maintain a naval presence at such a distance; cf. I.95 and Hdt. IX.106, 114.

**the allies from Ionia and the Hellespont:** by their participation in the battle of Mycale on the side of the Greeks, they had revolted from Persia (see Hdt. IX.104). The mainland Greeks were thus left with the responsibility for their protection. By "allies from Ionia" Th. probably means the Asiatic Greeks in general, i.e., Dorians and others as well as genuine Ionians who alone were related to the Athenians (I.2, 6, 12). The *Hellespont* was the ancient name for the Dardanelles.

**Sestos:** situated on the Chersonese (Gallipoli), the western shore of the Hellespont, thus controlling the passage to the Black Sea and the corn-growing areas on its southern shore that were vital to Athens (for earlier Athenian conquests in this area see Hdt. V.94, VI.34ff., VI.137, and cf. VII.147; cf. also *A.E.* pp. xxii–xxiii and I.2n., 120n.). The siege of Sestos is the last action described by Herodotus (IX.114–18). Thus Th. picks up his narrative at exactly where Herodotus left off and, indeed, uses his words at this point.

**the winter:** of 479/8. Campaigning during the winter was unusual; cf. II.1n.

**the places where they had hidden them away:** Troizen, Aegina, and Salamis. Cf. I.18n. and see Hdt. VIII.41–42 for an account of the evacuation. The Athenians enjoyed retelling the story: see I.73–74, 144.

**the rebuilding of their city and their fortifications:** during the invasion of 480/79 Athens had been evacuated and abandoned to the Persians, who destroyed much of the city (I.18). The story of the rebuilding is told in detail, probably because of Th.'s fascination with Themistocles (cf. I.135–38) and because he regarded the fortification of Athens, which rendered the city immune from attack by land, as a significant stage in the development of its power. Th. had stressed the importance of defenses for a state's development and security in the Archaeology (I.2, 5, 7, 8); these walls played a vital role in the Peloponnesian War (II.13).

**I.90. their allies, who were alarmed . . . by the sudden growth of Athenian sea-power . . . their [the Spartans'] real fears:** here are the causes of the Peloponnesian War in embryo; cf. I.23, 88, 118, and I.69n. For the origins of Athenian naval power see I.14, 93n.

**the daring which the Athenians had shown in the war against the Persians:** especially at Salamis. Cf. I.73–74, 92.

**such as they had in Thebes:** for the surrender of Thebes to Persia see Hdt. VII.233. Again, Athenians later liked to make the point that they did not surrender to the Persians; see I.74.

**I.91. The Spartans believed what Themistocles said:** they were, it seems, easily deceived by Themistocles, who used the sort of ruse for which he was well known (cf., for instance, Hdt. VIII.75). This episode is very much in the anecdotal mode of Herodotus.

**Abronichus:** see Hdt. VIII.21.

**Aristides:** Themistocles was supported by the other leading statesman of the day (cf. *Ath. Pol.* 23). This goes to show that the schematized picture to be found in Plutarch (e.g., *Arist.* 2), with its contrast between a just, honest, aristocratic Aristides and a cunning, unscrupulous, democratic Themistocles is, at best, an oversimplification.

**I.92. the Spartans showed no open signs of displeasure towards Athens . . . secretly they felt aggrieved:** the Spartans contain their annoyance, but a rift is opening up between the two states (cf. I.90 and, for some evidence of it even during the war, Hdt. IX.7–8). For its later manifestations see I.69n.

**I.93. Piraeus:** the collective name for Athens' three harbors, Cantharus, the main harbor, Zea, and Munychia, some four miles to the southwest of the city and west of the Bay of Phalerum where previously the Athenians had beached their ships (Hdt. VI.116). Themistocles saw the Piraeus as the key to Athens' future greatness as a naval power. The long walls connecting the city with the harbor would be built during the First Peloponnesian War (I.107).

**his year of office as archon:** 493 according to Dionysius of Halicarnassus (VI.34). There were nine archonships, the highest offices in the Athenian state at this time. Themistocles was eponymous archon, the chief magistrate after whom the year was named.

**Indeed it was he who first ventured to tell the Athenians that their**

**future was on the sea:** for Themistocles' expansion of the Athenian navy see Hdt. VII.144; *Ath. Pol.* 22; Plut. *Them.* 4.

**I.94. Pausanias:** following the Greek victory against Persia the Spartans had returned to Greece but were still official leaders of the Greek forces, and after the winter Pausanias, who was acting as regent in place of his young cousin Pleistarchus, took command of an allied fleet.

**Cyprus:** presumably a Persian naval base that may have offered opportunities for obtaining booty (cf. I.96). Aristides and Cimon were in command of the Athenian contingent (Diodorus XI.44; Plut. *Arist.* 23, *Cimon* 6). If the Greeks won over **most of the island** on this occasion they cannot have held it for long, since the Athenians conducted at least three later expeditions against the island, in ca. 467 (Diodorus XI.60–61), in 459 (I.104), and in 449 (I.112). The fleet's second destination, **Byzantium** (modern Istanbul), is much easier to explain, controlling as it did the entrance to the Black Sea (on which see I.89n.).

**I.95. the Athenians . . . their own kinsmen:** for the colonization of Ionia by Athens see I.12n.

**dictator:** i.e., tyrant (or "sole ruler"). The word is used here in its later (and modern) sense; cf. I.13n.

**he was collaborating with the Persians:** the story of Pausanias' trials and downfall is dealt with at length by Th. in I.128–35. See also I.137n.

**there seemed to be very good evidence for this:** Th. presumably had a Spartan source; see V.26n.

**They regarded the Athenians as . . . friendly to themselves:** yet Th. has already mentioned an increase in tension between the two states (I.90, 92). There is further evidence on Athens' assumption of the leadership of the Greeks: the Athenians themselves later (I.75) cited Spartan unwillingness to carry on to the end the war against the Persians, and Xenophon (*Hellenica* VI.5) and Plutarch (*Arist.* 23) support Th.'s statement that the Spartans handed over the command willingly; *Ath. Pol.* 23 is ambiguous but is probably best taken as meaning that the Spartans did not wish to continue the fight; the Athenian Euphemus, speaking at Camarina in 415/4, puts the emphasis slightly differently (VI.82), while Herodotus (VIII.3) says that the Athenians took the command from the Spartans, advancing the arrogance of Pausanias as justification for their action; finally, Diodorus (XI.50) records a debate in Sparta in which great resentment was expressed at the loss of the command, and this was followed by the suggestion that war be declared against Athens to recover it, though the assembly was dissuaded by a certain Hetoimaridas from undertaking such action. Diodorus places the debate in 475/4, but his chronology is notoriously untrustworthy, and such a debate, if genuine, would seem to belong to the period immediately following the Athenian assumption of the leadership of the Greeks, i.e., 478/7. Th.'s failure to mention the debate described by Diodorus (especially as he would have been on the lookout for early indications of ill feeling between Athens and Sparta) is disturbing, though no more so than some other omissions from the Pentecontaetia. The story of the debate makes sense in the light of Spartan irritation over their failure in the affair of the Athenian walls, not to mention friction between the two states during the war (I.92n.). Would the Spartans have accepted the loss of power and face with resignation, as Th. suggests? The most likely answer is that they were divided over the matter, as we see in this debate and on other occasions in the following years (I.69n.).

**I.96.** Despite its brevity, this chapter is one of our main sources of information on the early organization of the Delian League (a modern name: see n. later in this chapter, **Delos**). Other writers and some inscriptions, especially the so-called tribute lists (they are in fact lists of the firstfruits, the one sixtieth of the tribute paid to Athena) add much to what Th. says here. See *A.E.* pp. 17–29 and the introduction to the tribute lists, *A.E.* 58–65. See also the Penguin translation, app. 1, pp. 607ff.

**Athens took over the leadership:** as if it was doing no more than assuming control of an enlarged Hellenic confederacy (the organization of Greek states formed in 481 to meet the Persian threat: see Hdt. VII.145ff., 172). However, that fresh oaths were administered to the Ionians (Plut. *Arist.* 25) suggests that a new league of "the Athenians and their allies" is being formed.

**the Athenians assessed the various contributions:** tribute was brought by the allies to Delos and kept in the league treasury there by the **Hellenic Treasurers** (Gk. *Hellenotamiae*), who were Athenians.

**the Athenians . . . decided which states should furnish money and which states should send ships:** instead of paying tribute, some member states contributed a number of ships to the allied navy. Known examples are Naxos (I.98), Thasos (I.101), and Samos (I.117), as well as Chios and Lesbos (the only states still contributing ships in 431; see I.19). In due course, it seems, most states were given the choice between providing ships and paying tribute in money, and the majority opted to pay tribute on grounds of convenience; see I.99, VI.85.

**the object being to compensate themselves:** de Ste. Croix (1972, 302) has pointed out that this and similar translations are misleading. The Gk. actually says not "the purpose" or "the object" but "a" (not "the") "pretext," implying that the true purpose (certainly as far as Athens was concerned) was quite different. At III.10 the Mytilenean ambassador at

Olympia expresses what may have been the general feeling of the allies at the time: "the object of the alliance was the liberation of the Hellenes from Persia." His words are not as trustworthy as a direct comment from Th., but to judge by the early actions of the league, its initial aim seems to have been to expel all Persians from Greece, the Aegean, and its eastern seaboard and, by unifying the strength of the Greeks throughout that area, to prevent further Persian infiltration and a third Persian attack on Greece. Indeed fear of Persia is mentioned as a motive by the Athenians themselves at I.75 (though whether we should take these words at face value some fifty years after the event is another matter), and in 415 Hermocrates the Syracusan claimed that the aim of the Ionians in accepting the leadership of Athens was to seek vengeance against Persia (VI.76). However, we should not underestimate the importance of the quest for booty: the wealth of Persia was legendary, and a desire to (at least) recoup some of their expenses in the war could explain the allies' presence in distant waters (e.g., Cyprus) in the early days of the league (though a different interpretation of Th.'s language in this sentence suggests that he is talking not so much of plundering as of destroying). If the Athenians needed a pretext, presumably their true motive was the quest for empire or at least a desire to dominate the new league.

**460 talents:** such a figure seems on the high side, especially as many of the totals deduced from the tribute lists (the records of the quotas paid to Athena, which start in 454 when the empire had grown and more states were contributing money rather than ships) are not much bigger, while some are lower. Various theories have been advanced to explain Th.'s figure. It could be that the first assessment was for some reason exceptional and following payments lower: certainly it is not unknown for a state to have its tribute reduced. It is also worth remembering that the figure of 460 talents is an assessment, which may not have been paid in full, whereas the figures deduced from the tribute lists represent receipts. Further, the figure of 460 talents may have represented both money and ships (a possibility rejected by Hornblower [1991, 145]) whereas the tribute lists record only monetary contributions. Nor can we be certain that Athena received her share of all payments made or that all payments to her were recorded on the tribute lists. Another theory recently revived (Powell 1988, 14) is that the initial assessment included a contribution from Athens. In the light of these uncertainties, of the incomplete state of the tribute lists, and of the figure of 600 talents given by Th. (II.13) for the tribute at the outbreak of the Peloponnesian War, a figure of 460 talents for the first assessment is at least feasible. We must remember that we have only the vaguest knowledge (see Plut. *Arist.* 24) of the procedures employed and no knowledge of the tribute paid in the years between the first payment and 454, when the first offerings were made to Athena. Tradition has it that the initial contributions were assessed by the Athenian Aristides and met with universal satisfaction. Th. does not refer to him here, though he is mentioned in connection with the tribute in the Peace of Nicias (V.18).

**Delos:** selected to be the headquarters of the new league, a perfect choice for both practical and sentimental reasons: it was a small island (and thus not a major power in its own right), in a central position in the Cyclades, with a good harbor. In earlier times the Athenians, Ionians, and islanders had conducted a festival there in honor of Apollo, who, according to one legend, was father of Ion, the eponymous ancestor of the Ionians. After the purification by Pisistratus (I.8n.; Hdt. I.64), the Delian Games had been held regularly (III.104n.).

**representative meetings:** the league's assemblies were held at Delos, and every member state was represented. We know virtually nothing about these meetings. From a brief and difficult reference in III.10 it looks as if there was one chamber in which each member state, whatever its size, had an equal vote, but that despite this Athens was able to dominate the meetings (presumably by putting pressure on the large number of small states). In the constitution of the second Athenian confederacy in the fourth century Athens was not a member of the allies' assembly but had a vote equal in authority to the combined vote of the allies. This was a bicameral (twin-chamber) arrangement, and some modern historians believe that the Delian League also had two chambers. For further details of the league's meetings and a discussion of when they ceased see *A.E.* pp. 28–29.

**I.97. originally independent states:** on independence, Gk. *autonomia*, cf. I.67n.

**I shall now describe:** I.89–96 have contained an introduction to the Pentecontaetia, an explanation of its purpose, and a lengthy, almost relaxed, account of events from the end of the Persian War to the establishment of the Delian League. I.97 contains a second introduction, as it were, at the point where the league is about to take its first united action. The narrative style from this point is much tighter.

**until the beginning of the Peloponnesian War:** in fact the Pentecontaetia takes us only as far as the revolt of Samos of 440/39; see I.89–117, introductory n.

**Hellanicus:** a native of Lesbos, who was an older contemporary of Th. and an Atthidographer (writer of an Attic History, or "Atthis"). His work was published at about the end of the war and survives in fragments.

**but he has not given much space to the subject and he is inaccurate in his dates:** Th. thus gives further reasons for his decision to write the Pentecontaetia, in addition to that supplied at I.89. This passage is widely considered to be a later insertion. The irony of Th.'s comments on Hellanicus' account is often pointed out: these are precisely the criticisms one is tempted to make of Th.'s own record of the same period, though his dates are not so much inaccurate as nonexistent (cf. I.98n.). Cf. I.21 for further evidence of Th.'s polemical attitude toward other writers. For a suggestion that Th. was critical of other aspects of Hellanicus' approach see Hornblower 1987, 83–85.

**At the same time the history of these years will show how the Athenian Empire came into being:** the true purpose of the Pentecontaetia (cf. I.89).

**I.98. The first action:** Th. provides us with no fixed dates in the excursus. There are probably two explanations for this: first, Th. may have been writing when absent from Athens (he was exiled in 424: see IV.104–7, V.26) and thus may have had no access to official records; second, a date would be expressed in purely local terms (see II.2n.) and thus would mean little or nothing to a foreigner. We can be confident that Th. knew some dates from the period: the Thirty Years' Truce can easily be dated to the year 446/5 from II.2, and thus the Samian War can be dated too (I.115). For other events that Th. could have dated see *H.C.T.* 1:389–92. For a brief survey of the chronological problems of the Pentecontaetia see Rhodes 1985, section III.

**Eion:** at the mouth of the Strymon in the northwest of the Aegean. The town was well known to Th.: not only was it in his home country, Thrace, but during his generalship in the Peloponnesian War he saved it from the Spartan Brasidas (IV.102–7). Eion (along with Doriscus, further east) was retained by Persian forces after the main army had returned to Asia. Herodotus records a much fuller account of the Greek capture of Eion and the valiant efforts of the Persian commander to defend it (VII.107). Cf. Plut. *Cimon* 7, and for the date, 476/5, see *T.D.G.R.* 62. On the importance to Athens of the area (in particular Amphipolis, a few miles up river, at the crossing of the Strymon) see IV.102, 108.

**Cimon:** the Athenian general most responsible for the consolidation of the league in its early days. See also I.100, 102n., 108n., 112n. His father, **Miltiades,** had been the victor at Marathon.

**made slaves of the inhabitants:** the usual fate of the defeated in war; cf. the case of Scyros (next n.), and see III.36n.

**Scyros:** an Aegean island on the direct route between the Hellespont and Euboea. It was, according to Plutarch (*Cimon* 8), the base of pirates who preyed on shipping in the area; it was important to Athens in particular that the seas should be free of pirates because of its dependence on foreign trade and especially on imported grain (cf. I.2n. and, on piracy, I.4–8, II.32, 69). This episode brought great kudos for Cimon, who, in response to a Delphic oracle, brought the supposed bones of Theseus back from Scyros to Athens for burial. Plut. *Theseus* 36 enables us to date this episode also to 476/5, when Phaedon was archon.

**Dolopians:** relations of the Dolopians of Thessaly; cf. II.102, V.51.

**and colonized the island themselves:** with cleruchs (III.50n.; cf. *A.E.* 133–41), another reflection of its importance and evidence of Athens' use of the allied fleet in its own interests.

**Carystus:** on the southeastern tip of Euboea. Its population had, under pressure, cooperated with the Persians (Hdt. VIII.66) and had already been punished for their Medism by paying a fine to Themistocles (Hdt. VIII.112) and later suffering the devastation of their territory (Hdt. VIII.121). However, unlike the other cities of Euboea, Carystus was unwilling to join the Delian League and had to be conscripted by force. Th. gives no date: it would be some time in the latter half of the 470s.

**Naxos:** its attempted secession (on the date see I.137n.) presumably contravened the original oath of loyalty to the league, and this gave the confederacy the legal right to prevent its withdrawal, by force if necessary. Further details of the revolt Th. either did not know or considered unimportant; they are therefore omitted. Thus we do not learn why Naxos wished to secede in the first place or how, precisely, the island was punished.

**the original constitution of the League was broken:** closer to the Gk. would be "in contravention of the established rule," by which Th. may mean the natural right of self-government.

**lost its independence:** the Gk. (from the noun *douleia,* "slavery") means "was enslaved," though this is not to be taken literally. The islanders' freedom would have been curtailed in some way. They may also have lost their defenses and fleet.

**the process was continued in the cases of the other allies:** the Naxos episode set the pattern that would be followed in many other instances and is thus crucial to our understanding of how the league was turned into an empire. In the interests of brevity Th., always selective in approach, will not give full details of, or even mention, every instance. Some general comments follow.

**I.99.** Th.'s account of the first revolt prompts him to step outside his chronological framework to look ahead to the period when Athens was in full control of the league. He discusses briefly the changes in the relationship between Athens and its allies that put Athens in this dominant position.

**The chief reasons for these revolts were failures to produce the right amount of tribute or the right numbers of ships, and sometimes a refusal to produce any ships at all:** Th.'s thought processes are compressed here. Mention of an intervening stage—the Athenian pressure that, when brought to bear on the allies as a result of their failures, led to revolts—is delayed until the next sentence. The Gk. translated as "a refusal to produce any ships at all" is more likely to mean "desertion during a campaign" or, more vaguely, "failure to fulfil military obligations," as it is translated at VI.76, where fighting among the allies themselves is proffered by the Athenians as an excuse for depriving their allies of their independence.

**the Athenians as rulers were no longer popular:** cf. I.77n.

**For this position it was the allies themselves who were to blame:** only insofar as their apathy made it easier for Athens to oppress them. Cf. the words of Hermocrates the Syracusan: "the Hellenes in the mother country . . . have been enslaved through not supporting each other" (VI.77). For a victim's view of the process of divide and rule by which Athens turned the league into an empire see III.10. Spartan inactivity had also made things easier for the Athenians, according to the Corinthians (I.68ff.); cf. VIII.96, where the Spartans are described as "remarkably helpful enemies."

**Because of this reluctance . . . most of them . . . had assessments made by which . . . they were to pay a corresponding sum of money:** cf. I.96n., **the Athenians . . . decided.** No doubt the Athenians encouraged this trend. Cf. Plut. *Cimon* 11.

**the Athenian navy grew strong:** not quite what the Gk. says, which is something more like, "the navy grew strong for the Athenians."

**I.100. Next:** however, Diodorus (XI.60 = *A.E.* 16) and Plutarch (*Cimon* 12; see also *T.D.G.R.* 68) give brief accounts of campaigns in Asia, which may belong to the early 460s. Diodorus says that many cities of Lycia and Caria were brought into the league, some voluntarily, some by force, while Plutarch states that "Asia from the Ionian coast to Pamphylia he [Cimon] made completely empty of Persian forces." We also know from Th. (I.130) that there were Persian forces in Byzantium during the 470s. Finally, we must remember that the Persian governor of Doriscus held out against the Greeks for some time and that other Persian forces in Thrace and the Hellespont had to be expelled (Hdt. VII.107; cf. Aristophanes *Wasps* 1097–98). This evidence suggests that the impression given by Th., that in the years following Eion there was little trouble from Persia and that the gathering of Persian forces at Eurymedon was a bolt out of the blue, is misleading. But it would be missing the point to criticize Th. for the inadequacy of his account: see I.89–117, introductory n.

**the battles of the river Eurymedon in Pamphylia:** Cimon's finest hour and the justification of his anti-Persian campaigns, though he came under attack from his enemies not long after (Plut. *Cimon* 14, *Per.* 9). The episode probably belongs to the period 469–466. All we can be certain of is that it comes before the revolt of Thasos in 465. Plutarch (*Cimon* 13) put the Peace of Callias (I.112n.) soon after Eurymedon.

**the entire Phoenician fleet of 200 triremes:** a mistranslation, suggesting that the fleet was only 200 strong and that every vessel was either captured or destroyed. Much closer to the Gk. is "as many as 200 Phoenician triremes in all," i.e., from a larger total. Plutarch (*Cimon* 12) discusses the size of the fleet, quoting two figures, 350 and 600. The Persians depended heavily on the Phoenicians for naval forces; see I.16n.

**the revolt of Thasos:** the date of the revolt is one of the few in the Pentecontaetia that can be established with some certainty. Th. (IV.102) dates the foundation of **Amphipolis** (see I.98n., **Eion**) twenty-eight years after the massacre at **Drabescus.** We know that Amphipolis was founded in 437/6 (*T.D.G.R.* 62). The disaster at Drabescus therefore occurred in 465/4, and thus the rebellion of Thasos almost certainly began in 465 and ended in 463.

**markets on the mainland:** Thasos and the Thracian mainland opposite were rich in timber and precious metals; for the importance of the area to Athens see IV.108. On the wealth of Thasos see Hdt. VI.46.

**10,000 colonists:** an exceptionally large number, further reflection of the importance of this area to Athens.

**I.101. The Spartans . . . promised to do so:** for Spartan ill feeling toward Athens since the end of the Persian Wars see I.69n., 95n. Th. seems very sure of his information: he presumably had a Spartan source; cf. V.26n.

**without informing Athens:** the promise was clearly kept secret, otherwise Cimon would not have been able to persuade the Athenians to help Sparta against the helots (I.102).

**the earthquake which happened then:** a famous and particularly devastating earthquake (cf. Plut. *Cimon* 16). Earth tremors, common in Greece, are mentioned a number of times by Th.; see II.8n.

**Ithome:** not a walled town, but a fortified camp in a strong position from which the helots could raid the surrounding country in guerrilla attacks.

**the helots:** inhabitants of Laconia and Messenia who had been reduced to serfdom by the Spartans, whom they vastly outnumbered (cf. VIII.40). The constant threat of helot revolt had a strong influence on Spartan policy (cf. IV.41, 55; V.14) and in particular curtailed their foreign activities. The Spartans' fear of the helots sometimes drove them to desperate measures (see, e.g., IV.80; *T.D.G.R.* 13). On occasions, however, particularly when induced by an offer of freedom, helots could give loyal service to Sparta: see, e.g., IV.26. For instances of freed helots (Gk. *neodamodeis*) fighting for Sparta see V.34, VII.19, VIII.5.

**the perioeci:** literally "the dwellers around," not slaves or serfs, but free members of communities around Sparta, who were, however, subject to some Spartan control. They had a good record of loyalty to Sparta: they fought in the Spartan army and were sometimes given positions of responsibility (e.g., VIII.6, 22n.).

**the famous war:** two wars, in fact, in the eighth and seventh centuries, in which Sparta conquered Messenia (*T.D.G.R.* 9, 12).

**the Athenian terms:** these will have left Thasos considerably weakened, and it did not cause trouble again. Cf. the punishment of Samos at I.117.

**the mine there:** Th. himself possessed the right to work mines on the mainland (IV.105).

**I.102. their allies, including the Athenians:** see n. later in this chapter, **the original treaty of alliance.**

**Cimon:** he supported a policy of dual leadership for Greece and was generally sympathetic to Sparta. He persuaded the demos to help its "yoke fellow" (Plut. *Cimon* 16) and led a force of four thousand hoplites to Ithome (Aristophanes *Lysis.* 1137–44 = *T.D.G.R.* 67).

**siege operations:** the Spartan army, so successful in pitched battles because of its discipline, was unable to cope with this kind of warfare, partly because the Spartans had never developed the necessary techniques, partly because they could not afford to be away from home long enough to starve the enemy into surrender. The Spartans would have been aware of Athenian skill in this type of operation (and their own lack of it) from events in the Persian Wars (Hdt. IX.70, 102).

**the first open quarrel between Athens and Sparta:** though there had been some ill feeling behind the scenes by this time; see I.90, 92, 95n.

**The Spartans . . . grew afraid of the enterprise and the unorthodoxy of the Athenians . . . and feared that . . . they might listen to the people in Ithome:** on Athenian enterprise cf. I.70. It looks as if the Athenians showed some sympathy for the helots and were themselves (though hoplites, traditionally conservative) in a revolutionary frame of mind. This would not be surprising in the light of what was happening in Athens at the time. Th. ignores the reforms of Ephialtes (*Ath. Pol.* 23–27; Plut. *Cimon* 15, *Per.* 9), presumably because they would be irrelevant to the stated purpose of the Pentecontaetia. It is particularly unfortunate that he chooses to be silent on the political situation in Athens at this time. It was in many ways the end of one era and the beginning of another: the conservative, backward-looking attitudes and pro-Spartan policy of the last two decades were abandoned, new alliances were adopted, a radical step was taken in the development of Athenian democracy, and Pericles, who would be predominant in Athenian politics for a quarter of a century, was now coming to the fore.

**a different nationality:** i.e., Ionian/Dorian; cf. I.124n.

**merely declaring that they had no further need of Athenian help:** if the Spartans set out to insult the Athenians, it is not easy to see why. They must have realized that the philo-Laconian Cimon would be the first to suffer, and if their apparent inaction in the opening years of the First Peloponnesian War was the result of indifference, they were not seeking conflict. But we cannot ignore the promise made to Thasos. The truth lies in the complexities of Spartan politics, which are beyond us: opinion in Sparta on the subject of relations with Athens was, no doubt, divided on this occasion, as it was throughout the period (cf. I.69n.). The episode demonstrates the failure of Cimon's pro-Spartan policy of dual leadership for Greece. His ideals and policies were based not on the solid foundation of hard political fact but in the Panhellenic sentiment that had been created by the emergency of the Persian invasion and was, in reality, neither deep nor durable. He would presently be ostracized (Plut. *Cimon* 17; on ostracism see I.135n.).

**the original treaty of alliance which had been made against the Persians:** in 481; see Hdt. VII.145, 172.

**Argos:** Sparta's long-standing rival in the Peloponnese. In fact, Th. describes Argos as an enemy of Sparta at this time, which suggests that the two states were actually at war. This—or perhaps some time in the 450s during the First Peloponnesian War—is now seen as the best context for the battle of Oenoe (in the Argolid), mentioned not by Th. but by Pausanias (I.15.1, X.10.3), who wrote a description of Greece in the second century A.D. He writes that a combined Athenian-Argive army defeated a Spartan force in a battle in Argive territory. See Meiggs 1972, 96–97, 469–72. The dramatist Aeschylus refers to the alliance in *Eumenides* 762ff.

**the Thessalians:** they could offer Athens the best cavalry in Greece. For earlier Spartan interference in Thessaly (in the 470s) see Hdt. VI.72. For Athens' later relations with Thessaly see I.111 and II.22; see also I.107n.

**I.103. after ten years' fighting:** a notorious chronological difficulty. Th.'s text states that the helots surrendered "in the tenth year," yet he places the end of the revolt in sequence before the defection of Megara to Athens, the Egyptian expedition, and the beginning of the First Peloponnesian War, which belong to the period ca. 460. Thus, if the helot revolt lasted some nine years and finished about 460, it started in about 469, which is where some sources put it (see *T.D.G.R.* 67). However, Th. has already linked its outbreak with the revolt of Thasos, which is firmly dated to 465 (I.101n.). Therefore, either the revolt did not begin in 465/4, it did not end ca. 460, or it did not last over nine years. It is generally agreed that to move either the beginning or the end of the revolt to ensure a full nine or ten years for it would interfere too much with Th.'s order of events. A widely accepted solution is to substitute "fourth" or "fifth" for "tenth," assuming some corruption in the transmission of the text. All this assumes that in the Pentecontaetia Th. always puts events in strict chronological order and never looks ahead to anticipate the outcome of an episode he is describing; see I.89–117, introductory n.

**Naupactus:** recently taken by Athens, it was situated on the northern side of the mouth of the Corinthian Gulf, close to its narrowest point (on which see II.86). It thus occupied a vital strategic position, controlling the entrance to that important stretch of water. It became a major naval base for Athens in the Peloponnesian War. See also *T.D.G.R.* 135.

**which they had recently taken from the Ozolian Locrians:** the Gk. is in fact more likely to mean that the Locrian seizure (on which see *T.D.G.R.* 47) rather than the Athenian was recent. Th. does not wish to go into detail.

**Megara:** its position on the Isthmus of Corinth was of strategic value to Athens for two reasons. First, it afforded access to the passes of the Geraneia range of mountains that stretched across the isthmus; these passes, difficult at the best of times (see I.107, but note the Corinthian seizure of the Megarid, described at I.105), could be manned by Athenian troops to restrict land links between Sparta and its allies in central Greece and to reduce the possibility of Spartan invasions of Attica via the Megarid. Second, Megara controlled two ports, **Nisaea** on the Saronic Gulf and, more importantly, **Pegae** on the Corinthian Gulf, which would give the Athenians easier access to Naupactus and enable them to put greater pressure on Corinth, the greatest naval power in the Peloponnese. For an instance of the use of Pegae in this war see I.111. Megara eventually returned to the Peloponnesian alliance (I.114), and Nisaea and Pegae were given back under the terms of the Thirty Years' Truce (I.115)

**a war concerning the frontier boundaries:** see I.15n.

**the Corinthians began to conceive such a bitter hatred for Athens:** rapidly increasing tension soon leads to war. Corinthian ill feeling is also a major factor in the outbreak of the Peloponnesian War (e.g., I.67–71, 120–24), though Corinth was by no means antagonistic toward Athens between the wars (I.40n.).

**I.104. Marea, the town south of Pharos:** at the western extremity of the Nile Delta.

**Artaxerxes:** the unpopular Persian monarch Xerxes had died in 465 (probably in August) and the accession of Artaxerxes to the throne was followed by a period of unrest that Athens now exploited. A further incentive for Athens will have been the rich, corn-growing areas of the Nile valley.

**a campaign against Cyprus:** evidently important, but we know no more about it (for further evidence of Athenian interest in Cyprus see I.94n., 112). Clearly Cimon had not been alone in his determination to continue the war against Persia and extend Athenian interests in the east. There were some, it seems, who saw such a campaign as the logical sequence to the victory at

Eurymedon (albeit delayed by the revolt of Thasos), and who perhaps even regarded Eurymedon not as the conclusion of a long struggle to defend Greece against Persia but as the opening act of a new offensive designed to push the Persians further back and take territory (and booty: cf. I.96) from them.

We have further, epigraphic evidence for Athenian intervention in Egypt at this time in the form of a casualty list of the Erectheid tribe (*T.D.G.R.* 78). Listed are the names of 177 men of this tribe who died "in the wars in Cyprus, in Egypt, in Phoenicia, at Haliae, in Aegina, and at Megara." This is probably a list of the dead from the first year of the First Peloponnesian War, 460/59. We have no other reference to fighting in Phoenicia, but it is reasonable to assume that Athenian troops landed there during the Cyprus campaign.

**Memphis:** just south of the southern point of the Nile Delta. The account of the Egyptian campaign is continued at I.109.

**I.105. At this time, too, the Athenians sent out a fleet:** thus we are plunged into the so-called First Peloponnesian War. Th. implies the Athenians began proceedings, but we cannot be sure (see next n.). The early actions of the war involve states situated around the Isthmus of Corinth and the Saronic Gulf: Athens, Corinth, Epidaurus, Aegina, and Megara (cf. the situation in 432/1: see I.67n.). No mention is made of the Spartans at this time, though of course Th. may be including Spartan forces when he talks of "the Peloponnesians."

**Haliae:** on the eastern shore of the Argolic Gulf, close to the southern tip of the Argolid. It had a good harbor. Herodotus (VII.137) mentions a Spartan seizure of Haliae for which this attack could have been a retaliation, but as he gives no date we cannot say which came first.

**a force of Corinthians and Epidaurians:** an inscription (see Griffin 1982, 62) suggests that the Sicyonians were there too. They and the Corinthians are prepared to campaign at some distance from home to minimize Athenian influence in the Saronic Gulf and eastern Argolid. This is another possible context for the battle of Oenoe (I.102n.), with Athens supporting its new ally, Argos.

**Cecryphalia:** a small island in the Saronic Gulf, a little west of Aegina.

**war broke out between Athens and Aegina:** large, powerful, and Peloponnesian, Aegina was too close to Athens for comfort. Pericles (Plut. *Per.* 8) called it "the eyesore of the Piraeus." Diodorus (XI.70.2) records that Aegina had in fact been a member of the league before this war and that this was a revolt, but this is not widely accepted. See, for instance, Meiggs 1972, 51–52. For the surrender of Aegina see I.108.

**At the same time the Corinthians and their allies . . . moved down into**

**the Megarid:** cf. I.103n. Th., having described several campaigns with a minimum of detail, gives a very full account of the next episode, the battle in the Megarid between Corinthian and Athenian troops. This is perhaps because he was particularly impressed by Athenian determination and resourcefulness on this occasion. No doubt this was a well-known story in Athens. This victory confirmed Athens' domination of the Megarid for the time being. It is worth noting that on only one occasion in this war did the Spartans march through the Megarid with the intention of invading Attica, and that was at the very end of the war, when Megara had abandoned Athens in favor of the Peloponnesians. This illustrates the importance of this area to the safety of Athens (though, of course, that interpretation assumes that the Spartans wished to invade Attica; they may not have done so).

**the old men and the very young:** men of eighteen or nineteen years and over fifty. Cf. V.75.

**Myronides:** a general famous in Athens down to Th.'s time and after (Aristophanes *Lysis.* 801 and *Ecclesiazusae* 303).

**I.107. two long walls . . . one to Phalerum and one to Piraeus:** the Athenians would have been aware from events at Ithome that the Spartans would be unable to capture a walled city by storm. But Athens could, theoretically, be starved into surrender. This risk could be avoided only by establishing a link between the city and the port at Piraeus, which would give to the inhabitants of the city permanent, safe access to the sea and seaborne trade. Thus the Athenians would be able, if they so wished, to avoid the need to fight a land battle with Peloponnesian forces, as Pericles would advise at the outbreak of the Peloponnesian War (e.g., II.13). Phalerum, an open bay east of Piraeus, where the Athenians had beached their ships in earlier times (Hdt. VI.116), was included in the fortifications. Some time later, perhaps in the following decade, another wall was constructed parallel to the Piraeus wall, thus making it a double wall (*T.D.G.R.* 79). Plutarch (*Cimon* 13) claims that the foundations were laid in Cimon's time. See I.93 for the early development of the defenses of Athens and Piraeus.

**the Phocians started a campaign against Doris:** Phocis was a friend of Athens (III.95). Doris was believed to be Sparta's original Greek homeland: according to tradition the Dorians (I.12n.) resided for some time in Doris before moving south into the Peloponnese.

**the Spartans came to the assistance of the Dorians:** this appears to be the Spartans' first participation in this war (unless they contributed to forces described by Th. simply as "the Peloponnesians"). The size of the Spartan force is surprising: if indeed they had been slow to join the war initially, they now overcame their reluctance (and perhaps were by this stage more fully recovered from the helot revolt) and showed full commitment to it. Racial sentiment (I.124n.) may have played some part in the Spartans' thinking on this occasion, but they had previously shown an interest in this region (see, e.g., Plut. *Them.* 20) and would do so again (I.112). This interest may be connected with Delphi (I.25n.) and a wish to have influence in the amphictyony, the organization of twelve central and northern Greek states that managed the oracle.

**1,500 hoplites of their own:** the figure is considered high for genuine Spartiates; the forces perhaps included perioeci (I.101n.).

**King Pleistoanax:** cf. I.114n., II.21.

**If they went by sea:** as they had done on their first journey? It would not have been difficult to avoid Athenian ships in the **Gulf of Crisa** (Corinthian Gulf) once, but a return journey by sea was considered impossible because the Athenians would certainly be on the lookout for them. See next n.

**the Athenians would be able to sail up with their fleet and stop them:** a preferable interpretation of the Gk. is that the Athenians had in fact already sailed up and were thus in a position to stop them.

**nor did the route across Geraneia appear to be a safe one, since the Athenians held Megara and Pegae:** see I.103n.

**[I.108].** The chapter number 108 is misplaced in the Penguin translation: it should immediately precede the paragraph beginning, **The battle was fought at Tanagra . . .**

**a party in Athens who were secretly negotiating with them [the Spartans]:** we can assume from the assassination of Ephialtes (*Ath. Pol.* 25) that such groups were particularly active after the passing of his reforms.

**their whole army:** the size of the Athenian contingent is not given; for numbers of troops available to Athens at the beginning of the Peloponnesian War see II.13.

**14,000:** Pausanias (on whom see I.102n.) describes a golden shield set up at Olympia by the Spartans as a memorial of their victory. Its inscription mentions "the Argives, Athenians, and Ionians" as the defeated parties; it looks as if members of the Delian League fought with Athens at Tanagra (Pausanias V.10.4 = *T.D.G.R.* 80; cf. M.L. 35, 36). The allies included the Thessalians, but the relevant sentence is missing from Warner's translation. It reads: "Thessalian cavalry also went with the Athenians according to their alliance [I.102], though in the action they deserted to the Spartans." Athens and Thessaly were allies again by the time of the Peloponnesian War: see II.22.

**I.108. Tanagra:** other sources add some interesting details to Th.'s account. A fragment of the Greek historian Theopompus (mid-fourth century) states that before five years of Cimon's ostracism had elapsed he was recalled to Athens to conclude a peace (*T.D.G.R.* 76). Plutarch (*Cimon* 17–18, *Per.* 10) says that Cimon turned up at Tanagra to fight for Athens and dispel any rumors that he was connected with the oligarchic plot to betray Athens to Sparta. He was not allowed to fight, but his friends did so and died bravely. In remorse the Athenians summoned him back, whereupon he immediately put an end to the war. Although Diodorus (XI.80) talks of a four-month truce after Tanagra, we know of no peace until the five years' truce of 451 and of no activity of Cimon in Athens in the intervening years. See I.112n.

**cutting down some of the plantations:** this illustrates the importance of olive oil to the ancient Greeks; the destruction would have caused considerable hardship, especially as olive trees grow very slowly. Cf. IV.84n.

**The Athenians, on the sixty-second day after the battle, marched into Boeotia:** it is typical of the Athenians' determination at this time that they recovered so quickly from their failure at Tanagra and turned defeat into victory so decisively. Their success at **Oenophyta** was the beginning of their so-called land empire. They were now able to occupy Boeotia, Phocis, and Locris and thereby establish a land link with Naupactus. We should remember that at an unknown date during this war the Athenians took control of or came to an agreement with Achaea (I.111, 115). They thus controlled most of the land bordering on the Corinthian Gulf, including, of course, the Megarid. This must have made life particularly difficult for Corinth. But otherwise Athens seems to have gained little benefit from its occupation of central Greece. Boeotia and Phocis supplied troops for an Athenian expedition to Thessaly (I.111), but the tribute lists do not record payment of tribute by the mainland cities of Boeotia, and it will have overstretched Athens' resources to maintain control over the area. This was done by interfering in local politics, supporting pro-Athenian elements (including oligarchies when convenient: see Old Oligarch 3.11 = *A.E.* 108), exiling extreme opponents (I.113), and taking hostages. Some democracies were established, according to Aristotle (*Politics* V.2.6), but these do not seem to have worked to Athens' satisfaction. Athenian occupation of this region came to an end in 447: see I.113.

**Myronides:** see I.105n.

**Long Walls:** see I.107n.

**Aegina:** as with Boeotia, Sparta could offer no support. The islanders were heavily punished and compelled to pay a sizable tribute (thirty talents). For further details of Aegina's position after 457 see *A.E.* 156, a decree that records arrangements made for the island. It seems to mention an Athenian garrison. Aegina remained a tribute-paying subject until its population was removed by Athens early in the Peloponnesian War (II.27).

**Tolmides:** see *T.D.G.R.* 84 and I.113n.

**the Spartan dockyards:** at Gytheum, on the coast of Laconia to the south of Sparta.

**Chalcis:** on the coast west of Naupactus and the mouth of the Corinthian Gulf.

It was perhaps around this time that Athens entered into an alliance with the Sicilian town of Egesta (*T.D.G.R.* 81). This early sign of Athenian interest in the west, whether for commercial, imperial or other reasons, foreshadows later Athenian policy. It was followed up in the next decade by alliances with Rhegium and Leontini (III.86; *T.D.G.R.* 124, 125; I.36n.) and by Athenian participation in the foundation of Thurii (*T.D.G.R.* 108). See also I.44n.

**I.109. Meanwhile . . . in Egypt:** the account of the Egyptian expedition is resumed from I.104.

**all the chances and changes of war:** a constant theme in Th.; see I.120n.

**a large army:** Diodorus and Ctesias, a Greek doctor who resided at the Persian court in the fourth century, give figures of three hundred thousand and five hundred thousand but these must be vastly exaggerated (*T.D.G.R.* 72).

**I.110. this great venture of the Hellenes came to nothing:** it would seem that some 250 ships and their crews were lost in Egypt, the original 200 and the relieving squadron of 50. This would explain Th.'s language: he talks of a major disaster. Ctesias, however, states that the Athenian contingent numbered only forty (*T.D.G.R.* 72). Whatever the correct figure, Th.'s numbers seem high: after all, the Athenians were fighting a war on the domestic front, they had an empire to police, and they were besieging Aegina. How could they do this with two hundred ships in Egypt? Moreover, Th. talks of a Hellenic rather than an Athenian disaster and says that the original fleet of two hundred consisted of both Athenian and allied ships (I.104). This is confirmed by an inscription (*T.D.G.R.* 77) recording the presence of a Samian contingent. Likewise, the relieving squadron, **fifty triremes from Athens and the rest of the league,** also contained some allied ships. Thus the purely Athenian losses may not have been as great as appears at first sight. For a full discussion see Meiggs 1972, 473–76.

Certainly Athens seems to have had the resources to overcome some serious problems in the empire in the years following the failure in Egypt. There is evidence to suggest that the Persians were keen to follow up their victory in Egypt by moving westward, perhaps into the Aegean. It is probable that it was in 454 that Athens moved the league treasury from Delos to Athens, perhaps through fear of the arrival of a Persian fleet in the Aegean (see *A.E.* p. 58 n. 2). For evidence that the proposal to move the treasury came from the Samians see Plut. *Arist.* 25. What we can be sure of is that the first quotas to Athena were recorded in 454: a fragment of the first quota list includes the name of the archon for that year (*T.D.G.R.* 85). Other evidence from the tribute lists, supported by inscriptions, suggests that some cities on the eastern coast of the Aegean were in a state of revolt from Athens in the late 450s; see *T.D.G.R.* 92 = *A.E.* 130 and *T.D.G.R.* 71 = *A.E.* 106, which mentions Persian involvement.

**Cyrene:** close to the Mediterranean coast of Libya, well to the west of Egypt.

**Amyrtaeus:** he held out for some time; see I.112.

**the marshes:** in the lower Nile Delta.

**the Mendesian mouth of the Nile:** on the eastern side of the Nile Delta, north of the town of Mendes.

**the Phoenician fleet:** see I.16n.

**This was the end of the great expedition against Egypt:** Th. concludes by stressing the enormity of the disaster. Since we can date the beginning of the Egyptian expedition to 460 (I.103n.) and it lasted six years, its conclusion is fixed at 454. For the second, much briefer phase of Athenian involvement in Egypt see I.112.

**I.111. Thessaly:** Athens' willingness to intervene here can be explained, at least in part, by the defection of the Thessalian cavalry (I.107n.). This expedition was a failure (as so often, Greek forces were unable to take a walled town), but by 431 Athens had renewed its alliance with Thessaly (II.22).

**a force of Boeotians and Phocians, who were now their allies:** see I.108.

**Pharsalus:** the major town of southern Thessaly, a flat area where cavalry could be exploited to the full.

**Pericles:** Th.'s first reference to the great statesman, though the Pentecontaetia is not the place for Th. to discuss him. See I.127n., 139; I.139–46, introductory n.

**Xanthippus:** the victor at Mycale (I.89).

**Pegae:** see I.103n. Pericles first landed at **Sicyon** (as Tolmides had done: see I.108) and then with the help of some **Achaeans** (though no alliance between Athens and Achaea has been mentioned) sailed against **Oeniadae** ("always anti-Athenian": see II.102) in southern Acarnania; on this occasion too the Athenians failed to take a walled town. This expedition, along with that of Tolmides, illustrates the concern felt by Athens to maintain a strong presence in this important area, to support its forces and allies on the coast of the gulf, and to keep it open for Athenian shipping.

**I.112. Three years later:** on the rather imprecise evidence provided by Th. Pericles' expedition is generally dated to 454 and the **five years' truce** to 451. We have seen, however, that Theopompus links the conclusion of peace with the recall of Cimon, which was due at about this time, but which Theopompus and Plutarch put much earlier (*T.D.G.R.* 76; cf. I.108n.). The sources are irreconcilable and something has to give. Wherever we put the recall of Cimon, the five years' truce should probably remain at 451, which is also the date of Sparta's thirty years' peace with Argos (V.14, 28).

**Cyprus:** as a result of the two agreements discussed in the previous n. the position in Greece became much more stable and the Athenians, probably under the influence of Cimon, returned to the offensive against the Persians. Cf. I.94n.

**Amyrtaeus:** see I.110. The Athenians maintained their influence in Egypt: Plutarch (*Per.* 37) tells how King Psammetichus of Egypt sent a generous gift of grain to the Athenian people in 445/4.

**a fleet of Phoenicians, Cyprians, and Cilicians:** cf. I.16n.

At this point in Th.'s narrative belongs the so-called Peace of Callias (for an alternative date see I.100n.). This peace is the subject of one of the greatest and most enduring debates in the study of Greek history (it began in the fourth century B.C.). Full documentation of the sources can be found in *T.D.G.R.* 95, which also lists some important modern works on this contentious issue. If the peace is genuine Th.'s failure to mention it is inexplicable, even granted that his excursus is unfinished. Indeed, his silence at this point is one of the strongest arguments against the historicity of the peace (though its existence is perhaps implied elsewhere; see, e.g., III.33n., VIII.56n.). Whether or not terms were formally agreed on, it seems clear that from this time until the last decade of the fifth century, when they intervened in the Peloponnesian War on the side of Sparta, the Persians acquiesced in the existence of the Athenian empire and left it largely unmolested (though there is evidence of occasional Persian interference, e.g., Pissuthnes' support of the Samian rebels, mentioned at I.115). A later treaty made during the Archidamian War was ignored by Th. (*T.D.G.R.* 138; IV.50n.); this could be a renewal of an earlier agreement.

**the sacred war:** a campaign fought over the possession of Delphi (I.25n.; "Delphia" in the Penguin is a misprint), which had fallen under the control of Phocis at some stage, perhaps after it came to terms with Athens (I.111). Sparta's quick success was once again rapidly reversed by Athens. A further switch will have occurred following the collapse of Athens' land empire: both Delphi and Phocis supported the Peloponnesian side as the

Peloponnesian war began (I.118, II.9). The sacred war, because of its special circumstances (the Spartans and the Athenians did not actually come to blows), was not regarded as an infringement of the truce between Athens and Sparta, though it would have done nothing to improve relations between them. For Athenian links with Delphi at this time see *T.D.G.R.* 82.

**I.113. the exiled party:** cf. I.108n.

**under the command of Tolmides:** according to Plutarch (*Per.* 18), Tolmides' reaction to the rebellion in Boeotia was considered hasty and was publicly condemned by Pericles. Tolmides was killed on this campaign.

**evacuating the whole of Boeotia:** such was the end of what has come to be known as Athens' land empire. See I.108n. and de Ste. Croix 1972, 315. The Athenian defeat can be dated to 447, shortly before the revolt of Euboea (I.114n.).

**I.114. Euboea revolted from Athens:** in 446 (II.2). Euboea, with its rich, fertile plains, was important to Athens as a haven and a source of food (cf. II.14). Th. stresses Athens' reliance on the island at the time of its revolt in 411 (VIII.96). It is probable that many of the major cities of the island had been members of the Delian League from the early days, though Carystus had had to be coerced into joining (I.98). Enforced membership of the league and payment of tribute, along with the expulsion of some leading citizens (I.113), are in themselves adequate explanation of the revolt, but Diodorus (XI.88) also mentions that Athens had sent some cleruchs to Euboea (under Tolmides and therefore before 447). Discontent will have been aggravated by the loss of land involved in the establishment of an Athenian cleruchy.

**Megara . . . revolted:** for its strategic importance see I.103n. Athens maintained control over Nisaea and Pegae for the moment: they would be handed back as part of the Thirty Years' Truce (I.115). An Athenian inscription recording how Pythion of Megara led three tribal detachments from Pegae to Athens (*T.D.G.R.* 101) almost certainly refers to this episode.

**the Athenian garrisons:** a detachment of Athenian troops stationed in Megara to ensure its loyalty to Athens; see I.103. This practice was widespread; cf. the case of Samos (see I.115 and *A.E.* p. 130–31.

**Corinth, Sicyon, and Epidaurus:** enemies of Athens in this war who had acted in concert earlier; see I.105n.

**the Peloponnesians . . . invaded Attica:** for earlier Peloponnesian thoughts of invading Attica see I.69n.

**King Pleistoanax:** his decision to abandon the invasion was attributed at Sparta (and Athens) to bribery (II.21, V.16; cf. Plut. *Per.* 22–23; *T.D.G.R.* 104).

**Eleusis and Thria:** on the main route between the Isthmus of Corinth and Athens.

**peace terms:** Euboea was treated harshly to prevent a further rebellion of this important neighbor. The Hestiaeans were dealt with most severely because they had killed an Athenian crew (Plut. *Per.* 23 = *A.E.* 117; see also *A.E.* 115, 116): they were driven from their land and one thousand Athenian cleruchs were settled there. We know much more about the treatment of Chalcis and Eretria (not mentioned by Th.), since detailed decrees survive that describe the terms imposed on them (Chalcis: *A.E.* 119 = *T.D.G.R.* 103; Eretria: *A.E.* 121 = *T.D.G.R.* 102; see also *A.E.* 120, 122). In the case of Chalcis the city was not to be destroyed nor was the population to be forced out, though Plutarch (*Per.* 23) reports that the Hippobotae, the wealthy ruling class of knights, were expelled. The decree accords the Chalcidians some judicial privileges but demands of them complete loyalty and obedience. An oath is to be taken to the Athenians alone (rather than to "the Athenians and their allies," the customary formula), and this includes a promise to denounce anyone who stirs up revolt against Athens. The Eretrian Decree includes an identical oath. This ominous development illustrates the Athenians' determination to ensure complete loyalty and their openness in acknowledging that the Delian League was now an Athenian empire.

**I.115. a thirty years' truce:** the terms had perhaps been agreed on before the Spartan withdrawal. Th. here briefly mentions only one feature of the truce: he lists the places that Athens was compelled to give up, **Nisaea, Pegae, Troezen, and Achaea.** It comes as something of a surprise, after the defection of Megara, to see that the Athenians still occupied Pegae and Nisaea; in the case of the latter, perhaps the few Athenians who had escaped the massacre at Megara (I.114) were still holding out. Even more surprising is the reference to Athenian possession of Troezen and Achaea: Th. has told us nothing of their original conquest by or agreement with Athens (though he mentioned Achaeans fighting on Athens' side at I.111). Sparta's demand for the restoration of their independence is quite understandable: Athenian occupation of areas within the Peloponnese was bound to be seen as provocative.

Sparta may have bargained from a position of strength when the terms of the truce were decided on, but the Athenians were not completely cowed. They retained some key positions, including Naupactus, Euboea, and Aegina, though Aegina's status seems to have been the subject of some special provision (I.67, 139, 140). Sparta did not attempt to pressure the Athenians into freeing the Greeks but acknowledged their supremacy over them, on condition that the Athenians did not interfere in the Peloponnesian

League. The Spartans' main concern was for their own security as leaders of the Peloponnesian League and their position as the supreme military power on the Greek mainland. The Thirty Years' Truce assured them that position (as far as Athens was concerned at least), and they were content with that agreement, recognizing that for the moment they could achieve little more. The truce, if adhered to, would allow the two signatories to coexist peacefully, each supreme in its own sphere: a permanent peace on these conditions would perhaps have suited Sparta well. For a full list of the terms of the truce see de Ste. Croix 1972, 293–94.

**In the sixth year of the truce:** i.e., 441/0. Cf. I.118n. on the gap.

**war broke out between Samos and Miletus:** this seems to have been a typical quarrel between Greek states over border territories (cf. I.15n.). **Priene** lay between the two and bordered on Samos' mainland possessions. Samos was one of only three members of the Delian League that still contributed ships rather than money (cf. I.96n.; the others were Chios and Lesbos). Miletus was an Athenian subject: it had defected, unsuccessfully, in the late 450s (I.110n.) and possibly again in the 440s (its name is missing from the fragments of the tribute lists for 445–443; see Meiggs 1972, 563). The situation was serious for Athens: see VIII.76. In another context we learn that the Peloponnesians considered intervening in the revolt but decided against doing so on the advice of the Corinthians (I.40, 69n.).

**various private individuals . . . who wished to set up there a different form of government:** presumably along democratic lines; i.e., it had previously been oligarchic. It was standard practice during the Peloponnesian War to call in the Athenians in support of democracy (III.82.1).

**So the Athenians . . . established a democracy there:** one of the devices employed by Athens to assert control in troublesome subject states. It was expected that the demos would, out of gratitude and a sense of affinity with the Athenian democracy, be loyal to Athens; according to Diodotus, speaking in 427, this was in fact the case (III.47). There was probably no ideological intent: the Athenians would support oligarchies when it suited them (see I.108n. on Boeotia and the Old Oligarch 3.11 on Miletus).

**Lemnos:** a northern Aegean island and an Athenian cleruchy before the Persian Wars (Hdt. VI.136–40).

**Pissuthnes:** his action would seem to contravene at least the spirit of the Peace of Callias (I.112n.). Whether he acted with the approval of the Great King (Darius) is unclear. Pissuthnes would cause more trouble for Athens in 430: see III.34.

**the Persian Governor:** the Persian empire was divided into provinces (satrapies), each administered by a governor (satrap, a term not used by Th.), who often exercised considerable independence. **Sardis,** some seventy miles inland in central Asia Minor, was the main town of Pissuthnes' satrapy.

**the troops in the Athenian garrison and the Athenian officials:** on the troops see I.114n. The officials (Gk. *archontes*) were Athenian representatives stationed in subject states who upheld Athens' interests in matters of policy and government; see *A.E.* pp. 124–26.

**Byzantium:** cf. I.94n., 117.

**I.116. the Phoenician fleet:** i.e., the Persian fleet; see I.16n.

**Pericles and nine other commanders:** the ten generals (Gk. *strategoi*); see I.48n.

**Chios and Lesbos:** see I.96n.

**I.117. Thucydides:** not the historian (nor Pericles' rival Thucydides, the son of Melesias).

**Hagnon:** see II.58n.

**Phormio:** see I.64n.

**terms of surrender:** these presumably included the reestablishment of the democracy, but it did not last; see VIII.21, 73. For a fragment of Athens' treaty with Samos, including the oaths taken by each side, see *T.D.G.R.* 115. Despite the harshness of the terms, Samos was loyal to Athens in the Peloponnesian War, at the end of which the Samians were formally honored by Athens (*T.D.G.R.* 166). Cf. the terms imposed on Thasos (I.101).

**to pay reparations in instalments at regular intervals:** the Gk. translated as "reparations" is literally "the money spent" (on the war), i.e., a full indemnity. Plutarch (*Per.* 28) talks of "a heavy fine," paid in part at once and in part at fixed intervals. Other literary sources (e.g., Diodorus XII.28 and Nepos *Timotheus* I.2) put the cost of the campaign at 1,200 talents, but an inscription (*T.D.G.R.* 113) gives 1,400 talents. Cf. the more than 2,000 talents spent on the siege of Potidaea (II.70). These vast expenses bear witness to Athenian determination to prevent the spread of disaffection within the empire. It appears from this inscription that the Athenians had to borrow from monies dedicated to Athena to finance this war.

With the successful conclusion of the Samian War the Athenian empire enters what appears from our meager sources to be a relatively trouble-free phase. Th. has demonstrated, not, it must be admitted, to our complete satisfaction, how the Delian League, a voluntary union of independent Greek states, has been converted into an empire, firmly controlled and totally dominated by Athens. The Samian episode, described in so much detail, serves as the climax of the process begun by the subjugation of Naxos (I.98), and Th. can now return to his detailed narrative of events immediately preceding the outbreak of war.

## I.118–25. The Allied Congress at Sparta

This is the meeting of the Peloponnesian League foreshadowed at I.87. Only one speech is recorded, that with which the bellicose Corinthians wind up the debate. Many of their arguments will not stand up to close scrutiny, but their rhetoric is powerful and the majority of their listeners are already convinced. Several of the points raised by the Corinthians are "answered" in Pericles' speech at I.140–44; see I.139–46, introductory n.

**I.118. It was only a few years later:** Th. stops in 439 and jumps to 435, just as he ignored the period 445–441. These gaps are puzzling: in 446/5 the Athenians and the Peloponnesians agreed to live and let live; in 433 the Athenians believed there would be a war (I.44; cf. I.36n.). Are the events described in I.24–44 sufficient to explain the change? Has Th. proved the case he put forward in I.23?

**the affair of Corcyra, the affair of Potidaea:** see I.24–65.

**the other occurrences:** the complaints of Megara, Aegina, and others; see I.67.

**causes for the war:** i.e., "the reasons for breaking the truce and declaring war which were openly expressed," as opposed to "the real reason *[alethestate prophasis]* for the war" (I.23).

**The Spartans . . . did little or nothing to prevent it:** though they had been ready to do something in 465 (I.101) and 440/39 (I.40); see I.69n.

**being traditionally slow to go to war, unless they were forced into it:** cf. the criticism of Spartan character advanced by the Corinthian delegate in the debate at Sparta in 432, I.68ff.

**wars in their own territory:** the literal translation of the Gk. is "domestic wars" or "wars near home." The helot war of the late 460s is insufficient to explain long-term Spartan inactivity, and Th. is probably referring to wars fought during the first fifteen or so years of the Pentecontaetia that were connected with the development of democracy in some Peloponnesian states and had threatened the security of the Peloponnesian League. See I.135n. Th. had no reason to mention these wars: see I.89–117, introductory n.

**the Athenians began to encroach upon Sparta's allies: allies** might be better translated as "alliance" (the Gk. can mean either); this wording would make it clearer that Sparta is acting out of self-interest (cf. I.88), not out of an altruistic concern for the welfare of its allies.

**they also sent to Delphi:** cf. I.25n. The Peloponnesians have decided that the Athenians have broken the treaty, but they are not yet fully committed to war. However, they could confidently expect the god's support: see I.112n., **the sacred war.**

**if they fought with all their might:** the oracle hedges its bets, as usual.

**I.119. to take their votes on the question of whether war should be declared:** had things got this far yet? See I.125n.

**Potidaea:** still under Athenian blockade (I.65, II.70).

**I.120. They have already voted for war themselves:** not quite; see I.87.

**and have summoned us here to do the same thing:** see I.67n. on Sparta's constitutional powers as leader of the Peloponnesian League.

**those who live inland or off the main trade routes . . . will find it much more difficult to secure an outlet for their exports:** suggesting that it was already difficult? As far as the Aegean, especially the Hellespont area, is concerned, there is some evidence that Athens attempted to exert some control over trading activity (*A.E.* pp. 133–36; cf. Old Oligarch 2.12: "the Athenians will not permit our competitors to take their produce elsewhere; if they try to do so they will be excluded from the sea"). In particular, Athenian interest in the grain trade goes back a long way (I.2n., *A.E.* pp. xxii–xxiii). The Corinthians may even have feared that the Athenians might attempt to conquer Sicily (there is no evidence for this in the 430s, but they were considering the idea in 427: see III.86), and this could have posed a threat to their trading there. For further evidence of Athenian interference in Aegean trade see the decree recording its relations with Methone and Macedon (*T.D.G.R.* 128 = *A.E.* 159), which includes a reference to Athenian control of the Hellespont (*Hellespontophylakes* in line 37). See also Old Oligarch 2.11–12. During the war even Spartan commercial interests would be adversely affected: see IV.53.

The case has been argued that the Peloponnesian War originated from trade rivalry, in particular between Corinth and Athens, and indeed that Athens' main motive in its imperial expansion was to ensure its corn supply. See I.44n. The theory, of course, requires us to modify considerably the interpretation of events offered by Th. and to assume that he missed the point of the Corinthian activity he describes in so much detail in the years 435–431. It is now discredited: see, for instance, de Ste. Croix 1972, 214–20; Kagan 1969, 239–41.

**Wise men certainly choose a quiet life:** not the Athenian attitude to life, as the Corinthians have already said (I.70). The Gk. for **wise** is the adjective from *sophrosyne* (I.32n.).

**Many badly planned enterprises have had the luck to be successful:** and equally, rational calculation (Gk. *gnome* or *logismos*) is often overturned by chance (Gk. *tyche*) and the unexpected. For further references to the role of luck and the unpredictable nature of human affairs see I.78, 84, 140; II.11, 61, 64; III.45, 59; IV.12, 14, 18, 30, 55, 62, 64; V.102; VII.61; VIII.24. Within this rather loose and unreliable framework man in Th. is responsible for his own actions. Nothing is assigned (as in Herodotus, for instance) to gods. For a full treatment of the subject see Edmunds 1975.

**I.121. we are the victims of aggression:** cf. some of the arguments advanced by the Corinthians at I.68; see also I.144 and II.61 for a similar claim made by Pericles.

**we are superior in numbers:** cf. I.81n.

**the existing resources of our alliance:** these were meager according to Archidamus (I.80, 83). The Peloponnesians had no common fund (I.19). Cf. Pericles' comments on Peloponnesian finances at I.141.

**funds in Olympia and in Delphi:** monies and gifts deposited as offerings at the temple of Zeus at Olympia and the oracle. Olympia was in Elis, an ally of Sparta, and Delphi (I.25n.) supported the Peloponnesians (I.118). It appears to be taken for granted by the warring parties that they would have access to these funds, though there is no record of any borrowing taking place.

**on mercenaries rather than on her own citizens:** Athenian warships were crewed by both citizens and mercenaries (i.e., paid foreigners), as Pericles acknowledges (I.143), and occasionally by slaves (e.g., I.55). Cf. I.10n. The force sent to Sicily in 415 had a large mercenary element: see VI.22, 43; VII.57, 63.

**The chances are that, if they once lose a battle at sea, it will be all over with them:** Th. will no doubt have seen this as another example of naive optimism that could be so damaging when it intefered with political judgment (cf. V.14 and VII.28 for expectations at the beginning of the war). For further examples of wishful thinking and unjustified dependence on hope see III.3, 97; IV.65; V.102, 104; VI.13, 24, 31; VII.48, 77. Note in particular Th.'s general comment at IV.108: "the usual thing among men is that when they want something they will, without any reflection, leave that to hope, while they will employ the full force of reason in rejecting what they find unpalatable." Cf. a reluctance to believe unpalatable news (VI.32, 35; VIII.1) and a willingness to rely on uncorroborated information (VI.8, 65). Cf. also the words of the Spartans at IV.17–18 and those of Diodotus at III.45. Pericles stressed the importance of "estimating what the facts are and thus obtaining a clearer vision of what to expect" (II.62). Cf. Hermocrates, a speaker in the Periclean mold (VI.32). See also I.86n.

**education . . . nature:** another sophistic contrast. Cf. I.32n.

**I.122. foster revolts among their allies:** not as easy as it sounds, as the Peloponnesians discovered when they tried to support the revolt of Mytilene in 428; see III.26ff. Brasidas was later much more successful: see IV.81ff.

**build fortified positions in their country:** from which raids on enemy territory could be conducted. This policy (Gk. *epiteichismos*) was not tried in the early years of the war but was put into practice with devastating effect by the Athenians at Pylos (IV.2ff.) and the Spartans at Decelea (VII.19ff., following the advice of Alcibiades at VI.91). Cf. Pericles' comments at I.142.

**boundary disputes:** a common cause of wars in the Greek world. Cf. I.15n.

**they brought freedom to the whole of Hellas:** what of the Athenian contribution?

**a dictator state:** literally "a tyrant city," a vivid and emotive expression. Cf. I.124, where it is used again, and I.13n.

**we made it a principle to put down despots:** i.e., tyrants; cf. I.18n.

**I.123. the god, who has himself promised to support us:** Apollo at Delphi; see I.118n., II.54.

**all the rest of Hellas:** mere rhetoric, of course, but see II.8.

**It is not you who will be the first to break the treaty:** the Peloponnesians themselves later (VII.18) admitted that they had been in the wrong in rejecting arbitration, but on this occasion they were in no mood for legal niceties. Cf. I.28, 78.

**I.124. Dorians . . . Ionians:** an attempt to stir up racial hatred. Racial sentiment certainly figures in Th., often in speeches (e.g., I.95, 102; III.86, 92; IV.64; V.9; VI.20, 77, 80, 82; VII.5; VIII.25), and to some extent the combatants divide along racial lines. But racial considerations are generally subordinate to political interests: at VI.85 the Athenian Euphemus says, "ties of blood exist only when they can be relied upon; one must choose one's friends and enemies according to the circumstances on each particular occasion"; cf. Th.'s comments at the beginning of VII.57 and the words of Hermocrates at IV.61.

**that dictator city:** or, closer to the Gk., "tyrant city," the expression used in I.122. See I.13n.

**I.125. The Spartans had now heard everyone's opinion and put the vote city by city to all their allies:** further evidence of procedures—and of Sparta's control over them—in the congress of the Peloponnesian League. The allies had one vote each according to Pericles (I.141), with Sparta probably not voting (its wishes would already be clear enough). A majority vote was enough to secure a decision (cf. V.30).

**The majority voted for war:** the clear impression given at I.119 is indeed that the question to be voted on at this meeting is whether or not to go to war, but Th. is perhaps anticipating events again here; the allies may have decided no more than that the treaty has been broken (as did the Spartans at I.87) and thus will attempt negotiation before resorting to war; cf. I.88n.

**their present state of unpreparedness:** cf. Archidamus' earlier speech, especially I.82.

**a year, or rather less, went by before Attica was invaded and war openly broke out:** it comes as something of a surprise, after the display of Peloponnesian hostility toward Athens, that war was delayed for almost a year (though Archidamus had hoped for two to three years: see I.82). And then the initiative came not from Sparta but from Thebes (II.2), while Archidamus was working for peace even as he led the first invasion of Attica (II.12, 18). It looks as if, even after the allied decision that the treaty had been broken, the debate continued.

## I.126–38. A Digression: The Stories of Cylon, Pausanias, and Themistocles

The account of the embassies draws Th. into some uncharacteristic digressions. The inclusion of the stories of Cylon, Pausanias, and Themistocles is something of a puzzle: anecdotal and, at times, naive, the three stories are in the fashion more of Herodotus than of Th., who, in his introduction (I.22), stated his intention to exclude from his work a "romantic element" (Warner's translation) or storytelling. Th. perhaps had in mind Herodotus' habit of digressing to tell an interesting tale. He would have regarded such stories as likely to distract the reader from the serious purpose of his work. Gomme (*H.C.T.* 1:27) regarded the whole section as an excursus, "for his [Th.'s] purpose quite unnecessary," and suggests (431, 447) that he was unable to resist the temptation to indulge his interest in biography. Other explanations of the presence of these episodes have been advanced: that Th. wished to correct other versions of these events that he considered mistaken or unsatisfactory (he does this on other occasions: cf. I.20, 97) or even that he was keen to demonstrate that he could tell a story as well as Herodotus.

But the stories of Pausanias and Themistocles have some bearing on the war and its causes. They should be seen in conjunction with I.89–95, which give details of the activities of Pausanias and Themistocles in the period immediately following the Persian War. These two men, "the most famous people of their day in Hellas" (I.138; cf. the introductions of Pericles at I.127, 139), one Athenian, one Spartan, had saved Greece in the Persian invasion, Themistocles at Salamis and Pausanias at Plataea. They continued to influence the fortunes of Greece after the war: Themistocles, who had turned Athens into a naval power (I.93), consolidated its strength by ensuring that city walls were rebuilt, while Pausanias was responsible for the Spartan withdrawal from the command of the Greek fleet, thus offering Athens the leadership of the Greeks. Between them these two men bear much of the responsibility for the direction of Greek history after the Persian Wars.

Th.'s account of Pausanias and Themistocles illustrates his interest in political leadership. Pausanias and Themistocles were leaders of great ability but with equally great flaws of character—arrogance, overambition, and the ability to make enemies easily. Th. points this out clearly in the case of Pausanias (I.95, 132) but says nothing of these failings in Themistocles (our evidence is in Plut. *Them.* 3, 5, 18, 21) and does not condemn his Medism. His silence may be due to more than straightforward admiration for Themistocles; he perhaps considered that his downfall was to be attributed not so much to failings in Themistocles himself as to a mistake on the part of the Athenian people (see I.135n.). His emphasizing of Themistocles' talents stresses the folly of the Athenians. The episode thus anticipates an important theme in Th.'s account of the war: the volatile and sometimes irrational nature of the Athenian demos, often manifested in its treatment of its leaders (II.65n.). Indeed, the case of Themistocles reminds us of another remarkable Athenian, also a man of exceptional ability, Alcibiades, whose alienation from his city was so damaging to it.

The stories of Pausanias and Themistocles (and, indeed, of Cylon) are stories of leadership gone wrong. They throw into sharp relief the qualities of Pericles, Th.'s ideal statesman, who dominates the closing chapters of bk. I (see I.139n.). Thus outstanding individual figures complement the essentially collective and impersonal action of the Corcyra and Potidaea episodes and the Pentecontaetia, to round off a full explanation of the causes of the war and to look forward to some of the features of its course. Overlong and anecdotal they may be, but these passages add to our understanding of the war and its causes; we should not condemn them as irrelevant.

**I.126. a good pretext for making war:** almost as if the Spartans required further assurance of the justice of their case.

**In former times:** in the late seventh century, ca. 630.

**the Olympic Games:** see I.6n.

**dictator:** i.e., tyrant; cf. I.13n.

**went to Delphi to consult the god:** Apollo; cf. I.25n.

**he had won a victory at the Olympic Games:** in 640, according to the lists of victors.

**the Diasia:** held annually in March or April.

**nine archons:** see I.93n. Herodotus (V.71) disagrees with Th. on the government of Athens at this time.

**the Dread Goddesses:** the Eumenides or Kindly Ones, whose altars were just below the entrance to the Acropolis, on the Areopagus.

**the men who killed them and their families:** the Alcmaeonids, who were driven out of Athens in 508 by Cleomenes, king of Sparta (525–488). See Hdt. V.70, 72.

**I.127. Pericles, the son of Xanthippus:** see I.111n. Th. reintroduces Pericles (previously mentioned only in the Pentecontaetia: I.111, 114, 116–17). The introduction of Pericles into the main narrative seems overdue: Th. chooses the moment at which he is embarking on his account of the prewar negotiations and discussions of strategy to emphasize Pericles' predominance in Athenian politics and to note his hostility to Sparta and his support of war, factors that are largely responsible for the direction of Athenian policy from this point on. Pericles is introduced again in similar terms at the end of I.139 and thereafter will dominate Th.'s narrative until his death, which is recorded at II.65.

**of course they knew . . . they thought:** as often, Th. claims to be privy to Spartan thinking; cf. V.26n.

**connected with the curse on his mother's side:** Pericles' mother, Agariste, was a member of the Alcmaeonid family, which was descended from Megacles, who as chief archon was responsible for the killing of Cylon's supporters. Thus his descendants were accursed and this Spartan demand was directed against Pericles.

**urging Athens on to war:** the Gk. actually includes the definite article—"to the war"—which de Ste. Croix (1972, 65) regards as evidence that war was an acknowledged certainty; clearly this is not so: cf. I.88n., 125n. As to Pericles' motives, he may have felt that it would be better if war came sooner rather than later, on the grounds that Athens stood a better chance of winning under his leadership: he was probably in his late sixties in 431 and could not expect to lead Athens (or live) much longer. He knew well that the volatile and energetic Athenian demos needed a firm guiding hand. His words "What I fear is not the enemy's strategy but our own mistakes" (I.144) suggest that he believed that the greatest danger to Athens in the war lay in weak or misguided leadership, which would allow Athenian ambition to overreach itself.

**I.128. Taenarus:** a promontory in the southern Peloponnese. Located there was an altar of **Poseidon,** the god who caused earthquakes; this was an asylum for helots (I.101n.).

**the Spartans had . . . raised up some helot suppliants from the altar of Poseidon . . . and killed them:** a great sacrilege. Cf. I.24n.

**the great earthquake in Sparta:** of 465; see I.101.

**the goddess of the Brazen House:** Athena Chalkioikos on the acropolis of Sparta. See also I.134.

**Pausanias:** for his earlier activities see I.94–95.

**Gongylus of Eretria:** he had Medized (defected to Persia) during the Persian Wars and had been rewarded with the revenues of some towns in Asia Minor (cf. Themistocles at I.138).

**the text of which, as was afterwards revealed:** Th. appears to be quoting from Pausanias' letter to the king, though skeptics accuse him of gullibility or even invention; it is not easy to imagine how Th. could have seen this letter or a copy of it, though he might have had Spartan friends in high places (cf. V.26n.).

**I.129. satrapy:** see I.115n.

**in our house . . . neither night nor day:** rather grand expressions, the first typically oriental, which suggest the letter may be genuine, but see I.128n. Cf. *T.D.G.R.* 35.

**I.130. he thought even more of himself:** the humbling of human pride is a favorite theme of Herodotus, who perhaps would have depicted the fate of Pausanias in terms of the hybris/nemesis nexus, whereby humans are punished for their arrogant behavior by the vengeful anger of the gods. But for Th. such ideas have no part to play in history: the downfall of exceptional individuals can for him be satisfactorily explained by their own failings—or, in the case of Themistocles perhaps, by the misjudgment or malice of others.

**This was one of the chief reasons why the allied forces turned towards the Athenians:** see I.95, with n.

**I.131. Troad:** a region of Asia Minor, to the south and southwest of the Hellespont and to the north of Lesbos; it included the city of Troy. The exact site of **Colonae** is uncertain, but it was probably on the coast south of Troy.

**prolonging his stay abroad for no good reason:** the duration of Pausanias' second stint in the east is uncertain; see I.137n.

**skytale:** a wooden staff used by the Spartan authorities for sending coded messages to their officers abroad, who needed another skytale to decode the message. This should imply that Pausanias still had some official capacity, perhaps as a regent for Pleistarchus (I.132).

**bribery:** see II.60n.

**the ephors (who have the power to imprison the King):** cf. I.18n.

**I.132. Leonidas:** the Spartan king who commanded the three hundred Spartans at Thermopylae, defending the pass against the Persian invaders in 480, and died there.

**the tripod in Delphi:** an offering to Apollo, a golden tripod on a bronze column that took the form of three intertwined snakes, commonly called the Serpent Column. Engraved on its bronze coils are the names of the thirty-one states that contributed to the defeat of the Persians. The column still exists in Istanbul. See also Hdt. IX.81; M.L. 27 = *T.D.G.R.* 59.

**It was also reported that Pausanias was intriguing with the helots, and**

**this was in fact the case:** there was a lack of evidence for the charge of Medism (see opening sentence of this chapter) but Th. is certain on this point (see V.26n.). This was perhaps Pausanias' real offense.

**He was offering them . . . full rights as citizens:** the consensus is that Pausanias is unlikely to have gone this far.

**their usual practice . . . cast-iron evidence:** the Spartans are typically cautious. There is perhaps a contrast implied with the Athenian attitude toward Themistocles; see I.135n.

**They say:** qualifications of this kind (cf. "it is said," I.134, 138) tend to be associated with details of which Th. is not quite sure.

**Argilus:** near Amphipolis in Thrace.

**the boy friend of Pausanias:** homosexual relationships (often between an older man and a youth) were quite acceptable in Greek eyes and figure frequently in Greek literature. See Dover 1978.

**I.133. Taenarus:** see I.128n.

**I.134. the temple of the Goddess of the Brazen House:** see I.128n. and, on the use of temples as sanctuary, I.24n.

**the Caeadas:** a cavern near Sparta.

**as is shown by an inscription on the pillars there:** Th.'s words suggest that he had seen it for himself; cf. V.26n.

**I.135. he had been ostracized:** for Themistocles' ostracism and banishment see *T.D.G.R.* 65. Ostracism was a form of temporary exile. The victim, selected by the assembly, had to leave Attica for ten years but did not lose his property or citizen rights.

**he . . . was living in Argos, though he often travelled about in the rest of the Peloponnese:** Argos was a Spartan enemy, and Themistocles may well have had a hand in the foundation of an anti-Spartan league in the central Peloponnese at this time (not recorded by Th.; see Bury and Meiggs 1975, 202–3); the Spartans would naturally have been very eager to be rid of him. The Athenians seem willing to believe the worst of Themistocles, while Plutarch (*Them.* 22) attributes their persecution of him to malice and jealousy.

**I.136. Corycra, which honoured him as a benefactor:** see Plut. *Them.* 24.

**he was on one occasion so hard pressed:** the following story is particularly Herodotean in flavor, the sort of thing Th. normally eschews: see I.126–38, introductory n.

**'It is true,' he said . . . :** the use of direct speech (extremely rare in Th. outside full-scale debates) gives the episode greater impact.

**I.137. Naxos . . . Artaxerxes, the son of Xerxes, who had recently come to the throne:** the revolt and siege of Naxos (I.98) are usually dated to the late 470s or early 460s, yet we know from Persian sources that Artaxerxes came to the throne in 465. Th. certainly does not give the impression that it was a matter of years between Themistocles' flight across the Aegean and his sending of a letter to Artaxerxes. It is not impossible that the revolt of Naxos and Eurymedon took place in the same campaigning season, 466/5, to be followed "some time later" (I.100) by the revolt of Thasos, but such compression seems unlikely. Some later sources (mentioned in Plut. *Them.* 27) say that Themistocles came to Xerxes, not his son. This would solve the problem, but at the cost of jettisoning what would generally be regarded as the more reliable authority. Then one manuscript of Plutarch (*Them.* 25) says that the siege Themistocles encountered was that of Thasos (465–463; see I.100). This solves one problem but appears to create another: if Themistocles left Greece in, say, 466/5, then Pausanias will have occupied Byzantium for much longer than Th. might be taken to imply at I.131 (though in fact he gives no hint of the length of Pausanias' occupation of Byzantium and a prolonged stay is possible; see *T.D.G.R.* 61). But this solution too involves rejecting Th., this time in favor of Plutarch.

**The letter was as follows:** cf. I.128n. on Pausanias' letter.

**the good I did then:** for Themistocles' secret messages to Xerxes see Hdt. VIII.75, 110.

**the warning to retreat:** a mistranslation of the Gk. which means 'the warning of the retreat,' i.e., that the Greeks were intending to withdraw from Salamis.

**I.138. Themistocles learned . . . the Persian language and . . . the manners of the country:** a rare achievement for a Greek and further evidence of Themistocles' adaptability.

**Themistocles was a man who showed an unmistakable natural genius . . . quite exceptional . . . beyond all others deserves our admiration:** high praise from Th., leaving the reader with a strong impression of the rarity of a man such as Themistocles and, by implication, an equally strong impression of the folly of the Athenians. The word translated as "genius" (Gk. *synesis*) is elsewhere translated as "intelligence"; see I.79n.

**his forecasts of the future were always more reliable than those of others:** the supreme political skill. (Cf. the words of Nicias in the Sicilian debate: "success comes from foresight," VI.13). Other politicians in Th., e.g., Pericles (II.65) and Hermocrates (IV.59–65, VI.33–34), demonstrated a clear understanding of events, but none, not even Pericles, was credited with foresight to the same degree as Themistocles.

**Magnesia in Asia:** the Magnesia on the river Maeander, which became Themistocles' base, where he even issued his own coinage.

**It is said that his bones were . . . brought home by his relations:** the Gk. in fact says, "his family say that his bones were brought home." Pausanias (i.e., the writer: see I.102n.) reports that they were buried in Attica (I.1.2, I.37.1).

**the most famous people of their day in Hellas:** thus are the mighty fallen, Th. seems to conclude. A comparison with Pericles, who in the following chapter is described as foremost among the Athenians of his time, is perhaps implied; cf. I.139–46, introductory n.

## I.139–46. The Spartan Ultimatum and Pericles' Reply

Th.'s account of the background to the war reaches its climax with a speech from the greatest Athenian statesman, Pericles. It is no coincidence that his introduction follows the story of Themistocles. Like Themistocles, Pericles is "the leading man of his time among the Athenians" (I.139; cf. I.127). Th.'s summaries of the two men (I.138, II.65) suggest perhaps that in terms of sheer intelligence Themistocles was superior, but Pericles, unlike Themistocles, was known for his integrity and was far more adept in his handling of the demos. Moreover, while Themistocles was a Medizer, Pericles was a patriot, "a man who never sought power from any wrong motive." He managed to combine his ambition with love of and service to his country and was thus successful where Themistocles was not. Of the Spartan and Athenian leaders from the past and present presented in the second half of bk. I, Pericles is the most consistently successful. He is, for Th., a paragon of responsible leadership. He has the ability and force of character to unite the Athenians behind him—to plan a coherent war policy, convince the people of its appropriateness, and carry it into practice.

It has been suggested that this speech is largely a Thucydidean composition, on the grounds that it contains examples of "telepathy," i.e., answers points made in other speeches (in this case that of the Corinthians at the allied congress) that the speaker would not have heard. E.g., the Corinthian suggestion that the Peloponnesians borrow money from Olympia and Delphi to attract sailors in the Athenian navy by higher rates of pay (I.121) evokes a response from Pericles in I.143. Cf. also "building fortifications in Attica" (I.122, 142) and "improvement of Peloponnesian seamanship" (I.121, 142).

The reader who is alert to these echoes is understandably suspicious. It would not, however, have required any great insight on the part of an Athenian to realize what strategies were available to the Peloponnesians in the event of war. It is also possible that Pericles got to hear something of the deliberations that took place in Sparta: he had Spartan friends, and communications between the two states remained open (I.146).

**I.139. Potidaea:** see I.56–65.

**Aegina:** see I.67n.

**war could be avoided if Athens would revoke the Megarian decree:** such a concession would not satisfy Sparta's concerns about Athens' growing power (I.23, 88, 118). The offer is disingenuous; Sparta is merely establishing "a good pretext for making war" (I.126). This proposal presumably accounts for the widespread view found in Athens in the early years of the war that the decree was a major cause of it (see references to Aristophanes at I.67n.).

**Peace is still possible if you will give the Hellenes their freedom:** thus Sparta enters the war as the upholder of Greek liberty; cf. II.8n. The Gk. says not "freedom" but "autonomy," a vague concept, on which see I.67n. Pericles replies at I.144.

**Many speakers came forward:** but only the speech of Pericles is recorded by Th. Nor does he give a reply to Pericles' speech of II.60–64. It may be that other speakers had little or no influence on the course of events, but we must consider the possibility that Th. is keen to leave us with the clearest possible impression of Pericles' supremacy (cf. I.127). Th. says little about internal Athenian politics during the lifetime of Pericles.

**most powerful both in action and in debate:** i.e., in words and deeds, the components of political life; see I.22n. This is a description of a consummate politician. Other sources support this comment on Pericles' oratorical ability: the contemporary comedian Eupolis wrote, "a kind of persuasion sat upon his lips. Thus he and he alone of the orators used to bewitch his hearers and leave his sting in them" (frag. 94.5–7). Cf. Plut. *Per.* 8, 15; *T.D.G.R.* 74. Pericles himself was not too modest on the subject: see II.60. A fuller account of Pericles' qualities can be found in II.65.

**I.140. my views are the same as ever . . . I must give you exactly the same advice as I have given in the past:** Pericles' consistency contrasts with the volatility of the Athenian demos; cf. II.61n. Th. has not mentioned any earlier statements by Pericles, though he has said that he was "urging Athens on to the war" (I.127).

**the enthusiastic state of mind . . . is not retained when it comes to action:** Pericles' concern that Athenian resolve might weaken under pressure proves to be well founded: see II.59ff.

**I call upon those of you who are persuaded by my words:** not entirely a polite formality, but a reminder that not even Pericles could rely on the automatic acquiescence of the assembly. On persuasion see I.22n.

**the resolutions which we are making all together:** Pericles will soon be reminding the demos of this fact; see II.59n., 64.

**There is often no more logic in the course of events . . . and this is why we usually blame our luck when things happen in ways that we did not expect:** see I.120n.

**arbitration:** cf. I.28n., 78n.

**I.141. The Peloponnesians cultivate their own land themselves:** not strictly true of the Spartans, of course—the helots did it for them. This should not be taken to mean that there were no imports of foodstuffs to Peloponnesian states: see I.120, III.86, IV.53.

**they have no financial resources:** Sparta's allies did not pay tribute into a common fund; cf. I.19n. For the importance of capital reserves cf. I.7, 11; II.13.

**the wars they fight against each other are . . . short affairs:** cf. I.15n.

**wars are paid for by the possession of reserves:** cf. the words of Archidamus at I.80, 83.

**if, as is likely to happen, the war lasts longer than they expect:** as it will; see V.14, VII.28.

**In a single battle the Peloponnesians and their allies could stand up to all the rest of Hellas:** Pericles is well aware of Peloponnesian military superiority, a factor that plays a crucial role in the formulation of his strategy; see II.13n.

**they have no central deliberative authority:** Athens by this stage had full control of the Delian League's decision-making processes, but decision making within the Peloponnesian League was, as bk. I has made clear, a slow process. For the workings of the congress of the Peloponnesian League see I.67n.

**they all have equal votes:** as had originally been the case with the Delian League (I.96n.).

**I.142. their building fortifications in Attica:** Gk. *epiteichismos,* the long-term occupation of fortified positions in enemy territory; see I.122n. Pericles envisages such action by the Athenians only as a form of retaliation, but it was tried later with some success (at Pylos; see IV.2ff.).

**by receiving deserters:** the Spartan occupation of the fortress of Decelea in 413 encouraged desertion by Athenian slaves on a massive scale; see VII.23.

**And as for seamanship:** Pericles was right about the difficulties of acquiring naval skills; see, e.g., the victories of Phormio against much larger fleets in the Corinthian Gulf in 429/8 (II.83ff.).

**we shall be blockading them with strong naval forces:** it is not clear how Pericles hoped to achieve this. Athens did not have the resources to blockade the Peloponnesian coastline.

**I.143. Olympia . . . Delphi:** the treasuries of Zeus at Olympia and Apollo at Delphi; cf. I.121n.

**the foreign sailors in our navy:** cf. I.121n.

**higher rates of pay:** the standard rate was a drachma per day; see III.17n., VI.31.

**resident aliens:** metics; see II.13n.

**outlawed from their own cities:** Pericles is claiming that, since such men came from states within the Athenian empire, the Athenians would be able to prevent them from returning home.

**the destruction of a part of the Peloponnese will be worse for them than the destruction of the whole of Attica would be for us:** this will not prove to be the case; see, e.g., II.21, 59.

**Sea-power is of enormous importance:** cf. I.3–4. On Pericles' war policy see II.13n.

**the loss of men's lives:** of course, Pericles could not predict the plague (cf. II.64). For the extent of Athenian losses see III.87.

**Men come first:** cf. I.74n.

**I.144. ultimate victory:** not exactly what Pericles claimed; see II.13n.

**if only you will make up your minds not to add to the empire while the war is in progress:** the advice is repeated at II.65. In fact Cephallenia was conquered in the opening year of the war (II.30) and Epidaurus was almost captured in 430 (II.56). Melos was attacked unsuccessfully in 427 (III.91). The first expedition to Sicily (III.86) was not a serious attempt at conquest (despite some overambitious hopes: see IV.65), but the second was disastrous (II.65, VII.87; technically the main Sicilian expedition was initiated in peace time, but Nicias cannot have been the only Athenian who suspected that the fighting was not yet over).

**What I fear is not the enemy's strategy, but our own mistakes:** there is no need to see this as a later insertion designed to demonstrate Pericles' foresight; see I.127n.

**her [Sparta's] orders for the expulsion of aliens:** a long-standing practice of the xenophobic Spartans; cf. II.39.

**we will give their independence to our allies if they had it at the time that we made the treaty:** Pericles' response to the ultimatum of I.139; see n. there. On "independence," Gk. *autonomia,* see I.67n.

**the kind of government that suits Spartan interests:** i.e., oligarchy; cf. I.18n., 19n.

**war is being forced upon us:** cf. I.121n.

**they abandoned even what they had:** when in 480 the Persians had made their way through central Greece the Athenians took to their ships, abandoning their city to the invader and returning after their victory at Salamis; cf. I.89n.

**by wisdom rather than by good fortune:** the contrast (I.32n.) is between the Gk. *gnome* (I.79n.) and *tyche* (I.120n.)

**I.145. The Athenians considered that his advice was best:** i.e., there had been other speakers who disagreed with Pericles. Cf. I.139n.

**they were willing, according to the terms of the treaty, to reach a settlement:** this offer of arbitration was the legally correct course of action, as the Spartans later acknowledged (VII.18).

**I.146. without heralds:** i.e., there was not yet a state of war, in which heralds would be required. Cf. I.29n., II.1.

# Book Two

## II.1. Introduction

**between Athens and her allies on the one side and the Peloponnesians and their allies on the other:** a more complete and accurate description of the war than that given at I.1; see n. there.

**There was now no further communication . . . except through heralds:** i.e., the period mentioned in I.146 had come to an end. A further step toward war had been taken.

**it continued without intermission:** this makes it clear that Th. is referring to the so-called Archidamian War of 431–421, which concluded with the Peace of Nicias. See I.1n. He does not regard the uneasy armistice of 423/2 as an intermission.

**I have recorded the events as they occurred each summer and each winter:** the obvious advantages of this procedure outweigh its disadvantage, i.e., that it forces the historian to separate an account of, say, a campaign lasting several years into an equivalent number of sections. Episodes within a single year are similarly divided (e.g., the Athenian raids on the Peloponnesian coast in 431 are discussed at II.17, 23, 25, and 30; for some later adjustments to his method see VIII.45n.). Th. separated the year into summer and winter, i.e., into campaigning and quiet seasons, and notes the passing of each. By "summer" he means the period from spring to autumn inclusive, i.e., about eight months, generally starting in early March. But there is some inconsistency in Th. over the beginnings and endings of seasons, and it is unclear whether they were variable or determined astronomically and thus fixed.

## II.2–6. The Theban Attack on Plataea

Plataea, a small Boeotian town, lay close to the Attic-Boeotian border, some thirty miles from Athens and eight from Thebes. It had long been an ally of Athens. This in itself was irritating to Thebes, leader of the Boeotian confederacy and a member of the Peloponnesian League, but an additional consideration for Thebes was Plataea's position. The town was situated on two important routes, one being the pass between Attica and Boeotia past Mt. Cithaeron (mentioned at III.24), the other being the land link between Thebes and the Megarid and thus the Peloponnese. Thebes had been pressing Plataea to join the Boeotian confederacy for almost a century: see III.55; Hdt. VI.108. That Th. should open his account of the war with the most recent development in the long-running but relatively unimportant story of the enmity between these two communities is something of a surprise: neither of them was accorded prominence in bk. I, and the episode, though representing a further deterioration in relations between the Athenian and Spartan blocs, is of less significance for our understanding of the outbreak of war than the first Peloponnesian invasion of Attica that follows it.

The account of the attack on Plataea is a nice example of Thucydidean reporting. The writing is taut and vivid without being melodramatic. Also of interest are the aggravation of a dispute by stasis (a recurrent feature of Th.'s work, already seen in Epidamnus at I.24ff.) and the massacre of the Theban prisoners, recalling Th.'s comments on the unprecedented suffering caused by this war (I.23) and foreshadowing later atrocities, including the cruel revenge of the Thebans on the Plataeans (III.68). It is noticeable too that the very first action of the war illustrates the point made by the Athenian delegate at Sparta about the unpredictable nature of warfare (I.78; cf. I.120n.): so much of what happens in this episode is the consequence of chance, ignorance, and events beyond human control. For the siege and capture of Plataea by Sparta and for the political and moral issues raised by its fate see II.71–78; III.20–24, 52–68.

**II.2. The thirty years' truce . . . the reconquest of Euboea:** of 446/5; see I.114–15.

**In the fifteenth year:** 431. There was no standard system of dating in the ancient world. Each city-state had its own method of identifying the year of an event, which usually involved linking that event to a particular office-holder of that year; e.g., the method of identifying a year in Athens was to say "in the archonship of *x*." The archonship was peculiar to Athens and thus the information would be useless to an outsider. Likewise the names of the months varied from state to state. Th. rejected this method on the further ground of its inaccuracy: see V.20 (cf. his criticism of Hellanicus at I.97). Th. is anxious to date precisely the first clear breach of the treaty (cf. II.7n., VII.18): he links the attack on Plataea to a major international event, the truce of 446/5, and a more recent incident, the battle at Potidaea (I.62) in, perhaps, October 432; he gives the year in Athenian, Argive, and Spartan terms and, for good measure, the season of the year. For further discussion of his method see Finley's introduction to the Penguin translation, p. 22. The attack on Plataea would have occurred in early April 431 (see II.4n.), since Pythodorus' archonship expired on ca. 10 June (though Th.'s figures, "two months" and "six months," and thus the date are disputed).

**the priestess-ship of Chrysis at Argos:** the Argives reckoned by the number of years the priestess of Hera had held office.

**ephor:** see I.18n.

**a Theban force of rather over 300 men:** four hundred, in fact, says Herodotus (VII.233). The initiative in the war was taken neither by the Athenians—this is hardly surprising in view of their determination not to be the first to break the truce—nor by the Spartans themselves, but by the Thebans. Were Sparta's allies becoming impatient? See I.125n. Archidamus had hoped to stall for two to three years (I.82).

**Boeotarchs:** see IV.76n.

**a Plataean party:** wealthy aristocrats (III.65).

**getting rid of their own political opponents:** stasis again (I.2n.).

**(since Plataea had always been hostile to them):** the hostility between Plataea and Thebes is mentioned rather late and is still unexplained. Plataea, originally a Boeotian foundation (III.61), had, since 519 (III.68), been a loyal friend and ally of Athens (III.55).

**while it was still peace time and war had not yet actually broken out:** cf. II.7, 19n.; VII.18; contrast V.20n. We are told later (III.56, 65) that the attack on Plataea occurred during a religious festival, a time when, out of respect for the gods, acts of war would not normally be entered upon.

**their proper traditional place in the League of all Boeotia:** thus in Homer (*Iliad* II.504) Plataea is included among the cities of the Boeotian confederacy.

**II.3. in the night they could not see what had really happened . . . in the night they would not be so confident:** cf. II.4n., **the darkness.**

**II.4. the women . . . on the roofs . . . hurled down stones and tiles:** as they did in the fighting in Corcyra in 427 (III.74). Women feature rarely in Th., and when they do, it is usually in scenes of chaos and confusion. On attitudes toward women in fifth-century Athens cf. II.46n.

**it had been raining hard all night:** Th. mentions the rain not at the beginning of the passage but only when it becomes relevant, adding to the urgency of his account.

**most of them having no idea:** confusion and panic occur frequently in episodes of fighting in Th. Cf., e.g., II.84; III.77, 108, 112; IV.113; VII.44.

Panic during battles will have made Th.'s search for the truth more difficult, since he often relied on participants or eyewitnesses for information (I.22).

**the darkness:** this added to the panic; cf. Th.'s general comment at VII.80. Night fighting was uncommon for this reason: see VII.44. For some operations by night see III.112, IV.135.

**the mud:** streets in ancient Greek towns were generally unpaved.

**a moonless night at the end of the month:** the Greek month, of course, i.e., ca. 8 April.

**II.5. the river Asopus:** the border between Theban and Plataean territory (Hdt. VI.108).

**This is the Theban account . . . The Plataeans, however, do not admit . . . Whatever the truth may be:** a nice example of Th.'s point (I.22) that different eyewitnesses give different accounts of the same event. Unusually, he is reluctant to decide between the two versions.

II.7–17. Resources and Preparations for War

**II.7. the treaty had quite obviously been broken:** before the attack on Plataea, each side had claimed the other's actions to be a breach of the treaty, but there had been no undisputed violation. But was this considered the first act of war? See II.19n.

**any other foreign power:** Aristophanes (*Acharnians* 61–127, dated to 426) describes the return to Athens of an embassy sent to Persia. We also hear of Spartan embassies to Persia in 430 (II.67) and 425/4 (IV.50). Athens probably concluded a treaty with Persia in 424/3 (M.L. 70 = *T.D.G.R.* 138). For Athenian alliances with Sitalces of Thrace and Perdiccas of Macedon in 431 see II.29, and for Spartan alliances with northern states see II.80.

**500 ships:** Peloponnesian hopes of getting together such a navy seem unrealistic; the accuracy of the figure has been doubted. The western states did not intervene in Greece until after the Sicilian expedition.

**a certain sum of money:** in comparison with Athens, the Peloponnesian League was at a serious financial disadvantage; cf. I.19, 80, 83, 141–42. For some later contributions to the Spartan war effort see *T.D.G.R.* 132.

**Corcyra, Cephallenia, Acarnania, and Zacynthus:** genuine allies of Athens rather than subject members of the Delian League; Th. notes the distinction at II.9. Athens had been interested in this northwestern part of Greece for some time (e.g., it settled helots at Naupactus in 461/0: see I.103), though it was the Corinthians who had settled the area with colonies in earlier times. The region would be an important theater of operations in the Archidamian War.

**Corcyra:** for its agreement with Athens, which resulted in conflict between Athens and Corinth in 433, see I.44. Despite its lavish promises (I.36), Corcyra provided only limited assistance to Athens during the war: see II.25; III.94; VII.26, 57.

**Cephallenia:** the island west of the mouth of the Corinthian Gulf. It was won over by the Athenians in the first year of the war (II.30) and was of assistance to them in 427 (III.94). It had previously supported Corinth in its intervention at Epidamnus (I.27).

**Acarnania:** to the north of the mouth of the Corinthian Gulf. It had been an Athenian ally since Phormio's undated expedition (II.68) and supported Demosthenes in his Olpae campaign (III.105–14). For a discussion of the area see II.102.

**Zacynthus:** south of Cephallenia. It assisted Corcyra and Athens in 433 (I.47), though not an ally of Corcyra at the time (I.31), and proved a faithful ally in the war: see II.66, III.94, VII.31.

**II.8. Nothing . . . was on a small or mean scale:** Th. stresses the enormity of the war once again. Cf. the opening words of Archidamus' speech at II.11.

**great numbers of young men who had never been in a war and were consequently far from unwilling to join in this one:** the period between the end of the First Peloponnesian War (446) and the dispute concerning Corcyra (433) seems to have been relatively quiet; Th. records only the revolts of Samos and Byzantium of 440/39 (I.115–17). On youthful inexperience as opposed to the (supposed) wisdom of the aged cf. I.42, 72. It was the young among the Athenians who most wanted to attack the Peloponnesian invaders (II.21; cf. Archidamus' thoughts at II.20), and it was the youthful Alcibiades who was so keen to attack Sicily (VI.12, 17). Cf. Athenagoras on the headstrong youth of Syracuse (VI.38f.). The old often stand for caution, restraint, and experience: cf. Archidamus' opening words at I.80 and II.11; see also VIII.92 ("The elder men did what they could . . . "). Nicias makes rhetorical use of the distinction at VI.12–13. But in the Sicilian debate Th. notes that the impetuousness of the young is fatally combined with the complacency of the old (VI.24).

**all kinds of prophecies and . . . oracular utterances:** the seriousness of the situation is emphasized by reference to oracles and natural disasters, which Th. has already said were particularly prolific during the war (I.23). Many people regarded them as signs of impending doom, but for the moment Th. suspends judgment ("This was said and thought to be . . . "). In due course Th. shows considerable skepticism about oracles (see, e.g., II.47, 54; V.26: "one solitary instance of their having been proved right"), on the grounds that they claimed to predict what could not be predicted and because they had an undue influence on human affairs. For further examples of omens, prophecies, and prodigies see II.17, 21; VI.27; VIII.1.

**an earthquake:** Th. records a number of natural phenomena that occurred during the war, including eclipses (II.28, IV.52, VII.50), earthquakes (I.101; III.87, 89; IV.52; V.45; VI.95; VIII.6, 41), inundations (III.89), eruptions (III.116), and coastal deposition (II.102); the great plague (II.47–54, III.87) might be added. Some are noted because they affected the course of events (e.g., the plague, mentioned at III.87, and the eclipse of 413, mentioned at VII.50), but many he seems to mention out of scientific interest. Occasionally he will even speculate on the causes of such phenomena (see, e.g., III.89; cf. II.28 and the remarks on forest fires at II.77). The spirit of scientific inquiry, which is first seen in Ionia in the sixth century, was thriving in the Athens of Th.'s day. At the same time there was some vigorous resistance to new ideas, belief in the gods remained widespread, and, as Th. often makes clear, superstition was rife (see, e.g., the case of Nicias discussed at VII.50 and Plutarch's interesting comments in *Nicias* 23).

**Delos:** the sacred island of the Ionians; see I.96n.

**the liberation of Hellas:** a genuine ambition or mere propaganda? On liberation see, e.g., I.139 and Brasidas' campaign in the north in 424 (e.g., IV.85, 114, 120). In 425, however, during the Pylos episode, the Spartans were willing to abandon their campaign for Greek freedom in return for the men captured on Sphacteria (IV.17–20) and in 412/11 they were prepared to sacrifice the freedom of the Asian Greeks to Persia in return for its support in the war (VIII.18, 37, 58; cf. Lichas' argument at VIII.43).

**States and individuals alike were enthusiastic to support them [the Spartans] in every possible way:** cf. Archidamus' assertion that Sparta enjoyed widespread support in Greece (II.11). But these claims are not borne out by Th.'s narrative; cf. I.77n. Even after the failure in Sicily disaffection in the empire was not as widespread as Th. makes out (VIII.2n.).

**both in speech and action:** see I.22n.

**from those who wished to escape from her rule or from those who feared that they would come under it:** again fear is the dominant motive; cf. I.75n.

**II.9. On the side of Sparta:** next Th. gives us a list of the antagonists on each side in the war. Such catalogs were conventional (cf. *Iliad* II.494–877, Hdt. VII.61–99; also Th. VII.57–58) but Th.'s brief list is disappointingly inadequate as a source of information about the war. He also fails to exploit its literary potential to strengthen the impression given in the surrounding narrative that great events are taking place. **Argives:** Argos had made a thirty years' truce with Sparta in 451 (V.14). **Achaeans:** Achaea had been on Athens' side in the First Peloponnesian War but had returned to the Peloponnesian fold in 446 (I.111, 115). The **Megarians** had gone over to Athens ca. 460 (I.103) and rejoined the Peloponnesians in 446 (I.114); for their part in events just before the war see I.67n. **Boeotians:** see II.2–6. **Locrians:** these are the inhabitants of Opuntian Locris in the northeastern part of central Greece, as opposed to the Ozolian Locrians in the southwest (who were pro-Athenian: see III.95) and the Epizephyrian (= Western) Locrians of southern Italy (who were anti-Athenian). **Phocians:** on Athens' side in the First Peloponnesian War: see I.107–8, 111–12; cf. III.95. **Ambraciots:** see I.26, II.68. **Leucadians:** see I.26. **Anactorians:** see I.55. On the Athenian side the areas of the empire mentioned are similar to those used on the tribute quota lists for the organization of the collection of tribute. **Chios** and **Lesbos** were the only members of the empire still retaining the privilege of contributing ships (I.19). Both would revolt and be suppressed during the course of the war. **Messenians in Naupactus:** the helots settled there by Athens, ca. 461 (I.103). **Melos:** included in the assessment of 425 (*T.D.G.R.* 136), though not conquered until 416 (III.91, V.16). Melos made a contribution to the Spartan war fund in 427 (*T.D.G.R.* 132). **Thera:** assessed to pay tribute in 425 (*T.D.G.R.* 136; cf. 133). **Corcyra:** see II.7n. The allies of both sides in Sicily and Italy are omitted from the list, as is Thessaly (an Athenian ally).

**II.10. the invasion of Attica:** undertaken annually in the early years of the war to destroy property, farms, and crops. Thus the Peloponnesians hoped to ensure a quick and decisive victory (cf. V.14, VII.28), though Archidamus had had his doubts (I.81).

**two-thirds of its total force:** the usual proportion; cf. II.47, III.15. We have no reliable figures for the size of the Peloponnesian army. Plutarch (*Per.* 33) puts the number at sixty thousand, but this is generally rejected as being too high, though it is undisputed that Peloponnesian land forces were greater in number than the Athenian land forces; see I.81n.

**Archidamus:** cf. I.79n. The Peloponnesian army was traditionally led by one of the Spartan kings, and since Pausanias, the son of the banished Pleistoanax (II.21), was still young, Archidamus, though aged, leads this first invasion.

**made the following address:** rather too precise (as is "spoke as follows," which Warner frequently uses); see I.31n. Prebattle or precampaign speeches are commonly found in the works of ancient historians. They tend to include a number of generalizations, rhetorical commonplaces, and emotive appeals to stir the audience into action. It is tempting to ask, especially when the speech was delivered by a non-Athenian in foreign territory, how Th. could have known what was said. Presumably such speeches consist largely of "what in my [Th.'s] opinion was called for by the situation" (I.22).

**II.11. we are in greater numbers . . . than ever before . . . the city against which we are moving is at the height of her power:** another reminder, at the climactic moment, of the unprecedented magnitude of this war, this time from a participant in it; cf. I.1, 23.

**For the whole of Hellas is . . . , because of the general hatred against Athens, wishing us success:** an exaggeration? Cf. I.77n., II.8n.

**it may seem that . . . there is little risk of our enemy coming out to meet us in battle:** Sparta's prospects of success depend on this happening. Pericles knows this full well and will refuse to oblige.

**There is much that is unpredictable in war:** see I.120n.

**we ought to consider it very likely that they will come and meet us in battle:** even Archidamus could be prone to wishful thinking. Cf. I.121. He was right the first time: see n. earlier in this chapter, **it may seem that . . .**

**People grow angry when they suffer:** true, they will (II.22, 59), but Archidamus, despite his friendship with Pericles (II.13), underestimates his grip on the Athenian demos. Pericles will be able to prevent the Athenians from acting impulsively. On the contrast between passion and rational control see I.86n.

**II.12. Before making any further move he sent Melesippus:** Archidamus is still keen to avoid an outbreak of war; cf. I.125n., II.18n.

**Melesippus, the son of Diacritus, a Spartan:** a Spartiate, in fact (on the term see IV.8n.). He had also been on an earlier mission to Athens: see I.139.

**the Athenians refused him admission:** Pericles remains determined to show no sign of weakness and to make no concession. On his constancy cf. I.140; II.13 ("he gave just the same advice as before"), 61n.

**This day will be the beginning of great misfortunes to Hellas:** a vivid scene that adds to the drama of the opening of the war, but something of a cliché and not Th.'s usual style.

**II.13. one of the ten Athenian generals:** see I.48n. and cf. I.116. Pericles' power and influence rested not so much in his office as in his long record of success in politics and the confidence he enjoyed among the demos. He was elected general each year from 443–429 (Plut. *Per.* 16).

**Archidamus, who happened to be a friend of his:** there was nothing unusual in friendships between Athenians and Spartans. Cimon, for instance, was well known in Sparta and a keen philo-Laconian, even calling his son Lacedaemonius (I.45; cf. Plut. *Cimon* 16). Th. himself seems to have been well acquainted with Spartans and to have used his connections as sources for Spartan matters (V.26). The institution of the proxenia (II.29n.) also encouraged friendships.

**the proclamation about driving out the curse:** see I.126–27.

**he gave just the same advice as he had given before:** see also I.142–44 and II.65 (in a sentence toward the bottom of p. 163 in the Penguin translation). Pericles' policy, cautious and essentially defensive, was based on his recognition of Peloponnesian military superiority and of Athens' need to preserve its dominance on the sea and thus keep the city safe and the empire intact. He envisaged only limited offensive action: the raids on the Peloponnesian coast could be severe (e.g., II.56), but the damage would be isolated; one or two strategic acquisitions would be made early in the war (II.26, 32), but they did not weaken the Peloponnesians' overall position; the raids on the Megarid (II.31, IV.66) would be destructive but would not lead to the defection or capture of Megara by which Athens would be able to hinder Peloponnesian invasions of Attica; Athenian cavalry would carry out damage-limitation operations in Attica during the Peloponnesian invasions (e.g., II.19, 22; III.1).

How then, it might be asked, did Pericles propose to win the war? Warner's translation of the Gk. verb *periesesthai* as "ultimate/final victory" (I.144 and the last sentence of II.13; cf. II.65, V.14, VIII.106) is perhaps misleading. There was no possibility that the Athenians would win an outright victory over the Peloponnesians, since they would not face them in a full-scale battle. The Gk. verb can also be translated as "survive" or "win through," perhaps a more suitable rendering in this context. Thus Pericles hoped to convince the Peloponnesians of the Athenians' invincibility and the futility of making war on them. He would also have known that divisions existed in Spartan politics and would have been aware from Archidamus' eleventh-hour attempts at negotiation that there was still a strong antiwar faction in Sparta. Pericles might reasonably have hoped that two or three years of fruitless activity would produce a sufficient shift in Spartan and Peloponnesian opinion to swing the balance against war.

**the money paid in tribute by her allies:** see I.19, 96, 99. Archidamus had recognized Athens' superior financial position: see I.80, 83.

**Pericles encouraged confidence:** he seems to have believed that the war could be financed from existing revenues. Th. does not mention that Pericles underestimated the duration and the cost of the war and that tribute increases were necessary (IV.50n.).

**600 talents:** such a figure is too high for the *phoros* (tribute) alone, which, since the 450s, had not totaled more than about four hundred talents in a single year. The figure of six hundred perhaps includes not only tribute but all other types of income from subjects: rents, dues, taxes, contributions, and perhaps even reparation payments.

**the Propylaea:** the monumental entrance to the Acropolis. Its surviving accounts cover the years 437–433 (M.L. 60 = *T.D.G.R.* 118). Once the Parthenon was largely completed it seems that priority was given to the Propylaea, but it was never finished.

**other public buildings:** in particular the Parthenon, which was constructed between 447 and 433; the building accounts survive (M.L. 59 = *T.D.G.R.* 120).

**Potidaea:** still under siege; see I.56–65. For the conclusion and cost of the campaign see II.70.

**the spoils taken from the Persians:** in the Persian Wars of 480/79 (I.23n.). They included the throne of Xerxes and the saber of Mardonius, his general.

**the statue of Athene herself:** the great ivory and gold statue of Athene, built by Pericles' friend Pheidias and housed in the Parthenon. It was dedicated in 438. See M.L. 54 = *T.D.G.R.* 114.

**13,000 hoplites:** they will have been recruited mainly from the Zeugitae (the third of the four divisions of Athenian citizens established by Solon in 594/3 on the basis of wealth in the form of produce from land; see III.16n. and *Ath. Pol.* 7.). The same total is given in II.31. For a discussion of these figures and their implications for the total population of Athens see Rhodes 1988, 271–77; Hansen 1981. On hoplites see I.10n. Athens had no organized force of light-armed troops (see IV.94), but poorer citizens and foreigners were employed for this purpose on an ad hoc basis (e.g., II.31, IV.90).

**the eldest and youngest of the citizens in the army:** military service was compulsory between ages eighteen and fifty-nine; "eldest" probably means aged fifty to fifty-nine, "youngest" eighteen to nineteen. These men perhaps came from all four Solonian classes, which would explain the larger total. For an occasion when these troops were used in battle see I.105.

**resident aliens:** Gk. *metoikoi,* "metics"; foreigners who registered after a certain period of residence in Attica and were obliged to fight. There are no ancient numbers of metics; modern estimates hover (fairly uncertainly) around ten thousand.

**The wall of Phalerum:** a single wall from the city to the far end of the bay of Phalerum, which was east of Piraeus. The first of the **Long Walls** was built in the 450s; see I.93n., 107n. Later, possibly in the late 440s, a wall was built parallel to the Piraeus wall, thus making it a double wall, to make communications with the port safer.

**his usual arguments:** the facts and figures are followed by the sort of rhetoric with which Th. feels his reader is now familiar.

**II.14. even the wood-work:** the plain of Attica was not rich in woodland, though timber was available in the mountains around Athens (e.g., Cithaeron; see II.75, 77). Good quality timber for shipbuilding had to be imported; cf. IV.108n.

**Euboea:** see also II.26. The island, an important member of the empire, had revolted some fifteen years earlier (I.114). Cf. VII.28; VIII.1, 95–96.

**II.15.** A digression into Athenian prehistory: the hero **Theseus'** unification (synoecism: see I.10n.) of the separate communities that originally occupied Attica. **Cecrops,** supposed to have been the first king of Athens, **Erectheus,** a later king, and **Eumolpus** are mythical figures. **Eleusis** was the home of the Eleusinian Mysteries, dedicated to Persephone and Demeter.

**intelligent:** cf. I.79n.

**Evidence for this:** as in the Archaeology (I.3n.), Th. fails to distinguish between history and myth but does not accept tradition uncritically; hence he undertakes his quest for evidence, on which see I.21–22.

**Dionysus:** the god of wine and festivities. At his festival in **the month of Anthesterion** (literally the time when the flowers blossom, i.e., the beginning of spring) the new wine was opened and tried.

**Ionians who came from Athens:** see I.12n.

**the tyrants:** Pisistratus and his sons; see I.13n., 18n.

**the Acropolis is still called 'the city':** *acropolis* in Gk. means "high city."

**[II.16].** The chapter number 16 is misplaced in the Penguin translation: it should immediately precede the paragraph beginning, **For a long time . . .**

**had only recently re-established themselves:** some fifty years ago, in fact, at the end of the Persian Wars.

**It was sadly and reluctantly that they now abandoned their homes:** surely the words of a humane and sympathetic eyewitness; see my introduction, under "Conclusion."

**his own city:** life for the inhabitants of the countryside of Attica revolved around the deme (II.19n.), and it, rather than the city of Athens, was the immediate focus of their attachment.

**II.17. the temple of Eleusinian Demeter:** at the foot of the Acropolis, north of its western end.

**the Pelasgian ground:** on the west side of the Acropolis. On **Pelasgian** see I.3n.

**a Pythian oracle:** the Pythia was the priestess of Apollo at Delphi (I.25n.).

**there was not enough room for them:** Th. gives more details of the squalid living conditions in II.52, where he points out that they were a factor in the rapid spread of the plague.

**a fleet of 100 ships:** the Athenians now prepare for their first retaliatory attack on the Peloponnese, as planned by Pericles (I.143). See II.23, 25, 30–31, with II.13n.

## II.18–33. The First Peloponnesian Invasion of Attica and the Athenian Response

**II.18. Oenoe:** its exact location is unknown, but that it was on the Boeotian border makes it clear that the Peloponnesians took a roundabout route from the Isthmus of Corinth to the north instead of the direct route from Megara along the coast to Eleusis. We are not told why: perhaps it was to secure a further link with Boeotia and to give the Athenians even more time to come to terms. The Peloponnesians arrive at Eleusis by this circuitous route in II.20.

**spent much time with nothing to show for it:** for Spartan ineptitude in siege operations cf. I.102.

**II.19. no herald appeared from Athens:** Pericles remains steadfast; see II.12n.

**The invasion began about eighty days . . . Archidamus, the son of Zeuxidamus:** Th. begins his account of the invasion of Attic territory (the attack on Oenoe does not seem to count) in a formal manner, giving precise details of its date and a full introduction of Archidamus, even though he has recently been mentioned. It is as if Th. regards this as the first act of war—i.e., full-scale war: the attack on Plataea had taken place in peacetime (II.2n.) and had involved not the major participants themselves but only their allies. In V.20, however, he seems to take the attack on Plataea as the first act of the war; see n. there.

The Peloponnesian invasion of Attica is the point of no return. We have waited some time for it: the chapters describing the buildup to it since Plataea (10, 12, 14, 17, 18) have been interspersed with delays: a discussion of resources, plans, and attitudes (7–9), a speech (11), further material on resources and strategies (13), and a digression (15–16). The effect is to create tension and to stress the momentous nature of the occasion.

**a detachment of Athenian cavalry:** for their role in Pericles' war policy see II.13n. The cavalry were wealthy Athenians, who would be keen to protect their country estates: see II.65n. Cf. II.22, III.1.

**Cropia:** a deme west of **Acharnae** (II.20n.) and north of **Mount Aegaleus** but its exact site is unknown.

**The Streams:** possibly the border between Athens and Eleusis.

**demes:** local communities in Attica, about 150 in number, which provided a basis for administration and a local focus of loyalty, especially for citizens who lived outside Athens. Under Cleisthenes' reforms of 508 demes became subdivisions of the *trittys,* three of which (one from each of the three regions of Attica: the town, the coast, and the interior) constituted a tribe, the main unit of political organization in the fifth-century democracy. It became common practice to identify oneself by one's demotic, or deme name, rather than by the patronymic ("son of . . . ").

**II.20. Acharnae:** a large and populous deme some seven miles north of Athens. The citizens of Acharnae are represented by Aristophanes in his *Acharnians* as in favor of an aggressive approach to the war.

**His hope was . . . :** Th. claims to know what went on in Archidamus' mind; see V.26n.

**a population of young men that had never been exceeded:** cf. II.8n.

**3,000 hoplites:** out of a total of thirteen thousand, the number given at II.13. The figure of three thousand is generally considered too high for a single deme. An attractive emendation to the Gk. text is to read *politai* (citizens) instead of *hoplitai* (hoplites).

**II.21. Pleistoanax:** see I.114. He was recalled in the nineteenth year of his exile (V.16).

**they felt outraged:** cf. "their angry feelings," II.22. For Periclean control of public anger see II.60, 64–65.

**especially the young:** see II.8n. Archidamus had predicted their reaction (II.20).

**prophets . . . prophecies:** their appearance is again associated with tension and uncertainty; cf. II.8n.

**they abused him for being a general and not leading them out to battle:** Pericles was, of course, only one of ten generals (I.48n.), though no doubt preeminent among them.

**and put on him the whole responsibility for what they were suffering:** another suggestion of Pericles against the rest. The people are conveniently forgetting the facts; they were prone to this sort of behavior; cf. II.65n., **as is the way with crowds.**

**II.22. he [Pericles] summoned no assembly or special meeting of the people:** this cannot be taken at face value, since Pericles himself had no such authority. It may mean that Pericles, as one of the ten generals (who had the power, perhaps in conjunction with the prytaneis [see IV.118n.], to summon—or not to summon—assemblies), successfully argued against the summoning of an assembly because of the emergency created by the invasion. Or Th. may be referring not to a proper assembly but to a meeting of the men under the generals' command: the power to summon such a meeting would of course belong to the generals. Th. tends to talk of Pericles as if he had unrestricted powers; cf. II.21n., 65n., and, on the general's powers, II.59n.

**under the influence of anger rather than of reason:** see I.86n. on the distinction.

**He did . . . send out cavalry:** see II.19n.

**Phrygia:** its exact site is uncertain, but it was probably a few miles north-east of Athens.

**Boeotian cavalry:** note the (possibly exaggerated) claim of its importance to the Peloponnesians made by Hippocrates at IV.95.

**the old treaty:** we do not know the date of Athens' alliance with Thessaly, though it must be some time after the unsuccessful Athenian expedition to Thessaly in 457/6 (I.111). For an earlier alliance see I.102. Th. was capable of describing as "ancient" (or perhaps just "old") an alliance of less than twenty years: see III.86n.

**II.23. laid waste some of the other demes:** for the sparing of the sacred olive trees during the invasion see *T.D.G.R.* 127.

**Mount Parnes and Mount Brilessus:** mountains to the north of Athens. Mt. Brilessus is generally known as Mt. Pentelicon.

**the Athenians sent off round the Peloponnese the fleet of 100 ships:** see II.17n.

**On board the ships there were 1,000 hoplites:** see I.10n.

**Proteas:** joint commander of the Athenian fleet in the Corcyra campaign of 433; see I.45.

**for as long as their supplies lasted:** probably three to four weeks.

**Oropus:** an important port for vessels going to and from Euboea: cf. VII.28.

**the Graean territory:** the coast of northern Attica opposite central Euboea.

**II.24. a special fund of 1,000 talents:** the money would not be used until 411 (VIII.15).

**other funds:** see II.13.

**a special fleet of 100 triremes:** Athens' dependence on its fleet has been emphasized a number of times (e.g., I.140ff., II.13). Warships were equipped at the expense of private individuals, their **captains** (trierarchs): this was a form of public service that wealthy men could offer the state. What happened to these vessels is unknown: they do not seem to have been available after the Sicilian disaster (VIII.1).

**II.25. Corcyra:** one of the few occasions on which Corcyra offered any assistance to Athens (see I.44 for their alliance). Cf. II.7n.

**Brasidas:** a Spartan of unusual initiative and imagination who would play an important part in formulating and carrying out Spartan policy in the Archidamian War. Cf. IV.81n.

**II.26. Euboea:** whither the Athenians had dispatched their sheep and cattle for safekeeping at the beginning of the Peloponnesian invasion (II.14).

**Thronium:** on the Locrian coast opposite the northern end of Euboea. Cf. the occupation of Atalanta (II.32).

**II.27. accusing them of having been largely responsible for the war:** unreasonably (this is not the impression given in I.67, 139–40), but truth is the first casualty of war. The Athenians had to be sure that Aegina, which dominated the Saronic Gulf, did not fall into enemy hands. It could also be useful for raids on the Peloponnesian coast. For Aegina's incorporation into the Delian League see I.105, 108. It was restored to its original inhabitants in 405 (Xenophon *Hellenica* II.2.9).

**Thyrea:** in Cynuria in the northeastern Peloponnese; see V.14n. The Aeginetans formed a buffer between Laconia and Argolis.

**the earthquake and the revolt of the helots:** in 465; see I.101.

**II.28. the beginning of a new lunar month:** when earth, moon, and sun are so positioned as to make an eclipse of the sun possible. Thus Th., though tentative, is right. Greek thinkers understood the causes of eclipses (Plut. *Nicias* 23). For Th.'s interest in natural phenomena see II.8n.

**II.29. Abdera:** on the coast of Thrace, northeast of Thasos; it was a member of the Delian League.

**Sitalces . . . King of Thrace:** see II.95–101, IV.101.

**representative:** Gk. *proxenos,* a man who in his own state acted on behalf of another state to support its interests. Alcibiades throws some light on the workings of the institution of the proxenia at VI.89. Some Athenian proxenoi intervened vigorously in local affairs on behalf of Athens: see the cases of Nicias (II.85) and Peithias (III.70).

**Tereus who married Procne:** In this brief digression Th. seems anxious to deny the connection with Teres and to clarify a confused point. The Thracian connection may have added interest for Th., who had a Thracian background (see my introduction, under "The Life of Thucydides"). Cf. II.15 and the Archaeology (I. 2–19) for a similar rationalizing method.

**Perdiccas:** see I.56n.

**had his son Sadocus made an Athenian citizen:** a rare honor, granted here to secure the relationship.

**peltasts:** lightly armed, highly mobile troops, equipped with a small shield and javelin. They would be especially useful in mountain and guerrilla warfare. Athens did not maintain a force of light-armed troops: see II.13n.

**persuaded the Athenians to give Therme back to him:** see I.61 for its capture by the Athenians in 432.

**Phormio:** see I.64n.

**II.30. the Athenian fleet of 100 ships:** see II.17n.

**Sollium:** a Corinthian colony in Acarnania, on the coast south of Anactorium.

**Acarnanians:** see II.7n.

**Astacus:** on the coast of southern Acarnania.

**Evarchus:** see II.33 for his restoration.

**Cephallenia:** see II.7n. Its capture would appear to contravene Pericles' advice not to add to the empire during the war (I.144).

**II.31. resident aliens:** metics; see II.13n.

**the Megarid:** an important element in Athens' limited offensive operations would be a twice-yearly invasion of the Megarid (IV.66) and a blockade of Megara by sea (II.93). See I.103n. for the strategic importance of this area and II.13n. on Athenian strategy. For ill feeling between Athens and Megara and the importance of the Megarian Decrees as a cause of the war see I.67, 139, with nn.

**the plague:** see II.47ff.

**10,000 hoplites . . . the 3,000 at Potidaea:** making thirteen thousand, the figure given in II.13 for Athens' field army (excluding cavalry). Three forces at Potidaea totaling 4,600 have previously been mentioned (I.57, 61, 64); some troops had clearly been withdrawn.

**3,000 hoplites from the resident aliens:** to make up for the three thousand at Potidaea.

**light armed troops:** see II.13n.

**when Nisaea was captured by the Athenians:** in 424 (IV.66–69).

**II.32. pirates:** cf. I.98n.

**Euboea:** cf. II.14, 26.

**II.33. Evarchus:** see II.30.

## II.34–46. The Funeral Speech

It was established Athenian practice by the late fifth century to hold a public funeral in honor of all those who had given up their lives in war for the common good. The main element of the ceremony was a speech in praise of the dead, delivered by a prominent citizen.

It is impossible to assess how accurate a reflection of the original is Pericles' speech. This is not only because, like all Th.'s speeches, it would have been reworked by the historian; it is, in addition, the earliest extant funeral speech and the only complete example surviving from the fifth century. Fourth-century equivalents suggest a standard pattern for the genre, comprising an introduction; a comment on the speech as an institution; wide-ranging praise of the dead, glorifying their deeds and sacrifice; consolation of the mourners; and a dismissal. But Pericles' speech goes well beyond this formula: it is a eulogy of Athens itself, a glorification of its achievements and an affirmation of its promise. The Athenians have created a way of life and an organization of their state in which the rights of the individual and the needs of the community are in harmony; the citizens of Athens, totally committed to it, are prepared to fight and die to maintain this uniquely balanced and productive society. The speech is intended to promote among Athenians a full appreciation of what it means to be Athenian and thus to unite them in loyalty to the state and to each other in a war fought to protect Athenian culture and civilization. For this reason it is addressed to Athenian citizens only: metics, who fought and died for Athens, are ignored; women are mentioned only to be immediately excluded.

While we may agree with Pericles that the Athenians were an exceptionally gifted people, the picture presented by him here is, of course, idealized, almost romantic in its portrait of political and personal perfection. The essence of this style of oratory was to give unstinted praise in language designed to stir the emotions. Pericles adapts the genre to his own requirements and delivers a speech that sets forth a vision of an ideal society. It contains numerous generalizations and rhetorical flourishes, much that is detached from the world of everyday experience and that would not stand up to close scrutiny. The forceful logic and gritty realism found in Pericles' policy speeches are replaced here by majestic pronouncement. The magnificence of the speech reveals the oratorical power and versatility of Pericles. We see him too as the supreme statesman, a man of vision and authority, and a man who, above all else, loved his country.

For Pericles the speech will also have had a more immediate, political purpose. His war policy was unpopular (II.21), and this was an opportunity to unite the Athenians in support of it. It was not successful: see II.59, 65. On the genre of the Funeral Speech see Ziolkowski 1981.

**II.34. their annual custom:** in fact the Gk. means "ancestral custom" or "traditional custom." We do not know when the practice began.

**the bones of the fallen:** the custom was to burn the bodies at the site of the battle (e.g., VI.71) and bring the bones back to Athens.

**each tribe:** the ten political divisions of the Athenian citizens, created by Cleisthenes in 508.

**foreigners:** i.e., resident aliens (metics, II.13n.) and other noncitizens, permitted to attend this meeting (and to fight and die for Athens) but ignored in this speech (except for a brief reference at the end of II.36). On Athenian openness see II.39.

**women:** see I.46n.

**the most beautiful quarter:** the Ceramicus (the potters' quarter), outside the Sacred Gate. The road from this gate is lined with tombs.

**The only exception:** in fact there were others, e.g., Plataea (Hdt. IX.85). On **Marathon** see I.18n.

**a man chosen by the city for his intellectual gifts and for his general reputation:** who else on this occasion but Pericles, already twice introduced (I.127, 139) as the foremost Athenian statesman?

**II.35. speech . . . action:** see I.22n., 32n. The antithesis figures widely in this speech. Here, as elsewhere, Pericles argues that words cannot do justice to the actions of the dead.

**II.36. In this land of ours there have always been the same people:** or so, as a matter of pride, the Athenians claimed, whereas most other Greeks, in particular the Dorian Spartans, had originally been immigrants. Cf. I.2.

**subjects familiar to you:** including the Persian Wars, on which see I.73n.

**I shall say nothing about the warlike deeds by which we acquired our power:** Pericles will instead focus on the nature of the society that their power and talents have enabled the Athenians to create. But war is never far away: Athens' freedom, on which its achievements depend, must be maintained by vigilance, courage, and sacrifice (II.42–43).

**foreigners:** see II.34n.

**II.37. a model to others:** after the reforms of Ephialtes (462/1) a number of Greek states adopted democratic constitutions, often under pressure from Athens (e.g., Erythrae; see *T.D.G.R.* 71).

**democracy:** Gk. *democratia,* literally "people-power." The word is a fifth-century coinage, used at this time in contrast to oligarchy, the rule of the few. Pericles expresses pride in Athenian democracy, but it was Th.'s view that the democratic process at Athens was on the point of decline (II.65nn.); even Cleon would be critical (III.37–38).

**private disputes . . . public responsibility:** Athenian democracy, Pericles argues, combines fulfillment of private needs with the demands of public duty. But the war will reveal a tension between public and private; see II.65.

**not membership of a particular class:** most commentators take the Gk. to mean "not in rotation," which was the method by which most offices in Athens were filled. Pericles is asserting that talented men could still achieve high office through election: this was the means by which the generals were appointed. He seems to be defending the Athenian democratic system against the charge that it discriminates (by the use of annual rotation and the lot) against men of ability. Cf. Old Oligarch I.2–3.

**No one . . . is kept in political obscurity because of poverty:** payment for service in office had been introduced in the late 460s (or perhaps the early 450s) but was not sufficient to allow the poorest citizens to make a political career for themselves. Moreover, it is probable that the Thetes (I.10n.) were barred from some offices.

**just as our political life is free and open, so is our day-to-day life:** cf. the remarks of Cleon at III.37 ("fear and conspiracy play no part . . .") and of Nicias at VII.69. But it was not all sweetness and light, as Pericles himself knew: several of his friends had been attacked in the courts in recent years as a means of undermining his domination of Athenian politics (Plut. *Per.* 31–32).

**those unwritten laws which it is an acknowledged shame to break:** those fundamental moral principles that make for a civilized society—laws that the Athenians themselves will soon be breaking: see II.52–53 (with a verbal echo, "the most shameless methods," in chapter 52).

**II.38. various kinds of contests:** the chief festivals, such as the Panathenaea and the Dionysia, when business ceased. There were something like 150 festival days in the Attic year.

**all the good things from all over the world:** Athens' control over the sea gave it access to distant markets, in Italy and Sicily, Egypt, the Middle East, and the Black Sea. The ready availability of luxury goods to Athenians is confirmed by a critic of the democracy, the Old Oligarch (2.7). Cf. I.81, I.120n.

**II.39. our city is open to the world:** hence the presence of foreigners at this very gathering (II.34n.). But Pericles' sweeping statement should not cause us to forget that since his citizenship law of 451 (*Ath. Pol.* 26) only free adult males of pure Athenian descent had enjoyed the privileges of citizenship.

**deportations:** also referred to by Pericles in I.144. Cf. V.68 on Spartan secrecy.

**the most laborious training in courage:** Spartans were trained rigorously from an early age in military skills, and according to Nicias (VI.11), "military honour was the be-all and the end-all of their existence."

**the Spartans . . . bring all their allies with them:** e.g., II.10.

**we . . . do the job by ourselves:** Pericles omits mention of the use of mercenaries and the assistance of allies.

**II.40. Our love of what is beautiful:** following the building program initiated in the early 440s (II.13n.) Athens had by now the finest public buildings of any city in Greece and provided a strong contrast to Sparta, where the citizens had neither the money nor the desire to adorn their city in this way (cf. I.10). Athens had also become the intellectual center of Greece, while the "new learning" was conspicuously absent in Sparta (cf. I.84n.).

**does not make us soft:** Pericles presents Athenians past and present as resilient and determined, never soft; the Gk. for soft occurs again at II.42 ("No one of these men weakened . . .") and II.43 ("a humiliation caused by his own slackness"). But before long Athenian determination will wilt and Pericles, faced with the task of reviving it, will employ the vocabulary of softness (translated as "lack of moral fibre," II.61) to sting the Athenians into action. Cleon too will charge the Athenians with softness in his efforts to persuade the Athenians to adhere to their decision to execute the Mytilenians ("a kind of weakness," III.37; "do not grow soft," III.40).

**a man who takes no interest in politics . . . has no business here at all:** the working of the Athenian democratic system depended on the participation of the citizens. Cf. II.37, 63n.

**we do not think that there is an incompatibility between words and deeds:** cf. I.22n.

**the worst thing is to rush into action before the consequences have been properly debated:** a point made in the debate at Sparta in 431; cf. I.78n.

**estimating them beforehand:** close scrutiny of the facts and careful forethought were features of Athenian policy making under Pericles, according to Th. Cf. Pericles' definition of intelligence at II.62. But to estimate the risks beforehand is precisely what Th. believes the Athenians failed to do in the case of Sicily (VI.1).

**We make friends by doing good to others:** Pericles offers no examples. Perhaps he has in mind the recent alliance with Corycra or Athenian support of democrats in subject states.

**II.41. an education to Greece:** in what sense? The context suggests that Pericles has in mind the character of the Athenian citizen and the organization of the Athenian state. This is one of many striking expressions in this speech.

**each single one of our citizens . . . the rightful lord and owner of his own person:** there is much interplay in this speech between individual and state, the rights of the former and obligations to the latter.

**no subject can complain of being governed by people unfit for their responsibilities:** Pericles is on shaky ground in this elevated passage. Events will reveal the irony of this claim. Indeed, only months later, Pericles will tell the Athenians that their empire is "like a tyranny" (II.63).

**Future ages will wonder at us:** cf. I.75n., **fear . . . honour . . . interest.**

**the praises of a Homer or of anyone else whose words may delight us for the moment:** we are reminded of Th.'s comment at I.22 that he has no time for such fleeting pleasures. In fact, Th. has a high regard for Homer: see I.3. Cf. too the remarks of Cleon at III.38.

**whose estimation of the facts will fall short of what is really true:** cf. Th.'s remarks at I.21 on the unreliability of poets and other writers. Both the politician and the historian seek the truth: see II.62n.

**our adventurous spirit:** cf. the words of the Corinthians at I.70. Pericles' war policy required that this essential feature of the Athenian character be curbed: see I.144.

**II.42. my words of praise for the dead:** Pericles returns to the essential element of a funeral oration.

**words . . . the courage and gallantry:** in effect, the words/deeds antithesis again; see II.35n.

**the doubtful hands of Hope:** see I.121n.

**II.43. We who remain behind:** the remainder of the speech is an appeal to the living, who must devote themselves to the city for which their loved ones have died.

**fall in love with her:** another striking phrase, even more striking in the original, which literally means "become her lovers."

**II.44. I shall not commiserate:** Pericles acknowledges past sacrifice but is concerned to urge his audience to look to the future with courage and confidence.

**many changes and chances:** a recurrent theme in Th.'s work; see I.120n. Pericles and Th. seem to concur on this point.

**as the poet said:** no particular poet is referred to. In fact, the Gk. means simply "as some say"; the thought was probably a commonplace.

**II.45. a hard struggle in front of you:** once more Pericles is looking to the future and does not pull his punches.

**II.46. the duties of women:** Pericles will be brief; indeed, he seems reluctant to mention the subject of women at all. What he says to the mothers, wives, and daughters of the dead seems patronizing and unsympathetic. Kinder interpretations have been advanced by modern scholars, but we must take what we read at face value: Pericles is putting women in (what he regards as) their place, which is somewhere out of sight.

The position of women in Athenian society and the attitudes of that society toward them are contentious issues. It is dangerous to generalize about half the population of fifth-century Athens, not least because the evidence on which such generalizations must be based was produced by members of the other half. What we do know is that women had no formal role in war and politics. But the idea that they spent all their time indoors is more likely to represent a male fantasy than the reality of day-to-day life. For some source material in translation see *C.A.* 112–41. On women in Th. see II.4n.

**their children will be supported:** orphans were brought up at public expense, an arrangement perhaps introduced by Solon (archon in 594/3).

## II.47–55, 57. The Second Peloponnesian Invasion of Attica and the Plague

In Th.'s time there was a great deal of interest in medical science (and in the natural sciences generally: see II.8n.), and he decided to write up this unique episode not only because of the plague's effect on Athens' conduct of the war but also for its intrinsic interest and the potential usefulness of a full account. Modern authorities have disagreed on the extent to which Th.'s account is technical. Comparisons between Th.'s description and the surviving writings of the famous fifth-century physician Hippocrates of Cos reveal similarities in vocabulary, but it is difficult to prove that Th.'s terminology is less akin to fifth-century colloquial speech than to contemporary medical jargon. It is perhaps safest to consider Th. a well-informed layman on this matter.

The plague is an ideal vehicle for conveying Th.'s formidable powers of observation, analysis, and description: the result is an impressive and moving artistic achievement. An account of the physical symptoms and the psychological impact of the disease is followed by some discussion of its social consequences, the collapse of civic responsibility and a general degeneration of behavior. These social problems are thrown into clearer relief by the juxtaposition of the Funeral Speech and the account of the plague. In the Funeral Speech Athens had been held up as a model state, whose energy had been harnessed for the common good to create a truly civilized mode of life. The reader had been swept up in the grandeur of its ideas and its language: now the vision is shattered as the fragility of Athenian civilization is exposed and Pericles' ideal society disintegrates. We see a similar breakdown during the stasis in Corcyra (III.69–85, especially 82–84).

As for the identity of the disease, suggestions have included measles, bubonic plague, typhus, smallpox, influenza complicated by toxic shock syndrome, and, most recently, the Ebola virus. It is unlikely that we shall ever be certain. The disease could indeed by extinct by now. For a recurrence of the plague in 427/6 and the numbers of casualties see III.87.

**II.47. the Peloponnesians and their allies, with two thirds of their total forces as before, invaded Attica:** having given a full account of the first invasion (II.10–12, 18–23), Th. sees no need to go into detail on the second (or successive) invasion, though this one will be particularly damaging. His brief account is completed in II.55, 57.

**Equally useless were prayers . . . oracles:** see II.8n. Th. returns to this subject at the end of his description of the plague: see II.53–54.

**II.48. so they say:** a formula often used by Th. when he is not prepared to vouch for the information.

**how it could first have come about or what causes can be found . . . I must leave that to be considered by other writers with or without medical experience:** again Th. is cautious and will not indulge in speculation. He will do no more than what he can do with certainty, i.e., record what he saw.

**knowledge of which will enable it to be recognized, if it should ever break out again:** Th. has already expressed the hope that his work will be found useful (I.22), but he leaves it unclear as to how recognition of the disease will be helpful to those who encounter it in the future.

**I had the disease myself and saw others suffering from it:** Th. leaves us in no doubt about his qualifications to write this episode but, typically, says no more about his personal involvement. His own experiences and suffering must account in part for the sympathetic tone of his account.

**II.49. that has been given a name by the medical profession:** this phrase perhaps suggests that Th. was familiar with medical writings but did not wish to get too technical.

**II.50. Evidence for this may be found in the fact . . . :** as always, Th. seeks to support his point with evidence; see my introduction, under "The Aims and Methods of Thucydides."

**II.52. the removal of the people from the country into the city:** see II.14, 17.

**The temples . . . were full of . . . dead bodies:** it was an act of sacrilege to allow a death (or birth) to take place in a temple; cf. I.134 and the purification of Delos at III.104.

**men, not knowing what would happen next to them:** the plague illustrates as well as any other incident in Th. mankind's inability to control their environment. The role of chance in human affairs has already been cited a number of times (I.120n.). Now it intervenes dramatically to alter the course of events.

**became indifferent to every rule of religion or of law:** under the immediate threat of death, the conventions of civilized behavior were abandoned. Note that, whatever Th.'s own religious beliefs may have been, he recognizes the social value of religion; cf. "No fear of god . . ." (II.53), "fellowship in a religious communion" (III.82n.), "no oath sworn . . . " (III.83).

**II.53. Seeing how quick and abrupt were the changes of fortune:** cf. II.52n.

**acts of self-indulgence . . . pleasure . . . the pleasure of the moment:** Th. notes a similar response to the pressures of the civil war in Corcyra ("the pleasure of their own party at that particular moment," III.82). See II.65n., **adopted methods of demagogy.**

**As for what is called honour . . . so doubtful was it whether one would survive to enjoy the name for it:** something of a mistranslation. The Gk. means "no one was keen to strive after what was considered honorable because he was not sure he would not die before he achieved it."

**As for the gods, it seemed to be the same thing whether one worshipped them or not:** not a literal translation and certainly not evidence that Th. believed in the gods. Th.'s suggestion here that human attempts to communicate with and influence the divine are ineffectual ties in with his attitude toward oracles (II.8n.).

**II.54. people naturally recalled old oracles:** relying on the uncertain in their quest for certainty; cf. II.8n., 47.

***War with the Dorians:*** for racial undertones in the war see I.124n.

**the oracle that was given to the Spartans:** see I.118.

**II.55. Meanwhile the Peloponnesians . . . :** see II.47n., 57.

**the Paralian district:** the coastal regions of southwest Attica.

**Laurium:** a few miles north of Cape Sunium, the southern tip of Attica. The mines were an important source of revenue to the Athenians. It is unlikely that the Peloponnesians would have done them much damage in a short stay, but they were one of their objectives in the later occupation of Decelea (VI.91).

## II.56. The Athenian Attack on Epidaurus

**Pericles . . . was organizing an expeditionary force of 100 ships against the Peloponnese:** as he had done in 431; see II.17n. On the size of the force see VI.31.

**4,000 citizen hoplites:** i.e., forty per ship, though the usual complement was ten; cf. I.10n., II.23.

**Fifty ships from Chios and Lesbos:** see II.9n.

**they seemed likely to capture the place:** to do so would have constituted a considerable departure from Pericles' policy, which excluded expansion of the empire during the course of the war (I.144; cf. II.13n.). The size of the force is not easy to explain, but we must assume that the purpose of this expedition was the same as that of the others: to inflict as much damage as possible on the coastal towns of the Argolid (northeast Peloponnese) and to give a boost to Athenian morale. For an exception, a conquest, see II.30.

**II.57. this invasion lasted longer than any other:** cf. III.26.

## II.58. Athenian Activity in the North

**Hagnon:** he was the founder of Amphipolis (IV.102, V.11) and had a distinguished career.

**Cleopompus:** see II.26.

**Pericles' colleagues in the higher command:** i.e., the *strategoi;* see I.48n.

**the Chalcidians:** enemies of Athens since 432, when they supported the revolt of Potidaea (I.58). For further action (by Sitalces) against them see II.95ff.

**Potidaea, which was still being besieged:** for the conclusion of the siege see II.70.

## II.59–64. The Speech of Pericles

Th.'s attention is again focused on Pericles and the issue of political leadership, but now there is tension between leader and led, and in his final appearance Pericles struggles to assert his authority. The vision of civic harmony and the democratic ideal expressed in the Funeral Speech are further undermined by flaws in the democratic process that emerge with the increasing strains of war.

**II.59. Now they began to blame Pericles for having persuaded them to go to war:** the people made the decisions but would not take responsibility for them; what is more, says Th., Pericles had anticipated this outburst (as he claims in his opening words at II.60; cf. I.140). It had happened before: see II.21 and cf. II.65n., **as is the way with crowds.**

**They were then in a state of utter hopelessness, and all their angry feelings turned against Pericles:** the emotion of the people is again (cf. II.22) contrasted with the clear, rational vision of Pericles. This is not the sort of reaction to a setback that one would have expected from Athenians as described in the Funeral Speech.

**He [Pericles] therefore, since he was still general, summoned an assembly:** cf. II.22n.

**II.60. I expected this outbreak of anger . . . since I understand the reasons for it:** Pericles adopts an attitude of superiority in his opening words. If he hoped to cow his audience he was not entirely successful: Th. comments that "the general ill feeling against him persisted" (II.65). A similar attitude can be found elsewhere in this speech. Pericles was known for his aloofness (see Plut. *Per.* 7).

**one who has . . . ability . . . to see what ought to be done and to explain what he sees, one who loves his city and one who is above being influenced by money:** a combination of intelligence, political expertise, and honorable motives, the intellectual and moral qualities of Pericles acknowledged by Th. at II.65. On bribery see next n. but one.

**A man who has the knowledge but lacks the power clearly to express it is no better off than if he never had any ideas at all:** a reflection on the importance of the spoken word in Athenian society; cf. I.22n.

**but not able to resist a bribe:** the Old Oligarch (3.3) records that bribery was widespread in Athenian politics and this is confirmed by frequent reference to bribery in the major fifth-century authors. Cf. Cleon at III.38, 40 and Diodotus at III.42; also IV.65 on the alleged bribing of generals, VII.48 on Nicias' fears (despite his wealth) of a trumped-up charge of bribery, and Th. on "private ambition and private profit," II.65n. For references to bribery among Spartans, other Greeks, and foreigners see I.109, 131; II.21, 97, 101; III.11n.; IV.114; V.16; VII.86; VIII.45.

**II.61. As for me, I am the same as I was:** consistency of attitude and policy is another feature of Pericles' statesmanship—which is perhaps what we would expect from one who has just presented himself as a man of powerful intellect and high principle. Cf. the opening words of his first speech at I.140, II.12n., and Cleon's words at III.38.

**It is a policy which entails suffering:** cf. I.23 on the suffering brought about by the war.

**When things happen suddenly, unexpectedly, and against all calculation:** a theme running throughout Th. See I.120n.

**II.62. With your navy:** on numbers of Athenian ships see II.13, III.17n. The Archaeology (I.2–19) stressed the point that a navy was one of the bases of power in the Greek world.

**intelligence . . . which proceeds not by hoping for the best . . . but by**

**estimating what the facts are, and thus obtaining a clearer vision of what to expect:** the mark of the astute politician (cf., e.g., Themistocles at I.138), but not a characteristic of the Athenian demos. The language recalls Th.'s explanation of his methods and aims as a historian (I.22–23), suggesting a link in his mind between history and politics. On "hoping for the best" see I.121n.

**II.63. the hatred which we have incurred in administering it [the empire]:** cf. I.77n., V.95.

**Nor is it any longer possible for you to give up this empire . . . it is certainly dangerous to let it go:** cf. the remark of the Athenian delegate at Sparta at I.75. Power can limit freedom as well as expand it: cf. I.70n.; V.95, 97; and Sparta's position vis-à-vis the helots, discussed at IV.80.

**political apathy . . . those who are politically apathetic:** Gk. *apragmosyne* (I.32n.). Pericles condemns those who shun participation in politics. Cf. II.40n., II.64n.

**Your empire is now like a tyranny:** it was natural for Athens' enemies to make such a claim (e.g., I.122), but now an Athenian can make this admission in public. The brutal frankness of Pericles the pragmatist is in stark contrast to the lofty idealism of Pericles the visionary, who delivered the Funeral Speech. He is, though, doing no more than following his own principles: "seeing what ought to be done and explaining what he sees" (II.60) and "estimating what the facts are, and thus obtaining a clearer vision of what to expect" (II.62). Cleon in the Mytilene debate, when he too is trying to persuade the demos to face reality and to act consistently, says that the empire actually is a tyranny (III.37).

**it may have been wrong to take it:** but the moral issue is beside the point. Cf. Cleon's speech in the Mytilene debate, especially III.40: "whatever the rights or wrongs of it may be."

**II.64. you who came to the same conclusion as I did about the necessity for making war:** another sharp reminder that the assembly, not Pericles alone, made the decision to fight. It seems that the point was not well received: see II.65.

**Athens has the greatest name in all the world:** cf. I.75n.

**the plague, something which we did not expect:** see I.120n.

**has spent more life and labor in warfare than any other state:** cf. Pericles' comments on Athenian energy in II.41 and the words of Athens' enemies, the Corinthians, at I.70, with n.

**people who are politically apathetic:** yet another swipe at those who favor *apragmosyne;* see I.32n., II.63n.

**Do not send embassies to Sparta:** cf. II.59.

## II.65. Some Reflections on Pericles and His Successors

Pericles has, with difficulty, got his way and presented an optimistic view of the future. The people of Athens have put aside personal sufferings and rallied. At this point Th. chooses to look ahead to show that any revival is temporary and that Athens will lose the war. Moreover, not the enemy, but the Athenians themselves will be the cause of their destruction. In Th.'s view the crucial factor is the demise of Pericles, and it is Pericles who holds this long, rather chaotic chapter together.

If Th. appears to labor Pericles' virtues—and we may feel that they have already been amply demonstrated with an impressive introduction in I.139 (see n.) and three speeches—that is because this chapter is a kind of obituary to him. Th., writing after the end of the war, is reviewing the whole of the period he has covered, perhaps half his lifetime. An exile for the last twenty years of the war, he has watched from afar as Athens tore itself apart and wasted its strength and opportunities. He looks back, perhaps with some nostalgia, to the days of what he saw as Pericles' wise and responsible leadership. He is irritated by the inconstancy of the people but is much more angry with those politicians who dominated Athenian politics after Pericles' death; he attacks them repeatedly—and imprecisely—for their incompetence and their failure to put the interests of the city before personal ambition. The contrast in this chapter between the unfailing, paternal guidance of Pericles and the destructive demagoguery of his (unnamed) successors—between his vision and their shortsightedness, his integrity and their reckless ambition—is absolute and, surely, simplistic in its polarization. We must acknowledge a lapse here in Th.'s objectivity and judge both Pericles and his successors only by their policies and actions.

**public policy . . . as private individuals:** the strains of war reveal a tension between the interests of the state and those of individuals. The distinction, applied to Pericles' successors, is fundamental to Th.'s thinking in this chapter. Cf. II.37n. and n. later in this chapter, **private ambition and private profit.**

**the richer classes:** they would have constituted the cavalry, who were used to restrict Peloponnesian devastation during invasions (II.13n.) and who would have paid extra taxes to finance the war (III.19).

**they had condemned him to pay a fine:** for what exactly we do not know; cf. Diodorus XII.45 and Plut. *Per.* 35, where it is said that he was also deposed from the generalship. Th. could have given us details of Pericles' offense and punishment but is interested only in the fact that he was soon reinstated.

**as is the way with crowds:** cf. IV.28 ("the Athenians behaved . . . "), VI.63

("just as large numbers . . . "), VIII.1 ("like all democracies . . . "). The changeability of the people is in stark contrast to its leader's constancy. Th. regards it as one of the failings of the Athenian demos that its treatment of its leaders and generals was inconsistent, often hasty, and at times unfair. He himself, of course, suffered at their hands (V.26). Cf. the treatment of the generals at Potidaea (II.70) and of Pythodorus, Sophocles, and Eurymedon (IV.65), as well as the anxieties of Demosthenes (III.98, 114) and Nicias (VII.14, 48). The most extreme example is, of course, the execution of the six generals after the battle of Arginusae in 405 (Xenophon *Hellenica* 1.7). The case of Nicias shows that fear of popular displeasure could influence policy—on this occasion with disastrous consequences. Advisers of the demos also suffered when their policies did not produce the hoped-for results (cf. II.21, VIII.1, the words of Diodotus at III.43, and Old Oligarch 2.17). On Pericles see also II.59–60. For another example of popular inconstancy see III.36, with the comments of Cleon in III.37. See also I.86n. For the Spartan response to failure in their military leaders see II.85n. It is in reference to a Spartan that Th. makes the general comment in V.17: "during a state of war those in the highest position must necessarily get blamed for every misfortune that took place."

**they reelected him:** i.e., either they reinstated him to the generalship of 430/29 (though Th. has not mentioned his deposition: see n. earlier in this chapter) or, more likely, they elected him general anew for the following year.

**and put all their affairs into his hands:** suggesting that indeed **power was really in the hands of the first citizen,** but see n. on these words later in this chapter, explaining that both statements are misrepresentations.

**during the whole period of peace-time when Pericles was at the head of affairs:** i.e., presumably the period between the end of the First Peloponnesian War (446/5) and the outbreak of war in 431, in particular after 444/3, when Pericles' arch rival Thucydides, the son of Melesias, was ostracized (Plut. *Per.* 14). Plutarch (*Per.* 16) also records that Pericles was elected *strategos* for fifteen years in succession during this period, though there were indirect attacks on his leadership in the 430s (*Per.* 31–32).

**he appears to have accurately estimated . . . his foresight with regard to the war became even more evident:** foresight seems to have been for Th. the supreme expression of intelligence and the mark of political genius (cf. I.138), but he has gone too far here: see n. later in this chapter, **Pericles had said.**

**He survived the outbreak of war by two years and six months:** i.e., he died ca. September 429, but Th. anticipates his death in this "obituary" chapter (see my introductory n. to this chapter).

**Pericles had said that Athens would be victorious:** for exactly what

Pericles said see II.13n. For further details of Pericles' war policy see I.140–44, II.13. Th. clearly believed that Pericles' policy could have won the war for Athens if it had been given the chance; however, events proved that Pericles underestimated Spartan perseverance and that his policy was inadequate in two major areas, strategy (see n. later in this chapter, **did the exact opposite**) and finance (II.13, IV.50n.). Th.'s purpose in looking ahead to the end of the war is to contrast the character and policies of Pericles, who, he believes, could have won the war, with those of his successors who lost it.

**his successors:** presumably those politicians who were preeminent in the years following Pericles' death, such as Cleon, Hyperbolus, and Alcibiades (but surely not Nicias?). The sharp and unconvincing distinction made by Th. between Pericles and his successors (who are anonymous here and all tarred with the same brush) raises doubts about Th.'s judgment where Pericles is concerned. Suspicions are reinforced by Th.'s vagueness over **matters which apparently had no connection with the war and private ambition and private profit.** Cf. text later in this chapter, **a number of mistakes,** though only one instance is given and that is qualified. See my introductory n. to this chapter. On Pericles' successors in general see Connor 1971.

**did the exact opposite:** clearly an exaggeration, since some elements of Periclean policy (such as the firm control of the empire) were retained. Th. is therefore referring in particular to plans to add to the empire and, above all, as he makes clear later in this chapter, to the Sicilian expedition of 415, though there had been earlier reversals of Pericles' policy, such as the first attempt on Sicily in 427 (III.86, IV.65) and the fighting of large-scale land battles such as that at Delium in 424/3 (IV.90ff.). Th. is in effect claiming that greed (Gk. *pleonexia,* literally "grabbing at more": see III.82n.) brought the Athenians down. He does not mention that the failure of Pericles' policies drove his successors to try different ideas and that they enjoyed some notable successes (e.g., at Pylos; see IV.2ff.).

**private ambition and private profit:** the antithesis of that sense of community that was at the heart of the Funeral Speech. Cf. n. earlier in this chapter, **public policy . . . as private individuals,** and cf. text later in this chapter, **personal intrigues . . . quarrelling among themselves . . . their own internal [= private] strife.** On corruption in public life at Athens see II.60n. Where Warner, in his translation, writes later in this chapter of Pericles' "integrity" the Gk. actually says that Pericles could not be bribed. On corruption in Athenian public life see II.60n.

**intelligence:** Gk. *gnome,* described by Connor (1984, 55) as "that untranslatable combination of intelligence, planning, and resolve." It has two opposites in Th.: passion (Gk. *orge*), on which see I.86n., and chance (Gk. *tyche*), on which see I.120n. See also I.79n.

**integrity:** the Gk. says he could not be bribed at all; cf. II.60n. on bribery.

**It was he who led them rather than they who led him:** surely a generalization, since Pericles cannot have been entirely immune to public opinion. See, for instance, Aristophanes *Peace* 606ff.

**he was under no necessity of flattering them:** literally "he did not speak to give them pleasure," as opposed to his successors who did precisely that, according to Th. later in this chapter.

**he was so highly respected that he was able to speak angrily to them:** on Pericles' oratorical powers see I.139n.

**when he saw that they were going too far in a mood of over-confidence . . . when they were discouraged for no good reason:** i.e., he discouraged emotion and tried to get people to look at the facts—his own approach (II.62).

**in what was nominally a democracy, power was really in the hands of the first citizen:** an exaggeration, as recent events had made clear. In the Athenian democracy ultimate power lay in the hands not of any individual but of the citizen voters. By "first citizen" Th. means that member of the assembly who had won the most influence by the success of the policies he had promoted; there was no such official position.

**adopted methods of demagogy:** the Gk. says something more like "began to give the conduct of affairs over to the pleasure of the people," the implication being that policy was made according to whim rather than rational forethought, that long-term needs were sacrificed to immediate and ill-thought-out desires. For Th. such instant and rather mindless gratification has no place in politics: cf. the antithesis between passion and calculation (I.86n.) and his comment on the behavior of the extremists in the stasis in Corcyra: "there one standard was the pleasure of their own party at that particular moment" (III.82; for the resort to pleasure in extremis cf. II.53); see also IV.108, where Athens' allies are prompted to revolt by "the pleasurable excitement of the moment." Cf. too Th.'s attitude toward his writing ("my work is not a piece of writing designed to meet the taste of an immediate public," I.22; see n. there) and his acerbic comments on other, lighter forms of literature (I.21). Even Cleon called the Athenian demos "victims of your own pleasure in listening" (III.38).

**a number of mistakes:** though Th. gives only one and qualifies it.

**amongst which was the Sicilian expedition:** of 415–413, recounted in bks. VI–VII.

**the mistake was not so much an error of judgement with regard to the opposition to be expected:** yet in VI.1 Th. makes it clear that the Athenians were biting off more than they could chew. But note the words "not so much . . . as": Th. is not completely denying an error of judgment in the first place but asserting that mismanagement during the expedition was a greater factor in its failure. He recognizes the importance not only of establishing causes but also of assessing their relative weight. He uses the same formula at I.88.

**as a failure on the part of those who were at home to give proper support to their forces overseas:** Warner (in the Penguin translation, p.164 n. 28) comments that the explanation given here by Th. for the failure of the Sicilian expedition is not borne out by the narrative of bks. VI–VII. How has he interpreted Th.'s words? They need not imply that the Athenians failed to send additional troops when they were requested. Indeed, Th. makes it clear that this is precisely what they did do (VI.74, 93; VII.15). The Gk. could just as easily be translated "the Athenians made decisions that were not in the interests of the force they had sent out." This could well refer to the recall of Alcibiades; if so, the Athenians, having selected a trio of incompatible generals, then allowed factional wrangling to prejudice further the success of the expedition. Th. might also have had in mind the failure to recall Nicias when he was ill (VII.16).

**And yet, after losing most of their fleet . . . they none the less held out for eight years:** the manuscripts in fact say "three years," but this is clearly wrong (numbers were frequently mistaken in the copying process). "Eight years," i.e., 412/11–405/4, is perhaps the best alternative, with the Athenians surrendering in the ninth. Despite his strictures of the demos, Th. has some respect for its resilience: cf. VIII.1.

**with revolutions already breaking out in Athens:** stasis, I.2n. Th. describes the antidemocratic revolution of 411 in VIII.48ff.

**who were now reinforced by the Sicilians:** but by only twenty-two ships (VIII.26).

**Cyrus, son of the King of Persia:** the satrap (I.115n.) of Lydia, Phrygia, and Cappadocia who gave considerable help to the Spartan admiral Lysander and inflicted the final defeat on Athens at Aegospotami on the Hellespont in 405.

**an easy victory for Athens:** Pericles perhaps did not make quite such a rash prediction; see II.13n.

## II.66. The Peloponnesian Expedition against Zacynthus

**an expedition with 100 ships against . . . Zacynthus:** a considerable stepping up of Peloponnesian pressure on Athens. The fleet is a large one by Peloponnesian standards (II.7n.). Following Athenian demoralization (II.59), the Peloponnesians were keen to press home their advantage. For Athenian interest in this western area see II.7n.

**Cnemus:** cf. II.80ff.

**of the officer class:** i.e., a Spartiate; see I.18n.

## II.67. The Peloponnesian Embassy to Persia

**Aristeus:** see I.60n.

**a man from Argos called Pollis . . . acting on his private initiative:** because Argos was neutral in the war; see II.9. Pollis is otherwise unknown.

**with the object of persuading the King of Persia to provide money and join the war on the Spartan side:** so that the Peloponnesians could make use of his (i.e., the Phoenician) navy in the Aegean; cf. II.7, IV.50. On the Peloponnesians' need for money cf. I.80n.

**Sitalces:** for his alliance with Athens and the grant of Athenian citizenship to his son see II.29.

**Potidaea:** see I.56–65; II.58, 70.

**Pharnaces, son of Pharnabazus:** satrap of northwest Asia Minor; cf. I.129, VIII.6n.

**put them all to death and threw their bodies into a pit:** evidence, perhaps, of a decline in standards, brought about by the increasing pressures of war.

**the Spartans killed as enemies all whom they captured:** the Spartans were no better than the Athenians. During their intervention in the revolt of Mytilene (III.32) it was pointed out to the Spartans that to kill Athenian allies was "not the right way to set about the liberation of Hellas."

## II.68. The Ambracian Attack on Amphilocian Argos

**Ambraciots:** colonists of Corinth (II.80), listed among the allies of Sparta in II.9.

**Amphiaraus:** one of the Seven against Thebes who attacked Oedipus' son, Eteocles. Again Th. accepts as historical material we would regard as mythological. Cf. I.3n.; II.15n., 102n.

**It was from these Ambraciots . . . that they [the Amphilocians] first learned the Hellenic language, which they still speak:** yet they were of Greek origin. Th. does not explain. The translation could be slightly misleading: the word translated as "still" should be translated as "now," raising the possibility that the Amphilocians originally spoke one Hellenic language (or dialect), switched to another under the influence of the Ambraciots, and continued to speak this down to Th.'s time. See Hammond 1967, 419.

**Acarnania:** see II.7n. The date of Phormio's expedition is unknown. It has been suggested that it took place in the 430s and was anti-Corinthian in intent and thus a factor in the outbreak of war, but this is no more than guesswork. For the continuation of the war in this area see II.102n., III.102, 105–14.

**the alliance was first formed between the Athenians and the Acarnanians:** though Oeniadae remained hostile (II.102).

## II.69. Further Athenian Activity

**Naupactus:** see I.103n. For Phormio's famous victories in the Gulf of Corinth (**Gulf of Crisa**) see II.83–92.

**Caria and Lycia:** Athenian control over these distant areas had been difficult to maintain, and the tribute from them had declined considerably by the 430s. A second force was dispatched in 428 but was also destroyed (III.19).

## II.70. The Surrender of Potidaea

The story is continued from II.58 and a brief mention in II.67.

**The Peloponnesian invasions of Attica had failed to make the Athenians withdraw their troops:** the Peloponnesians had had excessively high hopes of the invasions in general; see V.14.

**cases of cannibalism:** another example of the extremes of savagery and suffering brought about by the war; see I.23. Cf. the famous statement in III.82: "But war is a stern teacher; in depriving individuals of the power of easily satisfying their daily wants, it brings most people's minds down to the level of their actual circumstances."

**2,000 talents:** cf. 1,400 talents as the cost of the Samos campaign of 440/39 (M.L. 55 = *T.D.G.R.* 113). The figures for Athens' income given in II.13 put these expenses in context. It is not surprising that Athens needed to raise extra revenues (III.19, IV.50).

**The following terms were agreed upon:** the strength of Athenian feeling toward Potidaea is reflected in the harsh terms imposed on the inhabitants. For the earlier difficulties that had prolonged the siege see II.58.

**The Athenians, however, blamed the generals:** not the first time—and not the last—that the assembly is overcritical of its generals in the field. See II.65n. But the generals were not demoted: Xenophon and perhaps his colleagues remained in office (II.79).

**thinking that it was possible to have secured an unconditional surrender:** in which case the inhabitants could have been killed or sold into slavery.

**Later they sent out colonists:** one thousand according to Diodorus (XII.46). A dedication made by the departing colonists survives: M.L. 66 = *T.D.G.R.* 129.

## II.71–78. The Siege of Plataea

**II.71. the Peloponnesians and their allies . . . marched against Plataea:** for the importance of Plataea and the earlier Theban attack on it see II.2n. Th. does not explain why the Spartans chose to attack Plataea now. They might have been under pressure from Thebes (cf. III.68) and were probably reluctant to enter Attica because of the plague.

**Pausanias, the son of Cleombrotus:** his career after the Persian Wars is described in detail by Th. in I.94–95, 128–35.

**the battle that was fought near our city:** the battle of Plataea, against the Persians, 479.

**an independent state:** see I.67n. on the Gk. *autonomia*.

**II.72. the work of liberation:** see II.8n.

**then do what we have already asked:** Th. has made no mention of this suggestion. Cf. III.64, 68.

**remain neutral:** this may look like a generous offer since combatants in war are naturally disposed to force others to join their side (e.g., Melos in 415, which is refused permission to be neutral at V.94–95). But the Plataean reservations are surely well founded.

**your fruit trees:** for their value cf. IV.84n.

**II.73. in all the time that we have been their allies:** since 519 (III.68, final sentence).

**nor will they desert you now:** in the event, the Athenians did precisely that. To have helped would have gone against Pericles' policy (II.13n.). The broken promise adds to the pathos of the Plataeans' plight.

**II.74. Gods and heroes . . . of the land of Plataea:** local divinities who were believed to protect Plataea; cf. IV.87. A formal and solemn opening.

**these people had first broken their engagements with us:** the oath they took to help bring freedom to Greece; see II.72. The Plataeans might reasonably have assumed that this had been binding only against Persia; the Spartans are claiming that the Plataeans are duty bound to join in the struggle against Athens for Greek freedom.

**II.75. First, using the trees . . . :** every aspect of the Plataean episode gets the full treatment from Th. We should not forget that he was a soldier and had a keen interest in military operations of all kinds. For other tactical innovations see IV.100, VII.36.

**continuously for seventy days and nights:** this seems too long; the figure may (as often) be corrupt.

**II.76. siege engines:** battering rams.

**II.77. the expense of a long siege:** cf. the cost of the Athenian siege of Potidaea, discussed at II.70n.

**great forest fires on the mountains:** Th. seems to go out of his way to mention this phenomenon, which provides him with an opportunity to offer a rational explanation of a natural event.

**it is . . . said:** Th.'s usual formula when he is not certain of his information.

**a thunderstorm . . . saved the situation:** again expectations are upset by chance; cf. I.120n.

**II.78. About the time of the rising of Arcturus:** the middle of September.

**The Plataeans had already sent to Athens their wives and children:** see II.6.

## II.79. The Athenian Defeat at Spartolus

**the Chalcidians in Thrace and the Bottiaeans:** allies of Potidaea in its revolt against Athens (I.58).

**Spartolus:** northwest of Potidaea.

**peltasts:** see II.29n.

## II.80–92. The War in Northwestern Greece; the Victories of Phormio

**II.80. Ambraciots and Chaonians:** cf. II.68.

**Zacynthus:** for a recent Spartan attack on it see II.66.

**Cephallenia:** see II.7n.

**Naupactus:** see I.103n. Phormio was based here, watching the entrance to the Corinthian Gulf (II.69).

**Cnemus:** see II.66.

**native troops:** the tribes listed here occupied the mainland opposite and to the north of Corcyra.

**Perdiccas:** see I.56n.

**II.81. if they failed to win it over by negotiation, to make an attack:** the Gk. says literally "if they did not persuade them with words, they would make an attempt with action"—the words/deeds antithesis again; see I.22n., 32n.

**II.82. The friendly tribe of the Oeniadae:** see II.102.

**II.83. the Crissaean Gulf:** the Gulf of Corinth.

**were equipped more as military transports:** thus they would be heavier and less easy to maneuver, a serious disadvantage in battle since the trireme was, in effect, a weapon; see I.14n.

**in circular formation:** this was to prevent the Athenians from using a tactic known as the *diekplous;* see I.49n.

**II.84. as his ships were the better sailers:** because the enemy ships were being used as transports (II.83n.).

**lacking experience:** cf. II.85n., 87n.

**dedicated a ship to Poseidon:** as god of the sea. Cf. II.92.

**II.85. an advisory commission:** Gk. *probouloi,* commissioners sent to buck up generals who had failed—and replace them if necessary. Cf. III.69, V.63, VIII.39. Like the Athenians (II.65n.), the Spartans could be hard on a general who was deemed to have let them down—even if he was a king (II.21; V.16, 63).

**Brasidas:** see II.25n.

**their first taste of naval engagements:** i.e., during this war.

**not taking into consideration the contrast between the long experience of the Athenians and the short training which their own crews had received:** ignoring the words of King Archidamus (I.80; cf. Pericles at I.142 and the Corinthians at I.121).

**their commander was instructed . . . to sail to Crete:** Th. does not openly condemn this decision, but his presentation of the episode—the urgency of the situation in the gulf, the true motives of **Nicias,** the time wasting, and the respite given to the Peloponnesians—makes his opinion of it clear enough. This is the first time Th. has mentioned Cretan involvement in the war. Needless to say, the ships arrive late: see II.92. Phormio's victories are all the more impressive.

**Athenian representative:** proxenos; see II.29n.

**II.86. in Achaea, where their land army had marched up to give them support:** though according to II.9 the Achaeans were neutral.

**the following appeal:** on prebattle speeches see II.10n.

**II.87. most of the luck was against us:** the lament of the defeated but hardly justified in this case.

**lack of experience . . . inexperience . . . you may lack the enemy's experience . . . This skill of theirs . . . all the skill in the world . . . their greater experience:** cf. II.85n.

**not . . . because of any cowardice:** cf. II.85: "the Spartans . . . concluded that the defeat was the result of cowardice."

**II.89. lack of sea room is a disadvantage:** because the Athenians will not have the space to carry out the maneuvers in which they excel.

**ramming:** by means of a bronze prow. To sink the enemy ship thus was the most efficient way for those with **superior seamanship** to defeat the enemy.

**to sail through the enemy's line and then wheel back on him . . . to fight a naval action as though it were a battle on land:** see I.49n.

**silence:** a mark of discipline and essential for hearing commands. Th. frequently notes the noise that accompanies the confusion of battle and makes matters worse (II.4n.).

**II.90. much against his will:** because he did not wish to be drawn into the narrow waters of the channel.

**Messenian land forces:** from Naupactus, I.103n.

**II.91. an unexpected and unlikely action:** human plans are subject to chance, as often in Th.; see I.120n.

**II.92. the Athenian fleet . . . from Crete:** see II.85.

### II.93–94. The Peloponnesian Attack on Piraeus

**II.93. an attempt on Piraeus:** the Megarians suffered invasions twice a year at the hands of the Athenians (II.31, IV.66) and no doubt hoped to put an end to them by delivering a shock attack on Athenian territory. It is certainly the sort of scheme that the adventurous Brasidas would have favored. The Peloponnesians had the enormous advantage of surprise on their side, especially after their recent defeat, and the port was unguarded. The idea was sound: they could have done untold damage to the fleet and dockyards. When the Peloponnesians tried again in the following year the Athenians were ready for them (III.15–16).

**the port of Athens:** Th. was not writing for Athenians only (I.1n.).

**rowlock thong:** a leather strap that held the oar in position.

**They were frightened of the danger:** following recent defeats the Peloponnesians lacked confidence at sea; cf. their abortive efforts to support Mytilene, discussed at III.29–33.

**they say that there was something about the direction of the wind:** literally "it is said that the wind prevented them"—perhaps a Peloponnesian excuse that Th. mentions only to cast doubt on by the formula "it is said."

**II.94. a panic broke out which was as great as any in the course of the war:** Th. again stresses the unexpectedness of the episode. By "the war" Th. may again mean the Archidamian War (I.1n.): there were many later panics in Athens on a greater scale. But perhaps we should not take Th. literally: even he was guilty of the occasional hyperbole.

**their ships . . . were letting in water:** to remain waterproof, an ancient ship required regular recoating with pitch.

## II.95–101. Events in Thrace and Macedonia

**II.95. Sitalces:** for his alliance with Athens see II.29; for his earlier support of Athens see II.67.

**Philip:** see I.57.

**Perdiccas:** see I.56n.

**Hagnon:** see II.58n.

**the Athenians also were supposed to support him:** they still hoped to bring Macedonia under control but failed to turn up (II.101).

**II.96. the Odrysians:** see II.29. Th. digresses to discuss the geography and inhabitants of Thrace, an area well known to him (IV.105). This is ethnography in the style of Herodotus.

**the area between Mounts Haemus and Rhodope:** a large area stretching from the northern shore of the Aegean and the Propontis in a northeasterly direction to the western shore of the Black Sea (**the Euxine Sea**). Haemus was west of the western shore of the Black Sea; the Rhodope range stretched northwest to southeast, north of the northern shore of the Aegean.

**the other Paeonian tribes:** north of Macedon

**Oscius:** its source is near that of the Strymon, but it flows north into the Danube.

**Nestus:** the river that enters the Aegean north of Thasos.

**Hebrus:** the river that enters the Aegean on its north coast at Aenus.

**II.97. Abdera:** on the Aegean coast northeast of Thasos.

**an equal amount of gold and silver was contributed in presents:** stories of Thracian wealth have been verified by archaeological finds in Bulgaria.

**unless one first produced a present:** bribery was prevalent among barbarians as among Greeks; cf. II.60n.

**the Ionian Gulf:** the Adriatic.

**in governing themselves wisely and in making an intelligent use of their resources they are below the average level:** cf. I.5n. on the tribes of northwest Greece and III.94 on the Aetolians.

**II.98. he set out against Macedonia:** for the geography of Macedonia the reader is referred to the maps in Hammond and Griffith 1972–79.

**his total force is said to have amounted to at least 150,000 men:** Th. is not prepared to vouch for the figure.

**II.99. Lower Macedonia:** i.e., coastal Macedonia, around the Thermaic Gulf.

**This part of the country . . . was first acquired . . . :** thus Th. enters on a brief digression on Macedonian history.

**Temenids from Argos:** the Macedonian royal house claimed to be descended from the Temenid branch of the Heraclids (I.12n.). Cf. Hdt. VIII.137–39.

**the Bottiaeans . . . the Chalcidians:** see I.57n.

**II.100. Archelaus:** King of Macedon, 413–399. Th. digresses briefly to summarize Archelaus' achievements. The passage suggests that at the time of writing Archelaus had been on the throne for some time, perhaps that he was nearing the end of his reign. This would mean that Th. was alive at the very end of the fifth century. To suggest that these words represent an obituary of Archelaus, i.e., that Th. is writing in 399 or later, is probably to push the evidence too far.

**II.101. since the Athenians . . . had not appeared:** see II.95. We can only speculate as to why they backed out: perhaps they decided they could not afford the troops because of the plague or were still reeling from the Peloponnesian attack on the Piraeus.

**So ended the expedition of Sitalces:** despite the size of his force—and Th.'s wealth of detail—Sitalces' campaign had no significant effect on the course of the war. The Athenians later made some use of Thracian mercenaries (e.g., IV.129), but the alliance with Sitalces was of little value to them.

## II.102–3. Phormio in Acarnania

**II.102. Astacus:** Athens had expelled the tyrant Evarchus from Astacus in 431 (II.30), but he had been restored by Corinth in the following winter (II.33). It looks as if Astacus was again friendly to Athens: perhaps Evarchus had been expelled for a second time.

**400 Athenian hoplites from the fleet:** see I.10n.

**Oeniadae:** for an earlier Athenian attempt to seize it see I.111; cf. III.7. It was brought over to the Athenian side in 424 (IV.77).

**silting up the channels, with the result that some of the islands have already become joined to the mainland:** the process known as coastal deposition. For Th.'s interest in a variety of natural phenomena see II.8n.

**Alcmaeon:** again (cf. II.29, 68) history and legend are happily mingled, despite Th.'s claim (I.22) that his work will lack a "romantic element."

**Amphiaraus:** see II.68.

**II.103. Phormio:** his final appearance; cf. III.7n.

# Book Three

## III.1. The Third Peloponnesian Invasion of Attica

**the Peloponnesians and their allies marched into Attica:** after a break in 429 (II.71). On their policy see II.10n.

**As on previous occasions, the Athenian cavalry went into action:** see II.19n.

## III.2–6. The Revolt of Mytilene

**III.2. the island of Lesbos:** of its five separate states **Methymna,** which supported Athens, was democratic. **Mytilene** was the largest; it had retained an oligarchic form of government. For the other three see III.18n. Lesbos had retained its independence up to this point and had contributed ships rather than money to the Delian League (e.g., I.116, II.56). Thus in II.9 it was placed in the list of Athens' independent allies rather than in the list of tribute-paying subjects.

**Even before the war Lesbos had wanted to revolt:** cf. III.13. Circumstances and date are unknown. Sparta's unwillingness to help is characteristic: see I.69n.

**Pontus:** the southern shores of the Black Sea, an area that supplied grain to many Greek states. See I.89n.

**people who represented Athenian interests:** *proxenoi;* see II.29n.

**making the whole of Lesbos into one state:** the process known as synoecism; see I.10n.

**the Boeotians, who were their kinsmen:** tradition had it that the original settlers on Lesbos came from Boeotia; cf. VII.57.

**III.3. the Athenians were suffering from the plague:** see II.47ff.

**the full force of the war which had only just broken out:** an unsatisfactory translation of some admittedly awkward Gk., especially the "only just":

the war is now in its fourth year. A better translation would be "the war that had recently broken out and was now at its height."

**rather through a process of wishful thinking:** see I.121n.

**the Malean Apollo:** a local divinity.

**The ten triremes of Mytilene . . . the provisions of the alliance:** nothing is known of this arrangement.

**Geraestus:** at the southern tip of Euboea.

**III.4. Malea to the north of the town:** Th. here disagrees with the Roman geographer Strabo, who put Malea south of Mytilene (XIII.2.2).

**III.5. the Imbrians, the Lemnians:** Imbros and Lemnos, islands in the north Aegean, were early acquisitions of Athens; on Lemnos see I.115n. Imbrians and Lemnians are often found in Th. fighting together on behalf of Athens; see, e.g., IV.28, V.8.

## III.7. Athenian Retaliation against the Peloponnesians and Activity in Northwestern Greece

**Phormio's son Asopius:** Phormio's popularity with the Acarnanians probably went back to his undated expedition described at II.68. We have heard the last of Phormio in Th., who gives no reason for his disappearance. He appears in Aristophanes (*Knights* 424, *Peace* 421) as a great seaman and popular captain. However, at his *euthunai* (the examination of a magistrate on the expiry of his term of office) he was fined, and when he could not pay the fine, he was deprived of his citizen rights; he was later reinstated by the people (*T.D.G.R.* 130). He was publicly honored by burial in the state cemetery (Pausanias I.29.3).

**Naupactus:** see I.103n.

**Oeniadae:** see II.102.

**Leucas:** the only island of any size in this area that remained on the Peloponnesian side. It had helped Corinth in its disputes with Corcyra (I.26, 46), contributed ships to the Peloponnesian navy (II.9), and been an important naval base for the Peloponnesian fleet during its operations in and around the Corinthian Gulf (II.80, 84).

## III.8–14. The Revolt of Mytilene Continued

**Olympiad:** the Olympic Games; see I.6n.

**Dorieus:** a famous athlete who won victories in the *pankration* (a rather violent combination of wrestling and boxing) in 432, 428, and 424. See also VIII.35.

### *III.9–14. The Speech of the Mytilenian Ambassadors at Olympia*

The bulk of this speech, chapters 9–12, is designed to prove that the Mytilenians were justified in rebelling from Athens. The speaker is aware, however, that this argument alone, no matter how convincingly presented, will not secure Peloponnesian support, and in chapter 13 he attempts to show that it is to the Peloponnesians' advantage to help Mytilene. That is to say, he attempts to demonstrate that justice and expediency coincide, as Cleon does later in the debate on the fate of the Mytilenians (III.37–40). The Mytilenians' speech is similar in structure to that of the Corcyraeans at Athens (I.32–36), also an appeal for an alliance. A detailed analysis of the speech can be found in Macleod 1983, 88–92.

**III.10. a conviction of honesty on both sides and a certain like-mindedness in other respects:** the first of the prerequisites of a harmonious alliance mentioned in the previous chapter.

**you withdrew from the leadership and the Athenians stayed to finish what was left to do:** criticism of the Spartans. Cf. the complaints made by the Corinthians in 432 at I.69. For the Spartan withdrawal after Mycale see I.94–96nn.

**But the object of the alliance was the liberation of the Hellenes from Persia, not the subjugation of the Hellenes to Athens:** this "object" is not mentioned by Th. in his discussion of the origins and aims of the league (I.96n.), but the claim is supported by the fact that many of the early activities of the league were directed against Persia.

**enslaving their own allies:** not to be taken literally; see I.98n., **lost its independence.**

**the multiple voting system:** this expression and what follows are difficult to interpret. It is widely accepted that each state had one vote but that Athens managed to dominate league meetings either because it exerted pressure on the large number of small states in the league or because these states sought Athenian protection against more powerful neighbors or because the populaces of these states looked to Athens for help against local oligarchs (or some combination of these three reasons). Cf. I.96n., **representative meetings.**

**Chios:** listed as a contributor of ships to the Athenian fleet in II.9; cf. I.19. Chios assisted Athens against Samos in 440/39 (I.116), against Epidaurus and other Peloponnesian states in the second Athenian attack on the Peloponnesian coastline (II.56), against Potidaea in 430 (II.58, VI.31), against Melos in 416 (V.84), and against Sicily in 415 (VI.43). However, although the Chians did not revolt from Athens until 411, there are signs that they offered support to Sparta and that Athens was suspicious of their behavior during the Archidamian War. Friendly Chians made a donation to the Spartan war fund, possibly in 427 (M.L. 67 = *T.D.G.R.* 132), and in 425/4 Athens, suspecting that the Chians were planning a revolt, ordered them to pull down some fortifications (IV.51).

**independent:** the Gk. is a cognate of *autonomia;* see I.67n. Cf. Cleon's comment at III.39, "they [the Mytilenians] had their own independent government."

**It seemed very unlikely that, after having brought under their control the states who were fellow members with us, they would refrain from acting towards us, too, in the same way:** i.e., it is only natural for powerful states to continue to extend their power, against the strong as well as the weak.

**III.11. it was natural for them to object to a situation where the majority had already given in and we alone stood out as independent:** for reasons why such an objection would be natural cf. the words of the Athenians to the Melians at V.95, 97. The Mytilenians understand the psychology of power.

**the only safe guarantee is an equality of mutual fear:** the second of the prerequisites of a harmonious alliance mentioned in III.9. Cf. III.12: "fear was the bond."

**we, who had votes like themselves:** see III.10n.

**they first led the stronger states against the weaker ones:** there is no suggestion of such an approach in Th.'s account of the early days of the Delian League (I.98ff.).

**they felt some alarm about our navy:** which might have numbered 50–70 ships.

**the trouble we took to be on good terms with the Athenian assembly and with their various leading statesmen:** an interesting admission, but we know no details.

**III.12. In wartime they did their best to be on good terms with us because they were frightened of us:** power brings security but also the fear of losing it.

**III.13. Indeed, we wanted to do so long ago:** cf. III.2n., I.69n.

**the Boeotians:** cf. III.2n.

**we . . . shall help in the work of liberation:** cf. II.8n. The Mytilenian case moves on from justice to expediency.

**Owing to . . . the expenses they have incurred, the Athenians are in a state of exhaustion:** the war has certainly been costly to the Athenians (II.70n.), but it is in the Mytilenians' interests to exaggerate: the Athenians had ships in reserve (II.24) and others besides (III.16) and were capable of raising additional revenues (e.g., III.19). For later financial measures see IV.50n.

**part of their fleet is sailing round your coasts:** see III.7.

**a large navy (which is the thing you need most):** if they are to promote rebellion among Athens' Aegean subject-allies. The ambassadors see the way to a Peloponnesian victory: by striking at the source of Athens' power and wealth (cf. the words of Archidamus at I.80, 83, and of the Ionian delegates to Alcidas at III.31). The Corinthians had given the same advice before the war broke out (I.122).

**III.14. the general good of all will be the result of our success:** the Mytilenians' concluding words are about expediency. Like the speech of the Corcyraeans at Athens, this speech comes to a climax with an urgent appeal to the self-interest of the audience.

### III.15–16. The Spartan Response

**III.15. two-thirds of their total forces:** the usual proportion; on numbers cf. II.10n.

**machines for hauling the ships across:** Corinthian territory bordered both the Corinthian and the Saronic Gulfs. To avoid sailing round the Peloponnese ships were dragged overland from one gulf to the other at the narrowest point of the Isthmus of Corinth, on a slipway known as the *diolkos*. Cf. VIII.7 and the similar arrangement at Leucas, mentioned at IV.8.

**so that they could attack simultaneously by land and sea:** the Peloponnesians were presumably inspired by the near success of their attack on Piraeus in the previous year (II.93–94).

**they were busy in harvesting their corn and tired of military service:** the Athenians too had begun to lose heart (II.59), as Pericles had predicted (I.140), but their spirits had been revived by Pericles (II.65).

**III.16. the knights and the Pentacosiomedimni:** the top two of the four wealth-based classes introduced as qualifications for office by Solon, archon in 594. Thus men of the third class, the Zeugitae, most of whom would be hoplites (I.49n.; cf. III.18), were pressed into service as rowers (usually recruited from among the lowest class, Thetes; see I.10n.), which suggests that Athens was short of manpower as a result of the plague.

**resident aliens:** metics; see II.13n.

### III.17. A Digression on Athenian Resources

**a hundred ships were guarding Attica, Euboea, and Salamis:** these are mentioned nowhere else in Th.; we would certainly expect to have heard of them during, for instance, the Peloponnesian attack on the Piraeus

(II.93–94). Another difficulty of this chapter is that it assumes that the siege of Potidaea is still in progress, whereas it came to an end in 430/29 (II.70). This chapter may be spurious (i.e., an interpolation by a later editor) or was perhaps misplaced (i.e., removed from its rightful place at some stage during the transmission of the text). If the latter, then to what year does it refer? A total number of 250 ships is given here; to this we should add the 100 in reserve (II.24), making 350. Yet the total in 431 was 300 (II.13): Th.'s expression **at the beginning of the war** cannot be taken quite literally. He must be referring to a time after the first year, but still early in the war, before the end of the siege of Potidaea in 430/29.

**two drachmae a day:** the payment of a drachma a day for the servants of hoplites in the forces besieging Potidaea may have been a special rate for troops on duty summer and winter, but we do not know enough of such matters to be certain. Payment for servants is not mentioned elsewhere, though Th. seems to suggest that it was common practice for a hoplite to be accompanied by a servant. The normal rate for both sailors and hoplites was probably one drachma per day (VI.8, 31; VIII.29), later reduced (VIII.45). The figure of three Aeginetan obols a day mentioned at V.47 was not pay but an allowance for food. For an explanation of Greek monetary values see the Penguin translation, app. 2, pp. 612–13.

## III.18. The Revolt of Mytilene Continued

**Antissa, Pyrrha, and Eresus:** three of the five independent states on Lesbos. Cf. III.2n.

**The hoplites rowed the ships themselves:** cf. III.16n.

## III.19. Athenian Efforts to Raise Money

**for the first time:** i.e., in this war; for an earlier instance see *T.D.G.R.* 119B, lines 17 and 19. No more such impositions are recorded by Th.

**a contribution of 200 talents:** an extraordinary tax levied on property (Gk. *eisphora*) to raise extra revenue. The rate of the tax is unknown: modern estimates seem to vary between 0.25 percent and ca. 2 percent, but they are guesswork, based partly on fuller fourth-century evidence.

**twelve ships to collect money:** it is unclear whether this is regular tribute or, like the *eisphora*, a special levy. Cf. II.69 for the difficulty of collecting money in these distant areas of the empire. For further similar missions see IV.50, 75, and for ships assigned to bring in tribute see *Ath. Pol.* 24.

The tribute quota lists suggest that there may have been an extraordinary reassessment of tribute in 428 and perhaps increases in 427 too. Further measures were passed in 426 to tighten up collection procedures (*T.D.G.R.* 133). But the *eisphora* and small-scale increases would not solve the Athenians' long-term financial difficulties. Far greater sums of extra revenue would have to be found if they were to continue to fight the war and keep the empire under control: see IV.50n. Cf. on financial matters III.33n., 39n., 46n. For the involvement of Cleon in Athens' financial affairs at this time see Aristophanes *Knights* 773–75.

**Lysicles:** referred to as a sheep seller by Aristophanes, but he was, in fact, one of Pericles' political heirs and married Aspasia. See *T.D.G.R.* 96.

**Anaia:** a site on the mainland opposite Samos occupied by hostile Samian exiles; cf. III.32, IV.75.

## III.20–24. The Siege of Plataea

**III.20. the Plataeans, who were still being besieged:** the story is resumed from II.78.

**no hope of help coming to them from Athens:** the offer was made at II.73.

**III.22. One of the Plataeans had knocked down a tile:** once again chance, in the form of a minor accident, has a decisive effect on events. Cf. I.120n., II.4n.

**The 300 troops:** they have not, in fact, been mentioned before.

**III.24. the shrine of the hero Androcrates . . . Erythrae . . . Hysiae:** all unknown. The episode is continued at III.52.

**the road to Athens in the direction of Cithaeron:** cf. II.1n.

## III.25–35. The Revolt of Mytilene Continued

**III.25. Pyrrha:** see III.18n.

**the forty ships:** see III.16.

**III.26. the forty-two ships:** unless this is an error, Th. is probably adding the two Mytilenian ships that might have joined Alcidas' fleet earlier (III.4–5). His inconsistency is perhaps the result of lack of revision.

**Cleomenes . . . Pausanias . . . Pleistoanax:** Pleistoanax had been exiled in 445 (II.21), and his brother, Cleomenes, acted as regent in place of his young son, Pausanias.

**III.27. the ships from the Peloponnese . . . continued to waste time:** the dilatoriness and ineffectiveness of Alcidas are mentioned or hinted at several times: cf. III.29, 31. Another, still less appealing side of him is revealed at III.32.

**the people . . . refused any longer to obey the government:** this conflict between the people and the authorities (probably an oligarchy) of Mytilene comes as something of a surprise, since we have assumed up to this point that the Mytilenian state was acting in unison. Was the revolt the act of a powerful, oligarchic minority? Had the demos been pro-Athenian all along? Cf. III.39n., 47n. On the greater issue of the popularity of the Athenian empire see I.77n.

**III.28. Athens was to have the right to act as she saw fit:** the terms imposed on Mytilene amount to unconditional surrender. The Athenians have power of life and death over their surrendered subjects.

**take refuge at the altars:** cf. I.24n.

**promising that he would do them no harm:** for their fate see III.35, 50.

**Antissa:** see III.18n. It had supported Mytilene in the early stages of the revolt, as had Eresus and Pyrrha, which are dealt with later (III.35).

**III.29. Teutiaplus:** his vigor and initiative are in sharp contrast to the feebleness of Alcidas; see III.27n.

**made a speech giving them the following advice:** the Gk. reads "said these things," rather than the usual and more vague "spoke along these lines" (I.31n.), but the difference is probably not significant.

**III.30. the unknown factor in warfare:** see I.120n.

**III.31. organizing revolt in Ionia . . . the greatest of her [Athens'] sources of revenue:** the tactics originally advocated by the Mytilenians (III.13n.).

**they would be welcomed everywhere:** the arguments of the Ionians imply the universal unpopularity of the Athenians; cf. I.77n.

**to involve her in more expense:** which Athens could ill afford at this time; see III.19n.

**Pissuthnes:** the satrap of Lydia; see I.115n.

**III.32. He therefore put out:** Alcidas scurries off home, pausing only to indulge in some tactless brutality. Sparta's uncharacteristic initiative is followed not merely by a failure to exploit opportunities but by doing more harm than good: a sad conclusion to its earlier commitment to support Mytilene. For another episode where Sparta's interests abroad were damaged by its harshness and tactlessness see III.93. Cf. II.67: "Indeed, at the beginning of the war the Spartans killed as enemies all whom they captured on the sea, whether allies of Athens or neutrals."

**Samians from Anaia:** see III.19n.
**the liberation of Hellas:** see II.8n.
**allies of Athens under compulsion:** see I.77n.

**III.33. the *Salaminia* and the *Paralus*:** two triremes used for state business and special missions. Their crews, who were on permanent call, enjoyed exceptional privileges.

**the cities of Ionia were not fortified:** presumably on Athenian instruction. This suggests that relations between Athens and Persia had been friendly. Cf. I.112n. on the Peace of Callias. Th. mentions as unwalled Clazomenae (VIII.31), Cnidus (VIII.35), Lampsacus (VIII.62), and Cyzicus (VIII.107). Cf. too the case of Chios (IV.51, VIII.14).

**he thought it a lucky thing:** Paches' relief that he was not compelled to blockade a Spartan fleet is a reminder of the cost of this sort of operation, which Athens could ill afford at the moment (cf. III.19n.).

**III.34. Notium:** Th. pauses to comment on another example of stasis (cf. I.2n.) in a Greek city-state.

**Colophon:** the Athenians had been forced to intervene in 447/6. For the extant regulations see M.L. 47 = *T.D.G.R.* 131.

**the time of the second Peloponnesian invasion of Attica:** early summer, 430; see II.47.

**Itamenes:** a Persian, otherwise unknown.

**Pissuthnes:** see III.31n. The **Arcadian . . . mercenaries** would be Greek professionals in the pay of Persia.

**Later the Athenians sent out settlers:** during the empire settlements were sometimes established so that the Athenians could maintain a presence in key locations. Cf. I.12n.

**III.35. Pyrrha and Eresus:** see III.18.
**whom he had placed in Tenedos:** see III.28.

## III.36–50. The Mytilenian Debate

**III.36. Salaethus:** see III.25. He seems to have been executed without a trial.

**in their angry mood:** the democracy at its worst; cf. II.65n., **as is the way with crowds.** There is now no Pericles in Athens to restrain popular anger: cf. II.21–22, 60, 65. The demos' change of heart will also be provoked by emotion.

**to put to death . . . the entire adult male population of Mytilene, and to make slaves of the women and children:** slavery was the fate of those defeated in war (for other instances see I.98), but such a massacre would be unprecedented.

**even though it was not a subject state:** see III.2n.

**people began to think how cruel and how unprecedented such a decision was:** the Athenian demos is not yet totally corrupted and will reverse its decision (III.49); on future occasions it will carry such a decision into effect (V.32, 116).

**the deputation from Mytilene:** see III.28.

**the Athenians who were supporting them:** Athenians with Mytilenian connections who would act in Mytilene's interests in Athens; cf. II.29n., **representative.**

**the authorities:** probably the prytaneis (II.22n.), rather than the generals.

**an assembly was called:** Th. provides us with the debate, or part of it, at which the second decision was taken. Why he chose the second rather than the first debate is unclear; it was, perhaps, because the second debate went beyond the particular question of the punishment of the Mytilenians to discuss some general aspects of the nature of (Athenian) power, a key theme of Th.'s work. See also III.49n.

**Cleon:** the author of the original motion and the most well-known of Pericles' immediate successors, though he may well have been prominent in Athenian politics for some time by 427 and kept in obscurity by Th. to emphasize the preeminence of Pericles. He was much disliked by Th. (see V.7, 10, 16), who no doubt had Cleon, among others, in mind when he compared Pericles so favorably with his successors (II.65). It is also possible that Th. and Cleon were personal enemies: Marcellinus' *Life of Thucydides* (46) reports that Cleon had a hand in Th.'s exile (V.26). No other politician receives such rough treatment from Th., though Hyperbolus comes close (VIII.73).

As for his policies, Cleon favored a vigorous prosecution of the war and an aggressive attitude to Athens' subjects. Such an approach was no more than the logical extension of Periclean policy, and Pericles himself, had he lived to face the later crises of the Archidamian War, would perhaps have been forced to resort to policies such as Cleon's. As leaders, indeed the most influential men of their times, both saw constancy of policy as a virtue and accused the Athenian demos of changeability and lack of resolution. Both were candid about the realities of Athenian power and the need to set aside moral considerations in order to pursue the interests of Athens.

But it suits Th. to contrast the two. He is keen to stress what he claims to be a decline in political leadership in Athens after the death of Pericles and presents Cleon personally and politically as a degenerate. Unfortunately, unprejudiced evidence on Cleon is lacking: of our other two main sources, one, Aristophanes, is more hostile than Th., and the other, Plutarch, is often derivative from Th. and Aristophanes. The best we can do is assess Cleon by his policies and actions, rather than accept Th.'s judgment of him.

**he exercised far the greatest influence over the people:** the Gk. says literally that he was "most persuasive" (cf. IV.21), another reminder of the importance in the Athenian democracy of the power of persuasion (Gk. *peitho;* see I.22n.), one of the skills taught by professional rhetoricians and the Sophists (I.32n.). This is not intended as a compliment by Th., who associates Cleon's persuasiveness with **violence of character** (the Gk. word is a cognate of the noun *bia,* force, often presented as the antithesis of *peitho*) and who disapproved of the goals for which Cleon employed his talents. Cleon's speech is aggressive, even bullying, in tone. Cf. Th.'s description of the Sicilian demagogue, Athenagoras (VI.35), and the Athenian Androcles (VIII.65).

### *III.37–40. The Speech of Cleon*

The speech falls into two parts: in chapters 37–38 Cleon attacks the decision of the assembly to reconsider the punishment of the Mytilenians, with many a swipe at the Athenian democracy and its failings; in 39–40 he restates the view that the appropriate penalty is death and argues that for Athens what is just coincides with what is in its interests (cf. the speech of the Mytilenians at Olympia at III.9–14). The speech is analyzed by Macleod 1983, 92–96; see also III.68n.

**III.37. a democracy is incapable of governing others:** i.e., democracy and empire are incompatible. Pericles in the Funeral Speech had presented them as essential features of Athenian society, but the democratic process had, according to Th. (II.65), degenerated since his death. According to Cleon, speech making is now a form of entertainment rather than the serious business of formulating policy.

**you are now changing your minds:** changeability is a characteristic of the demos in Th.; see, for instance, its treatment of Pericles at II.65.

**fear and conspiracy play no part in your daily relations with each other:** cf. Pericles at II.37.

**your empire is a tyranny:** not just "like a tyranny," as Pericles had said (II.63).

**who are always plotting against you:** cf. I.77n.

**a city is better off with bad laws, so long as they remain fixed:** the same argument is used by another persuasive demagogue, Alcibiades, at VI.18 (final sentence).

**lack of learning combined with sound common sense is more helpful**

**than the kind of cleverness that gets out of hand . . . states are better governed by the man in the street than by intellectuals:** cf. the sentiments of Archidamus at I.84. Cleon claims to distrust that very cleverness in speaking of which he is an arch exponent. On **sound common sense,** *sophrosyne,* see I.32n.; there is some irony in Cleon's commendation of this conservative virtue. He wishes to present himself as the champion of the ordinary man, down-to-earth and anti-intellectual, a contrast to the aloof and intellectual Pericles.

**some kind of a competition:** see III.38n.

**III.38. I have not altered my opinion:** another echo of Pericles (cf. I.140, II.61), though Pericles' refusal to change his mind is presented as firm consistency of policy based on a careful assessment of national interest, while Cleon's is a stubborn inflexibility. Further, while Pericles' ideas were durable, Cleon's policy is overturned within twenty-four hours.

**the injured party will lose the edge of his anger:** Cleon approves of acting in anger. Contrast Pericles at II.21–22, 60, 64–65 and Diodotus at III.42.

**It is obvious . . . :** is it?

**must have been bribed:** on bribery in Athenian public life see II.60n.

**these competitive displays:** the Athenians enjoyed the competitive aspect of oratory, as we see in some of Th.'s debates (e.g., IV.28). This is again an attack on the Sophists (I.32n.), who trained their pupils in the techniques of competitive speech making. Contests and formal displays were part of their method. See, e.g., Plato *Hippias Major* 282c = *C.A.* 214. It is this kind of public performance that Th. had in mind when he said that his work was "not a piece of writing designed to meet the taste of an immediate public," a translation that ignores the notion of competitive display present in the Gk.; cf. I.22n.

**as for action, you merely listen to accounts of it:** Cleon plays on what he claims to be an antithesis between words and deeds, demanding action rather in the way that Sthenelaidas had done in 432 (I.86). Diodotus later counsels against haste, arguing that words complement action (III.42; cf. Archidamus' point at I.82, 85).

**victims of your own pleasure in listening:** cf. II.65n., **adopted methods of demagogy.**

**professional lecturer:** in Gk. *sophistes,* "Sophist" (the only time that Th. mentions the Sophists directly). See I.32n.

**III.39. their own fortifications:** many states, in particular those guilty or suspected of revolt, had had their defenses destroyed, e.g., Thasos (I.101), Samos (I.117). See also III.33n.

**their own force of triremes:** some members of the league had forfeited their fleets after failed rebellions, others had allowed them to decline; see I.99.

**their own independent government:** Gk. *autonomia;* see I.67n. See also III.2n., 46n.

**a case of calculated aggression . . . They made up their minds to put might first and right second . . . making their unprovoked attack upon us . . . great prosperity . . . usually breeds arrogance:** much of what Cleon says about Mytilene, especially the generalizations he makes, could be applied equally to Athens.

**the fate of those of their neighbours who had already revolted:** e.g., Samos; see I.115–17.

**hopes that indeed extended beyond their means:** cf. I.121n.

**it is a general rule of human nature:** Diodotus later exploits similar generalizations from which to draw specific conclusions; see, e.g., III.45.

**Do not put the blame on the aristocracy and say that the people were innocent:** the precise attitude of the people, to both the revolt and their oligarchic government, is much disputed. They refused to obey orders after they had been given arms (III.27, 47).

**Meanwhile we shall have to spend our money:** which they can ill afford to do at the moment; see III.19n. On this point Diodotus is in agreement; see III.46.

**if our efforts are successful, we shall recover a city that is in ruins, and so lose the future revenue from it:** the Athenians are similarly pragmatic in their approach to the unyielding Melians; cf. V.91, 93.

**III.40. a large bribe:** cf. III.38n.

**just as I was at first so I am now:** unlike his listeners, of course, who have changed their minds—a sign of weakness, Cleon asserts. Cf. III.38n. and Diodotus' reply at III.42.

**To feel pity, to be carried away by the pleasure of hearing a clever argument, to listen to the claims of decency are three things that are entirely against the interests of an imperial power:** such brutal analysis of the exercise of power and self-interest appears every so often in Th. to keep the stark realities of imperial politics before our eyes. Cf. I.73–78, V.85–113. The first and third of these obstacles would in other circumstances, of course, be virtues; the second is a weakness on whose dangers Cleon has already spoken at length. These words suggest that many Athenians did feel pity for the Mytilenians; indeed, such feelings were the reason for the second debate (III.36).

**As for compassion, it is proper to feel it in the case of people who are like ourselves:** but it is inappropriate in the present case. In the following debate the Thebans will argue that pity is inappropriate in the case of the

Plataeans on the grounds that pity is reserved for unmerited suffering (III.67n.).

**I say that if you follow my advice, you will be doing the right thing . . . and . . . will be acting in your own interests:** justice and expediency coincide (as they had done in the speech of the Mytilenians) to require the harshest punishment of the rebels.

**If, however, whatever the rights or wrongs of it may be:** this point is presumably for the benefit of those who are not convinced by his argument that Athens has justice on her side. Could Cleon really have said such things in public, acknowledging the immorality of Athens' empire and advocating a policy of vengeance and harsh, unrelenting oppression? We must remember that the situation was desperate: a major Athenian ally had revolted; the Spartans had appeared on the scene; the whole empire and Athens' survival were at stake. Cleon's purpose is not to theorize about the nature of power but to examine the facts (following the practice of Pericles himself: see II.60) and to demonstrate to the demos where its interests lay; this was not an occasion to pander to the feelings of the sensitive. Cf. the Melian Dialogue (V.85–113), where Athens' purpose is equally pragmatic.

**III.41. Diodotus:** famous for this speech but otherwise unknown.

### *III.42–48. The Speech of Diodotus*

The structure of Diodotus' speech corresponds to that of Cleon's: chapters 42–43 are a reply to 37–38, 44–47 a reply to 39–40. Diodotus will argue that the task facing the assembly is not to judge the Mytilenians but only to assess the interests of Athens. See Macleod 1983, 96–101; III.68n.

**III.42. I do not blame those who have proposed a new debate:** Diodotus begins by refuting Cleon's opening comments on the inconstancy of the demos. His justification of the second debate leads Diodotus, as Cleon was lead by his opposition to it, to discuss the decision-making process at Athens in some detail. Whereas Cleon had advocated making decisions in the heat of the moment, Diodotus rejects action based on emotion in favor of reason, but, he maintains, conditions in the assembly often make this difficult. On several occasions he borrows Cleon's words to refute his point.

**anger:** cf. III.38n.

**anyone who maintains that words cannot be a guide to action:** as Cleon had argued. For Diodotus words are a means of dealing with a problem as much as action is; cf. I.22n. and Pericles at II.40.

**one with some personal interest at stake:** according to Th. (II.65) it was the particular fault of Pericles' successors that they pursued personal ambition at the expense of the city's interests.

**the uncertainties of the future:** another echo of Archidamus; cf. I.82.

**some good-sized pieces of misrepresentation:** skill in persuasion (Gk. *peitho;* cf. III.36n.) was unrelated to the pursuit of truth and could be used for good ends or bad.

**III.43. you turn upon the one man who made the original proposal:** cf. II.65n., **as is the way with crowds.**

**III.44. whether we are making the right decision for ourselves:** when Diodotus finally begins to discuss the case of the Mytilenians, in answer to the second part of Cleon's speech (39–40), we are perhaps surprised to find that his concern is neither with the humanitarian aspects of the issue nor with the guilt or innocence of the Mytilenians and the justice of the proposed punishment, but entirely with the practical interests of Athens. Thus, where Cleon distorted the concept of justice, Diodotus rejects it as irrelevant and advocates naked self-interest.

**III.45. Cities and individuals alike, all are by nature disposed to do wrong, and there is no law that will prevent it:** the distinction between *nomos* (law) and *physis* (nature) again; cf. I.76n. and the final sentence of this chapter. Cleon too uses such generalizations, at, e.g., III.39. Th. himself would surely have sympathized with Diodotus' sentiments: two of his most powerful pieces of direct analysis are devoted to episodes in which the collapse of legal and other sanctions is accompanied by human degeneracy at its most extreme (II.52–53, III.82–83).

**Hope and desire persist throughout . . . the idea that fortune will be on one's side:** see I.121n.

**III.46. to spend money:** again an Athenian concern for financial implications at this stage of the war; cf. III.19n.

**tried to assert its independence by revolting:** Diodotus appears, by implication at least, to contradict Cleon, who claimed that the Mytilenians were independent—it was freedom that they wanted (III.39; see n.). But the point should probably not be pressed.

**III.47. in all the cities the democracy is friendly to you:** not what Th. implies at II.8. Cf. I.77n.

**the democratic party at Mytilene, who never took any hand in the revolt . . . gave up the city to you:** there is some misrepresentation here; cf.

III.27. The people had used the threat of surrendering the city to Athens to blackmail the oligarchs.

**than that we should justly put to death:** a brief and isolated mention of justice, quickly dismissed as subordinate to self-interest. Cf. III.44.

**III.48. Do not be swayed too much by pity or by ordinary decent feelings:** here Diodotus borrows somewhat from Cleon (III.40) but is not so extreme (adding "too much"). Note, however, that he expresses no objection to the death penalty in principle or to the execution of the prisoners already taken, which he must surely have anticipated.

**III.49. the recent change of feeling:** see III.36.

**However, the motion of Diodotus was passed:** herein, perhaps, lies Th.'s reason for selecting the second debate rather than the first for inclusion. The initial decision, made in the heat of the moment, was an aberration, though certainly a sign of things to come (IV.122, V.16). The second debate more accurately reflects the mood of the Athenians at this stage of the war. Anger, resentment, and a quickness to panic are beginning to dominate Athenian debates, but for the moment the passions of the Athenians are still held in check by some feelings of humanity toward their subjects.

**they kept on rowing while they took their food . . . and rowed continually, taking it in turn to sleep:** not the usual practice. The crew normally ate and slept on land, since a trireme was not equipped with cooking or sleeping facilities.

**III.50. The Athenians also destroyed the fortifications of Mytilene and took over their navy:** standard procedure in such circumstances; cf. Thasos (I.101), Samos (I.117).

**instead of imposing a tribute:** it is surprising, in view of the cost to Athens of the revolt and Athens' overall financial situation at the time (III.19), that no tribute or war indemnity was imposed on Mytilene.

**except that belonging to the Methymnians:** they had not participated in the revolt (III.2).

**shareholders:** commonly called by their Gk. name, cleruchs, these were settlers from Athens who were given land in subject territories (cleruchies), often as a means of asserting control following a revolt. But these particular cleruchs did not take over the land themselves; the Mytilenians were allowed to keep it though they paid rent to the Athenians. It is generally assumed that the purpose of this unusual arrangement was to enable the Athenians on Lesbos to act as a garrison (I.114n.) to protect Athens' interests. The money from the 300 plots, paid to the sacred treasuries in Athens, would have amounted to about ten talents.

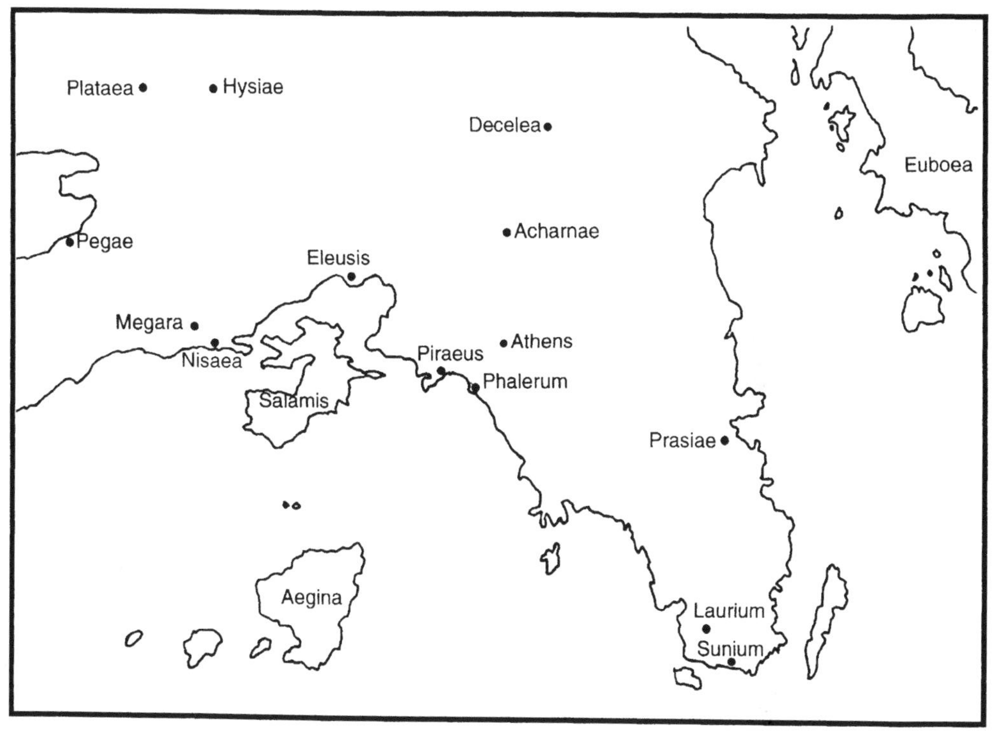
Plataea
Hysiae
Decelea
Euboea
Pegae
Acharnae
Eleusis
Megara
Athens
Piraeus
Nisaea
Phalerum
Salamis
Prasiae
Aegina
Laurium
Sunium

Map 1. Attica

Map 2. The Peloponnese

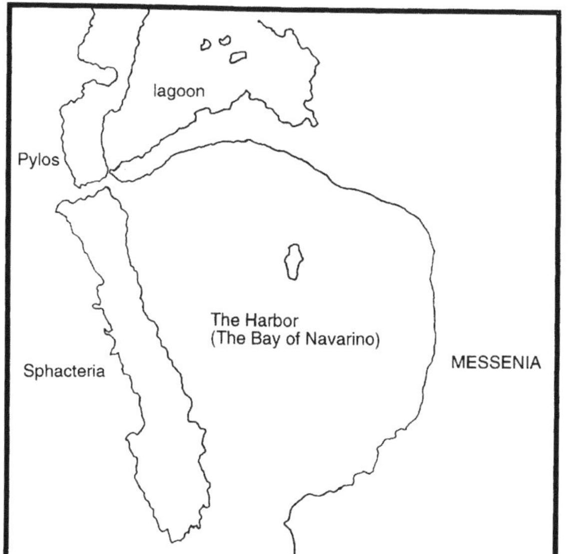


Map 3. Pylos and Sphacteria

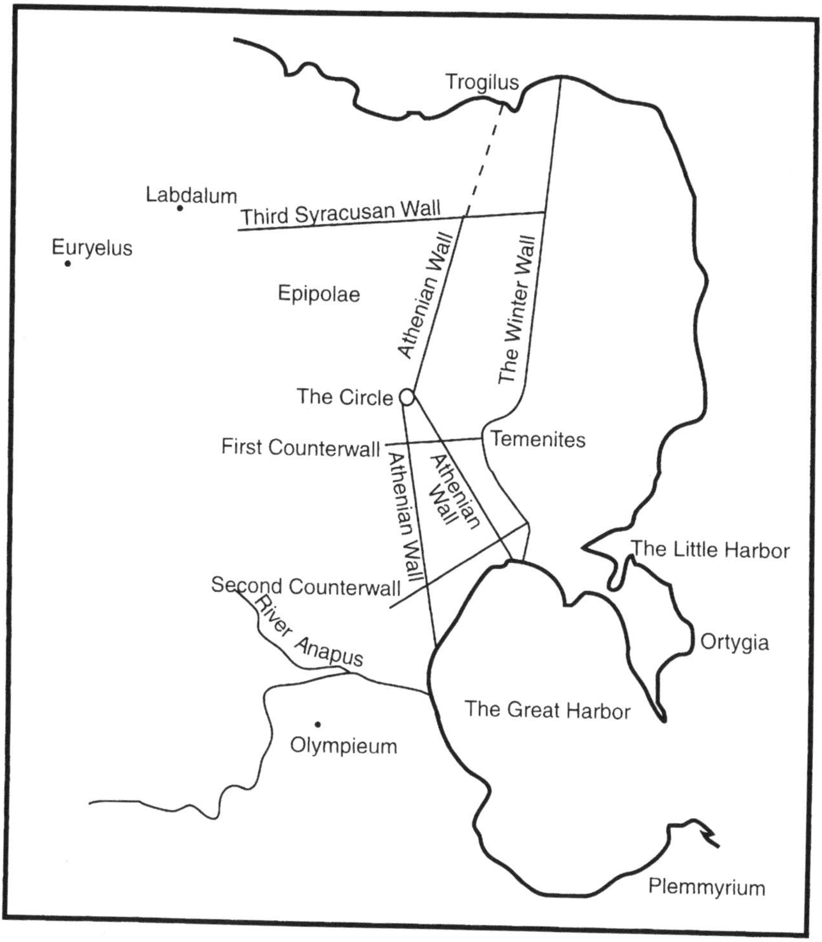

Map 4. The Siege of Syracuse

Map 5. The Eastern Aegean

But this arrangement seems to have been short lived. We have a fragmentary decree, difficult to date but usually put at about 425/4, which appears to return their lands and their rights to the Mytilenians (*A.E.* 169). If this reading is correct (the inscription is in very poor condition), then it looks as if the cleruchs were soon withdrawn and better relations were established with the former rebels. It may be that the Athenians had intended from the first that this novel arrangement should be temporary and that they would put an end to it when the war began to go better for them.

On the distinction between a cleruchy and a colony (I.12n.) see *A.E.* p. 118.

## III.51. The Athenian Attack on Minoa

**Nicias, the son of Niceratus:** best known as the opponent of Cleon and the reluctant general of the Sicilian expedition. He is generally regarded as a politician in the Periclean mold, but he was not from an aristocratic family, and his money, like Cleon's, came from business (the renting out of slaves, in fact). For his other activities in the Archidamian War see III.91; IV.42, 53–54, 129–31. Th. had a high regard for him: see VII.86.

**Minoa:** the point of this expedition was to put additional pressure on Megara, already under attack twice a year (IV.66), and to prevent a recurrence of the remarkable attack launched from there on the Piraeus (II.93–94).

## III.52–68. The End of Plataea

**III.52.** The story of Plataea is now resumed from III.20–24.

**his instructions from Sparta:** behind the Spartans' calculations lies an assumption that they will not win the war as quickly and as conclusively as they had initially hoped (V.14; cf. VII.28) and that they will eventually have to do some bargaining with the Athenians. This in fact turns out to be the case (V.17).

**the guilty would be punished:** i.e., those guilty of not helping Sparta in the war.

**who had been in charge of Spartan interests in Plataea:** i.e., was a proxenos; see II.29n.

### *III.53–59. The Speech of the Plataeans*

The Plataean speech is long and very moving. A number of factors contribute to the pathos of their situation: the Plataeans are the remnant of a small city that was the victim of an unprovoked attack from a stronger neighbor and more recently from a major military power; they have been abandoned by their allies and reduced after a lengthy siege; they have been tricked into surrendering; they know that their trial (such as it is) is a pretense, that the verdict has been decided in advance and is based not on considerations of justice but on political and military expediency.

The overriding aim of the Plataeans is to secure pity by an invocation of past services and a justification of past behavior. They employ a number of forensic techniques in this speech, e.g., the opening plea for sympathy, the claim that they are speaking the truth but face an uphill task, and the flattery of the judges. For a discussion of this debate see Macleod 1983, 103ff.

**III.53. Spartans, when we surrendered our city to you, we trusted you:** a stark, simple introduction: the essential facts and the Plataean error in a nutshell.

**a trial of this sort:** i.e., one in which the penalty does not fit the (so-called) crime and the issue has been decided in advance. So much for the Spartan offer of a "fair trial" (III.52).

**in order to gratify another state:** Thebes (III.68).

**III.54. we were not the first to break the peace:** it was the Thebans who attacked Plataea in peacetime (II.2–6; cf. III.56n.).

**we were the only state in Boeotia:** not true. Thespiae also fought against the Persians (Hdt. VII.132, 202). See also III.64n.

**the naval battle at Artemisium:** see I.23n.

**the battle fought on our own territory:** the battle of Plataea, in 479 (I.23n.), in which the Greek forces were led by the Spartan **Pausanias** (cf. I.130, II.71).

**every other enterprise undertaken by the Hellenes:** presumably the battle of Marathon during the first Persian invasion of 490.

**the earthquake, when the helots had revolted:** in 465; see I.101–2.

**III.55. we asked to become your allies:** in 519. See III.68; Hdt. VI.108.

**it was no longer honourable for us to forsake them:** the Plataeans will pay a heavy penalty for having put such a high value on honor. There is more talk of honor in the following chapters. How honorably are their allies, the Athenians (who had promised help at II.73), acting? In 415 the Melians will look to Sparta's sense of honor in the vain hope of assistance (V.104).

**they [the Athenians] . . . allowed us to share in some of the privileges of Athenian citizenship:** we do not know which privileges, but the Plataeans became to some extent "honorary Athenians," evidence of the closeness of the bond between the two states.

**III.56. It was not only in peace-time, but it was in the period of a religious festival:** and thus an act of impiety, the Plataeans argue. For the attack in peacetime see II.19n. and cf. III.65.

**in making them suffer for it:** an oblique reference to the Plataeans' killing of Theban prisoners (II.5). For the Theban response see III.66.

**the general law that one is always justified in resisting an aggressor:** the Plataean claim to justice is enshrined in a general law of human nature. Cleon and Diodotus had both invoked such general laws: see III.39, 45.

**It cannot be reasonable that we should now suffer:** a pathetic appeal. The Spartans have not come to Plataea to listen to reason.

**If you are going to take as your standards of justice your own immediate advantage and their [the Thebans'] hatred for us:** cf. the words of Cleon (III.40) and Diodotus (III.44); cf. also the words of the Athenians at Melos: "the standard of justice depends on the equality of power to compel and . . . the strong do what they have the power to do and the weak accept what they have to accept" (V.90; cf. I.76, IV.61).

**interests . . . right and wrong:** an important distinction (cf. I.32n.) in Th.'s work and the theme of the preceding Mytilene debate. Cf. text later in this chapter, **the right thing . . . the profitable thing.**

**if the Thebans do seem useful to you now:** cf. III.68.

**we were treated with peculiar distinction:** for the special honors accorded the Plataeans see II.71.

**III.57. an example of faith and honour:** presumably because of their declared mission to free the Greeks from Athens; see II.8.

**the tripod at Delphi:** see I.132n.

**our last hope:** see I.121n.

**III.58. we surrendered to you voluntarily, stretching out our hands as suppliants . . . Hellenic law forbids killing:** on the killing of suppliants cf. I.24n., and see II.5 for the Plataean killing of the 180 Theban prisoners.

**presenting garments:** clothes were a common form of offering to the dead.

**III.59. to relent, to look upon us with . . . compassion:** but pity has no place in war. For the Theban response see III.67n., and cf. Cleon at III.40 and Diodotus at III.48.

**how incalculable the future is:** a cliché in such circumstances; cf. the words of Archidamus at I.82 and of Hermocrates at IV.62, 64.

**while you liberate the rest of the Hellenes:** see II.8.

### *III.61–67. The Speech of the Thebans*

**III.61. after we had settled the rest of Boeotia:** at around the time of the Trojan War. Plataea's foundation date is unknown.

**from which we had driven out the inhabitants who were of different and mixed nationalities:** not a matter of shame, but simply the way in which superior powers work. On the racial factor see I.124n.

**they went over to the Athenians:** see III.55.

**did us much harm:** possibly in the campaign described in Hdt. V.77; *T.D.G.R.* 42.

**III.62. during the foreign invasion of Hellas:** the invasion of Xerxes in 480; see I.23n.

**collaborated with Athens:** the Gk. verb, an unusual one, means "to Atticize." It is perhaps intended to recall the verb "to Medize," used (e.g., at III.64) of those states that defected to the Persians (or Medes), and thus to suggest that the Plataeans too are traitors to Greece. Elsewhere, however, it is used by Th. without any such overtones, at, e.g., IV.133, VIII.38.

**an oligarchy, giving all men equal rights before the law:** this looks like a contradiction in terms, especially as the Gk. word *isonomia,* meaning "giving all men equal rights before the law," is usually associated with democracy. But it is not employed exclusively in this context, and elsewhere it describes political systems in which some were more equal than others. The translator's words "all men" are perhaps misleading: Th. cannot be referring to full democracy and may have meant that under an oligarchy equal rights were more widely enjoyed than under a "small group of powerful men," i.e., that they were enjoyed by members of the oligarchy, now free from a tyranny-like rule.

**a small group of powerful men:** Gk. *dynasteia,* a term of disapproval. Cf. IV.126n.; VI.38, 89 ("absolute power").

**dictatorship:** i.e., tyranny; see I.13n.

**moderation:** *sophrosyne,* here without its oligarchic overtones; see I.32n.

**when Athens was . . . attempting to bring our country under control:** in the early 450s; see I.108.

**internal dissension:** stasis; see I.2n.

**Coronea:** the battle that brought an end to the Athenian occupation of Boeotia in 447; see I.113.

**the liberation of the other Hellenes:** see II.8n.

**III.63. it is you Plataeans . . . who have done wrong to Hellas:** a reference to assistance (of which we know no details) given by the Plataeans to Athens in the period between the Persian and Peloponnesian Wars, when Athens turned the Delian League into an Athenian empire (I.98–99).

**III.64. you were the only ones who did not collaborate with Persia:** like the Plataeans (at III.54), the Thebans too omit mention of Thespian resistance to Persia, presumably because of ill feeling between the two states (IV.133).

**the alliance that existed in those days:** the alliance of Greek states formed in 481 to fight off the Persian invasion; cf. I.18n. It was abandoned ca. 461 (I.102).

**the conquest of Aegina:** ca. 457; see I.108n. Plataea's role is unknown.

**you were given an offer of immunity if you remained neutral:** see II.72.

**III.65. an . . . attack on your city in peace-time and during a religious festival:** see III.56n.

**men of substance from the best families . . . your traditional status as part of Boeotia:** see II.2n.

**III.66. we made a proclamation:** see II.2.

**an act of monstrous wickedness:** such as the Thebans and Spartans are now about to commit? See II.5.

**III.67. Coronea:** see III.62n.

**Pity is felt for unmerited suffering:** an answer to the Plataean appeal for pity at III.59. Cf. Cleon's claim that pity was an inappropriate response to the situation of the Mytilenians (III.40).

**deeds, not words:** Sthenelaidas (I.86) and Cleon (III.37–38) made use of the same antithesis. Cf. I.22n.

**III.68. the original treaty made with Pausanias . . . the same conditions of neutrality implied by the treaty:** see II.71–72.

**They therefore brought the Plataeans before them again:** a repetition, and a highly vivid one, of events described in III.52.

**Not less than 200 of the Plataeans . . . together with twenty-five Athenians:** there had been ca. 480 defenders originally (II.78), of whom 212 had escaped (III.24). About 40, therefore, had been killed in fighting.

**The women were made slaves:** the usual practice. Cf. the events in Torone described in V.3 and those in Melos described in V.116

**a large hotel:** for visitors to the temple.

**the Spartans acted so mercilessly towards the Plataeans . . . they**

**considered at this stage of the war the Thebans were useful to them:** as with Athens in the Mytilene debate, Sparta's overriding motive is self-interest. In this judgment Th. shows no doubt about Spartan motives; cf. V.26. on his knowledge of Spartan matters.

**in the ninety-third year after she became the ally of Athens:** Th.'s final comment is a reminder that Athens had been a long-standing ally of Plataea (the precise figure adds emphasis), but in the end Plataea had been allowed to perish.

We may ask ourselves why the Peloponnesian attack on Plataea and the initial negotiations (II.71–74), then the siege of the town (II.75–78, III.20–24), and finally the surrender, further negotiations, and the executions of the Plataeans (III.52–68) are recounted at such length. We have seen that Th.'s method is selective: some episodes are dealt with briefly, others are given very detailed treatment. Th. does not explain the criteria on which this process of selection is based, but we should look for some special significance in episodes such as the Peloponnesian attack on Plataea. After all, this was a small town that so far had played an insignificant part in the war. It occupied an important position (see II.2) but had not yet inconvenienced the Peloponnesians and, because of their military superiority, was unlikely to do so. Its existence was no more than an irritant to the Thebans. Yet the Peloponnesians chose to attack it, lay siege to it (a difficult operation at which they had little skill and that required long absence from home), and finally destroy it. It is perhaps this very insignificance of Plataea in the scheme of things and the disproportionate hostility of the Peloponnesians to it that aroused Th.'s interest.

The account of the destruction of Plataea follows hard on the heels of the Mytilene affair, and Th. surely intended that we should consider the two episodes together. In the Mytilene debate we have two speeches from two Athenians, each advocating a different way of achieving the same end, the best interests of Athens. The Mytilenians themselves, powerless and with no right to speak up for themselves, await their fate. An eleventh-hour change of heart among the Athenians produces a dramatic denouement to the episode. In the Plataean debate, the Plataeans, in a travesty of a trial, plead their own case. The Thebans respond, arguing that the heinous crime of killing prisoners must be punished by killing prisoners, while the Spartans observe, grimly assessing their advantage. This time there is no dramatic reversal; what might appear to have been an advantage to the Plataeans, the right they were granted to speak on their own behalf, turns out to have been of no use to them, and the death sentence is duly carried out. The two episodes raise common issues. In each debate we are accorded a clear vision of power, of the gap between the strong and the weak, and of the unscrupulous pursuit of self-interest, with pity and sentiment deliberately excluded from consideration. Each debate contains an earnest plea for the extermination of a community as an act of justice. The claims of the weak to justice and humane treatment are denied or distorted. The justice applied is the justice of the strong. Such distortion of values was seen by Th. as a symptom of moral and intellectual decay, and later in this book he will consider this issue in depth (III.83–84). The juxtaposition of the two episodes also has an ironical effect: while Athens, in the eyes of its enemies a harsh and tyrannical imperialist power, decides against inflicting the ultimate penalty on a rebellious subject, Sparta, the self-professed liberator of the Greeks, mercilessly destroys an insignificant Greek community in the pursuit of power.

But it is only a matter of time before Athens matches the cruelty of the Peloponnesians. Both episodes look forward to the Athenian siege of Melos in 416 (V.84–116). See my introductory n.

## III.69–85. Civil War in Corcyra

**III.69. The forty Peloponnesian ships:** see III.26n., 29ff.

**Brasidas . . . who had come to act as adviser to Alcidas:** cf. II.85n.

**The Athenians at Naupactus:** Phormio himself had returned to Athens in the spring of 428 (II.103). He died soon after. Asopius, his son, had conducted the twelve ships to Naupactus, though he himself was killed while returning from his expedition against Oeniadae (III.7n.).

**III.70. The revolution in Corcyra:** stasis; see I.2n. This was the first (III.82, 84–85) of many internal upheavals that occurred in Greek city states at this period and is selected by Th. for detailed treatment as an exemplar of its type; cf. III.85n.

**the prisoners who had been captured in the naval engagements off Epidamnus:** see I.54–55. They numbered ca. 250.

**800 talents:** an impossibly large figure; the text must be corrupt in some way.

**the original agreement:** a defensive alliance with Athens (I.44). So far Corcyra's direct impact on the war had been small (II.7n.).

**Peithias:** otherwise unknown.

**who had voluntarily offered to look after Athenian interests in Corcyra:** i.e., he was a proxenos, though in this case a voluntary (as opposed to hereditary, suggests Hornblower 1991, 468) proxenos, see II.29n., representative.

**Alcinous:** the king of Phaeacia in Homer *Odyssey* VI; see I.25n.

**one stater:** the Corinthian stater of three drachmae, about two Attic drachmae. See the Penguin translation, app. 2, pp. 612–13.

**took up their positions in the temples as suppliants:** cf. I.24n.

**III.71. the Corcyraean refugees in Athens:** those who had boarded the Athenian trireme (III.70).

**III.72. Aegina:** the island in the Saronic Gulf from which the Athenians had expelled the inhabitants in 431 (II.27).

**III.74. The women also joined in the fighting:** as they had done at Plataea; see II.4.

**The Corinthian ship:** see III.70.

**III.75. a force of twelve ships:** see III.69.

**500 Messenian hoplites:** see I.103 for the presence of Messenians at Naupactus.

**the whole state was to conclude an offensive and defensive alliance with Athens:** Corcyra already had a defensive alliance with Athens; see I.44. It is not confirmed that this new defensive and offensive alliance was in fact made, but it is implied later (VI.31n.).

**seated themselves as suppliants in the temple of the Dioscuri:** cf. I.24n. The Dioscuri were Castor and Polydeuces (Latin, Pollux), twin sons of Zeus and Leda. Their cult was widespread, especially in Dorian states.

**III.76. the harbour of Sybota on the mainland:** cf. I.50.

**III.77. the *Salaminia* and the *Paralus*:** see III.33n.

**III.78. the Peloponnesians formed their ships up in a circle:** cf. I.49n., **The fighting was . . .**

**a repetition of what had happened at Naupactus:** see II.84.

**III.79. Brasidas is said:** Th. is uncertain of his information. **Alcidas** is as cautious as ever: cf. III.31.

**III.80. a fleet of sixty Athenian ships:** sent, presumably, to ensure the loyalty of Corcyra to Athens.

**III.81. the Messenians:** see III.75n.

**persuaded about fifty of the suppliants there to submit to a trial:** the sort of trial, perhaps, which we saw in the case of the Plataeans. Th. stresses in particular the killing of suppliants in temples, an act of extreme impiety. Cf. I.24n.

**During the seven days that Eurymedon stayed there:** implying that he connived at the slaughter? Th. does not himself attach blame to Eurymedon: such things happen in war. Th. refers to Eurymedon as if we should know him, but this is in fact the first time he is mentioned.

**people went to every extreme and beyond it:** Th. often notes the extremes of behavior and suffering brought about by this war; cf. I.23.

### *III.82–84. An Analysis of the Nature of Stasis*

At the end of this long and complex narrative Th. pauses to offer some comments in his own right. This is not his usual practice—he prefers to let ideas develop from the words and actions of the participants in the war—but in two passages in bk. II Th. emerges from the background to offer his own analysis of the situation: first, in his comments on the devastating effects of the plague, a crucial time for Athens in the Archidamian war; second, in II.65, where he comments on the decay of Athenian politics and offers an explanation for Athens' failure in the war. We are perhaps expected to think back to these passages—and the vision of an ideal society that they surround—as we read this account of another society in the process of self-destruction.

Clearly the stasis in Corcyra was equally significant in his view: it was the archetype of many such conflicts whose cumulative impact on the whole Greek world was violent and destructive. Th. believed that in such critical circumstances, as during the plague, the essentials of human nature are most clearly visible. The normal conventions of civilized social behavior, which are taken for granted in peacetime, collapse when the pressures of war (and stasis can be the cruelest form of war: cf. Hdt. VIII.3, quoted at I.2n.) or some related crisis become too great and life deteriorates into a struggle for survival. Reason, the rule of law, and morality, the foundations on which an ordered society is constructed, yield to self-interest, fear, and passion. Thus, underlying the physical destruction of the state and its people is a moral degeneration that strikes at the very roots of civilized society. The analysis of the stasis at Corcyra picks out many features of the Mytilenian and Plataean episodes: the extremes of emotion and action, the lust for power and revenge, the distortion and misuse of language, the subordination of justice and decency to self-interest.

**III.82. practically the whole of the Hellenic world was convulsed:** cf. I.23.

**democratic leaders . . . oligarchs:** cf. I.2n., 19n. On the affinity between allied democrats and Athens and the hostility of oligarchs to Athens cf. the words of Diodotus at III.47. Contrast Th.'s remarks at II.8, where he talks of a general hostility to Athens. See also I.77n.

**each party:** not in any sense a modern political party, with a formal structure, an elected leader, and published policies, but a much looser, more fluid grouping.

**while human nature is what it is:** a proviso reminding us of the ultimate focus of Th.'s interest. Human nature provides the element of constancy in man's affairs. Cf. I.22, III.84.

**war is a stern teacher:** a better translation would be "a violent teacher" or Gomme's "a teacher of violence"—or perhaps Th. intended to convey both meanings. The personification is powerful. In war the usual techniques of civilized political intercourse (notably persuasion, which is at the heart of democracy) do not apply; force, driven by self-interest, reigns.

**new extravagances of revolutionary zeal, expressed by an elaboration in the method of seizing power and by unheard-of atrocities in revenge:** Th. has shown (e.g., in the Funeral Speech) how civilization has been fostered by courage, intelligence, inventiveness, and energy, with excess checked by restraint. During stasis these talents are used to promote evil ends, with all restraints removed.

**words, too, had to change their usual meanings:** to be precise, what Th. is asserting to have changed is not the meaning of words but the assessment of actions and the consequent application of the words used to express them. The misuse of language is a manifestation of the distortion of those fundamental values on which human social structures are founded. Language is seen to have no moral force; as part of a disintegrating society, it too disintegrates.

**any idea of moderation:** the Gk. is a cognate of *sophrosyne* (I.32n.), a desirable quality in better times but seen as the mark of a coward in a time of stasis.

**ability to understand a question from all sides:** literally "intelligence [Gk. *synesis;* see I.84n.] in everything," again normally a virtue, now a failing. Cf. text later in this chapter, **to plot successfully was a sign of intelligence and a victory won by treachery gave one a title for superior intelligence.**

**Family relations were a weaker tie than party membership:** Th. moves on to the damaging social effects of this intellectual and moral corruption.

**to acquire power:** Gk. *pleonexia,* literally "grabbing at more." See n. later in this chapter.

**fellowship in a religious communion:** implicit is a respect for the social and moral value of religion, though not necessarily belief in god. Cf. II.52–53 on the corruption caused by the plague.

**Revenge was more important than self-preservation:** the Corcyraean stasis shares many of the characteristics of a conventional war, but the passions are stronger. The anger and hatred of the extremists among the population are directed not at an outside enemy but against their domestic rivals.

**Love of power . . . greed . . . personal ambition:** these were the particular faults of Pericles' successors; cf. II.65n., **did the exact opposite,** and IV.21, where greed, Gk. *pleonexia,* is encouraged by Cleon ("winning still more").

**the safe and sound government of the aristocracy:** Gk. *sophrosyne* again, here used ironically; cf. I.32n.

**their one standard was the pleasure of their own party at that particular moment:** cf. II.65n., **adopted methods of demagogy.** The corruption in Corcyra is so deep that those involved can see only the pleasure of the moment, an instinctive human response to extreme pressure (cf. the reaction to plague conditions at II.53).

**As for the citizens who held moderate views, they were destroyed by the extreme parties:** cf. the way in which, during the Sicilian debate of 415, the minority of citizens who were opposed to the expedition kept quiet because of the fanatical enthusiasm of the majority (VI.24).

**III.83. The simple way of looking at things . . . the mark of a noble nature:** a forthright and rare statement of Th.'s own conservative moral values.

**two ideologically hostile camps:** see the beginning of III.82.

**no oath sworn that people would fear to break:** cf. III.82n., **fellowship in a religious communion.**

**III.84.** Further generalizations on the war in Corcyra that add nothing to what has already been said. This chapter is widely regarded as spurious—a later imitation of Th. that somehow found its way into the text.

**III.85. the people of Corcyra were the first:** this is often Th.'s method, to deal with one, frequently the first, instance of a phenomenon in depth and record later examples with the minimum of comment unless they are of particular interest; cf. the first rebellion against Athens (that of Naxos; see I.98) and the first Peloponnesian invasion of Attica (II.10–23).

**They then went up to Mt. Istone . . . and proceeded to make attacks on the party inside the city:** for the continuation of this episode see IV.2; for its conclusion, which is no less brutal than its course, see IV.46–48.

## III.86. The First Athenian Expedition to Sicily

**Laches:** a well-known figure, satirized by Aristophanes in his *Wasps.* He played a prominent part in arranging the Peace of Nicias (V.24, 43).

**all the other Dorian cities . . . had also been in alliance with Sparta:** see II.7; the alliance had been of little value to Sparta. On the racial factor cf. I.124n.

**the Chalcidian cities:** Naxos and Rhegium, founded, like Leontini itself, from Chalcis in Euboea.

**the Locrians:** not the Ozolian Locrians (who were pro-Athenian; see III.95, 101) or the Opuntian Locrians of central Greece (who were pro-Spartan; see II.9n.), but the Epizephyrian Locrians of southern Italy.

**The allies of Leontini:** or more precisely "the Leontinians and their allies." See I.36n. for the alliance between Leontini and Athens, which was, in fact, only some twenty years old.

**to prevent corn being brought in to the Peloponnese:** cf. I.120n.

**to make a preliminary survey:** such may have been the initial intention, but Hermocrates took the threat of Athenian conquest seriously (IV.61, 64), and the banishment of the two generals on the grounds that "they had been bribed to leave Sicily when it was in their power to take control of the island" suggests some enthusiasm in Athens for the idea (IV.65). Cf. Aristophanes *Knights* 173–74, 1302–5, produced in 424.

**to gain control of Sicily:** this goes well beyond the guidelines laid down by Pericles, which strictly forbade any additions to the empire during the war (I.144, II.65). Th. does not comment; indeed he offers no evaluation of Pericles' war policy at this stage, when there are signs that Athens is beginning to approach the war more aggressively; see III.91, 94ff. According to Plutarch (*Per.* 20–21, *Alcibiades* 17), there were even in Pericles' lifetime extremists in Athens who had immense imperialist ambitions. For Athenian aspirations in the second Sicilian expedition of 415 see VI.15, 90; Plut. *Nicias* 12.

**They . . . carried on the war:** for the course of the Sicilian expedition see III.88, 90, 99, 103, 115; IV.2, 24–25, 58–65. The account is fragmented for reasons of chronology (II.1n.).

## III.87. The Recurrence of the Plague at Athens

**the plague broke out:** for the original outbreak see II.47. For total numbers of Athenian hoplites and cavalry see II.13.

**Nothing did the Athenians so much harm as this:** what of the Sicilian disaster or Decelea? Th. should not be taken literally, unless he is referring only to the Archidamian War.

**the general mass of the people:** i.e., the Thetes, the lowest of the four Solonian wealth-based classes (III.16n.).

**many earthquakes:** see II.8n.

## III.88. The Athenians in Sicily

**the islands of Aeolus:** the Lipara Islands off the north coast of Sicily.

**Hephaestus:** the blacksmith god.

**Sicels:** non-Greek inhabitants of Sicily, who occupied the central and northern parts of the island; see VI.2.

## III.89. The Peloponnesian Invasion of Attica Fails; a Discussion of Tidal Waves and Earthquakes

**earthquakes . . . flood . . . inundation:** for Th.'s interest in natural phenomena of this kind see II.8n. An earthquake was regarded as a bad omen; hence the Peloponnesians ended the expedition. Cf. V.45n.

**Atalanta . . . the Athenian fortifications:** see II.32.

## III.90. Events in Sicily Continued

**I shall merely refer to what is most noteworthy:** Th.'s practice throughout, in fact, though his account of this expedition is particularly terse.

**Charoeades . . . Laches:** see III.86.

**Messina:** for the significance of the place, which controlled the narrow strait between Italy and Sicily, and for its recovery by Syracuse see IV.1.

## III.91. Athenian Activity in Greece and the Aegean

**the Athenians sent out thirty ships:** the policy of sending fleets to devastate the Peloponnesian coastline (II.13n.) is continued; see III.94.

**Demosthenes:** an eminent Athenian general from this point and responsible for a shift in the direction of Athenian war policy (e.g., III.95).

**Melos:** a Spartan colony (V.84, 89), which had so far remained neutral in the war, though the islanders had contributed to the Spartan war fund (*T.D.G.R.* 132; there are doubts about the date of this inscription). The Athenians resented their independence (cf. V.97, 99). The proposed addition of Melos to the empire, following hard on the heels of the decision to go to Sicily (III.86), shows that Pericles' advice not to add to the empire during the war has been abandoned. Perhaps even the moderates among the generals recognized the need for some change: the leader of this expedition was the cautious and conservative **Nicias** (III.51n.). This expedition fails, but Athens will try again: see V.84–116.

**Oropus:** on the northern coast of Attica, opposite Euboea; cf. II.23n.

**they were victorious in a battle:** a land battle, another departure from the spirit of Periclean policy. But having made a stand and flexed their military muscles, the Athenians quickly withdrew.

III.92–93. The Spartan Colony at Heraclea

**III.92. the Spartans founded their colony of Heraclea in Trachis:** an indication of a new Spartan initiative, though Sparta had a long record of interest in central Greece (e.g., I.107; Hdt. VI.72, 108). A motive not mentioned by Th. may have been a desire to exert influence at Delphi (already supportive of Sparta: see I.118, II.54) by acquiring a vote on the Delphic amphictyony, the organization responsible for the administration of the oracle. This foundation involved a commitment in an area close to Athens. It also opened up the way to Thrace and the Athenian allies in that area. It may well have been the brainchild of the imaginative Spartan general Brasidas, who had already realized that the best way to strike at Athens' interests was through its allies. He later undertook such a campaign in 424, using Heraclea as his base (IV.78).

**Euboea:** an important Athenian refuge that had so far in the war been secure from attack; see II.14n.

**they consulted the god at Delphi:** Apollo; cf. I.25n.

**with the exception of the Ionians, the Achaeans, and some other peoples:** further evidence of racial feeling, in particular between Ionians and Dorians; see I.124n.

**Thermopylae:** site of the pass defended against the Persians by three hundred Spartans in 480.

**III.93. they were originally very numerous:** Diodorus talks of ten thousand, including six thousand Spartans, but such figures, especially the second, are unrealistically high. The Athenians and their allies were able to get together ten thousand colonists for their settlement at Nine Ways (I.100, IV.102) in the 460s (which also failed).

**the governors sent out from Sparta . . . were very largely responsible for the decline:** unusual conditions could make Spartans nervous, tactless, and brutal. Cf. IV.80 and Alcidas at III.32, but contrast Brasidas. See also the remarks of the Athenians at the end of I.77. On Spartan governors cf. IV.132. On the later history of Heraclea see V.51–52, VIII.3n.; Xenophon *Hellenica* I.2.18.

III.94–98. Demosthenes in Western Greece

**III.94. Melos, the other Athenian fleet:** see III.91.

**Leucas:** see III.7n.

**Oeniadae:** see II.102.

**if he conquered them [the Aetolians], it would be easy to win over . . . all the other continental tribes:** this idea, along with Demosthenes' planned conquest of Boeotia, is a further shift away from Pericles' policy for fighting the war. Cf. III.86n.

**and, so it is said, speak a language which is almost unintelligible and eat their meat raw:** Th. is interested in the behavior of these barbarous western tribes (cf. I.5n.), but he will not vouch for the reliability of his information.

**III.95. to invade Boeotia by land:** if Boeotia could be taken it would give the Athenians control of the area to the north of the Corinthian Gulf and access by land to their allies in western Greece. Lack of Boeotian support would also make it more difficult for the Spartans to invade Attica. The plan ignored the lessons of history: Athens had held Boeotia before but had been unable to control it (I.108, 113).

**The Phocians . . . had always been friendly to Athens:** e.g., I.111–12, though in II.9 Th. reports that they supplied cavalry to the Spartans.

**against the will of the Acarnanians:** Demosthenes is offending some important Athenian supporters in this area by refusing to prosecute the siege of Leucas. The Corcyraeans are not prepared to get involved.

**Sollium:** captured by the Athenians in the first year of the war (II.30).

**300 Athenian citizens who were serving as marines:** on thirty ships (III.91), i.e., ten per ship, as usual; cf. I.10n.

**Oeneon:** see III.102n.

**the Ozolian Locrians:** see III.86n.

**III.96. the poet Hesiod is said to have been killed:** Hesiod was a Boeotian farmer who lived in the second half of the eighth century. He describes agricultural life of his time in his *Works and Days.*

**They had known about it from the time when the plans were first made:** one of Demosthenes' biggest mistakes was to underestimate his opponents.

**Nemea:** the well-known Nemea is in the Peloponnese.

**Potidania . . . Crocylium . . . Tichium:** their exact sites are unknown, but they are in southeast Aetolia, just north of the Locrian border.

**the most distant Ophionian tribes, the Bomians, and the Callians:** away to the north and northeast, but, again, their exact locations are unknown.

**III.97. They assured him that the conquest of Aetolia was a simple matter:** Demosthenes' enthusiasm gets the better of his judgment.

**capturing the villages one by one:** cf. I.5n.

**Demosthenes did not wait for the Locrian reinforcements:** a further error.

**light-armed javelin-throwers:** particularly mobile in mountainous terrain; cf. III.112.

**III.98. 120 hoplites:** these men were described in III.95 as marines, who are usually reckoned to be Thetes, while hoplites were generally Zeugitae; see I.10n.

**These Athenians, so many of them and all in the prime of life, were certainly the best men from the city itself who perished in this war:** another example of the extreme suffering endured in this war (I.23). The losses were more allied than Athenian, but the battle was disastrous for Athens, the inevitable climax of a badly planned campaign. Th.'s account is both dramatic and compassionate; cf. his tone at III.113, commenting on the conclusion of the Olpae campaign. By "this war" Th. may mean the Archidamian War only (I.1n.).

**Demosthenes . . . was afraid to face the Athenians:** not surprisingly. The demos could be vindictive even when a general was not at fault: see II.65n. Cf. III.105n. A second attempt on Boeotia by Demosthenes in 424/3 will also fail (IV.76, 89–101).

### III.99. Events in Sicily Continued

**Locri:** occupied by the Epizephyrian Locrians of southern Italy; see III.86n.

### III.100–102. The Peloponnesian Expedition against Naupactus

**III.100. 3,000 hoplites:** a sizable force. The Spartans take seriously the threat to their Aetolian allies.

**Heraclea:** see III.92.

**III.101. the Ozolian Locrians:** see III.86n.

**since the route to Naupactus ran through their country:** on the etiquette of taking a force through the territory of another state cf. Brasidas' journey through Thessaly at IV.78.

**Amphissa:** northwest of Delphi, toward the Aetolian border.

**III.102. Oeneon and Eupalium:** east and northeast, respectively, of Naupactus.

**Molycrium:** southwest of Naupactus.

**Calydon and Pleuron . . . Proschium:** approximately west of Naupactus, just above the mouth of the Corinthian Gulf.

**all the rest of the mainland would come over to the Spartan side:** Eurylochus is as easily convinced as Demosthenes. This expedition is much more ambitious than the earlier attempt on Acarnania (II.80).

## III.103. Events in Sicily Continued

**Sicels:** see III.88n.

**Inessa:** see VI.94n.

**acropolis:** literally "high city," an easily defended hill or outcrop of rock that would have been one of the attractions of the site for the original settlers and around which the city developed. The Acropolis of Athens is the most famous example, but many Greek cities had an acropolis.

## III.104. The Purification of Delos

**the Athenians . . . carried out ceremonies of purification on Delos:** home of Apollo and the Delian Games and once, of course, headquarters of the Delian League. On "purification" see I.8n. See also I.13, 96, and V.1, with nn. The episode provides brief but welcome relief from the savagery of war in an uncivilized region of Greece, as well as a reminder of the achievements of Greek culture that were being destroyed by the conflict. The purification would have had a political motive: the Athenians were consolidating their claim to be the leading Ionian city.

**no doubt because of some oracle:** see II.8n.

**the tyrant Pisistratus:** see I.13n., 18n.

**Polycrates, the tyrant of Samos:** see I.13n.

**the Delian Games:** clearly a revival of an earlier festival, now with an Ionian emphasis (other festivals, such as the Olympian and the Pythian, were at this time under Peloponnesian control). The festival included not only athletics but also music and poetry: the Greeks saw all such activities as competitive.

**the festival at Ephesus:** on the east coast of the Aegean. It might have been a festival in honor of Artemis or a major festival of all Ionians.

**Blind is the singer:** Homer, reputed to be from **Chios**; see I.3n.

**the difficulties of the times:** a reference to Persian pressure on Ionia, exerted as the Persians moved westward in the late sixth and early fifth centuries.

## III.105–14. The Peloponnesian Expedition to Acarnania

**III.105. The same winter the Ambraciots . . . :** Th. resumes his account of Eurylochus' expedition from III.102.

**Amphilocian Argos:** see II.68.

**Demosthenes, who had led the expedition into Aetolia:** for his disastrous failure and the reason why he had remained in the area see III.98, 102. He had probably lost his generalship as a result (and was thus acting in a private capacity in 426/5; cf. IV.2). His reputation among the Acarnanians seems to have recovered.

**the twenty Athenian ships:** not previously mentioned.

**Aristotle . . . Hierophon:** previously unmentioned and otherwise unknown.

**III.106.** The sites of the towns of this area are uncertain. The **Achelous** was the border between Aetolia and Acarnania. **Amphilocian Argos** was near the southeast corner of the Ambracian Gulf. **Olpae** was a little to the north of it.

**III.107. an ambush in a hidden pathway:** Demosthenes had learned from his experience of fighting in the mountains alongside the natives of the region.

**III.109. Menedaius . . . Macarius:** see III.100.

**III.112. the Messenians:** see III.75n.

**the Doric dialect:** spoken widely, with regional variations, in the Peloponnese.

**as it was still dark:** on night fighting see II.4n.

**their heavily armed opponents:** hoplite equipment and organization were of no advantage in mountain warfare. On the role of light-armed troops in rough terrain cf. III.97–98.

**III.113. "About two hundred," said the herald:** an exchange in direct speech, unusual (indeed, apart from the Melian Dialogue, unique) in Th., adding perhaps to the momentousness of the occasion.

**in all the war:** probably the Archidamian War (I.1n.); thus Th. would be writing this not long after 421.

**I have not recorded:** Th. is strangely coy about the number of dead, perhaps well over one thousand. It has been suggested that he was present on this campaign.

**III.114. 300 sets of armour . . . for Demosthenes:** the generosity of the spoils given to Demosthenes himself reveals the high regard in which he was held by Athenian allies in this area (cf. III.105). Stripping the dead and plundering enemy property were integral parts of Greek warfare and could be very profitable: see, for instance, VI.95.

**after the disaster in Aetolia, it was now . . . a much safer thing for him to return home:** see III.98.

**The terms were . . . :** i.e., a defensive alliance such as that concluded between Athens and Corcyra in 433; see I.44.

III.115. Events in Sicily Continued

**the Athenians in Sicily:** the story is resumed from III.103.

**Himera:** see VI.5, 62.

**Pythodorus . . . Sophocles:** for their later banishment and the fining of **Eurymedon** on the grounds of corruption during this campaign see IV.65. For the activities of Sophocles and Eurymedon before their arrival in Sicily see IV.2ff.

**Laches:** see III.86.

**the Locrian fort:** see III.99.

III.116. The Eruption of Mount Etna

**a stream of lava came down from Etna:** see II.8n. for Th.'s interest in natural phenomena.

**the first eruption for fifty years:** a precise or a round figure? Th. is not quite sure of his information: hence he begins with "It is said that . . . "

**since Sicily was colonized by the Hellenes:** in the second half of the eighth century (I.12n., VI.2–6).

# Book Four

## IV.1. Events in Sicily

**Messina:** the account of the Athenian intervention in Sicily is resumed from III.115. For the original surrender of Messina to Athens see III.90. Its defection was a serious blow to the Athenians. Syracusan fears that Athens might attempt to use the city as **a base against Sicily** were justified: see VI.50.

**Rhegium:** on the toe of Italy, roughly opposite Messina (cf. IV.24) and west of Locri, which was on the southern coast of Italy (cf. III.86n.). For Rhegium's alliance with Athens see I.36n.

**Party struggles:** stasis; see I.2n.

## IV.2. The Fifth Peloponnesian Invasion of Attica; Another Athenian Fleet Is Sent to Sicily

**before the corn was fully ripe:** about the beginning of May, slightly earlier than usual (cf. II.19, 47; III.1); see IV.6 for the consequences of this.

**Eurymedon . . . Sophocles . . . Pythodorus:** see III.115.

**the Corcyraeans in the city who were suffering:** see III.85.

**Demosthenes, since his return from Acarnania:** see III.114.

**held no official position:** one theory is that he had been dismissed from office after his failure in Aetolia, though there is no evidence for this. He clearly held no office for 426/5 (see III.105n.) and was probably reelected in the spring of 425, taking up office in the summer (IV.29). His precise position on this mission is unclear. After his success in Acarnania he clearly enjoyed some support among the Athenian demos. We would like to know what exactly he had in mind at this early stage and how he persuaded the assembly to grant him these unusual powers.

## IV.3–6. The Beginning of the Pylos Campaign

**IV.3. in what used to be the country of the Messenians:** see I.101, 103.

**The others, however, told him:** it is hardly surprising that the presence of Demosthenes, whose ideas were clearly at variance with the orders given to the generals, led to conflict. Demosthenes' plan was to occupy a position on the Peloponnesian coastline to incite rebellion among the helots and put pressure on the Spartans at home. This would, perhaps, prevent further invasions of Attica by Sparta. The idea had, in fact, been suggested by Pericles himself before the outbreak of war (I.142), but it was envisaged on that occasion only as a retaliation if the Spartans should establish an outpost in Attica, and it was never put into practice in Pericles' time.

**it had a harbour:** see IV.8n.

**IV.4. company commanders:** Gk. *taxiarchoi,* regimental officers in command of the quota of infantrymen supplied by each tribe.

**IV.5. The Spartans meanwhile had a festival:** such a festival prohibited military activity. There is considerable irony in the Spartans' initial casualness and misplaced confidence: this would prove for them one of the greatest disasters of the war.

## IV.7. The Athenian Defeat in Chalcidice

**Simonides:** otherwise unknown.

**Eion:** its site is unknown; it is not the Eion on the Strymon (I.98, IV.102).

**Chalcidians and Bottiaeans:** long-standing enemies of Athens (I.58).

## IV.8–23. The Pylos Campaign Continued

**IV.8. the subordinate towns nearest to Sparta:** inhabited by the perioeci; see I.101n.

**their sixty ships in Corcyra:** see IV.2.

**the isthmus of Leucas:** by which Leucas was joined to the mainland. On the dragging of ships across an isthmus cf. VIII.7n.

**Zacynthus:** an Athenian ally; see II.9.

**the harbour:** the modern Bay of Navarino. Th.'s description of the location as a "harbour" is something of a misnomer for what in fact is a very large bay, over three miles north to south, sheltered in places but elsewhere exposed to winds and waves from the open sea.

**the island of Sphacteria:** either Th. is mistaken about its length or the text is corrupt. The island is some twenty-five *stades* (ca. 4,500 yards) long, not fifteen (ca. 2,770 yards).

**narrow entrances:** the northern channel is something over one hundred yards wide at its narrowest point, clearly far more than what would be needed by **two ships abreast** (allowing about fifty feet per trireme, including oars, and some space between them). However, we cannot be sure—indeed it seems unlikely—that the topography of the area has not changed since Th.'s time. The southern entrance is some 1,400 yards wide, clearly a much greater space than that required by **eight or nine** triremes. See map 3.

**The Spartan plan was to block up the harbour entrances with lines of ships:** Th. does not say how many ships would be required; in fact the numbers would be impossibly large. It would appear that Th.—or his source—was unfamiliar with the site, got his facts wrong, and thus misunderstood Spartan intentions. For a reinterpretation of the text based on a detailed topographical survey of the area see Wilson 1979.

**420 hoplites:** this figure included a large number of Spartiates, members of the exclusive warrior caste who were the elite of the Spartan population. One hundred and twenty of these men were eventually captured (IV.38).

**helots:** see I.101n.

**IV.9. the triremes that remained out of the ones that had been left him:** three remained out of five (IV.5), two having been sent to Zacynthus (IV.8). From these ships and the Messenian vessels Demosthenes would have a force of about six hundred men. We do not know the size of his hoplite force (usually ten per ship: see I.10n.).

**a thirty-oared privateer:** on piracy see I.5, 98n. A **pinnace** is a small vessel with both sails and oars.

**spoke to them as follows:** on prebattle speeches see II.10n.

**IV.10. calculations are beside the point:** usually in Th. it is the need for careful judgment (as against blind hope) that is stressed; see I.121n. Demosthenes is perhaps afraid that his troops will be disheartened if they dwell on the dangers of their situation, though he himself proceeds immediately to calculate Athenian chances.

**who know from experience all about landing from ships:** as Th. notes (IV.12, 14), the situation is very unusual, with the Athenians on land and the Spartans on ships, but Demosthenes still manages to introduce the greater naval experience of the Athenians (I.142n.) into his speech, as an encouragement to his men.

**IV.11. There were forty-three [ships]:** though sixty were mentioned in IV.8. Th. seems to imply that this was their full fleet; perhaps some had been disabled and some were on the lookout for the Athenians.

**a regular Spartan officer:** i.e., a Spartiate; see IV.8n.

**exactly where Demosthenes was expecting it:** foresight is the mark of the astute leader in Th. and a prerequisite for success in war and politics; cf. I.138n. on Themistocles.

**It was Brasidas:** Th. again notes the courage and initiative of this Spartan general who plays such an important role in these middle years of the Archidamian War. Cf. II.25, IV.78ff.

**IV.12. It was indeed a strange alteration:** another example of the unpredictable element in warfare (I.120n.). Cf. IV.14n. and, for another reversal, IV.29. Th. notes such reversals in the position of the Athenians at Syracuse in 414/3; cf. VII.11, 56, 71, 75, with nn.

**Sparta chiefly prided herself on being a land power with an unrivalled army and Athens on being a sea power with the greatest navy in existence:** see I.18n. and, on Sparta's military reputation, IV.40.

**IV.13. Asine:** toward the southern end of the west coast of the Messenian Gulf.

**the Athenian fleet from Zacynthus:** summoned in IV.8.

**Chios:** see III.10n.

**nor had they blocked the entrances to the harbour, as they had meant to do:** they can have had no such plan; see IV.8n.

**IV.14. a reversal in the usual methods of the two sides:** cf. IV.12n.

**Both sides returned to their camps:** Th. has specifically mentioned that the Athenians had no base for their fleet (IV.13), and he does not make it clear where their camp was. There was nowhere suitable on Pylos for the Athenians to anchor a sizable fleet; Sphacteria and the bay were occupied by the Spartans.

**IV.15. to send ambassadors to Athens with a view to ending the war:** the Spartan population was small and dwindling. The earthquake of 465 will have accelerated the decline (I.101). There were no more than a few thousand Spartiates at this period (see Forrest 1980, excursus II, pp. 131ff.). They could not countenance the loss of 420 men, including a large proportion of Spartiates.

**IV.16. all their ships . . . with all other warships in Laconia:** the total, ca. sixty, is given toward the end of the chapter.

**IV.17. It is certainly our way not to use many words:** cf. I.86n.

**the mistake so often made by those who meet with some extraordinary piece of good luck and then go on pressing forward in the hope of**

**more:** precisely what the Athenians do, ignoring these ominous words at their cost; see IV.21n. On "hope" see I.121n.

**IV.18. the greatest reputation of any state in Hellas:** the whole speech reveals the Spartans' great concern for their city's honor. Cf. I.75n.

**True wisdom:** *sophrosyne;* see I.32n.

**as for war . . . its course is governed by the total chances in operation:** as Archidamus had warned the Spartans before war was declared (I.82). Cf. I.120n.

**the over-confidence which may spring from a success in war:** a recurrent theme in Th. The Athenians soon fall into the trap: see IV.65. One of Cleon's faults, in Th.'s view, was his excessive confidence: see V.7.

**IV.20. an unending hatred of you:** but not one that will prevent the Spartans from making peace with Athens in 421.

**they are not certain who began it:** hard to believe! The events of 431 (II.2–6) would be widely known by now.

**Think also of the advantages:** once more a speech requesting help ends on a thoroughly pragmatic note. Cf. the speeches of the Corcyraeans at Athens (I.32–36) and of the Mytilenians at Olympia (III.9–14).

**the rest of Hellas . . . will show us every possible mark of honour:** the Spartans are prepared now not only to abandon their struggle for Greek freedom (II.8) but to stand side by side with the Athenians as masters of Hellas. The following year they are proclaiming again that their mission is the liberty of Greece (e.g., IV.85). On honor see IV.18n.

**IV.21. Athens had wanted to make peace even earlier:** for Athenian peace proposals in 430 see II.59. And it was the Spartans who had turned down offers of negotiations before the outbreak of war (VII.18).

**winning still more:** the Gk. is akin to *pleonexia,* generally translated as "greed"; see III.82n. This is precisely what the Spartans had argued against (IV.17). For the further growth of Athenian confidence and ambition see IV.41, 65. But they will eventually regret this decision to reject an offer of peace (V.14).

**Cleon, the son of Cleaenetus, a popular figure of the time:** Th.'s description of Cleon suggests that this is his first appearance, whereas, in fact, he has already been introduced in similar language (III.36). This could be due to lack of revision of the text. The picture of Cleon presented in these chapters is clearly hostile, though Th. is forced to admit that Cleon fulfilled his promise (IV.39).

**who had the greatest influence:** literally "who was most persuasive"; see III.36n.

**the right reply:** significantly Th. does not grant Cleon a speech. The Athenians were now in the strongest position they had enjoyed since the outbreak of war. There was a good chance that they would be able to capture the prisoners and use them as hostages. Cleon preferred to build on Athens' advantage rather than bargain it away.

**the previous peace treaty:** the Thirty Years' Truce of 446/5, by which Athens surrendered **Nisaea, Pegae, Troezen, and Achaea**; for this and the difficulties Athens was in at the time see I.114–15. Achaea was, in fact, independent and did not belong to the Spartans, who thus could not return it. Th. perhaps means the goodwill and support of Achaea (which would seem to be readily transferable) rather than Achaea itself.

**IV.23. some other complaints which seemed hardly worth mentioning:** Th. clearly disapproves.

## IV.24–25. Events in Sicily Continued

**IV.24. Sicily:** the narrative of events is continued from IV.1.

**the Locrians . . . their hatred of Rhegium:** see IV.1n.

**Charybdis:** a dangerous whirlpool off the coast of Sicily, opposite the legendary monster Scylla on the Italian shore. See Homer *Odyssey* XII.

**the two great seas:** the Tyrrhenian is that off the west coast of Italy; the Sicilian is east of Sicily.

**IV.25. they then hurriedly retired . . . to their bases at Messina and Rhegium:** but the Syracusans (to whom "they" seems to refer) did not have a base at Rhegium, which was friendly to Athens. Nor will the Gk. as it stands allow us to assume that the Syracusans retired to Messina, the Athenians to Rhegium. There is a fault in the text.

**Camarina:** on the southern coast of Sicily; see III.86, VI.5.

**Archias:** otherwise unknown.

**the Chalcidian colony of Naxos:** see III.86, VI.3. The identity of the river **Acesines** is uncertain.

**Sicels:** see III.88n., 103.

## IV.26–41. The Pylos Campaign Continued

**IV.26. a difficult operation for the Athenians:** the Spartans occupied both Sphacteria and the mainland; the Athenians had only Pylos. The crews of seventy ships would total about fourteen thousand men to supply, in addition to those on Pylos. The shore was unsuitable for beaching triremes safely.

**poppyseed mixed with honey:** to prevent hunger, while **linseed** prevented thirst.

**IV.27. he declared that those who brought news from Pylos were not telling the truth:** according to Th. (V.16), slander was one of Cleon's political weapons. Its use on this occasion appears rather unintelligent.

**Nicias:** see III.51n. We have not previously been told of his involvement in the Pylos affair. It looks as if Demosthenes had requested reinforcements and Nicias had been appointed to command them.

**IV.28. The Athenians behaved in the way that crowds usually do:** Th. regards the assembly, particularly when it is in this sort of mood, as ill-equipped for making important decisions. He described the people's inconsistent treatment of Pericles in similar terms (II.65n.).

**the Lemnians and Imbrians:** see III.5n.

**peltasts:** see II.29n. Such troops would be invaluable in this sort of terrain.

**Aenus:** in the northeast corner of the Aegean. Cf. VII.57.

**This irresponsible claim:** Th. omits to mention that Cleon fulfilled his promise.

**the more intelligent members of his audience:** in the Gk. they are men possessed of *sophrosyne* (I.32n.), though there seems to be little of that quality in their behavior on this occasion—unless it is simply the fact that they are opposed to Cleon.

**IV.29. Demosthenes, one of the generals:** see IV.2n. Cleon chose him as colleague since he was on the spot and favored an aggressive approach to the war, as he did himself.

**finding themselves more the besieged than the besiegers:** another reversal (cf. IV.12n.), a further example of the unexpected in warfare (I.120n.).

**His own army, in spite of its size:** at least ten thousand (IV.32n.), though not all were well armed (IV.34).

**IV.30. These calculations of his:** Demosthenes learns from his mistakes, using the past to plan the future and relying on calculation rather than hope—characteristics of good leadership in Th.

**the Aetolian disaster:** see III.97–98.

**It happened, however, that one of the soldiers . . . accidentally set fire:** careful planning is again upset by an unpredictable mishap; cf. I.120n.

**the allies in the neighbourhood:** e.g., Zacynthus (II.9), Cephallenia (II.30), and Naupactus (I.103).

**IV.31. about 800 of them:** a trireme carried ten marine hoplites (I.10n.). Thus the fleet of seventy ships could furnish seven hundred.

**IV.32. the crews of rather more than seventy ships:** i.e., 70+ × ca. 110, if we exclude the ca. 60 in each ship from **the lowest rank of rowers** (I.14n.). The lightly armed troops mentioned here would total at least 2,000. In addition there were the hoplites mentioned in IV.31. A total of over 10,000 to face 420 (with accompanying helots: see IV.8).

**IV.33. the Spartans in their heavy armour:** the terrain did not suit hoplite equipment or tactics. See I.49n., III.112n.

**IV.34. they had been obsessed with the idea that they were actually going to attack Spartans:** Sparta's reputation as a land-fighting force was unequaled. See I.18; IV.12, 40n.

**IV.36. the battle of Thermopylae:** fought in 480 by the three hundred Spartans against the Persian invaders. **The path** is mentioned in Hdt. VII.213.

**IV.38. The Spartans order you to make your own decision:** not very helpful. The Spartans were keen to recover the prisoners (IV.41) but did not treat them well: see V.34. They are more concerned with their honor and reputation, their "image"; cf. the Spartans' speech at IV.17–20.

**440 hoplites had crossed over:** a misprint. The figure was 420 (IV.8).

**the Spartan officer class:** i.e., Spartiates; see IV.8n.

**IV.39. Cleon:** now a national hero, he was rewarded with the highest honors the state could bestow, front seats in the theater and meals at public expense (Aristophanes *Knights* 280, 702, 709, 766, 1404).

**however mad he may have been to have made it:** fair comment?

**IV.40. The general impression had been that the Spartans would never surrender:** the Spartans' military prowess and reputation and the undermining of that reputation are key features of this episode; cf. IV.12, 34. On the Spartans' obsession with their prestige as the foremost land-fighting force in Greece cf. the words of Nicias at VI.11: "military honor is the be-all and the end-all of their existence"; cf. too Pericles' words at II.39.

**the real Spartans:** Gk. *kaloi k'agathoi,* "the brave and good"—the mixture of courage and breeding on which the Spartiates prided themselves.

**IV.41. Pylos was firmly garrisoned:** the first instance in the war of the application of the policy of *epiteichismos,* the long-term occupation of fortified positions in enemy territory; cf. I.122n.

**what was in fact their old country:** see I.101, 103.

**the spread of revolution:** there had been a number of earlier helot revolts, the latest in 465 (I.101). See IV.80 on Spartan methods of repression.

**The Athenians, however, were aiming at gaining still more:** the policy of Cleon; see IV.21n.

**frequent representations were made to them:** cf. Th.'s comment at V.15, "the Athenians would not listen to any reasonable proposals."

IV.42–45. The Athenian Expedition against the Territory of Corinth

**IV.42. just after the events related above:** the Athenians are quick to follow up their greatest success yet by putting further pressure on key Peloponnesian positions.

**Nicias:** he will have been embarrassed by the success of Cleon. In view of their rivalry he was perhaps one of those who would not have been unhappy to see the attack on Sphacteria fail (IV.28).

**Chersonese . . . Rheitus:** on the coast of the northwestern corner of the Saronic Gulf. The **Solygian hill** and **Solygia** are a little inland. Th. does not explain the purpose of this expedition.

**In ancient times:** for the Dorian invasion see I.12n. According to legend, the Dorians reduced Corinth, expelled the Aeolian dynasty of Sisyphus, and assumed power.

**Argos:** the Argives "maintained friendly relations with both sides" (II.9), no doubt intervening when it suited them.

**those who lived beyond the Isthmus [of Corinth]:** presumably those to the northeast, toward Megara, who stayed there to protect their own territory. But the Gk. is obscure and the text perhaps corrupt.

**men who were away . . . in Ambracia and Leucadia:** see III.114.

**Cenchriae:** at the extreme northwestern corner of the Saronic Gulf, east of Corinth and southwest of **Crommyon,** which was on the southern shore of the Isthmus of Corinth, toward the border of the Megarid.

**IV.44. Mount Oneion:** in fact a mountain range, with Solygia at its eastern end, obscuring the view of the battle from Cenchriae.

**IV.45. Epidaurus:** see II.56 for an earlier attack.

**Methana:** on the neck of an isthmus, it could be held easily and seems to have been the main object of this campaign. This is another instance of *epiteichismos* (I.122n.).

**Troezen:** formerly allied to Athens but surrendered by the terms of the Thirty Years' Truce (I.115). The Athenians were clearly keen to recover it and to strengthen their position in this area (cf. IV.21, 118n.). Perhaps they were hoping to increase their influence at Argos. We know from Aristophanes (*Knights* 465–66) that Cleon had been making overtures to the Argives, whose truce with Sparta was due to expire in 421.

### IV.46–48. The End of the Civil War in Corcyra

**IV.46. Corcyra . . . the revolution:** see III.70–85, IV.2. Many of the features of Th.'s analysis of stasis at III.82 are exemplified in this shattering conclusion. It is another instance of the extreme cruelty and suffering brought about by this war (I.23).

**Ptychia:** its site is uncertain, but it was probably in front of the harbor.

**IV.47. Much of the responsibility for this must rest with the Athenian generals:** Th., who is not given to comments of this kind, is disgusted by the connivance and motives of Eurymedon and Sophocles.

**IV.48. this war:** Th. probably means the Archidamian War; see I.1n.
**Sicily, their original destination:** see IV.2.

### IV.49–57. Further Athenian Activity

**IV.49. Anactorium:** taken by treachery by the Corinthians from the Corcyraeans (I.55). Athens continues to put pressure on Corinth.

**IV.50. ships which were sent out to collect money from the allies:** arrears, presumably, or extraordinary contributions (since the regular tribute was brought to Athens by its subjects). Alternatively, the ships may be connected with a large increase in tribute at this time (*T.D.G.R.* 136; cf. 133). It is ignored by Th., perhaps because it proved Pericles' predictions wrong (II.13). Cf. II.69, III.19, IV.75.

**Eion, on the Strymon:** see I.98n.

**a Persian called Artaphernes, who was on his way to Sparta from the King of Persia:** for earlier Spartan embassies to Persia (also intercepted by Athens) see II.7, 67. Th. does not mention communications between Athens and Persia, but Aristophanes (*Acharnians* 65ff., produced in the previous year) describes a scene in which a messenger from the Great King (Darius) comes before the assembly. Sparta perhaps had more to gain from a Persian alliance: the possibility of using Persia's fleet to destroy Athens' control of the Aegean.

**the Assyrian characters:** the cuneiform (wedge-shaped) letters employed by the Persians.

**Artaxerxes, the son of Xerxes, had just died:** in 425/4. For Athens' treaty with his successor, Darius II, see *T.D.G.R.* 138.

**IV.51. Chios:** Athens' major surviving "free" ally (II.9). The Chians would be loyal from now on—i.e., until they revolted in 413 (VIII.5ff.). For details of Chios' participation in the war up to this point see III.10n.

**their new fortifications:** on the building of defenses as a preliminary to revolt cf. the case of Mytilene, mentioned at III.2, and see VIII.14n.

**IV.52. a partial eclipse:** for Th.'s interest in natural phenomena of this type see II.8n. This particular eclipse is also mentioned by Aristophanes in *Clouds* 584–85, where it is said to be a warning against the election of Cleon as *strategos*.

**Mytilene:** the story is continued from III.50. Like the Samian (IV.75) and Corcyraean (III.85) oligarchs, the Mytilenian exiles do not give up easily. Like the Samians also, they are cooperating with the Peloponnesians (as oligarchs generally did: see III.82). For the next stage of the story see IV.75–76.

**Rhoeteum:** on the coast of the Troad, just inside the western mouth of the Hellespont.

**2,000 Phocaean staters:** the Phocaean stater was probably worth a little less than an Attic stater. There were twenty-four drachmae to the stater. See the Penguin translation, app. 2, pp. 612–13.

**Antandrus:** on the northern shore of the Gulf of Atramyttium, which faces the northeastern side of Lesbos.

**the Actaean cities:** so called because they were on the coast (Gk. *acte*) of the mainland, near Lesbos.

**possessions of Mytilene:** until 427, when they were taken over by Athens; see III.50.

**IV.53. Cythera:** another site of particular importance to Sparta, which the Athenians now propose to garrison and from which they will conduct raids on the Peloponnesian coast.

**Nicias:** despite Cleon's victory at Pylos a number of "conservatives" were elected to the generalship for this year.

**the semi-independent class:** the perioeci; see I.101n.

**the port for merchant ships:** Sparta was to some degree dependent on trade, presumably in grain. Cf. I.120n. Possession of the island would enable the Athenians to hinder such trade, though a complete blockade would have been impossible.

**pirates:** see I.98n.

**IV.54. 2,000 hoplites from Miletus:** the figure is too large, perhaps a dittography, in error, of the two thousand in IV.53.

**Negotiations had been going on previously between Nicias and some**

**of the people of Cythera:** this sort of internal division was widespread in Greek cities by this time; cf. I.2n.

**terms so advantageous . . . to the Cytherians:** see IV.57.

**IV.55. a revolution against the government:** in particular, a helot revolt; cf. IV.41n.

**quite at variance with their normal way of doing things:** their hoplite force alone had been more than adequate in the past. Cf. IV.34n.

**a war fought on the seas:** cf. IV.12n.

**people who thought that every moment when they were not attacking was so much sacrificed:** that typically Athenian restlessness that the Corinthians had pointed out (I.70).

**the many unpredictable blows of fortune:** see I.120n.

**their morale collapsed:** the Athenians go to the opposite extreme (IV.65).

**IV.56. Cotyrta and Aphrodisia:** somewhere on the coast of Laconia, but their exact sites are unknown.

**the exiled people of Aegina:** see II.27.

**the earthquake and the revolt of the helots:** of 465 (I.101).

**they were subjects of Athens:** for Athens' conquest of Aegina in ca. 457 see I.105, 108. For further evidence of ill feeling see I.67, II.27.

**IV.57. the rest of the inhabitants of Cythera were to keep their own land:** some had, after all, cooperated with Athens (IV.54), and it would be risky to install cleruchs (III.50n.) so close to Sparta and so far from Athens.

**a tribute of four talents:** not excessive. Th. describes these terms as "advantageous" to Cythera (IV.54). The island was returned to Sparta under the terms of the Peace of Nicias (V.18), but it is interesting to note that Cythera fought on the side of Athens in the Sicilian campaign of 415–413 (VII.57).

**all the Aeginetans . . . were . . . to be put to death:** unlike Cytherans and Spartans, these prisoners were of no value as hostages. But so far the Spartans had exercised the greatest brutality in the war (see, e.g., II.67; III.32, 68), and more was to come from them (IV.80).

**the other Spartans from Sphacteria:** see IV.38.

### IV.58–65. Peace in Sicily

**IV.58. Sicily:** the conclusion to Athens' intervention; the narrative is resumed from IV.25 and the last sentence of IV.48.

**their claims in respect of matters in which they considered they were**

**being unfairly treated:** individual complaints, but Hermocrates sees beyond these; see IV.60n.

**Hermocrates:** a prominent figure in Syracusan politics during the second, great Athenian expedition to Sicily, described by Th. in bks. VI–VII. He is accorded two further speeches (VI.33–34, 76–80), and Th. expresses his admiration for him at VI.72.

**the most influential of all:** more literally "he was the most persuasive"; cf. I.22n., III.36n. As is sometimes his practice, Th. records only the decisive speech.

**IV.59. not . . . as a representative of a city of minor importance:** thus Hermocrates stamps his authority on the debate.

**the best one for Sicily as a whole:** cf. IV.60n.

**no doubt we shall go to war again:** cf. the outbreak of squabbles between Peloponnesian allies during the armistice of 423 (IV.133–34) and, of course, (as an illustration of the temporary nature of political alliances) the realignments that followed the Peace of Nicias. Hermocrates, a true pragmatist, has a sound understanding of human behavior, based on an intelligent assessment of experience. In this speech he conforms to Pericles' definition of intelligence by "estimating what the facts are and thus obtaining a clearer vision of what to expect" (II.62). Cf. VI.72.

**IV.60. if we are sensible:** *sophrosyne* again, the essential virtue of the wise and moderate (I.32n.). The words are repeated at the opening of IV.61 and in IV.64 ("if we are wise").

**not simply concerned with the private interests of each state:** Hermocrates' recognition of the wider issues, his broader vision, is among the things that distinguish him from the other delegates, who, it seems (IV.58), could not see beyond the immediate interests of their own states.

**with a few ships:** Th. uses the same words of the original fleet (IV.24), but such a description hardly fits the reinforcement of forty vessels (III.115; IV.2, 48).

**by nature we must be their enemies:** not for racial reasons but because it is natural for the Athenians to wish to extend their power by further conquests; see the following chapter and I.76n.

**under the cover of a legal alliance:** see III.86.

**will attempt to bring all of us under their control:** Hermocrates has no doubt of Athens' present or ultimate intentions (cf. III.86). This may be a reference to the expedition of 415 but is not necessarily so.

**IV.61. internal strife:** stasis; see I.2n.

**the Dorians among us are enemies to the Athenians:** apart from

Camarina; see III.86. On the racial factor see I.124n., III.86n. But Hermocrates sees that the search for power overrides racial affinities. Cf. text later in this chapter, **Athenian intervention has nothing to do with the races into which we are divided.**

**the Chalcidians:** see III.86n. for their identity and links with Athens.

**For men in general it is always just as natural to take control:** a fundamental aspect of the behavior of states and a key theme of Th.'s work. Cf. I.76n., V.105.

**war . . . peace . . . good excuse for their evil ends . . . good reason to go away without having attained them:** the translation cannot convey the antitheses achieved by choice of words and the word order in the Gk. There are numerous others in this speech. Cf. I.32n.

**IV.62. That imponderable element of the future:** see I.120n. Cf. "an inscrutable future" (IV.63), "the dangers of the future . . . fortune, which is out of my control" (IV.64).

**IV.64. There will be occasions, no doubt, when we shall go to war again:** cf. IV.59n.

**IV.65. Morgantina:** its exact site is unknown but was inland near the east coast of Sicily, between Syracuse and Catana.

**banished two of the generals:** the Athenians were often vengeful against generals whose performance had displeased them; see II.65n.

**on the grounds that they had been bribed:** Th. has not mentioned bribery before and passes no comment on this allegation. On bribery in Athenian public life see II.60n.

**when it was in their power to have taken control of the island:** this was not the original intention of the expedition to Sicily (III.86), nor, as far as we can tell (III.115), the aim of the reinforcements.

**Such was the effect on the Athenians of their present good fortune that . . . their strength was equal with their hopes:** see I.121n. Th.'s words sound an ominous note. The Athenian' success undermines their sense of their own limitations, and the qualities by means of which they built the empire (noted by the Corinthians at I.70) are becoming the vices that will destroy it (as Pericles had feared). Cf. the atmosphere in Athens during the Sicilian debate of 415 (VI.24). Aristophanes' *Knights* displays a similar mood in Athens at this time (174, 1303). But the decline is not immediate: see, e.g, IV.73. The buoyant mood of Athens is in marked contrast to the low morale of Sparta (IV.55).

**whether the forces employed were large or wholly inadequate:** in Th.'s view the latter is clearly the case on this occasion. Even on occasions when the forces are adequate, as in the second, great expedition to Sicily (VI–VII), mismanagement results in failure.

IV.66–74. The Athenian Attack on Megara

**IV.66. The Megarians in the city of Megara:** as opposed to the exiles mentioned in the next sentence. This is the first time we have been told that the Athenians conducted two invasions each year of the Megarid, though Th. mentioned regular annual invasions following the first attack in 431 (II.31).

**exiles at Pegae who had been driven out in a revolution:** stasis; see I.2n. The exiles have not been previously mentioned. The Athenians are eager to exploit this internal dissension in the hope of regaining control of Megara, which occupied an important position on the Isthmus of Corinth (I.103n.). They had controlled it in the 450s and early 440s, during which time they built **the long walls** to Nisaea on the Saronic Gulf (I.103).

**Pegae:** the Megarian port on the Corinthian Gulf that had been surrendered by Athens to the Peloponnesians in 446 (I.115; cf. IV.21).

**the leaders of the democratic party . . . entered into negotiations with the Athenian generals:** following the general pattern outlined at the beginning of III.82.

**IV.67. Minoa:** occupied by Athens in 427 (III.51).

**Plataeans:** presumably from the 212 who escaped to Athens in the winter of 428/7 (III.20–24).

**Athenian home guards:** Gk. *peripoloi,* translated at VIII.92 as "the militia." They may have consisted largely of young men undergoing military training.

**the trophy:** presumably the one mentioned in IV.68 or IV.72. See I.30n.

**IV.68. by putting on a lot of olive oil:** not the clearest means of identification, one would have thought.

**IV.69. They started from the wall which they held:** the long walls, mentioned in IV.66.

**IV.70. Brasidas:** see II.25n., IV.81, and, on his Thracian campaign, IV.78ff. Aware of the strategic significance of Megara, he takes immediate action.

**all the troops of his own command that had already been enrolled:** see IV.80 (final sentence, with n.).

**IV.72. the Boeotians:** the seizure of the Megarid by the Athenians would leave them isolated by land from their Peloponnesian allies. They will have been aware of pro-Athenian activity within their own cities (IV.76) and may have feared an Athenian invasion, as in 457 (I.108).

**IV.73. They had already gained most of their objects:** not as they are described in IV.66. But the Athenians recognize that discretion is the better part of valor.

**IV.74. The Athenians also returned home:** though they left a garrison in Nisaea (IV.118).

**they were condemned and put to death:** the polarization of political parties that resulted in stasis often led to extremes of recrimination (cf. the case of Corcyra discussed at III.82–84, and on stasis in general see I.2n.). Th. does not say how long the new regime lasted.

**a revolution led by a very few people:** the extremists were, as often, few in number but powerful through terror.

## IV.75. Athenian Activity at Antandrus and in the Pontus

**the Mytilenians . . . Antandros:** see IV.52 (where the spelling is "Antandrus"), with n.

**the Athenian ships sent out to collect tribute:** see IV.50n.

**Lamachus:** satirized by Aristophanes in his *Acharnians,* he is the future joint general of the Sicilian expedition (VI.8).

**the Pontus:** the Black Sea; see III.2n.

**Anaia:** see III.19n.

**[IV.76].** The chapter number 76 is misplaced in the Penguin translation; it should immediately precede the paragraph beginning, **The same summer . . .**

**Heraclea:** on the southern shore of the Black Sea and, like **Chaldedon,** a Megarian colony.

**a sudden flow of water caused by floods in the upper country:** on Th.'s interest in natural phenomena see II.8n.

## IV.76–77. Athenian Plans for an Attack on Boeotia

**IV.76. Demosthenes:** his next initiative was an attack on Boeotia, an idea he had conceived earlier in the war (III.95). The scheme was bold, typical of Demosthenes' enterprising approach to the war. Despite a previous failure and Athenian inferiority on land, he believed that Athens should attempt to win the war, rather than to merely "win through" it (II.13n.), and that to do so, risks had to be taken. Strategically, Demosthenes' attack on Boeotia is a logical follow-up to his success in the Peloponnese and his recent attempt on Megara. If successful, it would deprive the Peloponnesians of a major ally (Hippocrates notes the Peloponnesian use of Boeotian cavalry at IV.95) and would further depress Spartan morale (cf. IV.55). It would also relieve Athens of pressure on its borders and give it access by land to its allies in the west.

**intriguing with him . . . and introducing a democracy:** again following the trend described in III.82.

**overthrowing the regime:** yet another example of stasis (I.2n.). The Boeotian confederacy, headed by Thebes, consisted of free and independent states that elected the Boeotarchs, the eleven Commanders of Boeotia, including two from Thebes (IV.91), who were the supreme executive government of Boeotia. See also V.38n.

**Orchomenus . . . Chaeronea:** Athenian acquisitions in the First Peloponnesian War (I.108, 113).

**Minyan:** the Minyae were ancient inhabitants of Boeotia.

**Delium:** its exact site is uncertain, but it was on the eastern side of Boeotia, near the border of Attica. **Tanagra** was the site of the great Athenian defeat in 457 (I.108).

**IV.77. Oeniadae:** "the only place in Acarnania which had always been anti-Athenian" (II.102).

**Salynthius and the Agraeans:** allies of the Ambraciots; see III.106, 111, 114.

The narrative of the Delium campaign is resumed at IV.89.

## IV.78–88. Brasidas' Expedition to Thrace

**IV.78.** Th. interrupts his narrative of the planned attack on Boeotia to return to Brasidas, who is himself planning a major offensive against Athens. Thus these two important campaigns are interwoven. The effect is to make the Athenian attack on Boeotia appear rather misguided and irrelevant. Demosthenes, absorbed in his own ambitious designs of conquest, fails to see the threat posed by Brasidas, who is allowed to slip through to the north. While the attempt on Boeotia flounders, Brasidas, unopposed, efficiently undermines Athenian power in a vital area.

**Brasidas was on his way to the Thracian area:** see IV.70, 74.

**1,700 hoplites:** helots and mercenaries raised by Brasidas himself; see IV.70, 80.

**Heraclea in Trachis:** the Spartan colony founded in 427; see III.92–93.

**Pharsalus:** the major town of central, southern Thessaly. Later in the chapter we are told that **Thessaly had always been on good terms with**

**Athens** (cf. II.22); thus Brasidas was accused of traveling there **without the consent of the whole people.** But locally the government was **in the hands of a powerful class,** clearly oligarchs and sympathetic to Sparta.

**Melitia in Achaea:** i.e., Achaea Phthiotis, south of Thessaly and separate from it but subject to it.

**official representative:** proxenos; see II.29n.

**the Chalcidians:** see IV.79.

**Larissa:** the major town of northern Thessaly.

**Perdiccas:** he had urged Peloponnesian intervention (IV.79). Brasidas would not find him easy to deal with (IV.83). See I.56n.

**if the local form of government had been democratic . . . Brasidas would never have been able to go forward:** suggesting a firm ideological division between the warring parties. Cf. III.82.

**the river Enipeus:** it flows from Achaea Phthiotis into central and northern Thessaly.

**he knew of no quarrel between Thessaly and Sparta:** though Thessaly was friendly with Athens; see n. earlier in this chapter.

**Phacius:** in northern Thessaly, en route to the Thessalian border with **Perrhaebia,** which was separate from but subject to Thessaly.

**IV.79. the Thracian towns in revolt from Athens:** for the original revolt of Chalcidice and Bottiaea from Athens, which occurred in 432 along with the Potidaean revolt, see I.58.

**his past differences with the Athenians:** see I.56n.

**Lyncestians:** Macedonian neighbors of Perdiccas; see II.99, IV.83.

**IV.80. now that the Athenians were making their attacks on the Peloponnese:** in the period after Pylos; see IV.53–57.

**these allies were prepared to supply the army:** though Perdiccas, disgruntled, later reneged in part on this agreement (IV.83).

**they feared a revolution:** as in 465 (I.101).

**(Spartan policy with regard to the helots had always been based . . . on the idea of security):** the helots vastly outnumbered the Spartans, who, since the conquest of Messenia (I.101n.), had adjusted their way of life to ensure mastery of their serf neighbors. Thus Sparta's famed political stability (I.18n., 70n.) is seen to be based at least in part on brutality.

**700 as hoplites:** after the campaign they were treated well; see V.34 and cf. I.101n.

**The rest of his army:** about 1,000, since the total was 1,700 (IV.78).

**mercenaries whom he had raised from the Peloponnese:** i.e., he was given no regular Peloponnesian troops, despite the potential of his expedition. See IV.70 for the raising of the army. The Spartan authorities seem to have been interested more in ridding themselves of troublesome helots than in providing Brasidas with suitable forces, and they gave him little support (IV.108).

**IV.81. a great reputation for energy:** in this and other ways (e.g., his oratorical ability: see IV.84) he was not a typical Spartan (on the Spartan character see I.70n.). Th. pauses in his narrative to compliment Brasidas, whom he much admires, on his personal qualities and his contribution to Sparta's eventual success in the war. Cf. IV.108.

**when Sparta wanted to make peace:** in 422/1 (V.14–18).

**places to offer in exchange for those held by Athens:** see the treaty at V.18.

**the Sicilian expedition:** of 415–413, recorded in bks. VI–VII. After Athens' failure there was widespread disaffection among its allies in the Aegean.

**gallantry:** Gk. *arete,* a wide-ranging complimentary term, translated elsewhere by Warner as "high principles," "virtue," and "ability"; in a military context it often means "courage." Th. also accords *arete* to the Pisistratids (VI.54), Nicias (VII.86), and Antiphon (VIII.68).

**wisdom:** Gk. *synesis,* elsewhere translated as "intelligence"; see I.79n.

**He was the first to be sent out in this way:** Th. seems to have forgotten the tactless intervention of Alcidas in the Aegean; see III.26ff.

**IV.84. Acanthus:** situated on the northeastern shore of the isthmus linking Acte with the mainland.

**just before the time of the vintage:** late August.

**two distinct parties:** Brasidas distinguishes between the few and the many in Acanthus at IV.86. The loyalty of the demos to Athens is an exception to Th.'s general remarks in II.8. See I.77n.

**their fears for their fruit:** Brasidas prefers persuasion, but diplomacy was clearly supported by intimidation. Vines and olives were two crops that thrived in the generally poor Greek soil (I.2n.), and the Greeks depended heavily on them. Cf. the trouble the Spartans took in 457 to cut down trees on their return from the battle of Tanagra (I.108) and Archidamus' attempted use of the Plataeans' fruit trees as hostages (II.72).

**He was not at all a bad speaker either, for a Spartan:** he also speaks at length; for an example of "Laconic brevity" see the speech of Sthenelaidas at I.86, and cf. IV.17: "It is certainly our way not to use many words when few are enough."

**IV.85. the cause which we proclaimed at the beginning of the war:** see II.8n.

**the war at home has taken an unexpected course:** the Spartans had anticipated a quick victory (V.14; cf. VII.28), though Archidamus had warned them that their calculations were subject to chance (I.84). See I.120–1nn.

**through a foreign country:** Thessaly; see IV.78.

**Yet it was this same army of mine which the Athenians . . . would not venture to attack when I went to the relief of Nisaea:** an "untrue but attractive" statement, says Th. (IV.108). The two forces were not the same, and Brasidas had been as reluctant to fight as the Athenians. See IV.70ff. for the relief of Nisaea.

**IV.86. independence:** Gk. *autonomia,* an imprecise term; see I.67n.

**in case I should put the city into the hands of some group or other:** oligarchs, no doubt. The Spartans were known for installing pro-Spartan oligarchies where they could (I.19). Cf. the recent case of Megara, where the process had been accompanied by a massacre of the pro-Athenian element (IV.74).

**to enslave either the many to the few or the few to the many:** the two distinct parties of IV.84. The second of these alternatives seems particularly unlikely: as usual (III.82), the few, rather than the many, had called in the Spartans.

**IV.87. I shall call upon the gods and heroes of your country:** as Archidamus did before he laid siege to Plataea (II.74).

**I came here to help you:** "the very voice of empire-builders," comments Gomme. These words are immediately followed by a threat of force.

**two good reasons:** the first (and thus more pressing?) being the immediate interest of Sparta.

**the good of one and all alike:** in Sparta's view, of course. There was no unanimity even among the Acanthians about what their good was (IV.84).

**IV.88. voted by ballot:** the democratic process flourishes in Acanthus; this may account in part for its attachment to Athens.

**they made Brasidas pledge his own word:** the Acanthians remain mistrustful of his rhetoric, though they are convinced by his threats. Had they heard of events at Megara?

## IV.89–101. The Delium Campaign

**IV.89. Delium:** the account of the Delium campaign is now resumed from IV.76–77. The time is November 424.

**IV.90. resident aliens:** metics, originally to be used for defense only (II.13n.). They and the **foreigners** were presumably included to speed up the fortification of Delium. Many members of this force were not armed for fighting (IV.94).

**he . . . began to fortify Delium:** the policy of *epiteichismos;* see I.122n. See IV.76 for the intended role of Delium in the Athenian plans.

**the temple:** Athenian actions constitute sacrilege, according to the Boeotians (IV.97); for the Athenian defense see IV.98. Cf. I.24n.

**IV.91. the eleven Commanders of Boeotia:** or Boeotarchs; see IV.76n.

**Oropus:** in Athenian territory; see IV.99.

**IV.92. it is your tradition to fight a foreign army of invasion:** the Medism of the Boeotians in 480 is conveniently forgotten.

**Euboea:** an Athenian possession for some time. For its revolt and suppression by Pericles in 446 see I.114.

**how most of the rest of Hellas felt about Athens:** but see I.77n.

**while others fight battles with their neighbours for one frontier or another:** see I.15n.

**Coronea:** for the earlier Athenian occupation of Boeotia and the battle of Coronea that brought it to an end see I.108, 113.

**our internal quarrels:** stasis; see I.2n.

**the older ones . . . the younger ones:** on the distinction cf. II.8n.

**the god whose temple they have unlawfully fortified:** Apollo; see IV.76, 90.

**IV.93. peltasts:** see II.29n.

**the lake:** Lake Copais in central Boeotia.

**twenty-five shields deep:** to give the phalanx greater weight and solidity.

**IV.94. On the Athenian side the hoplites were drawn up eight deep:** the standard formation.

**nor did Athens possess any:** i.e., there was no official light-armed force in the Athenian army. Thus there is no mention of them at II.13; see n. there.

**IV.95. without the support of the Boeotian cavalry:** their part in the first Peloponnesian invasion of Attica is mentioned in II.22. The Peloponnesians had not invaded Attica since the Pylos campaign.

**Oenophyta . . . Myronides . . . masters of Boeotia:** see I.108.

**IV.96. the coming on of night:** which would put an end to the fighting; cf. II.4n.

**IV.97. delivered his message:** the lengthy exchanges that followed the battle illustrate some conventions of Greek warfare—and show how the combatants might attempt to exploit them to their advantage.

**the Athenians, however, had fortified Delium:** see IV.90n.

**IV.98. Hellenic law:** or rather, custom as traditionally accepted by all Greeks.

**the altars of the gods were the refuge:** see I.24n.

**as for the dead bodies, the Boeotian attitude was a great deal more irreligious than the Athenian . . . what was theirs by right:** to recover one's dead under a truce after a battle was a long-established and civilized custom of Greek warfare. Th. perhaps saw this deterioration of mutual respect as further evidence of a general decline in standards of behavior during the war.

**IV.100. javelin throwers and slingers:** i.e., specialist troops, but they do not seem to have been required; nor were the reinforcements of hoplites. Greeks generally had little confidence in their abilities in siege warfare.

**the Malian Gulf:** the large gulf north of western Boeotia, facing the northwestern tip of Euboea.

**the Peloponnesian garrison which had left Nisaea:** see IV.69.

**an engine constructed in the following manner:** Th. is very interested in the type of device described in this chapter; cf. his account of the siege of Plataea, II.75–77.

**IV.101. Sitalces:** see II.95–101.

## IV.102–8. Brasidas Captures Amphipolis

**IV.102. Brasidas:** the story of his northern campaign is resumed from IV.88.

**Amphipolis:** its strategic value for Athens lay in the fact that it controlled the only point in the area at which the Strymon could be crossed (IV.103, 108).

**Aristagoras:** instigator of the revolt of Ionia against Persia in 499; see Hdt. V.11, 124–26.

**Darius:** the king of Persia, who was advancing Persian frontiers westward at the time of the Ionian revolt.

**Thirty-two years after:** in 465; see I.100 for the disaster at **Drabescus.**

**Twenty-nine years afterwards:** a more accurate translation would be "in the twenty-ninth year," i.e., 437/6.

**Hagnon:** see II.58n.

**Eion:** cf. I.98n.

**called Amphipolis . . . because it was surrounded on two sides by the**

**river:** i.e., that is what the Gk. name means, though in fact the river was on three sides of the town.

**it was a conspicuous sight:** the town was built on a hilltop.

**IV.103. Arnae:** site unknown.

**Bromiscus:** some eighteen miles from Amphipolis.

**Argilus:** its site is uncertain. There were clearly divisions in the politics of the city, and some citizens had left for Amphipolis.

**The bridge was only lightly guarded:** a criticism of Eucles? The bridge was crucial, but we are told nothing about the number of troops available to Eucles.

**IV.104. the citizens [of Amphipolis] themselves were mistrustful of each other:** as a consequence of civil dissension. Cf. IV.106.

**It is even said that Brasidas would probably have taken the city there and then:** Th. is not prepared to vouch for this probability. It is perhaps intended to suggest that even if Th. had been at Eion he could not have saved Amphipolis if Brasidas had acted quickly.

**Eucles, the general from Athens who was there to defend the place:** further criticism of Eucles?

**Thucydides, the son of Olorus:** By using the third person (cf. I.1) and giving his father's name, as if he were talking about any Athenian, Th. conveys detachment and objectivity. But modern commentators have traced elements of self-defense in his account of the fall of Amphipolis. See in particular Westlake 1969, 123–37.

**Olorus:** see my introduction, under "The Life of Thucydides." Th.'s wealth and status in the area are noted in the next chapter.

**the author of this history:** literally "who wrote these things"; on the word *history* see I.1n.

**who was then at the island of Thasos:** why? What was he doing there? Why was he not at Eion? He does not say. He may have had genuine (i.e., Athenian, not personal) business in Thasos, but he would have known about the activities of Brasidas and should have been on hand. This was later the view of the Athenians (V.26), though we cannot always rely on their judgment in such matters (II.65n.). Th. was probably as surprised by the arrival of Brasidas as were the inhabitants of Amphipolis.

**about half a day's sail from Amphipolis:** optimistic. It may be that Th. is understating the sailing time between Thasos and Amphipolis, a distance of about fifty miles, thus implying that he could reach Amphipolis more quickly than he actually could.

**As soon as he heard the news:** presumably by some sort of signaling system.

**he set sail at once:** cf. IV.106n., **If the ships had not arrived so quickly.**

**the seven ships that he had with him:** a surprisingly small force, though his duties may have been only supervisory.

**IV.105. Brasidas . . . was alarmed . . . heard that Thucydides . . . had great influence . . . fearing that, once Thucydides had arrived, the people of Amphipolis would be confident . . . He therefore put forward very moderate terms:** an interesting attribution of feelings, expectations, and motives, reflecting well on Th.'s influence in Amphipolis.

**the gold-mines:** see I.100n.

**IV.106. late:** we are not told exactly when he set out and thus how long the voyage took; but Th. is careful to say that he arrived **on the same day.**

**If the ships had not arrived so quickly:** Th. is constrained to acknowledge Brasidas' tactical and diplomatic superiority but again makes the point that he arrived quickly and only a few hours too late and, of course, that he succeeded in saving Eion.

**IV.107. After this Thucydides organized the defence of Eion to keep it safe:** thus Th. diverts the reader's attention from his failure to save Amphipolis and contrasts his own success at Eion with Eucles' failure at Amphipolis—or is this taking suspicion of Th.'s motives too far? He is surely obliged to record what he did; otherwise he would leave the account incomplete.

**a number of boats:** clearly not triremes, but presumably fishing or merchant vessels acquired locally.

**Myrcinus:** northeast of Amphipolis. We know nothing more of the internal squabbles of this kingdom.

**Galepsus and Oesime:** on the mainland, west of Thasos.

**Perdiccas:** he had recently quarreled with Brasidas (IV.83) but is keen to cooperate with him following his latest achievement.

**IV.108. The place was . . . useful:** only now, after its loss, does Th. comment on the value of Amphipolis to Athens; cf. IV.102n.

**it supplied timber for ship-building:** the soil of Attica was too poor to grow trees suitable for shipbuilding; cf. VI.90n., VII.25, VIII.1n.

**provided that they got an escort from the Thessalians:** as Brasidas had done, though not without difficulty; see IV.78.

**Brasidas was behaving with great moderation:** further praise from Th. of this exceptional Spartan commander; cf. IV.81.

**wishful thinking . . . calculation . . . hope . . . reason:** on the contrast between desire and reason see I.121n.

**the Athenians had just been defeated in Boeotia:** see IV.89–101.

**the untrue, but attractive, statement of Brasidas:** see IV.85n.

**the pleasurable excitement of the moment:** see II.65n., **adopted methods of demagogy.**

**it looked for the first time as though they were going to find the Spartans acting with real energy:** cf. the Corinthian assessment of Spartan character at I.70.

**in winter:** military operations were normally kept to a minimum during the bad weather of the winter months (II.1n.), but this was an emergency.

**Brasidas sent messengers to Sparta asking for another army:** a reasonable request, given his successes and prospects. He had raised his force of 1,700 himself (IV.70, 80).

**the building of triremes on the Strymon:** the logical but ambitious next step after Brasidas' successes. Nothing came of it.

**The Spartans, however, did nothing for him . . . their leading men were jealous of him:** though they are happy enough to take advantage of his achievements (cf. IV.117). For possible Spartan suspicion of Brasidas see IV.132n. Again Th. seems privy to Spartan feelings and motives; see V.26.

IV.109–16. Brasidas in Chalcidice

**IV.109. the Megarians recaptured their Long Walls:** for their seizure by the Athenians see IV.69.

**Acte:** the most easterly peninsula of Chalcidice, about forty miles long and very rugged, especially toward **Athos,** at its end.

**the King of Persia's canal:** cut by Xerxes to facilitate the movement of his forces round the Aegean during his invasion of 480. See Hdt. VII.22–25.

**Pelasgian:** see I.3n.

**of the Tyrrhenian race:** the Tyrrheni or Tyrseni were, like the Pelasgi, probably early inhabitants of the northern Aegean area; at some stage they migrated to Etruria in Italy and became identified with the Etruscans.

**Bisaltians, Crestonians and Edonians:** cf. II.99–100. See also, on Edonians, I.100; IV.102, 107.

**IV.110. Torone:** the chief city of the middle peninsula, Sithonia, at its southern end.

**A few people there:** Th. again (cf. the case of Acanthus discussed at IV.84) makes it clear that it was only a minority of the inhabitants who wished to betray the city to Sparta. Cf. I.77n.

**Dioscuri:** Castor and Pollux, twin sons of Zeus and Leda.

**Twenty men had originally been detailed . . . but only these seven . . . had the courage to enter:** Th. often uses precise details such as these to dramatize an episode.

**Canastraeum:** the extreme point of Pallene, the most westerly of the three Chalcidic peninsulas.

**IV.114. they had not aimed at enslaving the city:** the word *enslaving* (Gk. *douleia*) is not to be taken literally; see I.98n.

**nor had they taken bribes:** on bribery cf. II.60n.

**had acted entirely for the good of Torone:** cf. Brasidas' words to the Acanthians, "I came here to help you" (IV.87n.).

**from now on they would be held responsible for anything done amiss:** as at Acanthus (IV.85–87), Brasidas follows an unexpectedly generous offer with an ominous note of warning.

**IV.116. thirty silver minae:** i.e., three thousand drachmae or half a talent, a surprisingly large sum to be offered to a single soldier for such an action. It would have been the equivalent of three thousand days' pay. The text may be corrupt at this point (as is often the case with numbers, since Greek writers used a system of letters and symbols that can easily be confused). For the Greek monetary system see the Penguin translation, app. 2, pp. 612–13.

## IV.117–19. The Truce of 423/2

**IV.117. an armistice for one year:** as in the period just before the Peace of Nicias in 421 (V.14), each side is disappointed with its achievements in the war so far and anxious to recoup its losses. Neither side will be satisfied with the results of the armistice.

**They were particularly anxious to get back the men:** i.e., the men captured on Pylos. This is the main Spartan priority at the moment, despite the possibilities to which Brasidas' success had given rise.

**IV.118. With regard to . . . :** this is clearly a record of the original document. How, where, and when Th. had access to it, especially as he was in exile by now, is unknown. See IV.122n.

**the temple and the oracle of the Pythian Apollo:** at Delphi. It was customary to begin a treaty with a clause establishing religious freedom (cf. V.18).

**those who have been guilty in respect of this treasure:** the plundering of the treasures (that is presumably what it is) is not referred to elsewhere.

**Coryphasium:** the Peloponnesian name for Pylos (IV.3). **Buphras** and **Tomeus** are unknown.

**Cythera:** occupied by Athens in 424; see IV.54, 57.

**Nisaea . . . Minoa:** see III.51; IV.69, 73, 109. The sites of **the temple of Nisus** and **the temple of Poseidon** are unknown.

**the Athenians are to retain the island:** the island is unidentified; there may be a fault in the text.

**the territory of Troezen:** we know nothing of the agreement made between Athens and Troezen, whose territory had been raided by Athens (IV.45).

**all heralds and embassies:** cf. I.29n.

**arbitration:** see I.28n.

**prytany:** the Council of Five Hundred at Athens (or the boule, the executive committee of the assembly: see Rhodes 1972) was made up of fifty men from each of the ten tribes. Each tribal group served as prytaneis, presiding officers, of the boule for one-tenth of the year (a prytany).

**the fourteenth of the month:** the date of the agreement is given according to the Athenian calendar here and in Spartan terms in chapter 119. In terms of the Julian calendar it would have been March or April 423.

**IV.119. a more general settlement:** this treaty was seen as a preliminary to a permanent agreement. This would, of course, involve an abandonment by the Spartans of their mission to liberate Greece from Athens.

## IV.120–28. The Campaigns of Brasidas Continued

**IV.120. Pallene:** the westernmost of the three Chalcidic peninsulas.

**The Scionaeans say that they come from Pellene:** note Th.'s antiquarian interest in the origins of cities (cf. IV.109, as well as the early chapters of bks. I and VI.).

**he would do them honour in every way:** but he will not protect them from a dire punishment at the hands of the Athenians (V.32).

**IV.121. The people of Scione were greatly heartened . . . a general feeling of confidence:** the people of Scione believe what they want to believe; cf. I.121n.

**IV.122. the commissioners who were carrying round the news of the armistice:** it was perhaps from these commissioners that Th. obtained details of the agreement.

**on the motion of Cleon:** cf. his speech on the Mytilenian rebels at III.37–40. Is this motion further evidence of "the violence of his character" (III.36)?

**IV.123. those in Mende who were working with Brasidas were few in number:** once again only a minority wished to revolt from Athens. Cf. the case of Acanthus discussed at IV.84 and that of Torone discussed at IV.110.

**IV.124. a second expedition . . . against Arrhabaeus:** for the first, which had resulted in a quarrel between the allies, see IV.83. Perdiccas was clearly still of the opinion that Brasidas' function was "to destroy those enemies whom he, Perdiccas, pointed out" (IV.83), and he was able to put pressure on Brasidas to cooperate, perhaps by reducing even further his support for his army (IV.83, final sentence).

**the Hellenes living in Macedonia:** the Macedonians were not Hellenes (cf. I.2n.), but many of the coastal cities were Hellenic foundations.

**the Illyrian mercenaries:** Illyria was northwest of Macedonia, toward the Adriatic coast.

**IV.125. one of those irrational panics:** panic is a frequent feature of battles in Th., especially at night. See II.4n.

**IV.126. Peloponnesians:** though the majority of his forces were not Peloponnesians but northern allies (IV.124).

**barbarian:** i.e., non-Greek. At the core of this speech is a Greek contempt for the disorderliness and indiscipline of foreigners; cf. I.5–6nn. The Spartans in particular prided themselves on their military prowess and discipline.

**you who come from states where it is not the many who rule the few, but rather the other way about, and where to fight and conquer has been the one and only basis of national power:** a translation based on a reading that has been emended on the assumption that Brasidas is referring to Spartan-style oligarchies. The text as it stands is translated as follows by Gomme: "for you do not at all come from states in which not many rule a few, but a few the many, having won their mastery [Gk. *dynasteia*] by military prowess." Gomme argues that Brasidas is referring to the situation among the enemy where narrow dynasties (*dynasteia* is a term of disapproval; cf. III.62) rule unwilling and largely unenfranchised subjects.

**IV.128. they unyoked and slaughtered . . . cattle:** the Peloponnesians are disciplined at first but can match non-Greeks for barbarity when pushed. Brasidas' words in the preceding chapter now appear somewhat hollow.

**a panic-stricken retreat by night:** see IV.125n.

**Perdiccas began to regard Brasidas as an enemy:** see I.56n., IV.132.

### IV.129–32. Athens' Response to Brasidas' Successes

**IV.129. Chios:** perhaps expected to demonstrate its loyalty after its recent suspicious behavior (IV.51).

**Nicias . . . and Nicostratus:** as at Cythera; see IV.53. On Nicias see III.51n.

**Methone:** for its special relationship with Athens see *T.D.G.R.* 128.

**IV.130. Indeed, the generals found it difficult:** like Brasidas' troops, who killed Macedonian cattle (IV.128), the Athenian rank and file need to satisfy their lust for vengeance. The generals offer generous terms to the people of Mende, perhaps recognizing that most of them had not supported the revolt (IV.123); they are also anxious to keep Mende loyal so that they can concentrate on Scione.

**IV.132. Perdiccas . . . the retreat from Lyncus:** see IV.128.

**they brought with them from Sparta . . . some quite young men . . . as governors of the cities:** it was clearly customary to confer such senior positions on older men. There was perhaps a shortage of suitable men because the prisoners from Pylos were detained in Athens. This is the first time we read of any Spartan governors for the cities that have rebelled from Athens, and their appointment seems to conflict with the autonomy promised to the cities by Brasidas (e.g., IV.86): more explanation is needed.

**so that this task should not have to be entrusted to the people available on the spot:** were Ischagoras and his men sent out to support Brasidas or to keep an eye on him and prevent him from acquiring too much personal power? Perhaps the latter: see IV.108n., **The Spartans however did nothing for him.**

## IV.133–34. Events in Boeotia and the Peloponnese

**IV.133. They had always wanted to do this:** just as they had long cast envious eyes on Plataea, whose destruction they eventually secured. They are, of course, doing no more than what in Th.'s view is natural, to rule wherever one can.

**the flower of Thespian youth had fallen in the battle with the Athenians:** IV.96. The Thebans see this not as a reason to be grateful to the Thespians for their sacrifice but as an opportunity to be exploited.

**the temple of Hera at Argos was burnt down:** an odd inclusion. **Chrysis** was also mentioned at II.2.

**IV.134. the Mantineans and Tegeans:** allies in the Peloponnesian War, of course, but during the armistice, like Thebes and Thespiae, they have time to pursue a private squabble. On Tegea see V.32n.

## IV.135. Brasidas at Potidaea

**Brasidas moved again and tried to seize Potidaea:** a breach of the truce by Brasidas, as was his reception of Mende and Scione. He claimed that the Athenians had been the first to break the agreement (IV.123).

# Book Five

## V.1. Further Purification of Delos

**up to the Pythian Games:** these took place in July/August, but the armistice had been concluded in March/April of the previous year for a year. It looks as if some words have dropped out of the text. Either the treaty was renewed for a shorter period on its expiry, or perhaps hostilities did not restart until some time after its expiry.

**Delos:** see I.8n., 96n.

**the previous ceremony of purification:** see III.104. Th. has no details of the **crime committed in the past,** possibly some offense in connection with rituals, but it produced among the population a **state of pollution,** i.e., a defilement resulting from some crime or impiety, for which atonement had to be made through fulfillment of a ritual obligation. For the moment the Delians were compelled to leave the island, but later they would be restored (V.32).

**Pharnaces:** the Persian governor, or satrap (I.115n.), of the Hellespontine region.

**Atramyttium:** on the Gulf of Atramyttium, facing the northeast corner of Lesbos.

## V.2–3. Cleon in Chalcidice

**V.2. Cleon got his way:** he had been eager for some time to punish the rebels in the north (IV.122), but Nicias had been responsible for the first stage of this important operation (IV.129).

**V.3. the Athenians from the ships had taken Torone:** Cleon's first action is a considerable success, but Th.'s description is perhaps rather cool. Brasidas' late arrival is not unlike that of Th. at Amphipolis (IV.106).

**they made slaves of the wives and children:** cf. III.68n. The punishment of Torone is much more severe than that of Mende (IV.130). Cf. the cases of Scione (V.32) and Melos (V.116).

**when peace was made:** see V.17–20.

**Panactum:** its precise site is uncertain. Its return will later be required by the Peace of Nicias (V.18), but the Boeotians will refuse to give it up (V.35ff.).

V.4–5. Further Athenian Involvement in Sicily

**V.4. the general agreement:** of 424; see IV.65.

**Leontini:** see I.36n., III.86n.

**the democratic party . . . The governing classes:** stasis (I.2n.) in the cities of Sicily continues; passions are so high (as is typical of internecine war: see III.82) that the governing classes prefer to see their city disappear than to consent to a **redistribution of the land.** It was in the Athenians' interests to maintain their influence in the west, in both Sicily and southern Italy (V.5), if they still had visions of conquering the island (cf. III.86, IV.65, VI.1).

**Camarina:** Dorian, but friendly to Athens (III.86, VI.5). **Gela** had been an enemy of Athens, **Catana** a friend.

**V.5. Locrian:** see III.86n.

**party strife:** stasis; see I.2n.

**Messina:** previously an Athenian ally; see IV.1.

V.6–13. Cleon and Brasidas at Amphipolis

**V.6. Eion:** a trading post at the mouth of the Strymon; see IV.102.

**Stagirus . . . Galepsus:** for their defection to Brasidas see IV.88, 107.

**Perdiccas:** see I.56n. and, for his alliance with Athens, IV.132.

**V.7. Inactivity made the soldiers discontented:** implying that Cleon could not control his men? Cf. IV.4, though here the soldiers' boredom is put to constructive use.

**the comparison between the daring and skill of Brasidas and the incompetence and weakness of their own commander:** Brasidas is depicted as the superior tactician in these chapters and as the master of his opponent. The reader must be cautious: is this depiction entirely fair? See III.36n. and cf. V.10, 16.

**they had been unwilling enough to follow even when they left home:** we would like more details, but Th. does not offer them.

**He was in the same confident frame of mind:** how did Th. know his frame of mind? Cf. IV.18n.

**at Pylos, where his success had convinced him of his intelligence:** the episode in which Cleon had captured the Spartiates isolated on Sphacteria in 425; see IV.2–40.

**V.8. he lacked confidence:** Cleon was overconfident, while Brasidas was aware of his own limitations.

**the Lemnians and the Imbrians:** see III.5n.

**made the following speech:** on prebattle speeches see II.10n. Cleon is accorded no parallel speech.

**V.9. Dorians about to fight with Ionians:** see I.124n. on the racial distinction.

**V.10. the Thracian Gates:** at the northeast corner of the town; **the first gate,** mentioned later in this chapter, was in the southeast. Both gates were in the long wall that defended the eastern side of Amphipolis.

**he did not wish to risk a general battle until his reinforcements arrived:** is this a sign of confidence?

**making it wheel round, and so exposing its unarmed side to the enemy:** the translation "unprotected" or "unshielded" would be clearer than "unarmed." Since the soldiers carried their shields on their left arms, as they swung to the left their right side was exposed to the enemy. Cf. V.71n.

**Here he [Brasidas] was wounded . . . Cleon himself had no intention of standing his ground:** Brasidas dies fighting, while Cleon dies running away. Again Th. claims to know what is going on in Cleon's mind.

**killed by a Myrcinian peltast:** the detail highlights the ignominy of Cleon's death. A peltast was a lightly armed soldier.

**V.11. Hagnon:** see II.58n.

**About 600 of the Athenians had fallen . . . the unforseen panic-ridden affair:** Th. notes the discrepancy in numbers of casualties and passes judgment on the battle in scathing terms—to support his condemnation of Cleon?

**V.12. Ramphias:** see I.139.

**Heraclea:** the Spartan foundation in Trachis (III.92).

**V.13. The Thessalians:** friends of Athens who had been far from happy about the passage of Brasidas through their territory (IV.78).

**Spartan opinion was, in fact, in favour of peace:** see V.15n.

V.14–19. The Peace of Nicias

**V.14. a serious blow at Delium:** in 424/3, a turning point in the Archidamian War. See IV.89–101.

**the . . . confidence . . . to reject previous offers of peace:** in 425, after Pylos (IV.21, 41).

**in the belief that their good fortune . . . would carry them through to final victory:** wishful thinking once again; see I.121n. Athenian overconfidence is noted by Th. at IV.65.

**they regretted that they had not seized upon the excellent opportunity of making peace after Pylos:** it was Cleon who had urged the rejection of peace proposals after Pylos, which is now mentioned specifically, perhaps to remind the reader of what now appears to have been a serious error; cf. V.15n.

**The Spartans . . . had found that the war had gone very differently from what they had imagined:** at the beginning of the war a quick Spartan victory had been widely expected (VII.28), though not by the shrewd Archidamus, who saw that such expectations were based on hope rather than on calculation (I.81).

**simply by laying waste her land:** cf. I.81n., II.10n.

**The disaster suffered on the island:** the loss of the Spartiates on Sphacteria in 425; see IV.2ff.

**Cythera:** for its capture by Athens see IV.53.

**helots:** for their desertion and the fear of revolution, as in 465 (I.101), see IV.41.

**the thirty years' truce between Sparta and Argos:** not mentioned earlier. For Argos' relations with Sparta and Argive neutrality in the war cf. V.22, 28, 36, 40.

**Cynuria:** a region on the borders of Spartan and Argive territory, about which there had been constant disputes (V.41). The Spartans had handed it over to the population of Aegina after they had been expelled from their homes by the Athenians (II.27, IV.56).

**some of the states in the Peloponnese had the intention of going over to Argos, as indeed they did:** see V.29.

**V.15. Sparta had begun to negotiate directly after their capture, but the Athenians . . . would not listen to any reasonable proposals:** Th.'s view of the rejection of peace proposals urged by Cleon. The recovery of the Spartiates had been Sparta's overriding concern throughout the campaign of Brasidas (IV.108, 117).

**the Athenians were then doing so well:** see IV.41, 65.

**the defeat at Delium:** see V.14n.

**the armistice for one year:** in 423; see IV.117–18.

**V.16. the two people who on each side had been most opposed to peace:** having dealt with motives for peace based on national considerations, Th. now turns to the personal motives of the leaders on either side. The clear implication of his comments on these men—whether, like Cleon and Brasidas, they were in favor of war, or, like Nicias and Pleistoanax, against it—is that powerful individuals used their influence to bring state policy into line with their private interests. And yet there can be little doubt that, e.g., Cleon and Brasidas supported war on the grounds of (perceived) national as well as personal interests. Moreover, it is difficult to see how Th. could be certain of the personal motives he ascribes to these characters. But he often illustrates the influence of private ambition on public policy. Cf. his comments on Pericles' successors at II.65 and on the motives of Alcibiades at V.43 and VIII.47.

**Brasidas because of the success and honour which had come to him:** again, how did Th. know? He has previously shown admiration for Brasidas and made it clear that his northern campaign gave new life to the Spartan war effort.

**Cleon . . . his slander of others:** Th. perhaps has Nicias (IV.27) and probably himself (V.26n.) in mind. On his hostility to Cleon cf. III.36n.; V.7, 10.

**Nicias . . . who had done better in his commands than anyone else of his time:** a personal judgment that should be seen in the context of Th.'s deep respect for Nicias (III.51n.).

**Nicias wished to rest upon his laurels, to find an immediate release from toil and trouble both for himself and his fellow citizens . . . He thought that these ends were to be achieved by avoiding all risks and by trusting oneself as little as possible to fortune:** hence his opposition to the Sicilian expedition and his unsuitability as its commander. Cf. the cautious tone of his speeches in the debate, VI.9–14, 20–23.

**Pleistoanax:** for his abortive invasion of Attica in 446 see I.114n., and for his exile and restoration see II.21.

**he . . . had bribed the priestess:** on bribery cf. II.60n.

**the demigod son of Zeus:** Heracles, from whom the Spartan royal houses claimed descent.

**he had built half of his house inside the grounds of the temple of Zeus:** for sanctuary; cf. I.24n.

**Lycaeum:** in Arcadia, near the Laconian border.

**their kings:** see I.18n.

**the time of the foundation of Sparta:** the date is (of course) unknown. Homer talks of Lacedaemon, ruled by Menelaus, and archaeology has demonstrated that there was a settlement on the site of Sparta in the Mycenaean period, which was destroyed ca. 1200. This will have been followed at some stage by the settlement of Dorian Sparta. The Spartan king lists went back to ca. 900 or a little earlier.

**V.17. during a state of war those in the highest position must necessarily get blamed for every misfortune:** cf. II.65n.

**building permanent fortifications in Attica:** the policy of *epiteichismos;* see I.122n. From such fortifications the Peloponnesians could continually raid the Attic countryside and thus force the Athenians either to come out to battle or to stay permanently in the city. The idea was not put into effect until 413 (VII.19).

**Nisaea . . . Plataea:** see III.52, IV.69. The surrender of neither could be described as **an agreement reached freely.**

**the Boeotians, the Corinthians, the Eleans, and the Megarians, who were opposed to what was being done:** the reasons why these Spartan allies refused to accept the peace are not given now but emerge from the narrative of events following the treaty. These are powerful and important members of the Peloponnesian League, and their unwillingness to accept the terms of the treaty negotiated by Sparta bodes ill for its success.

**V.18. With regard to the Panhellenic temples:** the opening of the treaty bears a strong resemblance to the opening of the armistice of 423 (IV.118), though the scope of the latter is limited to Delphi. On this occasion religious freedom throughout Greece is established at the beginning of the agreement.

**At Delphi the consecrated ground and the temple of Apollo and the Delphians . . . shall be governed by their own laws:** in an effort to establish their neutrality; Delphi had been pro-Spartan in the Archidamian War (I.118).

**The Spartans and their allies are to give back . . . :** the clauses concerning the status of Athens' former allies are confusing, perhaps because of some corruption of the text. **Amphipolis** is dealt with individually because of its uniqueness (it paid no tribute) and its importance to Athens (IV.108). There then seems to be a class of unnamed cities that are accorded certain privileges, though they are to be returned to Athens. A final group of cities are to be allies of neither side. These appear to be identified as **Argilus, Stagirus,** and **Acanthus,** which had all gone over to Brasidas during his northern campaign; **Scolus,** not mentioned elsewhere by Th.; and **Olynthus** and **Spartolus** (Chalcidian and Bottiaean, respectively), which had revolted from Athens in 432 (I.58). They are now to return to the status of tribute-paying members of the Delian League, though they are not to be military allies of Athens unless they so wish.

**the tribute fixed by Aristides:** see I.96, 99. This would have been lower than later assessments, especially the major reassessment of 425 (IV.50n.).

**independent:** Gk. *autonomous;* see I.67n.

**Mecybernaeans . . . and Singaeans:** not mentioned elsewhere by Th.

**Sanaeans:** Sane is mentioned once, briefly (IV.109), but this reference does not explain the city's inclusion in the treaty.

**Panactum:** for its capture by the Boeotians see V.3. They will refuse to give it up (V.35ff.).

**Coryphasium:** a local name for Pylos; see IV.3.

**Cythera:** see IV.53.

**Methana:** see IV.45.

**Ptelium:** not mentioned elsewhere by Th.; site unknown.

**Atalanta:** see II.32, III.89.

**Scione:** see IV.120–22, V.32.

**Torone:** see V.3.

**Sermyle:** not mentioned since I.65.

**With regard to . . . any other cities in Athenian hands, the Athenians may act as they think fit:** apart from some halfhearted efforts on behalf of a few of Athens' subject-allies, the Spartans' abandonment of the Greeks they set out to liberate is absolute.

**Olympia, Pythia, the Isthmus:** Panhellenic centers and sites of major Greek festivals. Pythia is Delphi.

**Amyclae:** see V.23n.

The reference in the treaty to a number of places not mentioned in Th.'s narrative suggests perhaps that he did not have a copy of the treaty before him when he wrote the history of this period and that, when he later got hold of one, he did not have the time (or the inclination) to rewrite the relevant portions of his narrative to remove the anomalies.

**V.19. the 27th day of the month . . . :** the date of the treaty is given in precise terms, both Athenian and Spartan, as one would expect. Each Greek state had its own method of dating; see II.2n.

**Those who took the oath:** since this is a copy of an agreement between Athens and Sparta the signatories are Athenians and Spartans. Similar agreements will have been made between Athens and those Peloponnesian states prepared to accept the terms.

## V.20. A Note on Chronology

**the City festival of Dionysus:** the major Athenian dramatic festival, held in March, in honor of Dionysus, the god of wine, festivity, and the tragic art. Most new tragedies and comedies were introduced on this occasion. Indeed, Greek drama had developed from the dithyrambic choruses sung at the festival of Dionysus. There was also a rural festival of Dionysus, held in December.

**just ten years, with the difference of a few days, after the first invasion of Attica and the beginning of the war:** Th.'s calculations on the length of the Archidamian War do not tally. The first invasion of Attica took place "at midsummer, when the corn was ripe" (II.19). The Peace of Nicias was made "at the very end of winter and the beginning of spring." The Archidamian War would thus appear to have lasted a few months less than ten years. It has been suggested that the words "the first invasion of Attica and" should be removed from the text and that the expression "the beginning of the war" should be taken to refer to the Theban attack on Plataea, which also took place "at the beginning of spring" (II.2)—a forced solution but the only way in which the difficulty can be resolved. But see II.2n., 19n., where Th. seems to regard the invasion as the beginning of the war and the attack on Plataea as happening in peacetime.

**any reckoning based on the names of magistrates in the various cities:** cf. II.2n.

**summers and winters . . . each of these being equivalent to half a year:** though campaigning took place over a longer period, roughly March to October. Cf. II.1n., V.26.

## V.21–22. The Aftermath of the Peace

**V.21. Ischagoras . . . Clearidas:** see IV.132.

**Philocharidas:** cf. V.44.

**V.22. those of them who had not accepted the treaty:** Boeotia, Corinth, Elis, Megara; see V.17.

**The Spartans . . . proceeded to form an alliance with Athens:** the reader is taken aback by the rapid pace of events and their irony: what better example could one have of the unpredictable element in politics and warfare (I.120n.)? Th. describes Sparta's motives for making an alliance, but not those of Athens.

**Lichas:** a famous and wealthy Spartiate; see also V.50, 76; VIII.39ff.

**Argos had refused to renew her treaty with Sparta:** see V.14. The Argives "hoped to gain the leadership of the Peloponnese" (V.28).

## V.23–24. The Alliance between Athens and Sparta

**V.23. a rising of the slaves:** the helots, of course, who were serfs rather than slaves (I.101n.). Cf. IV.80 for the part played in Spartan thinking by the danger of helot uprisings. No reciprocal arrangement is required: the Athenians do not seem to envisage a rising of their own slaves, though desertions on a massive scale occurred during the Peloponnesian occupation of Decelea (VII.27).

**the Dionysia:** the city festival of Dionysus; see V.20n.

**the Hyacinthia:** a Spartan festival, conducted at Amyclae, near Sparta, in the summer (V.41). It was held in honor of Hyacinthus, who was accidentally killed by Apollo.

**V.24. the men captured on the island**: i.e., on Sphacteria in 425; see IV.38. These important prisoners, the object of so much Spartan anxiety, are finally recovered. For their fate see V.34.

**the first war:** the Archidamian War; on the expression see I.1n.

**without intermission:** see II.1n.

V.25–26. Introduction to the Second Phase of the War

**V.25. the ten years' war:** another name for the Archidamian War; see I.1n.

**for six years and ten months:** if this period began with the peace of Nicias or the alliance (spring, 421), then it finished in the middle of the winter of 415/4, the winter whose end is recorded in VI.93. Nothing mentioned by Th. during that winter could be described as ending a period in which **they refrained from invading each other's territory.** There is probably an error in the figures.

**V.26. The history of this period:** a second introduction for the second phase of the war. It was clearly written after the end of the war, when Th. had decided that the two phases of warfare were best seen as a single war, interrupted by an uneasy peace. On the word *history* see I.1n.

**summers and winters:** see II.1n.

**twenty-seven years:** 431–404. The account of the years after 411 was completed by Xenophon in his *Hellenica.*

**the Mantinean and Epidaurian wars:** see V.53ff.

**the allies in the Thracian area continued hostile:** e.g., Scione, reduced soon after the treaty (V.32).

**the Boeotians were in a state of truce:** see V.32.

**for those who put their faith in oracles:** see II.8n.

**thrice nine years:** oracular language; cf. "thrice nine days" at VII.50.

**I lived through the whole of it, being of an age to understand what was happening:** these remarks are generally interpreted as defensive, presumably against some sort of charge that Th. lacked the experience to write on such a momentous subject. For his date of birth see my introduction, under "The Life of Thucydides."

**I was banished from my country:** Th. has nothing else to say on the subject. According to Marcellinus (*Life of Thucydides* 46), Cleon played a significant part in his banishment; if true, this would to some extent explain Th.'s hostility toward him. On the Athenians' treatment of failed generals see II.65n.

**for twenty years:** there was a general recall of exiles to Athens in 404. Pausanias (I.23.9) states that Th.'s recall was the subject of an earlier special decree, and Marcellinus (*Life of Thucydides* 32) suggests that he returned after the Sicilian defeat; it may be that the offer was made and its acceptance assumed by Marcellinus, whereas in fact Th. turned it down, presumably preferring to wait for a more suitable moment.

**my command at Amphipolis:** see IV.104ff.

**particularly on the Peloponnesian side:** Th. seems to have been well acquainted with Sparta and its people. He certainly visited the place (I.10, 134) and had detailed knowledge of its workings and history (see, e.g., his knowledge of Spartan procedures at IV.38 and of Spartan policy at IV.80–81) and of some of its darker secrets (IV.80; cf. V.68 on secrecy, II.39n.). He admired the Spartan character: see VIII.24.

## V.27–32. Diplomatic Activity in the Peloponnese

**V.27. the embassies . . . which had been summoned to discuss these matters:** see V.17.

**a defensive alliance:** cf. I.44n.

**V.28. their treaty was on the point of expiring:** see V.14, 22. This had been a factor in Sparta's desire for peace.

**they hoped to gain the leadership of the Peloponnese:** cf. V.40.

**the reputation of Sparta had sunk very low:** Th.'s concentration in the latter part of bk. IV on Brasidas' achievements in the north and the pressure these put on Athens tends to obscure the fact that nearer home the Spartans enjoyed very little success in the period between Pylos and the Peace of Nicias. See, for instance, IV.55.

**the Attic war:** i.e., the Archidamian War; see I.1n.

**V.29. the Mantineans:** a glimpse of their activities was offered at IV.134.

**a democracy like their own city:** a common political system was something of a bond (cf. I.19n.) but (like shared racial background: see I.124n.) was subordinate to self-interest.

**the part of the treaty with Athens where it was laid down that no breach of oath would be involved:** this, in fact, is a clause in the alliance (V.23), not the treaty.

**enslave:** not to be taken literally; cf. I.98n., **lost its independence.**

**V.30. it was expressly laid down that a majority vote of the allies should be binding on all:** as we saw in the vote for war in 432 (I.125).

**Sollium:** taken by Athens in the opening year of the war (II.30n.); **Anactorium** was captured in 425 (IV.49).

**when Potidaea first revolted:** in 432 (I.58).

**their oath to the allies:** see I.71n.

**V.31. Lepreum:** a place "on the frontier between Laconia and Elis" (V.34); by "Laconia" Th. means here the area previously called Messenia. Lepreum was of minor importance, but an irritant to Elis. See V.49–50 and, on border squabbles in general, I.15n.

**to Olympian Zeus:** i.e., to the sanctuary of Zeus at Olympia.

**Spartan arbitration:** see I.28n.

**they brought forward the agreement:** there is no record of it elsewhere. It appears to have been an arrangement between Peloponnesian states securing rights of members to territory they possessed at the opening of the war against occupation by fellow members. At the beginning of the Peloponnesian War there may have been minor border squabbles (cf. I.15n.) between members of the Peloponnesian League that they agreed to put aside for the duration of the major conflict. Cf. Hermocrates' advice to the Sicilians in 424 (IV.63–64).

**the Attic War:** the Archidamian War; see I.1n.

**the Chalcidians of Thrace:** they were presumably disillusioned with Sparta and were looking elsewhere for support against Athens.

**The Boeotians and Megarians . . . did not suffer from Spartan interference:** both had strongly oligarchical governments and supported Sparta; see III.62n. on Boeotia and IV.74 for Megara's recent adoption of an oligarchy following the intervention of Brasidas.

**they thought that the democratic government at Argos would be less congenial to their own aristocratic governments than was the constitution of Sparta:** cf. V.29n.

**V.32. Scione:** for its earlier history and its revolt from Athens see IV.120–23, V.2.

**They put to death the men of military age, made slaves of the women and children:** cf. the cases of Torone (V.3) and Melos (V.116).

**gave the land to the Plataeans:** the city of Plataea had been destroyed by Sparta in 427 (III.68).

**They also brought the Delians back again to Delos:** they had been expelled during the armistice of 423 (V.1).

**the importance of Tegea:** a major Spartan ally whose defection would seriously weaken the Peloponnesian League.

**a ten days' truce:** cf. V.26.

## V.33. The Spartan Campaign against the Parrhasians

**the Parrhasians:** they occupied the western part of the plain of the river Alpheios.

**one of their political parties had asked for Spartan help:** it would have been the oligarchs if the pattern outlined at the beginning of III.82 is being followed.

**Sciritis:** north of Sparta between the rivers Eurotas and Oinous; see V.67n.

## V.34. Events at Sparta

**the helots who had fought with Brasidas:** see IV.80. Th. tells us nothing more of **the already freed helots** (Gk. *neodamodeis;* see I.101n.).

**Lepreum on the frontier between Laconia and Elis:** see V.31.

**they might start a revolution:** Spartan stability (I.18n.) was, perhaps, not all it seemed.

**They were therefore deprived of the rights of citizenship:** Sparta's treatment of the men taken on Sphacteria perhaps comes as something of a surprise, in view of their status (cf. IV.8n., 38) and the efforts of the authorities to recover them. But they had let Sparta down and damaged its reputation (V.28). They did not deserve a hero's welcome.

## V.35–39. Further Diplomatic Activity

**V.35. the Dians:** cf. IV.109.

**Acte:** the easternmost of the three peninsulas of Chalcidice. The Gk. translated as **in Athos** is presumably corrupt: Athos is at the end of the peninsula. See IV.109.

**they held on to the other places:** Cythera, Methana, and so on, listed in V.18.

**Panactum:** see V.3.

**Cephallenia:** Athenian since the first year of the war; see II.30.

**V.36. different ephors:** on the office see I.18n. This is a reminder that attitudes and thus foreign policy in Sparta could change from one year to the next. Cf. Sparta's inconsistency in its attitude toward Athens between the Persian and Peloponnesian Wars (I.69n.).

**they asked the Boeotians to hand over Panactum:** it is not quite clear why the Boeotians should be prepared to give up Panactum, unless it is a price they are prepared to pay to put Sparta in a stronger position in a war with Athens. Cf. V.39.

**V.37. their government:** the Boeotarchs, or Commanders of Boeotia; see IV.76n.

**V.38. the four Councils of Boeotia:** not mentioned elsewhere by Th. They were the supreme authority in matters of foreign policy, but it looks as if the Commanders of Boeotia were able, on some issues, at least, to manipulate them. On this occasion, however, they were cautious and unwilling to go along with even the first stage of the commanders' plans.

**V.39. Mecyberna:** mentioned in the treaty (V.18).

**the Boeotians . . . began to dismantle . . . Panactum:** for their reasoning see V.42.

## V.40–51. The Alliance between Athens and Argos

**V.40. the Argives had begun to fear that they were going to be isolated:** an anxiety not entirely grounded in logic: why should they think that **Sparta had persuaded the Boeotians to destroy Panactum,** when this would antagonize Athens? One of the Spartans' main ambitions at the moment was to recover Pylos (V.39); it is unlikely that they would deliberately provoke Athens. Indeed, they did not do so: in V.42 Th. is quite clear that the Boeotians had acted "on their own account."

**their refusal up to now to renew the treaty with Sparta:** see V.14, 22, and, for Sparta's desire to renew it, V.36.

**their ambition to become leaders of the Peloponnese:** cf. V.28.

**Tegea:** see V.32n.

**V.41. the Cynurian land:** see V.14n.

**There have been constant disputes about this district which is on the frontier between the two states:** arguments over frontiers were a frequent cause of war in the Greek world; see I.15n.

**Thyrea:** see II.27n.

**as had once been done in the past:** ca. 550; see Hdt. I.82.

**the Hyacinthia:** cf. V.23n.

**V.42. the Boeotians had acted on their own account . . . Sparta had made a separate alliance with the Boeotians:** cf. V.39.

**previous undertakings:** see V.35.

**V.43. Alcibiades:** a relation of Pericles and a member of a prominent Athenian family, he was coming to the forefront of Athenian politics at this time, and he plays a major role in the war from now on. On this occasion

Alcibiades is motivated partly by policy considerations, his support for an alliance with Argos, but much more space is devoted to **considerations of his own dignity.** Cf. Th.'s attribution of personal motives to Brasidas, Nicias, and Cleon in V.16 and to Alcibiades again in VI.15 and VIII.17; see also his views on the part played by the intrigues of unscrupulous, self-seeking politicians in Athens' defeat in the war (II.65).

**Clinias:** killed at the battle of Coronea in 447/6 (Plut. *Alcibiades* 1) and possibly the proposer of the so-called Decree of Clinias, which tightened up tribute payment in the Athenian empire (*T.D.G.R.* 98).

**a man who was still young in years:** Alcibiades would have been in his midthirties at this time. Cf. Nicias' charge against him at VI.12.

**(or would have been thought so in any other city in Hellas):** positions of distinction were reserved for senior politicians in many states (e.g., Sparta: see IV.132). There were age qualifications for office in Athens, but any capable man could achieve prominence in the assembly.

**He did not like . . . paying no attention to him:** as he later tells the Spartans (VI.89).

**the Spartans had negotiated the treaty through Nicias:** see V.16.

**Laches:** leader of the first Athenian expedition to Sicily (III.86) and proposer of the armistice of 423 (IV.118).

**his family had looked after Spartan interests in Athens:** see II.29n., **representative,** and for further evidence of the link see VIII.6.

**a post which his grandfather had given up:** Th. does not give the reason, but the abandonment of the relationship will probably have occurred just before or during the First Peloponnesian War (460–446). The grandfather was also called Alcibiades.

**which he himself wanted to take on again:** see VI.89, where Alcibiades claims that he did in fact take up the position again when the Spartans were in trouble at Pylos.

**his attentions to the prisoners captured on the island:** the Spartiates seized on Sphacteria in 425 (IV.38). Alcibiades' involvement is not mentioned elsewhere by Th., though Alcibiades claims credit for his efforts on behalf of the Spartans at VI.89.

**V.44. who was a sister democracy:** see V.29n.

**Philocharidas:** he had supported the agreement between Athens and Sparta (V.21).

**Endius:** a long-standing friend of Alcibiades (VIII.6).

**V.45. the Council:** the boule, or Council of Five Hundred (IV.118n.), one of whose functions was to receive foreign embassies.

**the following expedient:** how credible is the story? It is not made clear why the Spartan ambassadors should have trusted Alcibiades or how he convinced them he had the authority to carry out his promises.

**there was an earthquake and this assembly was adjourned:** it was standard practice to bring public proceedings to an end in such circumstances.

**V.46. Xenares:** see V.36–38, 51.

**V.47. The Athenians . . . the Eleans:** there would probably have been three separate treaties, one each between Athens, on the one hand, and Argos, Mantinea, and Elis, on the other. Fragments of an Athenian copy survive and, apart from some minor variations, confirm Th.'s version (Tod 1946 72).

**three Aeginetan obols:** equivalent to rather more than four Attic obols, an adequate ration allowance. See III.17n. and the Penguin translation, app. 2, pp. 612–13.

**The Council . . . Prytanes:** see IV.118n. "Prytanes" is a misspelling in the Penguin translation and should be "Prytaneis." Little is known of the various officers in Argos, Elis, and Mantinea who were to take the oath. Chief magistrates in a number of Peloponnesian towns were called **Demiurgi** (literally "workers of the people").

**the great Panathenaeic festival:** see I.20n. "Panathenaeic" is a misspelling in the Penguin translation and should be "Panathenaic."

**V.48. Corinth, though an ally of Argos:** see V.31.

**the . . . alliance concluded previously:** not specifically mentioned before by Th., though at the end of V.46 he does refer to the three states as "the Argives and their allies."

**offensive and defensive . . . purely defensive:** see I.44n.

**the first alliance which was purely defensive:** see V.27–28. The Corinthians are not prepared to join the alliance just negotiated between Athens, Argos, Elis, and Mantinea, since it could involve them in a war against Sparta. They are far more interested in changing Spartan policy concerning the peace, the original cause of their separation from Sparta (V.25, 27).

### *V.49–50. The Olympic Festival of 420*

**V.49. Olympic Games:** see I.6n. Interference in the games for political reasons is clearly not a new phenomenon. Olympia was in Elean territory, and the Eleans administered Olympic law, the regulations concerning the sanctuary and games of Olympia.

**the wrestling and boxing:** the *pankration,* an event combining wrestling and boxing.

**the temple:** of Olympian Zeus, in whose honor the games were held.

**Lepreum:** see V.31n.

**Phyrcus:** its site is unknown but is obviously in Elean territory.

**the Olympic truce:** in force for the duration of the games, to enable participants from warring states to compete; cf. the Isthmian truce mentioned at VIII.9–10.

**two minae:** the usual figure for the ransom of a hoplite. On Greek monetary values see the Penguin translation, app. 2, pp. 612–13.

**V.50. The Eleans . . . were . . . afraid that the Spartans might use force:** there was more at stake in the Olympic Games than participation in athletics.

**Harpina:** in the Alpheios valley, not far from Olympia.

**Lichas:** see V.22n.

**there was an earthquake:** see V.45n.

**V.51. Heraclea:** see III.92–93.

V.52–62. Campaigns in the Peloponnese

**V.52. incompetence in governing the place:** cf. III.93. Th. does not mention Heraclea again, but relations between Boeotia and Sparta soon improved (V.57), and the place may have been returned.

**Alcibiades . . . went into the Peloponnese:** this expedition achieved little, but Alcibiades showed some personal initiative, an eye for an opportunity, and an ability to win friends and influence people. We are reminded of Brasidas, though we cannot compare this little foray with his great expedition to the north.

**one of the generals:** see I.48n.

**Patrae:** close to the mouth of the Corinthian Gulf, a little inland. Alcibiades was presumably intending to establish a pro-Athenian base.

**Achaean Rhium:** roughly opposite Naupactus. The epithet *Achaean* is added to distinguish it from the other Rhium on the northern shore of the gulf. Cf. II.86.

**V.53. Epidaurus:** on the southern shore of the Saronic Gulf. Its capture would render navigation in the gulf even more difficult for Corinthian ships, though, of course, it would not have been easy since the Athenian occupation of **Aegina** (II.27). Athens had attacked Epidaurus in 430 (II.56).

**Scyllaeum:** the promontory at the end of the peninsula that formed the southeastern shore of the Saronic Gulf.

**V.54. Leuctra:** its precise site is unknown. **Mount Lycaeum** is in western Arcadia, northwest of Sparta. The expedition may have been a response to the Argive attack on Epidaurus. Elis or even Mantinea may have been its ultimate objective.

**the sacrifices for crossing the frontier:** standard procedure among the Spartans (cf. V.55), as indeed were sacrifices in Sparta before departure.

**they called each day the fourth from the end of the month:** in this farcical manner they pretended that the sacred month Carneus, in which military expeditions were banned, had not yet arrived.

**V.55. representatives of the cities:** these are not identified, nor is the purpose of the meeting given, though something can be deduced from what follows.

**V.56. Agesippidas:** he does not appear so incompetent now (cf. V.52). This expedition through Athenian waters is a considerable achievement.

**the treaty, where it was laid down that neither party should allow an enemy to go through its territory:** see V.47. "Territory" appears to include maritime as well as continental possessions. The Athenians now openly declare that the Spartans have broken their word, in that they have not carried out the terms of the treaty. Thus they retaliate with raids from Pylos.

**the helots of Cranii:** the helots withdrawn by Athens from Pylos had been settled at Cranii in Cephallenia (V.35). For their raids on Spartan territory see VI.105. They seem to have been assisted by some Athenians (V.115).

**V.57. In the middle of the next summer:** 418.

**in the rest of the Peloponnese some states were in revolt:** cf. I.18n.

**including the helots:** helots are used as soldiers on this occasion (cf. IV.80, VII.19), rather than as orderlies to the Spartan hoplites.

**From Boeotia came 5,000 hoplites:** the Spartans now seem to be on good terms again with Boeotia (cf. V.52).

**V.58. the Nemean road:** Nemea is some four miles southeast of **Phlius,** where the Spartan allies were assembling, and about thirteen miles (as the crow flies) north of Argos. **The plain** is the Argive plain, north of the city of Argos. The site of **Saminthus** is unknown.

**V.59. the five generals:** little is known of the internal civil or military arrangements at Argos, though these five commanders may be connected with the five Argive companies or divisions mentioned in V.72.

**who represented Spartan interests at Argos:** i.e., was a proxenos; see II.29n.

**V.60. Agis . . . acted on his own responsibility:** a Spartan king in command of an army had absolute power, but cf. V.63n.

**the Charadrus:** a dry riverbed that formed part of the defenses of the city.

**by taking refuge at the altar:** cf. I.24n.

**V.61. After this, reinforcements arrived from Athens:** their late arrival is not explained.

**Alcibiades, who was there as ambassador:** for his enthusiasm for an alliance between Athens and Argos see V.43.

**Orchomenus:** some twenty miles west and a little north of Argos.

**hostages of their own:** these were children; see V.71.

**V.62. Lepreum:** see V.31n.

**Tegea:** a more appropriate target; see V.32n.

## V.63–74. The Battle of Mantinea

**V.63. so many allied troops of such a high quality:** cf. V.60.: "the finest Hellenic army that had ever been brought together."

**carried away by passion in a manner quite unlike themselves:** in a manner, in fact, more typical of an Athenian assembly.

**10,000 drachmae:** see the Penguin translation, app. 2, p. 612. These were probably Aeginetan drachmae, an impossible sum for any but the most wealthy to repay.

**ten Spartans of the officer class:** i.e., Spartiates; see IV.8n. Th. has mentioned officers acting as advisers before (see II.85n.), but none who advised a king. There is no sign of them later (VIII.5, 9).

**he should not be empowered to lead an army out of the city:** the restriction on his power is not very clear nor is its relationship to the offense he is deemed to have committed. Agis certainly remained in absolute command during the campaign: see V.66. But Spartan kings were clearly not omnipotent: cf. I.18n.

**V.64. helots:** again used as soldiers; cf. V.57.

**Orestheum in Maenalia:** up the Eurotas valley, northwest of Sparta.

**enemy-occupied country:** since the capture of Orchomenus.

**V.65. At this point one of the older men in the army:** a picturesque touch but Th. is surely right to cast doubt (**because he himself had suddenly changed his mind**) on this anecdote as an explanation for Agis' actions.

**V.67. Sciritae:** from Sciritis in Arcadia (V.33n.); they were employed as cavalry scouts.

**the helots who had been freed:** see IV.80 for their original number (seven hundred) and enrollment and V.34 for their grant of freedom.

**the right wing:** the position of honor in the battle line.

**V.68. The Spartan army looked the bigger:** this perhaps suggests that the two armies were roughly equal in size. It is easy enough to calculate the numbers in the Spartan army from the information given by Th. If the front rank consisted of 448 (4 × 4 × 4 × 7) men and they were drawn up eight deep, the total would be 8 × 448 = 3,584. (This was not the full size of the Spartan army: a sixth of their force, the youngest and oldest members, had been sent back to guard their homes: see V.64.) In addition, there were six hundred **Sciritae**; contingents from Heraea, Maenalia, and Tegea (mentioned in V.67), whose total numbers are not given; and possibly the three hundred knights mentioned in V.72. The allied contribution could probably have matched Sparta's (on the size of the Spartan population see IV.15n.). The total was probably around nine thousand.

The Athenians (with one thousand hoplites and three hundred cavalry; see V.61), the Mantineans, the Cleonaeans, the Orneans, and the Argives (with one thousand picked troops and the rest of their army) will have made up a force of no more than about eight thousand. Some commentators have found this figure impossibly small. It would mean, for instance, that the main Argive army was no bigger than about three thousand men, smaller than Sparta's. It has thus been argued that Th.'s text is at fault. Certainly his figures hardly tally with his concluding comment on the scale of the battle (V.74).

**The secrecy with which their affairs are conducted:** cf. V.26n.

**V.69. the generals . . . spoke to the troops:** Th. does not on this occasion give the prebattle speeches in full but merely summarizes the argument of each. See II.10n.

**slavery:** the word (Gk. *douleia*) is not to be taken literally. It is often used by Th. to mean political subjection. Cf. I.98n., **lost its independence.**

**V.71. his unarmed side:** in ancient times a soldier marching to battle held his shield in his left arm, thus exposing his right side. In trying to find protection behind the shield of the man on the right, each soldier moved over to the right, led by the man on the extreme right, who had no such source of protection and was thus keen to outflank the enemy's extreme left. On this occasion Agis, seeing that his left wing was in danger of being encircled, ordered it to move further left and took troops from the right to fill the gap in the middle thus created.

**two regiments taken from the right wing:** two regiments would be made up of over one thousand men, but Th. has already said that there were only "a few Spartans" on the right wing (V.67). Various solutions for the discrepancy have been proposed: none satisfies.

**V.72. the knights:** the king's bodyguard. At an early stage they were clearly cavalry, but now they were hoplites.

**the five companies:** see V.59n.

**V.74. the greatest battle that had taken place for a very long time among Hellenic states:** this comment has a bearing on Th.'s figures; see V.68n. He is perhaps thinking of Tanagra (I.107), where the numbers of troops were higher.

**Aeginetans:** i.e., Athenian settlers on Aegina (II.27).

**as for the losses among the Spartans themselves, it was difficult to find out the truth:** despite his familiarity with matters Spartan; cf. V.26n. Th. himself remarks that the Spartans were notoriously secretive (V.68).

V.75–81. The Aftermath of Mantinea; Sparta and Argos Make Peace

**V.75. the oldest and youngest troops:** sent back to Sparta in V.64. Cf. the case of Myronides and his force of the oldest and youngest Athenians, mentioned at I.105.

**allies from Corinth:** see V.64.

**the Carnean holidays:** cf. V.54n.

**the disaster in the island:** Sphacteria in 425 (IV.2ff.).

**lack of resolution:** or "slowness to act"; cf. I.70n., 71, 84, 118; IV.55; V.82.

**the Epidaurians took advantage:** for their war with Argos see V.53ff.

**V.76. a pro-Spartan party who wanted to overthrow the democracy in Argos:** cf. I.19n., III.82 (opening sentences).

**Lichas:** cf. V.22n.

**the official post of looking after the interests:** see II.29n., **representative.**

**Alcibiades happened to be in Argos:** see V.43n., 61.

**V.77. an agreement:** this document and the alliance (V.79) are in the Laconian dialect and thus are clearly copies of the originals.

**to the Orchomenians their children . . . to the Spartans the men they hold in Mantinea:** see V.61. Nothing is known of the **Maenalians.**

**Epidaurus:** see V.53ff., 75.

**V.78. their alliance with Mantinea, Athens, and Elis:** see V.47.

**V.80. their fortified posts in the Peloponnese:** including Epidaurus and, presumably, Pylos and Cythera.

**Perdiccas:** last heard of in 422 (V.6), as an ally of Athens. See I.56n. and, for his Argive origins, II.99.

**the Chalcidians:** Spartan allies, perhaps, since their revolt from Athens in 432 (I.58).

**the Athenians renewed their treaty with Epidaurus:** i.e., the Peace of Nicias, to which, as allies of Sparta, the Epidaurians would have sworn (V.18).

**V.81. The Mantineans:** they are unable to act independently of the new combination of Argos and Sparta. Th. does not identify **the cities** that they lose.

**the Spartan force went to Sicyon . . . and reorganized the government there on more oligarchical lines; afterwards the two forces . . . suppressed the democracy at Argos, replacing it with an oligarchical government favorable to Sparta:** standard Spartan behavior; see I.19n., V.29n.

## V.82–83. Counterrevolution in Argos; Athens and Perdiccas

**V.82. Dium:** for its refusal to cooperate with Brasidas in 424/3 see IV.109. It was clearly on bad terms with Athens by 421 (V.35).

**the democrats at Argos had formed into a party again:** the stasis in Argos is typical of the factional infighting that, in Th.'s view (I.2n.), was so destructive of Greek cities in this period. The Spartans, recently so confident and purposeful, are dilatory and indecisive when it comes to interfering in the domestic politics of their ally. The strength of democratic, pro-Athenian feeling in Argos should not surprise us. The oligarchs had got their way only because of recent reversals, and the presence of Alcibiades (cf. V.76) would have helped to maintain support for friendship with Athens.

**the Gymnopaedic festival:** another Spartan festival, held in midsummer.

**V.83. except the Corinthians:** the absence of the Corinthians from the campaign against Argos is mentioned but not explained. Th. does this sort of thing occasionally. Perhaps he would have supplied the missing information if he had had a chance to revise his work.

**Hysia:** a misprint in the Penguin translation; it should be "Hysiae," which is situated between Argos and Tegea.

**Perdiccas:** cf. V.80n. Th. has said nothing of the proposed expedition of Nicias and its abandonment because of Perdiccas' lack of support.

## V.84–116. The Melian Dialogue

The Athenian attack on Melos, like the Spartan destruction of Plataea in bk. III, is selected for extended treatment not because of its importance to the course of the war but for the issues raised in the accompanying negotiations. On this occasion the negotiations are presented not in the usual way, by antithetical speeches, but in a format unique in Th., a dialogue, a device usually associated with tragedy or philosophical discourse. Th. is clearly experimenting: unlike speeches, the dialogue form allows close discussion of individual points as they arise, while the cumulative impact of the Athenians' constant refutation of the Melians' arguments is (for the reader at least) overwhelming, adding to the dramatic intensity of the episode.

The essential characteristic of the dialogue is often said to be its abstractness, which has led to its being cited as the most "artificial" of Th.'s speeches (if it may be so called). It has thus been argued, or assumed, that it cannot have been written according to the principles enunciated by Th. in I.22. But we must not lose sight of the purpose of the dialogue: it may indeed contain some generalizations of an abstract nature and a tendency toward sophistic arguments (e.g., the discussion of honor and dishonor in chap. 111), which it is easy to declare artificial or inappropriate, but such arguments are presented not to further philosophical progress or score debating points but to convince those listening that they must act in a particular way. Seen in this context, they make sense. The dialogue is not an abstract, intellectual exercise but an attempt to solve a practical problem with the minimum inconvenience. It must be approached as the speeches in general are approached, following the guidelines laid down by Th. in I.22. We must assume that the thrust of the debate is genuine but that some of its arguments have been supplied by Th., though which and how many we cannot say.

Whatever we may feel about its composition, it is necessary to ask why Th. chose to recount this particular episode at such length. Above all, the dialogue is dominated by the fact of power—its character, its application, its consequences—and herein it goes to the heart of Th.'s thinking. The analysis revolves around some important sophistic issues, notably the conflict between justice and expediency and the *nomos* (law) / *physis* (nature) antithesis (I.32n.). These ideas are explored elsewhere in Th. (e.g., in the speech of the Athenians at Sparta in I.76 and in the Plataean debate in bk. III) and are found in the writings of other contemporary authors, particularly Plato (cf. Thrasymachus in *Republic* I and Callicles in the *Gorgias*). They were clearly current in intellectual circles at this time, as thinkers, Th. foremost among them, contemplated the ramifications of the manner in which Athens exercised her power.

Then, Th. clearly has something to say about the moral and psychological condition of the Athenians as an imperialist power. Some commentators have gone further, seeing the dialogue as evidence of a moral degeneration among the Athenians and contrasting their extremism on this occasion with the milder and more enlightened imperialism of Pericles as expressed in the Funeral Speech (e.g., II.41). But the Funeral Speech was not an occasion for analysis of the harsh realities of political life, and if we look at other Athenian pronouncements of that time (in particular I.75–76, from a speech delivered before the outbreak of war) we see an attitude very similar to that expressed in the Melian Dialogue. Moreover, not long after the Funeral Speech Pericles could assert in public that the empire was "like a tyranny" (II.63), while Cleon claimed that it actually was a tyranny (III.37). There is perhaps a little evidence for such a decline in the Mytilene episode, when the second debate was provoked by feelings of revulsion at the cruelty of the initial decision, which was then rescinded (III.36; cf. Cleon, "To feel pity . . . ," III.40), but even on this occasion the decisive arguments of Diodotus were couched entirely in terms of self-interest and the finer feelings were not so deep or widespread as to produce an overwhelming change of heart (III.49). The earlier phases of the war show no traces of a higher moral tone among the Athenians, and it is more likely that Th. was concerned with imperialism itself, a nasty business, as it always had been, whose true character emerges more clearly as circumstances drive the Athenians to ever harsher measures.

Here, as so often, Th. is interested in the attitudes of the oppressed as much as in those of their oppressors. This debate was the preliminary to a massacre. It was not the first such massacre committed by the Athenians (see the case of Scione mentioned at V.32), but on this occasion the victims to be were given the opportunity to save themselves from destruction. They rejected it, and the significance of this episode for Th. lies in part in the thinking behind this decision.

Finally, we must see the dialogue in relation to the episode that follows it, the Sicilian debate and expedition. It is surely a piece of deliberate artistry as well as a chronological coincidence that Athens' ruthless, precise application of power and self-interest at Melos is immediately followed by what was for Th. the supreme misjudgment of the Athenian democracy, an almost suicidal loss of contact with reality. A minor victory is followed by a major defeat, both arising from the same cause, a paradoxical aspect of Athenian power revealed by the dialogue: in some ways it limits, rather than enlarges, Athenian freedom of action. Melos is a small, insignificant state that presents no risk to Athens; yet the Athenians feel compelled to subdue it on the grounds that if they ignore it, or even accept an alliance with it, their subjects would regard that as a sign of weakness in them. The Athenians are prisoners of their power. It is fear that drives them on (cf. I.75n.): in the words of Euphemus, they "rule in order not to be ruled" (VI.87; cf. the words of Alcibiades quoted at V.91n.). The dialogue is a dramatic illustration of the tyranny of fear and the essential amorality of the imperialist mentality.

**V.84. Alcibiades:** he is still convinced that Athens' main chance of success lies in making trouble for Sparta in the Peloponnese, especially by strengthening ties between Athens and Argos. Cf. V.43, 52, 61, 76.

**300 Argive citizens:** for their fate see VI.61.

**Melos:** in the southwest of the Aegean. The reasons for Athens' expedition against this island are not given but have to be deduced from his account of the episode.

**six from Chios, and two from Lesbos:** see VI.43n. It was probably the Methymnians who provided the two Lesbian ships. The allies' contribution to the force was considerable: Athens was still suffering the effects of the plague.

**They had refused to join the Athenian empire like the other islanders:** cf. III.91. The Melians had been included in the tribute assessment of 425 (*T.D.G.R.* 136; IV.50n.) but had clearly been uncooperative. Earlier in the war they had perhaps contributed to the Spartan war fund (*T.D.G.R.* 132).

**when the Athenians had brought force to bear on them:** in 426; see III.91. Melian resistance on that occasion would contribute to increased Athenian determination now.

**The Melians did not invite these representatives to speak before the people but asked them to make the statement . . . in front of the governing body and the few:** hints of disagreement on Melos between democrats and oligarchs. Did "the few" fear that the people might support Athens?

**V.86. the likely end of it all will be either war, if we prove that we are in the right, and so refuse to surrender, or else slavery:** "slavery" (on the precise meaning of the word, Gk. *douleia,* see I.98n., **lost its independence**) is, in fact, the best they can hope for either way.

**V.87. save your city from destruction:** precisely what, in their view, the Melians are trying to do, but, of course, the Melians and the Athenians differ on how this might best be achieved. The Athenians present the situation in these terms to the Melians to make it clear to them that their only chance of survival lies in immediate surrender. This is the fact that they must look in the face.

**V.89. fine phrases:** the Athenians had used such language before, claiming a right to their empire on the very grounds that they now reject as being irrelevant and unconvincing (I.73–74). Cf. the words of Euphemus at Camarina in 415 (VI.83).

**you should try to get what it is possible for you to get:** the Athenians preach what they practice.

**when these matters are discussed by practical people:** another plea for realism.

**the standard of justice depends on the equality of power to compel:** by this the Athenians mean that there can be justice only between equals. If one state (or individual) is much more powerful than its opponent, then it will force its will on it, and the weaker state, which lacks the strength to enforce the claims of justice, will have no choice but to accept the will of the stronger. This is described by the Athenians as "a general and necessary law of nature" (V.105), an essential fact of human existence, impervious to considerations of justice and right.

**V.91. One is not so much frightened of being conquered by a power which rules over others:** the Athenians see little risk of defeat at the hands of Sparta. The prospect of rebellion within the empire is a source of greater concern to them, though we know of no specific threats to their security at this time.

**We do not want any trouble . . . we want you to be spared:** There is a touch of grim comedy in the frankness of the following interchange. The words of the Athenians are based on the premise that in a time of extreme peril the first priority of the living must be to find the surest means of staying alive; the Melians fail to grasp the point (V.92).

**V.94. So you would not agree to our being neutral:** in a conflict on this scale weak states are compelled to join one side or another. The Spartan offer to Plataea (II.72) had been an exception. Neutrality is also impossible for individuals: see III.82, final sentence.

**V.95. our subjects would regard that as a sign of weakness:** the Athenians were perhaps feeling generally insecure. At VI.18 Alcibiades says, "The fact is that we have reached a stage where we are forced to plan new conquests . . . because there is a danger that we ourselves may fall under the power of others unless others are in our power." Cf. the words of Euphemus at Camarina in 415 (VI.83, final paragraph; VI.87).

**V.96. fair play:** the Melians return to the notion of justice—in vain.

**V.97. they think that..those who still preserve their independence do so because they are strong:** making Athenian action imperative. It may be that some event, unknown to us, has brought Melos to the attention of the Greek world. Certainly the Athenians seem to suggest that the eyes of all are on them.

**V.98. we must try to persuade you:** the Melians, clutching at straws, are still trying to find arguments of a practical nature that will persuade the Athenians that their present behavior is, in fact, against their interests. The Athenians are not convinced.

**V.100. we who are still free would show ourselves great cowards and weaklings:** the Melians raise the issues of their self-respect and public opinion of them.

**V.101. This is no fair fight:** the Athenians reply that there can be no honor or shame in a struggle where the rivals are so unevenly matched. The issue of honor is a red herring.

**V.102. fortune sometimes makes the odds more level than could be expected:** cf. the words of Diodotus at III.45. Th. frequently shows that luck plays an important role in human affairs, especially in war (I.120n.), but that it is a mistake to rely on it.

**V.103. Hope, that comforter in danger:** see I.121n.
**prophecies and oracles:** see II.8n.

**V.104. the gods will give us fortune . . . we are standing for what is right against what is wrong . . . the Spartans, who are bound . . . for honour's sake . . . to come to our help:** the irony and the pathos of the Melians' words continue to mount.

**V.105. it is a general and necessary law of nature to rule wherever one can:** the Athenians have already (V.89n.) argued that the notion of justice has no place in the present debate, and they make no reply to the renewed Melian claim that they have right on their side. The Athenians claim to be following "a law of nature," a course of action that is, by definition, they argue, impervious to criticism on moral grounds. As far as they are concerned, they are now offering in support of their action convincing philosophical arguments that complement the justification of it on practical grounds already advanced. Both arguments focus on their power and the need to preserve, exercise, and increase it. To this need all other considerations are subordinate or irrelevant. The justification of power is power itself. Cf. I.76. The translation "law of nature" (literally "a compelling nature") blurs the sophistic distinction between *nomos* (law) and *physis* (nature) that is raised here; cf. I.32n.

**In matters that concern themselves or their own constitution the Spartans are quite remarkably good:** the Gk. says that they particularly practice *arete,* a virtue that combines honorable behavior in general and military courage in particular. At VI.11 Nicias says that *arete* is "the be-all and the end-all of the Spartans' existence."

**as for their relations with others . . . the Spartans are most conspicuous for believing that what they like doing is honourable and what suits their interests is just:** the argument resumes its sophistic tone. The Athenians are presumably referring to the Spartans' abandonment of the Greeks they set out to liberate.

**V.106. Their own self-interest will make them refuse to betray their own colonists:** again the Melians are forced to restrict their argument to the issue of expediency, so forcefully advanced by the Athenians.

**V.107. if one follows one's self-interest, one wants to be safe:** the Melians are easily outmaneuvered by the Athenians, who make the point that the Spartans will put their own security before all other considerations. Th. has himself said that "the Spartans were traditionally slow to go to war, unless they were forced into it" (I.118). Here it is clear that, despite what the Melians thought or hoped, there was no compulsion on the Spartans to come to their defense.

**V.108. we think that they would even endanger themselves for our sake:** again the Melians are deluding themselves. They are by no means close to the Peloponnese, though it is true that their island would be a useful base for a Peloponnesian fleet operating in the Aegean. The arguments based on their reliability or race (cf. I.124n.) were unlikely to be persuasive. The Melians had done little to support Sparta in the war and even now were happy to remain neutral (V.89, 94n., 112).

**V.110. they would turn against . . . those of your allies left unvisited by Brasidas:** in his campaign of 424 (IV.78ff.). The Melians continue to cling desperately to the unlikely prospect of Spartan intervention, if not in Melos directly, then as a diversionary tactic in some part of the Athenian empire.

**V.111.** A lengthy summary of the Athenian case, a final effort to convince the Melians that they cannot win the present conflict and that they must give all their attention to one question, i.e., How can they best preserve themselves and their city? The answer is inescapable: they should surrender to the Athenians. At this stage the Athenians ignore the question of justice, having already shown that it has no bearing on the present situation. Instead they present the facts of international politics in the starkest possible terms to bring home to the Melians the realities of their position.

**when you are allowed to choose between war and safety, you will not be so insensitively arrogant as to make the wrong choice:** foreshadowing Athens' own position and behavior in the next episode, the Sicilian debate.

**V.112. Our decision, Athenians, is just the same as it was at first:** the Melians cannot be persuaded by Athenian reason; their faith in the gods and the Spartans is unshakeable. There is some irony in their final words: they offer the Athenians the chance to make a treaty on their (Melian) terms. The two sides are as far apart at the end of the debate as they were at the beginning.

**V.115. the exiles from Argos:** see V.83.

**the Athenians at Pylos:** the Athenians had established a force of Messenians and helots at Pylos in 419/8 (V.56). Presumably some Athenians were there with them.

**V.116. the sacrifices for crossing the frontier:** cf. V.54n.

**there was also some treachery from inside:** for an earlier hint of division within the Melian population see V.84n.

**the Melians surrendered:** the failure to negotiate a settlement and the difficulties of the siege would have incensed the Athenians. Th. sees no need to dwell on the details of the massacre or to pass judgment on the behavior of the Athenians; indeed his language is very matter-of-fact (cf. his discussion of events at Torone at V.3 and at Scione at V.32). Plutarch (*Alcibiades* 16) records that Alcibiades was largely responsible for the harsh treatment of the Melians. For the restoration of the Melians in 405 see Xenophon *Hellenica* II.2.9.

# Book Six

## VI.1. The Decision to Attack Sicily

**the same winter:** 416/5.

**larger forces than those which Laches and Eurymedon had commanded:** though the fleet was the same size as its predecessor, sixty ships (VI.8). Laches was sent with twenty ships in 427 (III.86); Eurymedon brought forty reinforcements in 425 (IV.2).

**to conquer it:** cf. VI.6, 90; VII.75. The prospect of conquest had been in part behind the first expedition: see III.86, IV.65.

**They were for the most part ignorant:** previous contacts had, it seems, given the Athenians few opportunities for research. Th. seems to be implying that the Athenians were guilty of an error of judgment, though in II.65 ("the mistake was not so much . . . ") he denies that this was the prime cause of Athenian failure.

**they did not realize they were taking on a war of almost the same magnitude:** they will soon be fighting full-scale wars on two fronts. The point is exploited by Nicias in the debate (VI.10) and played down by Alcibiades (VI.17) and Athenagoras (VI.36). This double commitment is "what wore them [the Athenians] down more than anything else" (VII.28).

**The voyage round Sicily:** a distance of about five hundred miles.

**it is separated from the mainland by only two miles of sea:** the Straits of Messina between the northeast corner of Sicily and the toe of Italy. Cf. IV.24.

## VI.2–5. Sicilian History

Rather than enlarge on the strength and resources of the Sicilian cities, Th. digresses to explain their origins. The Archaeology (I.2ff.) illustrates the importance he attached to unraveling the complexities of early history to provide a context for his subject. Nor was Th. immune to the attractions of geography and ethnography, areas of particular interest to his predecessors. His source for this material is generally reckoned to be Antiochus of Syracuse, a fellow historian and contemporary, who wrote a history of Sicily to the year 424.

**VI.2. It is said . . . I cannot say . . . On these points we must be content with what the poets have said:** Th. generally likes to weigh the evidence and deliver his own judgment but cannot improve on the information offered by the poets (whom he tends to mistrust: see I.20) in relation to the earliest inhabitants of Sicily.

**according to the Sicanians themselves they were there first . . . The truth is, however . . . :** Th. confidently rejects Sicanian tradition but, characteristically, does not supply us with the reasoning behind his judgment.

**the Cyclopes and Laestrygonians:** mythical tribes found in Homer *Odyssey* IX–X.

**After the fall of Troy:** see I.9, with nn.

**Achaeans:** one of the names used for the Greeks in the works of Homer.

**Eryx and Egesta:** in the far northwest of Sicily. Egesta is also known as Segesta.

**Phocians:** from Phocis in central Greece.

**Opicans:** early inhabitants of central Italy, according to the tradition adopted by Th.; cf. his mention of Opicia at VI.4.

**the arrival of the Hellenes in Sicily:** in the second half of the eighth century; on Greek colonization in general see I.12n.

**Phoenicians . . . Carthage:** according to tradition Carthage had been founded by migrants from Phoenicia in the eastern Mediterranean.

**Motya, Soloeis, and Panormus:** the latter two are in the northwestern part of Sicily; Motya is an island off the western end of Sicily.

**VI.3. Naxos:** founded ca. 733, some fifty miles north of Syracuse.

**Apollo Archegetes:** Apollo the First Leader, who will have been consulted before the decision to colonize was taken; cf. I.25n.

**Syracuse was founded in the following year:** Syracuse, on the east coast of Sicily, was the island's major city in the fifth century. Its traditional foundation date, on which Th.'s other dates are based, is ca. 732.

**Heraclids:** see I.12n.

**Catana:** also on the east coast of Sicily, between Naxos and Syracuse. Founded ca. 728.

**VI.4. Trotilus . . . the river Pantacyas:** their identities are not certain, though they would not be too far from **Leontini** (founded ca. 728), which was a little inland, some twenty miles northwest of Syracuse.

**Thapsus:** a peninsula some seven miles north of Syracuse, near **Hyblaean Megara,** which was founded ca. 728.

**Gelon, the tyrant of Syracuse:** see I.14n.

**Selinus:** toward the western end of the southern coast of Sicily. Founded ca. 628.

**Gela . . . Acragas:** a little inland from the southern shore of Sicily, about forty miles apart. Acragas is also known as Agrigentum. Founded ca. 688 and ca. 580 respectively.

**Zancle . . . Rhegium:** cf. IV.24. No date for the foundation date of Zancle is given.

**pirates:** cf. I.5, 98n.

**Cumae:** an early foundation, from Chalcis in Euboea, on the west coast of Italy (Opicia: cf. VI.2n.), just north of the Bay of Naples.

**some Samians . . . on their flight from the Persians:** the story is recounted in Hdt. VI.22–24.

**VI.5. Himera:** on the north coast of Sicily, just west of its halfway point. Th. gives no foundation date.

**party struggle:** an early instance of stasis (I.2n.).

**Acrae . . . Casmenae:** west of Syracuse. Founded ca. 662 and ca. 642 respectively.

**Camarina:** founded ca. 597, on the southern shore of Sicily, southwest of Syracuse. The spelling "Camerina" used at times in the Penguin translation is incorrect.

**Hippocrates, the tyrant of Gela:** from 498 to 491.

## VI.6. Further Details of the Athenian Decision to Attack Sicily

**it was an island of this size:** Th. returns to the theme of VI.1.

**In fact they aimed at conquering:** the Gk. says that conquest was the "truest cause" *(alethestate prophasis)* of the expedition. This expression is also used of Spartan fear as the cause of the Peloponnesian War; see I.23n.

**their own kinsmen:** the Ionians of Leontini, allies of Athens.

**their newly acquired allies:** "newly" is not in the Gk. Th. would appear to be referring to the people of Egesta. An alliance between Athens and Egesta is recorded in *T.D.G.R.* 81, but its date is controversial.

**marriage rights:** when husband and wife were from different states, the question of the citizenship of the children had to be settled by agreement between the two communities; on this occasion Egesta and Selinus clearly could not agree.

**disputed territory:** a common cause of conflict between neighboring states; see I.15n.

**the alliance made in the time of Laches, during the war in which Leontini was concerned:** the alliance with Egesta (*T.D.G.R.* 81) as the context suggests, or another, with Leontini? Neither is mentioned by Th. in his account of the war in Sicily, 427–24 (III.86n.), but Athens had had an alliance with Leontini since before 433 (I.36n.), and this could be a renewal. On Laches see VI.1n.

**the Syracusans, who were Dorians . . . would come . . . to the aid of their Dorian kinsmen:** on the racial factor in the war see I.124n., VII.57.

**join the Peloponnesians:** as the Peloponnesians had hoped at the beginning of the war; see II.7n.

**the money . . . in the treasury and the temples:** for the storage of state monies in temples cf. II.13; *T.D.G.R.* 119.

### VI.7. Fighting in the Peloponnese and Macedonia

**(except the Corinthians):** they had not been happy with Spartan leadership since the Peace of Nicias of 421 (V.17; cf. V.83).

**Argos:** the Spartans had had the upper hand over their great Peloponnesian rival in recent years and had even established there a sympathetic oligarchical government (V.81), though they found it impossible to maintain (V.82–83, 116).

**Orneae:** some twelve miles northwest of Argos. It was an ally of Argos in 418 (V.67), and Sparta had clearly retained control of it since Mantinea.

**an Athenian force:** for Athens' alliance with Argos see V.47.

**Methone:** a member of the Athenian empire situated just north of Pydna on the Thermaic Gulf. It was particularly useful for Athens as a base from which to observe events in Macedonia. For evidence of a special relationship between Athens and Methone see *T.D.G.R.* 128.

**Perdiccas:** see I.56n.

**the Chalcidians in Thrace:** the Peace of Nicias had provided for their return to the Athenian fold, but that return had not occurred (VI.10).

### VI.8–26. The Sicilian Debate

**VI.8. sixty talents:** the equivalent of 360,000 drachmae. This sum, distributed among the crews of sixty ships (bearing two hundred men per ship: see I.14n.) for thirty days, gives one drachma per man per day. This was a typical wage for a skilled workman: see III.17n., VIII.29, and the Penguin translation, app. 2, pp. 612–13.

**commanders with full powers:** at such a distance they had to make decisions without reference to the assembly. The choice of one general rather than three was considered by the assembly, according to a fragmentary inscription (*T.D.G.R.* 146b, which also confirms the figure of sixty ships).

**Alcibiades:** see V.43n.

**Nicias:** see III.51n.

**Lamachus:** a general in 424 (IV.75) and an experienced soldier, he was perhaps expected to bridge the gap between the brilliant but unpredictable Alcibiades and the cautious Nicias. Aristophanes had poked fun at him in his *Acharnians* (produced in 425) but later called him a hero (*Frogs* 1039, produced in 405).

**to reestablish Leontini:** for its demise see V.4.

**Nicias had not wanted to be chosen for the command:** he disapproved of the venture and perhaps had had enough of war; see V.16.

**VI.9.** The renewal of war, like its initial outbreak, is preceded by debate. The decision to undertake the expedition to Sicily is seen against the background of some important features of Athenian politics: the damaging personal rivalries, the overwhelming imperialist ambition, and the influence of rhetoric in the decision-making process. Like the Mytilene debate in bk. III, the Sicilian debate is in fact a reconsideration of a decision already made. But in the Mytilene episode passions had cooled by the time of the second discussion; on this occasion passions run higher and the opposition is cowed into silence.

The speeches repay careful reading. Dover (*H.C.T.* 4:229) writes: "There is no debate in which Thucydides has given us so striking a representation of rhetorical technique at work . . . No statement or prediction or factual implication can be taken at its face value; everything is coloured; everything is exaggeration, insinuation, or half-truth." These were the conditions in which the Athenians made (or confirmed) this momentous decision. The episode illustrates what Th. saw as a decline in the democratic process at Athens since the days of Pericles (cf. II.65).

**no speech of mine could be powerful enough to alter your characters:** the character of the Athenian people, summed up by an outsider before the war began (I.70, with n.), is at the root of their success. Nicias fears it will also be their (and thus his) downfall. He has further thoughts on the Athenian character during this expedition: see VII.14, 48.

**it would be useless to advise you to safeguard what you have and not to risk what is yours already for doubtful prospects:** the policy that Pericles had persuaded the Athenians to follow at the beginning of the war. The Athenians are now going to opposite extremes, and Nicias would like to see a return to Periclean principles but considers it futile even to suggest it.

**VI.10. the peace treaty which you have made:** the Peace of Nicias of 421 (V.18).

**certain people here and in Sparta:** Alcibiades in Athens (V.43), Cleobulus and Xenares at Sparta (V.36).

**they only made the peace because of their misfortunes:** Spartan thinking before the peace is summed up in V.14–16.

**a number of points still not settled:** including the status of Chalcidice (mentioned later this chapter) and Amphipolis (V.21, 35) and Athenian raids from Pylos on Spartan territory (V.56, 115n.).

**There are some states . . . who have not yet accepted the peace terms:** Corinth, Boeotia, Elis, and Megara had been opposed to the peace from the beginning (V.17).

**Some of these are openly at war with us:** presumably a reference to Corinth (V.115).

**our truces with them are renewable every ten days:** referring to Boeotia (V.26).

**whom they would rather have had as allies in the past:** see II.7.

**the Chalcidians in Thrace:** cf. VI.7 with n.

**VI.11. (the possibility with which the Egestaeans are always trying to frighten you):** see VI.6.

**your successes . . . have now made you despise them and set your hearts on the conquest of Sicily:** cf. IV.21n.

**military honour is the be-all and the end-all of their existence:** cf. Pericles' comments at II.39, with n, and I.75n.

**who do not even speak our own language:** Gk. *barbaroi,* on which see I.3n. The Egestaeans were part of the non-Hellenic Elymi (VI.2).

**the oligarchical machinations of Sparta:** this imprecise charge, quickly dropped, is used to frighten the democratic Athenians. On Sparta's liking for oligarchy see I.19n.

**VI.12. only recently:** Nicias is telescoping events somewhat: the second and last outbreak of the **great plague** was in 427/6 (III.87; for the first, in 430/29, see II.47–54). Nevertheless, its effects would still have been felt in 415.

**exiles who are begging for assistance:** they were from Leontini, which was under pressure from Syracuse; see VI.6, 19.

**someone sitting here . . . too young for his post:** Alcibiades; on his age see V.43n. Nicias makes much of Alcibiades' youth in this speech; Alcibiades in his reply tries to turn his youth to his advantage. On the contrast between youth and old age in Th. cf. II.8n.

**entirely for his own selfish reasons:** thus Nicias presents himself by implication as a patriot, but according to Th. (V.16) his commitment to peace was not entirely altruistic.

**the horses he keeps:** for racing in competitions, an aristocratic activity.

**maladministration of public affairs:** cf. the accusations leveled by Th. at Pericles' successors in general (II.65).

**VI.13. this same young man's party:** i.e., his supporters, not a party in the modern sense.

**I . . . call for the support of the older men among you:** he will not get it; see VI.24. Old age tends to be associated with caution in Th.: see II.8n.

**Do not . . . indulge in hopeless passions:** for the response to this plea see VI.24. Often in Th. reason is overwhelmed by emotion, not least in democratic assemblies; cf. I.86n.

**success comes from foresight:** cf. Th. on Themistocles, I.138n.

**the Ionian sea . . . the Sicilian sea:** the former lay between northwest Greece and southeast Italy, the latter, to the south, between the Peloponnese and Sicily.

**VI.14. the president of the assembly:** Gk. *prytanis,* the chairman of the standing committee of the boule; cf. IV.118n.

**VI.15. Carthage:** it looks as if there was talk in Athens of greater conquests than Sicily; see VI.34, 90, and cf. III.86n.

**the downfall of the city:** the end of the Peloponnesian War in 404.

**dictator:** Warner's usual translation of the Gk. *tyrannos,* "tyrant"; see I.13n.

**his conduct of the war was excellent:** nothing Alcibiades has done up to this point would justify such a judgment, and Th. must be referring to later events. Alcibiades campaigned with the Athenian fleet from 411 to 406, when he went into exile again. His activities are described by Xenophon, who completed the history of the war in his *Hellenica.*

**VI.16. the Olympic games:** held in the previous year, 416. See I.6n.

**providing choruses:** wealthy citizens were required to support dramatic productions at festivals by paying for the costs of a chorus. This form of public service (called a liturgy, from the Gk. *leitourgia*) is to be found in other spheres, notably the fitting out of a trireme. Cf. VI.31n.

**I brought about a coalition of the greatest powers of the Peloponnese:** Alcibiades refers to the alliance of Athens with Argos, Elis, and Mantinea (hardly "the greatest powers of the Peloponnese"), which he arranged in 420 (V.43–47).

**Mantinea:** the battle of 418 in which Sparta defeated the Argives and their allies (V.63–74). For Alcibiades' role see V.61.

**they [the Spartans] have not even yet quite recovered their confidence:**

in fact their reputation (V.75) and their political position within the Peloponnese (where the Argive alliance collapsed: see V.77–81) benefited greatly.

**VI.17. Nicias [has] the reputation for being lucky:** Th. comments on the success of his career up to 421 at V.16.

**swollen populations made out of all sorts of mixtures . . . constant changes and rearrangements in the citizen bodies:** the tyrant Gelon (I.14n.) had boosted the population of Syracuse by transporting citizens from elsewhere (VI.5; Hdt. VII.156), and, of course, there had been earlier immigrations and movements (VI.2–5), but Alcibiades is clearly exaggerating.

**open sedition . . . violent party strife:** stasis; see I.2n. The point is acknowledged by the Syracusan Athenagoras at VI.38. According to Th. stasis was prevalent throughout "practically the whole of the Hellenic world" (III.82).

**non-Hellenic peoples who . . . will join us:** as indeed most of them did, confirms Th. (VII.58).

**our fathers left behind them these same enemies when they had the Persians on their hands as well, and so founded the empire:** in fact the Athenians and Spartans were still allies during the earliest days of the Delian League (I.98–99) and, indeed, until the late 460s (I.102).

**VI.18. to remain inactive:** the danger of inactivity (Gk. *apragmosyne* or *hesychia;* see I.32n.) is the theme of this chapter.

**racial distinctions:** the people of Egesta, who sought Athenian help (VI.6), were not Greeks (VI.2).

**we have reached a stage where we are forced to plan new conquests and forced to hold on to what we have got, because there is a danger that we ourselves may fall under the power of others unless others are in our power:** for the idea that the Athenians are trapped by their empire, which they must continue to consolidate and expand, cf. I.70n.; II.63; V.95, 97; VI.87.

**a combination where all sorts are represented—the inferior types, the ordinary types and the profoundly calculating types:** Nicias had played on the youth of Alcibiades and his supporters and had called for the backing of his older listeners; Alcibiades rejects that distinction, seeing his audience in terms of their ability and claiming the support of all.

**to defend itself not by speeches, but in action:** an important sophistic distinction (I.32n.), often used in this way by bellicose politicians in Th. (e.g., Sthenelaidas at I.86, Cleon at III.38).

**the way that men find their greatest security is in accepting the character and institutions which they actually have, even if they are not perfect:** cf. Cleon at III.37.

**VI.20. cities . . . not wanting the kind of change by which they would be glad to escape from some oppressive government and accept a new government on easier terms:** Athens had tended to depose oligarchies in favor of democracies among its subjects (cf. Aristotle *Politics* 1307b22, quoted at I.19n.), but the cities of Sicily were already democratic. Th. raises the issue again at VII.55.

**Naxos and Catana . . . their racial connection with Leontini:** they were all Ionian; cf. I.124n.

**seven other cities:** Syracuse, Selinus, Gela, Acragas, Messina, Himera, Camarina; cf. VI.4–5, VII.58.

**first-fruits:** a tithe of produce or cash equivalent paid to Syracuse by its subjects; cf. the tithe of one-sixtieth paid from the tribute by the Athenians to Athena (I.96n.).

**the number of their horses:** the Athenians took only thirty with them (VI.43) and, as Nicias feared, were outclassed by Syracusan cavalry (e.g., VI.71).

**they grow their own corn and do not have to import any:** unlike the Athenians, who imported much of their corn from the coastal regions of the Black Sea and elsewhere (I.2n., 120n.). Self-sufficiency in corn would be vital to the Syracusans if they lost control of the seas around Sicily.

**VI.21. It would be disgraceful if we were forced to retire or to send back later for reinforcements owing to insufficient foresight:** they will have to do both, of course. Nicias knows that "success comes from foresight" (VI.13), but despite his caution his foresight is inadequate.

**during the four winter months it is difficult even for a messenger to get to Athens:** it is in Nicias' interests to exaggerate. For travel by sea between Sicily and Greece during the winter see VI.74, 88.

**VI.22. a large army:** its composition is described in VII.57.

**any whom we can persuade or hire to come with us from the Peloponnese:** Argives (allies) and Mantineans and other Arcadians (mercenaries); see VI.43, VII.57. On Peloponnesian mercenaries cf. VIII.28.

**not every city will be able to receive a force as large as ours:** the Athenian force will hug the coastline of Italy on its voyage and will need to put in to shore at times for water and supplies. But Nicias is right: they will not be welcomed; see VI.44.

**the money at Egesta . . . is more likely to be there in theory than in fact:** again Nicias is right; see VI.8, 46.

**VI.23. we are going off to found a city:** the Athenian force is compared to a city (whose essential component is its citizens: see I.74n.). Cf. VII.75 ("they were like nothing so much as the fleeing population of a city"), 77 ("you yourselves . . . are a city already"). Athenagoras employs the same image at VI.37. In the absence of the expedition the polis of Athens goes into decline ("instead of a city it became a fortress," VII.28).

**I invite him to take the command instead of me:** a ploy favored by Nicias; cf. IV.28.

**VI.24. The Athenians . . . became more enthusiastic about it than ever . . . just the opposite of what Nicias had imagined took place:** a scene of tragic quality, heavy with irony and self-delusion. The Athenians' ignorance of Sicily (VI.1) is forgotten.

**The older men thought . . . :** wishful thinking is the source of much suffering in Th.; cf. I.121n. Early in the war Th. had drawn attention to the particular bellicosity of the young in Athens (II.21); now the old (usually cautious: see II.8n., VI.13n.) and the young alike are overwhelmed with enthusiasm for war.

**the average soldier himself saw the prospect of getting pay for the time being and . . . permanent paid employment in future:** the soldiers in the expedition would be paid by the state. Th. has little to say on the economic benefits of the empire for ordinary Athenians. Cf. I.77n.; Old Oligarch I.16–18; Plut. *Per.* 11–12.

**the few who actually were opposed to the expedition were afraid of being thought unpatriotic if they voted against it:** suggesting perhaps a decline in the democratic ideal from, e.g., the dizzy heights of the Funeral Speech.

**VI.25. transports . . . in whatever number was decided upon:** forty out of the one hundred triremes (VI.31). A transport was a trireme converted to carry troops.

**VI.26. lists of those to be called up:** taken from the list of men eligible for hoplite service kept by the state; see VI.43.

**the years of continuous war:** the Archidamian War; see I.1n.

**capital had accumulated as a result of the truce:** Th. frequently emphasizes the importance of capital, especially for a naval power (e.g., I.11–12). On the cost of this expedition see VI.31 and on the depletion of Athenian reserves, VIII.1.

## VI.27–29. The Mutilation of the Hermae and the Profanation of the Mysteries

**VI.27. Hermae:** square pillars with a head of Hermes, the god of travelers, carved on top and an erect phallus below. These pillars were a **national insti-**

**tution,** a distinctive feature of Athenian life (explains Th. for the benefit of his non-Athenian readers: cf. I.1n., II.34), and this (presumably) concerted act of sacrilegious vandalism was taken seriously (note the reference to the death penalty in VI.31).

**a revolutionary conspiracy to overthrow the democracy:** cf. I.107, VIII.45ff.

**VI.28. resident aliens:** or metics; see II.13n.

**mysteries:** secret rituals, performed at Eleusis (to the west of Athens) in honor of Demeter, the goddess of cereal crops, and her daughter Persephone. Their profanation was a second disturbing act of impiety.

**those who disliked him most:** Th. does not name Alcibiades' enemies, but see VIII.65 on Androcles; cf. too VI.89, VIII.53.

**their keeping a firm hold themselves of the leadership of the people:** according to Th. (II.65), this rivalry for preeminence between the politicians who came after Pericles led to the decline of Athens.

**the undemocratic character of his life:** cf. Nicias' accusations at VI.12.

**VI.29. the Argives and . . . the Mantineans:** for their alliance with Athens see VI.82, 84. See also VI.61.

## VI.30–31. The Expedition Sets Sail

**VI.30. Corcyra:** on its position on the coastal route to Sicily cf. I.44.

**the promontory Iapygia:** the most southeasterly point of Italy, across the **Ionian Sea** from Corcyra.

**VI.31. the force which Pericles took to Epidaurus:** in 430 (II.56).

**the same force which went against Potidaea with Hagnon:** also in 430 (II.58).

**to both the captains and the State:** the state provided the ships and paid the sailors, but each captain (Gk. *trierarchos*) fitted out and maintained his vessel at his own expense, as a form of public service (cf. VI.16n.).

**Every sailor received a drachma a day:** see VI.8n.

**thranitae:** the rowers who manned the uppermost of the three banks of oars on a trireme. In this position they probably had the hardest work and were exposed to the greatest danger; as a result their pay was higher than that of the other rowers.

**the rest of the crews:** apart from the other oarsmen, ten marines (I.10n.), and a small number of archers, a crew included a helmsman, a boatswain, a bowman, shipwrights, and a pipe player.

**a grand total of many talents of money:** Th. lays great emphasis on the vast cost of the initial outlay of this expedition, but more money will be needed; see, for instance, VI.74, 93; VII.15, 28. The expense of naval warfare and maintaining a naval empire is a recurrent theme of Th.'s work.

**And what made this expedition so famous . . . :** Th. concludes his account of the gathering of the forces by stressing the magnitude of both the enterprise and Athenian expectations, foreshadowing a disaster of similar proportions.

**VI.32. Corcyra:** cf. VI.30n.

## VI.32–41. The Debate at Syracuse

The scene moves to Syracuse, the main city of Sicily. A debate in the democratic assembly of Syracuse is recorded by Th. and, like its predecessor in Athens, is presented largely in terms of factional wrangling and personal rivalry between two leading politicians: Hermocrates, an impressive figure who had played a major part in the conclusion of the first Athenian campaign in Sicily, and the blustering, shortsighted Athenagoras, a demagogue in the mold of Cleon.

**VI.32 cont. At Syracuse news of the expedition arrived . . . but . . . none of it was believed:** just as the Athenians will refuse to believe news of the disaster when it reaches Athens in 413 (VIII.1). See also VI.35 and cf. I.121n. on wishful thinking in general.

**Hermocrates:** see IV.58n.

**He considered that he knew what the real facts were:** following Periclean principles; see II.62, final sentence.

**VI.33. because they are allies of Egesta:** see VI.6n.

**to restore Leontini:** see V.4, VI.8.

**a matter of accident:** the Gk. means something more like "against expectation."

**it was against Athens that the Persians set out:** Persian interest in Greece arose after Athens helped the Ionians in their revolt against Persia in the 490s (Hdt. V.97ff.).

**VI.34. Sicels:** see VI.2 for their identity and VI.45 for the implementation of Hermocrates' suggestion. The loyalty of the Sicels will be divided (VI.103).

**Carthage:** cf. VI.15n. No contact seems to have been made.

**Let us also send to Sparta and to Corinth:** see VI.73.

**you, with your stay-at-home habits:** criticism of the Spartan character; cf. I.70.

**meet the Athenians at Tarentum . . . and make it clear to them that . . . they will have to fight for their passage across the Ionian sea:** the modern consensus is that the Sicilians would have been easily defeated and that the proposal was not serious (or was never made). This, of course, would have implications for the genuineness of (at least this part of) the speech: see my introduction, under "The Aims and Methods of Thucydides."

**we failed to help the Spartans to destroy them:** the Peloponnesians had sought help against Athens from the western powers at the outbreak of war; see II.7.

**VI.35. As for the people of Syracuse, there were a number of conflicting opinions among them:** almost all of them based on wishful thinking (or no thinking at all). The democracy at Syracuse looks as ill-equipped to make important decisions as its counterpart at Athens.

**Athenagoras, a man who at that time had very great influence with the people:** literally "he was most persuasive," an echo of the introduction of Cleon at III.36; see n. there. And like Pericles' successors, Athenagoras is concerned more with domestic political intrigues than with the welfare of the state.

**VI.36. It is not likely that they would . . . take on a new war on just as big a scale:** precisely what they did, of course; cf. VI.1n. Athenagoras could not be more wrong: he tells the Syracusans what he believes they want to hear, rather than, like Hermocrates, relying on "the real facts" (VI.32).

**VI.37. they will not have any horses with them:** see VI.20n.

**even if they brought with them here another city as big as Syracuse:** cf. VI.23n.

**VI.38. the Athenians . . . I am quite sure . . . are occupied in safe-guarding their own possessions:** some irony here: again Athenagoras is entirely mistaken. His words remind us of the policy Nicias would have liked the Athenians to adopt but claimed it was a waste of time even to recommend (VI.9).

**our city . . . is involved in continual party strife:** the stasis (I.2n.) of which Alcibiades spoke (VI.17).

**dictatorships:** i.e., tyrannies; see I.13–14, with nn.; I.17. In fact, tyranny at Syracuse came to an end in 466.

**powerful groups:** Gk. *dynasteia,* a term of strong disapproval; cf. III.62n.

**you young men:** it looks as if they supported Hermocrates' proposal for action; cf. the headstrong youth of Athens who were eager to attack the Peloponnesian invaders in 431 (II.21). In the following chapter these young men (along with the rich) are accused of harboring oligarchic intentions. It is rhetorically effective for Athenagoras to associate youth with impatience and irresponsibility. See II.8n.

**that is against the law:** see V.43n.

**VI.39. There are people who will say that democracy is neither an intelligent nor a fair system:** Athenagoras proceeds to defend democracy, though neither the state of Syracusan politics as outlined by him nor his own glaring inadequacies as a politician are much of an advertisement for the system.

**the intelligent:** see I.79n.

**VI.40. this city of ours . . . the city . . . The city:** personification of the polis; cf. Nicias' sentiments at VII.77 ("It is men who make the city . . ."), and see VI.23n.

**VI.41. One of the generals . . . refused to allow any other speakers to come forward:** presumably by using his influence as a prominent citizen rather than by exercising any constitutional power; cf. the case of Pericles discussed in II.22n.

## VI.42–52. The Athenians Arrive in Sicily

**VI.43. fifty-oared ships:** a smaller and more old-fashioned vessel than the trireme; cf. I.14n.

**Chios:** still independent and in possession of its fleet; see I.19, II.9, VII.57. The **other allies** might have been Methymna (loyal to Athens during the revolt of Lesbos: see III.2, 5), Cephallenia, and Corcyra.

**the regular calling-up lists:** cf. VI.26n.

**the lowest property class (called thetes):** the lowest of the four wealth-based classes introduced by the Athenian lawgiver Solon in the 590s. They were provided with hoplite equipment at public expense. On their use as marines see I.10n.

**120 exiles from Megara:** see IV.74.

**thirty horses:** see VI.20n.

**VI.44. Tarentum and Locri:** neither could be expected to be sympathetic to Athens: Tarentum, in southeast Italy, was a Spartan colony, and Locri was an enemy of Athens in the earlier expedition (III.86, V.5).

**their Chalcidian origin:** see III.86n.

**VI.45. Garrisons were put into some of the cities of the Sicels:** as Hermocrates had advised (VI.34).

**VI.46. the promised sums of money:** see VI.6, 8, 62. Nicias had had his doubts about their existence: see VI.22.

**the people of Rhegium . . . had always been on good terms with Athens:** they were, in fact, allies; see I.36n., III.86.

**the temple of Aphrodite at Eryx:** in the extreme northwest of Sicily.

**Phoenician:** the Phoenicians were pre-Hellenic settlers in Sicily; see VI.2.

**VI.47. Selinus, which was the main objective of the expedition:** see VI.6, 8. Nicias seems prepared to carry out only the first of his instructions.

**VI.48. Messina . . . the gate of Sicily:** see IV.24.

**VI.49. Lamachus said that they ought to sail straight to Syracuse . . . It is at the beginning, he said, that every army inspires most fear:** Lamachus sees Syracuse as the main danger to Athens, as the Egestaeans had claimed (VI.6), and believes that an immediate victory over it is the key to conquering Sicily. Th. later expresses some sympathy with his ideas: see VII.42; cf. VI.63.

**Megara . . . It was uninhabited:** Hyblaean Megara; see VI.4.

**VI.50. Naxos . . . Catana . . . the river Terias:** on the east coast of Sicily, Naxos being the most northerly. The river Terias is the Fiume de San Leonardo.

**the great harbour:** Syracuse was sited on a large, natural harbor, the scene of the final great battle of this expedition.

**VI.52. saying that they were bound by oath:** it is unclear when they would have taken such an oath. It may be connected with the alliance between Athens and Camarina made "in the time of Laches" (VI.75), i.e., during the war of 427–424, in which Laches led the Athenian forces (III.86n.).

**the Syracusan cavalry:** see VI.20n.

## VI.53. Events in Athens

**the *Salaminia*:** see III.33n.

**complete rogues:** according to VI.28, the informers were "some resident aliens and some personal servants." Th. is not impressed with the thoroughness of Athenian investigations on this occasion. Contrast Spartan practice, discussed in I.132n.

**had arrested . . . some of the best citizens:** cf. VI.60.

**the dictatorship of Pisistratus and his sons . . . how oppressive it had**

**been in its later stages:** Pisistratus had finally seized power as tyrant (I.13n.) in 546 after having been twice expelled from Athens. He died in 428/7 and his eldest son, Hippias, succeeded him until he was driven out in 510. Hippias became more despotic after the murder of his brother, Hipparchus, by Harmodius and Aristogiton in 514. See Hdt. V.55–56, 62–65; *Ath. Pol.* 18–19. It was this final oppressive phase of the tyranny that was now recalled in Athens.

**but because of the Spartans:** on the Spartan policy of deposing tyrants and installing sympathetic oligarchies see I.18–19.

### VI.54–59. Digression: The Story of Harmodius and Aristogiton

**VI.54. a love affair:** on homosexuality between Greek men see I.132n.

**I shall deal with this in some detail, and show that the Athenians themselves are no better than other people at producing accurate information about their own dictators and the facts of their own history:** in other words, this is a digression, introduced to put the story right and show how easily the truth can become distorted. Th. made the same point in I.20, where he also used this episode as an example.

**high principles:** Gk. *arete;* see IV.81n.

**intelligence:** Gk. *synesis;* see I.79n.

**they greatly improved the appearance of their city:** major building works undertaken by the Pisistratids included the temples of Olympian Zeus and Pythian Apollo and the Nine Fountains mentioned in II.15.

**carried through their wars successfully:** wars against neighbors and overseas with Mytilene over Sigeum on the Hellespont, where Pisistratus sought to protect the Athenian trade routes (Hdt. V.94–95).

**made all the proper religious sacrifices:** most notably, Pisistratus instituted the City Festival of Dionysus, where Greek tragedy would develop out of choral performances. For his purification of Delos see III.104.

**they took care to see that there was always one of their family in office:** a fragment of an archon list (see next n.) from the period just after Pisistratus' death suggests that high office was also allowed to members of other leading families to win their support (*T.D.G.R.* 23c).

**the yearly office of archon:** see I.93n.

**the inscription on the altar in the Pythium:** the inscription survives; see *T.D.G.R.* 37.

**VI.55. this is something which I assert confidently on the basis of more accurate information than others possess:** note the extremely polemical tone. Cf. I.20.

**all the legitimate brothers:** Hippias, Hipparchus, and Thessalus.

**VI.56. carry a basket in a procession:** in religious processions young girls carried baskets containing offerings to the gods.

**VI.57. the Ceramicus:** the potters' quarter in the northwest of the city.

**the Leocorium:** a shrine dedicated to a little-known Attic hero, Leos.

**VI.59. Lampsacus:** on the Asian shore of the Hellespont. Its ruler, the tyrant **Hippocles,** was Greek but had Persian support.

**the Persian King Darius:** see I.14n.

**Alcmaeonids:** a distinguished Athenian family that had been opposed to and exiled by the Pisistratids; see Hdt. V.62.

**Sigeum:** see VI.54n.

**the expedition to Marathon:** see I.18n.

## VI.60–61. The Recall of Alcibiades

**VI.60. an oligarchy or a dictatorship:** more literally "oligarchy or tyranny," as if they were very much the same thing. In Greek terms they were not (on the popularity of tyrants see I.13n.), but by this stage both were seen as extreme, nondemocratic forms of government.

**an increase in savagery . . . more arrests:** the start of the deterioration was noted at VI.53.

**one of the prisoners:** the orator Andocides, whose speech *On The Mysteries,* delivered in 400 when he was defending himself against a charge of impiety, provides further information on the events of 415. For the imprisonment of suspects see VI.53.

**The death sentence was passed on all who managed to escape:** they were also deprived of their property; see *T.D.G.R.* 147.

**VI.61. the Argive hostages:** see V.84.

**the Mantineans and Argives:** see VI.29.

**Thurii:** in southeast Italy, founded in 444/3 by a number of Greek states, including Athens. See *T.D.G.R.* 108.

**Not long afterwards Alcibiades, now in exile, crossed . . . to the Peloponnese:** these few simple words belie the momentousness of this disastrous consequence of Athenian mismanagement (cf. II.65n., **as a failure on the part**).

## VI.62–71. Athenian Victory before Syracuse

**VI.62. the money:** see VI.6, 8, 46.

**the Tyrrhenian sea:** off the north coast of Sicily, facing Italy.

**Himera . . . the only Hellenic city in these parts:** it was Chalcidian; see VI.5.

**thirty talents . . . 120 talents:** again emphasizing the vast expense of this expedition and Athens' need to recoup some of its costs; see especially VI.31. The implications of the high price of warfare is an underlying theme in Th. from the Archaeology (I.2–19) onward.

**VI.63. after the Athenians had failed to make an immediate attack:** cf. VI.49n.

**(just as large numbers are apt to do when they feel confident):** we have recently seen the Athenian demos carried away by enthusiasm (VI.24); Th. now observes a similar phenomenon at Syracuse. Cf. II.65n., **as is the way with crowds.**

**VI.64. while they themselves had no cavalry at all:** what has happened to the thirty horses of VI.43?

**the Olympieium:** a sanctuary of Olympian Zeus, lying inland west of the Great Harbor and just south of the river Anapus.

**VI.65. The Syracusan generals . . . showed a remarkable lack of precaution and believed what they were told:** they were no more circumspect than the masses, it seems. Indeed, they virtually constituted a crowd themselves: there were fifteen of them, according to VI.72. Cf. I.121n. on wishful thinking.

**the river Symaethus:** about eight miles south of Catana.

**the Athenians were landing:** whether they landed south of the river, to its north, or on both sides is not made clear. The question is of some importance for an understanding of the tactics in the engagement to follow.

**VI.66. Dascon . . . the bridge over the Anapus . . . the road to Helorus:** Th. does not go out of his way to help his reader come to grips with the topography of Syracuse. Indeed, he writes as if the reader is familiar with it. No general survey is provided, and the location of a number of features (including these three) is uncertain. Th. does not say whether or not he had visited Syracuse.

**VI.67. eight deep:** as at Mantinea; see V.68.

**noncombatants:** carriers who supplied the forces with provisions.

**VI.68. Remember this, too: we are far from home . . . :** the pessimistic Nicias moves quickly from Athenian advantages to the dangers of failure. The impression that he is not the right man for the job is reinforced.

**VI.69. they might themselves be governed less oppressively:** Th. believed that Athens' power was widely and bitterly resented by its subjects (II.8, but see I.77n.).

**VI.71. They . . . sailed back to Catana:** thus giving the enemy what they most needed, time. See Demosthenes' judgment of Nicias' tactics at VII.42.

## VI.72–73. Syracusan Activity

**VI.72. Hermocrates:** already introduced at IV.58 and VI.32; see nn. there. Hermocrates stands out as one of the few great leaders of the period and bears comparison with Pericles (II.65). On his description as **remarkably intelligent** cf. I.79n.

**He now raised their spirits and refused to allow them to become despondent:** cf. Th. on Pericles: "When they were discouraged for no good reason he would restore their confidence" (II.65).

**what had done the harm:** Hermocrates looks at the facts (as he had done in the debate at Syracuse: see VI.32), analyzes the problems, and comes up with solutions. This is a Periclean model of intelligence, "which proceeds not by hoping for the best . . . but by estimating what the facts are and thus obtaining a clearer vision of what to expect" (II.62).

**the number of the generals:** see VI.65n.

**VI.73. They sent representatives to Corinth and to Sparta:** as initially suggested by Hermocrates (VI.34).

## VI.74. Athenian Activity

**They sent a trireme to Athens:** its mission was successful; see VI.93.

## VI.75–88. The Debate at Camarina

We have seen (e.g., in the case of Melos) that Th. is interested in the ways small states respond to the exertion of superior force by greater powers. He now draws our attention to the plight of the people of Camarina, allies of both the Athenians and the Syracusans, who are under pressure to join the conflict on one side or the other. But their efforts to win over the Camarinaeans draw the speakers into an argument over Athens' aims in Sicily and the origins and nature of the Athenian empire. The debate is thus the last of a series on the subject of imperialism and invites comparison in particular with the Athenian speech at Sparta in 432 (I.73–78) and the Melian Dialogue (V.85–113).

**VI.75. the Syracusans built a wall:** the so-called winter wall, which ran from north to south, with a westward bulge at its southern end to incorporate **the ground of Apollo Temenites,** a sanctuary located on the north-western side of the city. See map 4.

**Epipolae:** described briefly at VI.96. It is a large plateau, with an uneven and rocky surface, lying to the north and northwest of the city of Syracuse. It rises gently from east to west, though its edges are steep in places.

**the alliance made in the time of Laches:** see VI.52n.

**VI.76. destroying cities:** by removal or annihilation of their populations. The most notorious case was that of Melos, which occurred not long before this expedition set out (V.116). Cf. Hestiaea in 446/5 (I.114), Aegina in 431, Potidaea in 430 (II.70), and Scione in 421 (IV.122, V.32).

**their racial connection with them:** see III.86.

**Chalcis in Euboea:** its rebellion in 446 had been suppressed by Athens (I.114; *T.D.G.R.* 103).

**the alliance of Ionians and others racially connected with Athens:** in fact, other races were included, e.g., the Aeolians of Lesbos.

**voluntarily accepted Athenian leadership:** see I.95–96.

**to get their own back from Persia:** cf. I.96n.

**accusing some of failure to fulfil their military obligations:** for more details see I.99, with n.

**fighting among themselves:** e.g., Samos and Miletus; see I.115. This excuse is not mentioned at I.99.

**VI.77. the Hellenes in the mother country who have been enslaved through not supporting each other:** see I.99n.

**enslaved:** from the Gk. noun *douleia,* slavery, but the expression is not to be taken literally: see I.98n., **lost its independence.** Cf. "are always slaves" (VI.77), "become slaves at once" (VI.80), and "to be slaves themselves" (VI.82).

**sophistries:** Gk. *sophismata,* the tricks associated with Sophists (I.32n., III.38n.). This instance of this word is unique in Th.

**not Ionians . . . but free Dorians:** for the use of racial distinctions for rhetorical purposes cf. I.124n. Hermocrates had earlier stressed Sicilian unity (IV.61, 64).

**VI.78. (and superior powers are both envied and feared):** such envy and fear are at the heart of international relations in Th. and were, in his view, responsible for the outbreak of the Peloponnesian War.

**One cannot regulate fortune:** again Hermocrates and Th. think alike; see I.120n.

**VI.79. you have an alliance with the Athenians:** see VI.75.

**you were only bound to help them when they were the victims of aggression:** cf. Athens' defensive alliance with Corcyra of 433 (I.44).

**who are by nature hostile to you:** because they are Ionians.

**VI.80. the Ionians, our perpetual foes:** see VI.77n., **not Ionians.**

**become slaves:** see VI.77n., **enslaved.**

**VI.81. Euphemus, the Athenian:** otherwise unknown.

**VI.82. when he said that Ionians are always the enemies of the Dorians. That is quite true:** Euphemus agrees with Hermocrates (VI.80) on the issue of race but later makes a qualification: "ties of blood exist only when they can be relied upon; one must choose one's friends and enemies according to the circumstances" (VI.85).

**we broke free from the Spartan empire and from Spartan leadership:** the Gk. word *arche,* translated as "empire," can also mean "command" and would perhaps be better so translated here. Euphemus would thus be referring to Sparta's command of the Greek forces in and just after the Persian Wars.

**We ourselves were appointed to the leadership of those who had previously been under the King of Persia:** see I.95–96.

**in this way we are least likely to fall under the domination of the Peloponnesians:** thus in the next chapter Euphemus will claim that the Athenians' primary motive in holding their empire is fear.

**The fact is that these kinsmen joined the Persians . . . and . . . did not have the courage to revolt:** Herodotus (VIII.85) notes some Ionian support of the Persians at Salamis.

**to be slaves themselves:** see VI.77n.

**VI.83. We therefore deserve the empire which we have:** cf. the arguments advanced by the Athenian delegation in their speech at Sparta in 432 (I.73ff.).

**the largest fleet:** see I.74n.

**We are not making any dramatic statements such as that we have a right to rule because single-handed we overthrew the foreign invader:** cf. the words of the Athenian delegate at Melos in 416: "we . . . will use no fine phrases, saying . . . that we have a right to our empire because we defeated the Persians" (V.89). In fact, Euphemus has already offered a justification of the Athenian empire (VI.82).

**So now it is for our own security that we are in Sicily:** likewise the Athenians argued in 432 that the motives behind their imperialist activity were "security, honour, and self-interest" (I.76) and Alcibiades talked of security when supporting the expedition (VI.18).

**it is because of fear that we hold our empire:** cf. "we rule in order not to be ruled" (VI.87). Fear is the prime motive for war in Th. (e.g., I.23). Cf. I.75n.

**VI.84. when the Syracusan representative says . . . :** see VI.76.

**VI.85. ties of blood exist only when they can be relied upon:** see I.124n., VI.82n.

**The Chians and Methymnians provide ships and are independent:** see VI.43n.

**some allies . . . enjoy complete freedom, because they are in convenient positions round the Peloponnese:** e.g., Zacynthus, Cephallenia, and the Messenians at Naupactus.

**VI.86. When you asked for our help originally:** in 427 (III.86).

**we could not keep you under our control because of the length of the voyage and the difficulty of garrisoning large cities:** Euphemus adopts the arguments of the opponents of the expedition (VI.11).

**VI.87. in Hellas we rule in order not to be ruled:** fear again; cf. VI.83n.

**we are forced to intervene . . . our interventionism:** Gk. *polypragmosyne;* see I.32n. On the idea that Athens' power compels it to act in certain ways cf. Alcibiades' words at VI.18 ("we have reached a stage . . . "), with n.

**our general character:** cf. the analysis of the Athenian character expounded by the Corinthians at I.70 (with n.) and the comments of Alcibiades at VI.18.

**VI.88. for the future they thought it best to give their practical support . . . to Syracuse:** as they will do in due course (VII.33).

**Carthage:** cf. VI.15, 90, where the talk is of conquest rather than cooperation. No help seems to have been forthcoming.

**they also sent to Etruria . . . Messengers, too, were dispatched to the Sicels:** the responses were encouraging; see VI.103.

**their racial connection:** Syracuse had been founded by Corinth (VI.3).

## VI.88–93. Alcibiades in Sparta

**VI.88 cont. He had crossed . . . from Thurii in a merchant ship:** see VI.61. Unlike triremes, merchant ships were designed to cross the open sea; cf. I.44n.

**Mantinea:** see VI.16n.
**ephors:** see I.18n.

**VI.89. the position of official representatives for Sparta in Athens:** See II.29n., **representative**; V.43.

**the losses which you sustained at Pylos:** see IV.38.

**you negotiated through my personal enemies:** in particular, of course, Nicias; also Laches; see V.43.

**Argos:** cf. VI.16n.

**My family has always been opposed to dictators:** i.e., to tyrants (I.13n.). Alcibiades' mother's family, the Alcmaeonids, had helped to expel Hippias, the son of the tyrant Pisistratus (VI.59).

**democracy is the name given to any force that opposes absolute power:** thus Alcibiades attempts to justify his association with the Athenian democracy.

**absolute power:** Gk. *dynasteia;* cf. III.62n.

**It is people of this sort who have banished me:** on Alcibiades' enemies see VI.28n.

**VI.90. to attack the Carthaginian empire and Carthage:** cf. VI.15n.

**Italy is rich in timber:** Athens had to import the timber it needed for building ships; cf. II.14n., IV.108n.

**we should have blockaded the coast of the Peloponnese:** this is not possible; Alcibiades is exaggerating.

**VI.91. a force of troops that are able to row the ships themselves and to take the field as hoplites:** highly unusual; see I.10n.

**Decelea:** see VII.19. The idea of building fortifications in Attica had been considered before the war: see I.122n. with I.142.

**Laurium:** the site of Athens' silver mines in the southeast of Attica.

**what she gets . . . from the law-courts:** Th.'s meaning is not clear. The Gk. actually says "what they [the citizens of Athens] get" and may refer to payment for jury service, of which the Athenians will be deprived if they have to be constantly under arms in case of attacks from Decelea.

**VI.93. The Spartans . . . were still hesitating and examining the risks involved:** characteristic Spartan caution; cf. I.68ff., especially I.70n.

**Asine:** a suitable point for departure to Sicily, it was located on the Messenian Gulf in the southern Peloponnese.

**the Athenian trireme from Sicily:** see VI.74.

## VI.94. Athenian Operations in Sicily

**The Megarians, as I have already said, were driven out:** see VI.4, 49.

**the river Terias:** see VI.50n. **Centoripa** was ca. twenty miles northwest of Catana; **Inessa** and **Hybla** lay on the southern slopes of Mount Etna.

## VI.95. Events in Greece

**Cleonae:** some fourteen miles north of Argos. Th. does not explain the reason for this roundabout route.

**Here an earthquake occurred:** a bad omen; cf. III.89n., V.45n.

**the Argives invaded the border territory of Thyrea:** on disputes over borders as a cause of war see I.15n. On Thyrea cf. II.27.

**Thespiae:** another example of stasis; see I.2n. For an earlier Theban intervention see IV.133.

## VI.96–103. Athenian Successes at Syracuse

**VI.96. Epipolae:** see VI.75n.

**it is all within sight from inside:** incorrect, unless by "inside" Th. means, as Dover suggests, inside the city as enlarged by the wall built that winter (VI.75).

**VI.97. Leon:** its site is unknown.

**Thapsus:** see VI.4n.

**they made the ascent by way of Euryelus:** thus they came up through Epipolae northwest of Syracuse, heading for the fort at Euryelus, at the highest point of Epipolae, about five miles from the city.

**Labdalum . . . looking towards Megara:** i.e., on the northern edge of Epipolae.

**VI.98. Syca:** Gk. for fig tree, perhaps a familiar landmark. The **Circle** was well south of Labdalum, which was invisible from it (VII.3).

**VI.99. Trogilus:** modern historians identify it with the cove of Santa Panagia, north of Syracuse.

**a counterwall:** the first of three intended to prevent the Athenians from walling off Syracuse. It ran from the recently built Syracusan wall (VI.75) westward to a point south of the Circle.

**VI.100. the postern gate:** its position is unknown. Th. is again topographically unhelpful.

**the precinct of Apollo Temenites:** see VI.75n.

**VI.101. the river:** the Anapus, which flowed from the west into the Great Harbor.

**Lamachus:** his death, in a minor incident, leaves the unsuited and unfit Nicias in sole command.

**VI.102. Nicias . . . ill-health:** he had a disease of the kidneys (VII.15).

**VI.103. a double wall down to the sea:** i.e., two parallel walls, for additional protection, to the northwestern shore of the Great Harbor.

**many of the Sicels . . . now allied themselves with the Athenians . . . three fifty-oared ships from Etruria:** the help sought at VI.88. On fifty-oared ships see I.14n.

**overtures were made to Nicias:** see VII.48–49.

VI.104. Gylippus Sails for Sicily

**Gylippus and the ships from Corinth:** see VI.93.

**Leucas:** still pro-Peloponnesian; see III.7n. Gylippus moves up the west coast of Greece to make the crossing at its narrowest point. When he hears the alarming news, he sails instead across open sea (**the Ionian gulf**) to **Tarentum** in southeast Italy.

**two Leucadian and two Ambraciot ships:** both Leucas and Ambracia (on the mainland to the northeast of Leucas) were colonies of Corinth.

**sent an embassy to Thurii and renewed the rights of citizenship which his father had had there:** Gylippus' father, Cleandridas, had been exiled in 446/5 (Plut. *Per.* 22) and had gone to Thurii (VI.61n.).

**the Terinean Gulf:** to get to this gulf, which is on the west coast of Italy, Gylippus would have had to bypass Sicily. This is not the most obvious route to Tarentum: Th.'s geography is awry.

VI.105. Events in Greece

**the Spartans and their allies invaded Argos:** continuing the story from VI.95.

**their treaty with Sparta:** the treaty of 421 (V.18).

**raids from Pylos and at other points in the Peloponnese:** see V.56, 115; VII.18.

**giving Sparta a better reason for saying that she was acting in self-defence against Athens:** cf. VII.18.

# Book Seven

## VII.1–8. Gylippus and Events at Syracuse

**VII.1. Epizephyrian Locri:** see II.9n. It had refused the Athenians water and anchorage on their journey to Sicily (VI.44) and remained anti-Athenian.

**Archonidas . . . King over some of the Sicels . . . a friend of Athens:** on Sicel support of Athens cf. VI.103.

**700 of his sailors . . . who had been armed:** on the use of rowers as soldiers see I.10n.

**VII.2. the Corinthian fleet from Leucas:** see VI.104.

**the route which the Athenians had used first:** see VI.97.

**a double wall of nearly a mile down to the great harbour:** south from the Circle; see VI.103.

**the section from the Circle to Trogilus:** northward to the sea; see VI.98–99.

**VII.3. the high ground of Temenitis:** northwest of Syracuse, between the city and Epipolae; see VI.75n.

**Labdalum:** see VI.97n.

**VII.4. a single wall which started from the city and was to go at an angle up across Epipolae:** the third Syracusan counterwall, this time north of the Circle, extending from the wall built by the Syracusans during the winter (VI.75), in a westerly direction toward Euryelus. By "the city" Th. means the area enclosed by the winter wall, and by "an angle" he means at a right angle to the Athenian wall.

**Plemmyrium . . . opposite the city:** i.e., on the southern shore of the Great Harbor mouth, opposite Ortygia. Here the Athenians would be in a better position to observe Syracusan activity in the smaller harbor (which was entirely under Syracusan control), north of Ortygia.

**Most of the equipment was stored in them:** cf. VII.24.

**VII.5. between the two lines of fortifications:** i.e., south of the third Syracusan counterwall and north of the completed section of the Athenian wall.

**if Peloponnesians and Dorians could not feel certain of defeating . . . Ionians and islanders:** once again racial distinctions are used for rhetorical effect; cf. I.124n.

**VII.6. Next night the Syracusans achieved their object with their cross wall:** a key moment in the campaign; cf. VI.96. After their initial successes, the Athenians' position is rapidly deteriorating.

**VII.7. the other twelve ships:** see VI.104.

**VII.8. a desire to say something which would please the general mass of opinion:** the Athenian assembly did not like to hear bad news; cf. II.65n., **as is the way with crowds.**

### VII.9. The Athenian Attempt on Amphipolis

**Perdiccas:** see I.56n.

**Amphipolis:** lost to Sparta in 424 (IV.102–6) and never returned to Athens, despite the provisions of the Peace of Nicias (V.18). For its importance to Athens see IV.108.

### VII.10–15. The Letter of Nicias

**VII.10. The clerk of the city:** an official whose duty it was to read out documents to the assembly.

**It was as follows:** much the same formula as that used to introduce speeches (cf. I.31n.), which suggests that the letter is not a verbatim record of the original but has been written up by Th. according to the principles expounded in I.22.

**VII.11. the Syracusans, against whom we were sent out:** strictly speaking, Selinus had been the primary object of the expedition (VI.8; cf. VI.47) and further action was left to the generals' discretion, but in a frank address to the demos there is no point in disguising the fact that the Athenians' real motive was the conquest of Syracuse (cf. Lamachus' view at VI.49).

**we, who thought we were the besiegers, have become in fact the besieged:** the theme of reversal is prominent in Th.'s account of the Athenians in Sicily; cf. VII.56, 75, with nn.; IV.12n.

**VII.12. our fleet was originally in first-class condition:** a point strongly emphasized by Th. at VI.31.

**We cannot drag our ships on shore to dry and clean them:** which would make them lighter and more maneuverable.

**VII.13. our slaves are beginning to desert:** the context (the deterioration of the crews) suggests that these slaves were rowers, not personal servants of officers in the crews; see I.55n.

**As for the foreigners in our service, those who were conscripted:** from among Athens' subject-allies; see VII.57 and, on mercenaries in general, I.121n.

**the idea of high pay:** cf. VI.24.

**contrary to their expectations:** cf. the original enthusiasm and passion for the expedition (VI.24, 31).

**Hyccaric slaves:** from Hyccara, a Sicanian town on the northern coast of Sicily. For its capture and enslavement in 415 see VI.62.

**VII.14. you are by nature so difficult to control:** Nicias had already acknowledged his weakness in the face of Athenian determination (VI.9; cf. VII.48).

**if things do not turn out in the way you have been led to expect, then you blame your informants:** cf. II.65n., **as is the way with crowds.**

**VII.15. the original objects of the expedition:** Nicias does not expand. See VI.1, 6, 8, 47; VII.11n.

**I did you much good service:** cf. III.51n.

### VII.16–17. The Athenian Reaction to Nicias' Letter

**VII.16. the other two generals who had been chosen in Athens as Nicias' colleagues:** who were, unlike Menander and Euthydemus, members of the annually elected board of ten generals (I.48n.).

**the lists for calling-up:** see VI.26n.

**Demosthenes:** the eminent Athenian general of the Archidamian War. For his campaigns see in particular III.91, 94–98; IV.2ff., 76ff.

**Eurymedon:** he already had experience of service in Sicily from the first Athenian expedition (IV.2, 65).

**the time of the winter solstice:** mid-December 414.

**VII.17. Naupactus:** see I.103n.

### VII.18. Peloponnesian Plans

**as they had already decided to do:** see VI.93.

**Athens, with two wars on her hands:** cf. VI.1n.

**the Spartans considered that Athens had been the first to break the peace treaty:** the treaty of 421, the Peace of Nicias. For the Athenian breach see VI.105.

**the first war:** the Archidamian War; see I.1n.

**the Thebans had entered Plataea in peace time:** the Thebans were Spartan allies, and the Spartans felt some guilt by association. For the attack on Plataea see II.2ff.; on its timing see II.2n.

**the provision in the previous treaty that there should be no recourse to war if arbitration were offered:** the treaty referred to is the Thirty Years' Truce of 446/5 (I.115). On arbitration see I.78n.

**the disaster at Pylos and their other defeats:** Sparta's loss in 425 of Pylos and the men on Sphacteria (IV.2ff.) was followed by further defeats, e.g., at Cythera (IV.53–54).

**the Athenians had . . . laid waste to parts of Epidaurus and Prasiae:** see VI.105.

**whenever any dispute arose on doubtful points in the treaty:** the treaty referred to is the Peace of Nicias (V.18). In particular Pylos had not yet been returned to Sparta, nor Amphipolis to Athens.

## VII.19. The Fortification of Decelea

**At the very beginning of next spring, earlier than ever before:** March 413.

**they . . . proceeded to fortify Decelea:** as Alcibiades had advised (VI.91).

**freedmen:** freed helots, Gk. *neodamodeis;* see I.101n.

**Taenarum:** see I.128n. (where it is written "Taenarus").

**the twenty-five Corinthian ships which had been manned during the winter:** see VII.17.

## VII.20. Demosthenes Departs for Sicily

**according to the terms of the alliance:** the Athenian-Argive alliance of 420 (V.46–47) had been abandoned in 418/7 (V.78) but resumed soon afterward (V.82).

**Chios:** see VI.43n.

**the regular calling-up lists:** see VI.26n.

**Aegina:** occupied by Athens since 431 (II.27).

## VII.21–24. The Syracusans Capture Plemmyrium: The First Naval Battle

**VII.21. Athenian naval experience:** cf. Pericles' words at I.142–43. Athens' reputation for naval skill had been enhanced by some notable victories in the Archidamian War, e.g., those of Phormio (II.83ff.).

**when forced to do so by the Persians:** on the origins of Athens' navy cf. I.93n. and Pericles' words at I.142.

**VII.22. Plemmyrium:** see VII.4n.
**the smaller harbour:** north of Ortygia.

**VII.23. returned to their camp:** on the northwestern shore of the Great Harbor.

### VII.25. The Syracusans Follow Up Their Success

**Caulonia:** on the eastern side of the toe of Italy, northeast of **Locri** (VII.1n.).
**timber for ship-building:** cf. VI.90n.
**some Thespian hoplites:** from Thespiae in Boeotia; see VII.19.
**Megara:** cf. VI.49.
**their old dockyards:** on the northern shore of the Great Harbor.
**a ship of 10,000 talents burden:** an unlikely translation—it would imply too large a vessel—of some obscure Greek, which means "a ship capable of carrying ten thousand units of some [unknown] commodity."

### VII.26. Demosthenes Sails to Corcyra

**Charicles and the thirty Athenian ships:** see VII.20.
**as at Pylos:** see V.56, VI.105.

### VII.27–28. The Consequences of Sparta's Occupation of Decelea

**VII.27. peltasts:** lightly armed troops who wore no body armor.
**ever since Decelea had been first fortified:** at the beginning of spring 413 (VII.19).
**The previous invasions had not lasted for long:** the longest, that of 430, was forty days (II.57).
**the enemy were on top of them throughout the year:** Th. writes as if Decelea had been occupied for much more than three or four months (early spring to summer). Cf. "summer and winter, there was no end to their hardships," at VII.28.
**more than 20,000 slaves . . . deserted:** in fact, the Gk. says "had deserted," which suggests that they had done so by this time, July 413. Clearly this was a mass exodus and evidence of Athens' deteriorating fortunes.

**VII.28. Euboea:** on its importance to Athens see II.14, VIII.96.
**Oropus:** on the northern coast of Attica, opposite Euboea. **Sunium** is the southeastern tip of Attica.

**instead of a city it became a fortress:** cf. VI.23n.

**they had two wars on their hands at once:** cf. VI.1n. and text later in this chapter, **another war on the same scale.**

**the Athenians were becoming embarrassed financially:** despite some large increases in the tribute during the course of the war (*T.D.G.R.* 136; IV.50n.). Annual income from the empire in the years just before and during the Sicilian expedition is reckoned to be ca. nine hundred talents.

**they imposed upon their subjects a tax of five per cent on all imports and exports by sea, thinking that this would bring in more money:** than the tribute that the tax replaced. This would mean that annual seaborne traffic in the Athenian empire had a value of eighteen thousand talents (see previous n.).

**revenue was declining:** no details are given. It may be that income based on a tax on goods was considered more secure than a tribute exacted from subjects who could be expected to become increasingly reluctant to pay.

## VII.29–30. The Thracian Mercenaries at Mycalessus

**VII.29. the Euripus:** the narrow stretch of water between **Chalcis** on Euboea and the mainland. **Mycalessus** is a few miles inland in Boeotia.

**the Thracian race, like all the most bloodthirsty barbarians . . . :** cf. I.5n.

**a disaster more complete than any, more sudden and more horrible:** a point repeated at the end of the next chapter. The episode seems to have had a particular impact on Th. (himself of Thracian origin) as another example of the extremes of suffering occasioned by this war (I.23).

**VII.30. the Commanders of Boeotia:** see IV.76n.

## VII.31. Demosthenes and Eurymedon at Naupactus

**Demosthenes, as we have seen:** see VII.26.

**a merchant ship in which the Corinthian hoplites intended to sail across to Sicily:** for merchant ships taking the route across open sea to Sicily cf. I.44n.

**Alyzia:** on the coast of Acarnania, opposite Leucas. **Anactorium** was on the southern shore of the Ambracian Gulf, just east of its mouth.

**Eurymedon . . . as already mentioned:** see VII.16.

**Conon:** a distinguished Athenian general in the final years of the war and afterward. This is his only appearance in Th.

**his own eighteen:** though twenty were mentioned at Naupactus in VII.19.

**sailed to Corcyra, ordered them to man fifteen ships:** Corcyra had probably been a full ally of Athens since 427 (III.75n.).

VII.32. Events in Sicily

**the representatives from Syracuse who, as already related . . . :** see VII.25.
**Centoripa:** see VI.94n. **Alicyae** was north of Selinus.
**the Agrigentines:** Agrigentum (or Acragas) was neutral (VII.33). Passage through the territory of another state naturally required the permission of its inhabitants; cf. IV.78.

VII.33. Demosthenes and Eurymedon Reach Thurii

**the Camarinaeans:** previously uncommitted; see VI.88.
**practically the whole of Sicily, except for Agrigentum:** an exaggeration. Naxos and Catana fought on the Athenian side, as did the Egestaeans and most of the Sicels (VII.57–58).
**the Ionian Gulf . . . the headland of Iapygia:** see VI.30n.
**an old friendship with the local ruler, Artas:** its origin is unknown, as is that of the alliance with **Metapontum.**
**a revolution:** yet another example of stasis; see I.2n.
**an offensive and defensive alliance:** see I.44n.

VII.34. The Naval Battle at Naupactus

**the Peloponnesians in the twenty-five ships:** see VII.17, 19, 31.
**very little less than those of the Athenians:** the twenty-eight mentioned in VII.31 had now been increased to thirty-three, as we learn later in this chapter.
**Erineus in Achaea:** a bay some sixteen miles east of Patrae.
**the Athenians . . . had seven ships put out of action through being rammed head on:** cf. I.14n. There was no room here for the skillful maneuvers at which the Athenians excelled; the battle was rather like that between the Athenians and Corcyraeans in 433 (I.49n.).
**the Corinthian triremes, which had been built out wider:** by the reinforcement of the anchor blocks, or "catheads," one on each side of the bow, which tore into the outriggers of the enemy vessel and did much to disable it. Cf. Syracusan tactics, described at VII.36.
**the Corinthians counted it a victory if they were not thoroughly defeated, and the Athenians considered that they had lost if they did not win easily:** such had been the predominance of Athens in naval warfare; cf. VII.21n.

VII.35. Demosthenes and Eurymedon in Italy

**Locri:** see VII.1n.

## VII.36–41. The Second Naval Battle at Syracuse

**VII.36. cat-heads:** see VII.34n.

**the usual Athenian tactics . . . to row round and ram him amidships:** the *periplous;* see I.49n.

**no breaking through the line and wheeling back again:** the *diekplous;* see I.49n.

**this sytem of charging prow to prow:** as at Naupactus (VII.34). Cf. VII.40.

**VII.37. the Olympieium:** see VI.64n. Thus the Athenians are attacked from two sides, from east and southwest.

**VII.40. The Syracusans met their attack prow to prow . . . and with the specially constructed beaks of their ships stove in the Athenian bows:** as planned in VII.36.

**VII.41. dolphins:** fish-shaped iron weights hanging from beams that could be swung round over an attacking ship; the weight would then be dropped on to the ship, damaging or even, as here, destroying it.

## VII.42–45. Demosthenes and Eurymedon Arrive at Syracuse; Attack on Epipolae

**VII.42. about seventy-three ships:** the number is made up from the ships mentioned at VII.16, 20, 31, 33.

**from . . . her allies:** see VII.17, 26, 31.

**javelin-throwers . . . from outside [Hellas]:** see VII.33.

**For Nicias had appeared formidable enough when he first arrived:** if by "arrived" Th. means "arrived in Sicily," then Demosthenes has in mind the conference between the three generals, where a decision was made by which they lost the advantage of surprise. This was the point made by Lamachus (VI.49). Cf. VI.63. But the reference to Catana suggests a criticism of the Athenians' failure to follow up their initial victory. On this interpretation "arrived" would refer to the arrival of the Athenians before Syracuse. Either way, the main point is that Demosthenes did not wish to waste his advantages by indecision or procrastination and end up in the situation in which Nicias now found himself.

**the Syracusan counterwall:** see VII.6.

**VII.43. siege engines:** battering rams; cf. II.76.

**by way of Euryelus (the same route as that by which the first army had**

**ascended originally):** see VI.97. It looks as if Epipolae was in Syracusan hands following the success of their third counterwall.

**the 600 Syracusans:** see VI.96.

**The Boeotians:** from Thebes and Thespiae; see VII.19, 25.

**VII.44. it was difficult to find out from either side exactly how things happened:** Th. tells us (V.26) that his exile allowed him to talk to participants in the war on both sides. He stressed in I.22 that he cross-questioned observers carefully and was aware that "different eyewitnesses give different accounts of the same event." Even so, he usually weighs the evidence himself and presents us with his judgment; for another occasion (again involving night operations) when he found it difficult to sort out conflicting evidence see II.5n. Cf. too VIII.87.

**But in a battle by night:** cf. II.3–4n. on night fighting.

**the singing of the paean:** to sing the paean, or battle hymn, during the fight (as opposed to before or after it) was a particularly Dorian practice.

## VII.46–50. The Aftermath of the Battle on Epipolae

**VII.46. Acragas:** or Agrigentum; on its neutrality cf. VII.33.

**state of revolution:** stasis; see I.2n.

**VII.47. marshy and unhealthy ground:** ideal conditions for malaria and diseases carried by flies.

**while it was still possible to cross the sea:** it is only August; cf. VI.21n.

**those who were building fortifications in Attica:** at Decelea; see VII.19, 27–28.

**VII.48. There was also a party in Syracuse who wanted to betray the place to the Athenians:** cf. VI.103, VII.49.

**the Athenians would not approve of the withdrawal, unless it had been voted for at Athens:** Nicias had been appointed "with full powers" (VI.8) but feared the disapproval of the demos—not without cause: cf. II.65n., **as is the way with crowds.**

**whose judgements would be swayed by any clever speech designed to create prejudice:** rhetoric, whose object was to persuade rather than get at the truth, was a fundamental instrument of Athenian democratic procedure, and Nicias is doubtful of the objectivity of the assembly; cf. I.32n., III.38n.

**would say that the generals had been bribed:** the charge leveled against the generals of the first expedition to Sicily; see II.60n.

**knowing the Athenian character as he did:** cf. Nicias' remark, "you are by nature so difficult to control," in his letter to the Athenians (VII.14).

**he preferred to take his chance . . . and . . . to meet his own death:** and, it might have been added, to expose his army to a similar fate. But Th. is sympathetic to Nicias; cf. his final judgment on him at VII.86.

**They had spent 2,000 talents already:** the only indication of the vast expense incurred by the Syracusans. On Greek monetary values see the Penguin translation, app. 2, pp. 612–13.

**they depended more on mercenaries:** in fact, that was a large mercenary element in the Athenian force; see I.121n.

**VII.49. He knew that they were short of money:** the arguments of the previous chapter are repeated—evidence, perhaps, of lack of revision.

**Thapsus:** cf. VI.4n.

**the fleet would be able to fight in the open sea:** the advantage it had lacked in the Great Harbor; cf. VII.36.

**Eurymedon supported him:** whether Menander and Euthydemus (VII.16) had any role in these discussions is left unclear.

**VII.50. Gylippus and Sicanus now returned to Syracuse:** on their absence see VII.46.

**hoplites who had been sent out in the spring from the Peloponnese:** see VII.19.

**Cyrene:** a colony of Thera, which was itself a colony of Sparta.

**the Euesperitae:** inhabitants of the city now called Benghazi. **Neapolis** is identified with Nabeul on the eastern side of Cape Bon in Tunisia.

**an eclipse of the moon:** on 27 August 413. For other eclipses in Th. and his interest in all kinds of natural phenomena see II.8n., **an earthquake.**

**Most of the Athenians took this event so seriously . . . :** they were superstitious people, but, Th. implies, Nicias should have known better; cf. II.8n.

**divination:** the art of discovering the will of the gods, as practiced by **soothsayers,** who generally accompanied military expeditions.

**thrice nine days:** typically oracular language; cf. "thrice nine years," at V.26.

**So the Athenians . . . stayed on:** despite a shortage of provisions, not mentioned by Th. until VII.60.

## VII.51–54. The Syracusan Victory in the Great Harbor: The Third Naval Battle

**VII.51. the Athenian walls:** the eastern wall of the double walls.

**VII.52. they [the Syracusans] sailed out:** from their base in the northeastern part of the Great Harbor; they thus faced approximately west, the Athenians approximately east. **Eurymedon** would have sailed round the southern end of the Syracusan line, which was pushing the Athenians westward, and would have headed toward **the land,** i.e., Ortygia, and **the part of the harbour where there is a narrow bay,** i.e., its northern shore. He was thus separated from the rest of the Athenian fleet and his base.

**VII.53. beyond the shelter of their stockade and camp:** whether to the north or south is unclear. Reference to **the breakwater** and **the marsh of Lysimeleia** does not help, since the whereabouts of neither are known for certain.

**the Etruscans:** cf. VI.88, 103; VII.57.

## VII.55–56. Morale and Strategy

**VII.55. democracies like themselves:** a common political system could be a bond, but, like community of race, in the world of practical politics it was always subordinate to self-interest.

**They had been unable to make use of a fifth column:** cf. VII.48–49.

**or to offer the prospect of a change in the form of government:** cf. Nicias' warning in VI.20.

**VII.56. For them [the Syracusans] it was no longer a question simply of saving themselves:** the Athenians have been defeated on the element where they considered themselves supreme and are becoming the besieged instead of the besiegers. On the reversal of roles cf. VII.11n.

**The other Hellenes would be immediately liberated:** this underestimates Athenian resilience, which Th. noted at II.65. Cf. VIII.1.

**greatly would they be honoured:** on the pursuit of honor by Greek states cf. I.75n.

**There were other reasons, too, which made this struggle a glorious one . . . there had certainly never been so many peoples gathered together in front of a single city:** Th. returns to the momentousness of this campaign as its climax approaches. He had begun with the same point: see VI.31.

## VII.57–58. The Catalog of Allies

By Th.'s day a catalog of combatants was a standard feature of war literature. A list of the participants in the war as a whole has already been provided (II.9n.); a separate catalog of the allies participating in this, the single biggest campaign of the war, is now given (though a brief list has already been supplied at VI.43). It seems to have a number of purposes: to emphasize the magnitude of the episode (less in terms of numbers, already mentioned in

VII.56, than in the breadth and variety of geographical and racial origins of the participants); to point out the motives for their involvement (fear and self-interest, as usual in Th.); and, from a literary point of view, to create tension before the climactic moment of the expedition.

The allies are listed on a regional basis: on the Athenian side those from mainland Greece and the Aegean are dealt with first, followed by those from Italy and Sicily; on the Syracusan side Th. begins with the Sicilians (Greeks on the south coast, then those on the north coast, then non-Greeks) and moves on to Peloponnesians and Boeotians. Within this overall geographical framework the allies are subdivided on the basis of race and political status (e.g., free or subject).

**VII.57. not because of any moral principle or racial connection; it was rather because of the various circumstances of interest or of compulsion:** i.e., in effect, self-interest and fear lay at the heart of this campaign just as they had caused the Peloponnesian War itself. Cf. the point about a common political system at VII.55n. On race cf. I.124n.

**their colonists:** as opposed to tribute-paying subjects. On Athenian colonization see I.12n.

**Lemnians, Imbrians:** see III.5n.

**Aeginetans (that is, the people who were then occupying Aegina):** Athenian settlers in fact, since Athens had expelled the original inhabitants in 431 (II.27).

**the Hestiaeans:** also Athenian settlers, who had occupied Hestiaean territory since the suppression of the revolt of Euboea in 445 (I.114).

**independent:** on the concept of political independence (Gk. *autonomia*) see I.67n. The use of this term does not necessarily imply that the Chians accompanied the expedition entirely of their own free will.

**Chios:** cf. IV.51n., VI.43n.

**the Methymnians:** they had held aloof from the revolt of the rest of Lesbos in 428/7 (III.2) and had retained their navy, but they were compelled to serve.

**the Plataeans:** for their long-standing enmity with Boeotia see II.2n.

**Cythera:** occupied by the Athenians in 424 (IV.54), it should have been returned to Sparta according to the Peace of Nicias (V.18).

**The Corcyraeans:** on their long-standing hatred of Corinth see I.13, 24ff.

**The Messenians . . . from Naupactus:** see I.103.

**Pylos, which . . . was occupied by the Athenians:** since 425 (IV.2ff.). It too should have been returned under the provisions of the Peace of Nicias (where it is given its other name, Coryphasium). Cf. VI.105.

**a few exiles from Megara:** see VI.43. They had been forced out of Megara during the stasis of 424 (IV.66–74).

**their fellow Megarians from Selinus:** see VI.4.

**Argives:** see VI.43n.

**Aetolians:** enemies of Athens at their last appearance (III.94), but since recruited by Athens (probably by Demosthenes, who was in the area en route to Sicily: see VII.31).

**out of friendship for Demosthenes:** following his campaign of 426/5 (III.94–98, 100–102, 105–14).

**the revolutionary situation in which they were caught up:** on stasis in Thurii see VII.33.

**of those who did not speak Greek there were the Egestaeans:** see VI.2.

**most of the Sicels:** cf. VI.103.

**VII.58. Acragas which took no part in the war:** see VII.33. For the stasis there see VII.46, 50.

**freedmen and helots:** see I.101n.

## VII.59–71. The Final Naval Battle in the Great Harbor

**VII.60. senior officers:** Gk. *taxiarchoi,* one for each of the ten tribes.

**they had sent to Catana, telling them not to send provisions in:** this was not mentioned during the discussions about departure (VII.50) and makes the decision to remain all the more remarkable.

**to abandon the upper walls:** the wall south of the Circle, including the northern section of the double wall. The **cross wall** would connect the two arms of the double wall at a point close to the shore.

**shortage of provisions:** cf. n. earlier in this chapter, **they had sent to Catana.**

**VII.61. there is an unpredictable element in warfare:** see I.120n.

**in the hope that we, too, may have fortune with us:** now the Athenians must rely on hope, though recently they had told the Melians that hope was no more than a "comforter in danger" (V.103). On hope in Th. see I.121n.

**VII.62. a land battle on the sea:** see I.49n., VII.34n.

**altering the construction of our ships . . . the extra thickness of the enemy's prows:** see VII.34, 36.

**VII.63. though not really Athenians:** i.e., they are either metics (resident aliens; see II.13n.) or mercenaries (I.121n.). Nicias is surely generalizing in treating all the sailors as non-Athenian. His remarks in his letter (VII.13) imply that some of the sailors were Athenian citizens.

**admired for it throughout Hellas:** cf. I.75n.

**VII.65. Gylippus and the generals encouraged their men:** thus the speech that follows must be conflated from several different speeches.

**VII.66. to enslave Sicily:** i.e., to subdue it; on "enslave" see I.98n., **lost its independence.** Cf. VI.1n. The point is repeated at VII.68 and acknowledged by Th. at VII.75.

**to enslave the Peloponnese and the rest of Hellas:** cf. Alcibiades' claims at VI.90.

**VII.67. the attempts they are making to copy our own equipment:** the alterations to their ships; see VII.62.

**all the hoplites they will have on deck, contrary to their usual methods:** ten was the normal complement (I.10n.).

**VII.68. the bitterest of pains . . . the greatest of outrages:** Gylippus will have in mind the recent Athenian treatment of Melos (V.116). Cf. Athenian treatment of Torone at V.3 and of Scione at V.32.

**VII.69. And Nicias, half-distraught . . . :** as the tension mounts Th. focuses on the desperate Nicias and reports, in indirect form, his words of encouragement, now addressed to individuals, the ships' captains in whose hands success lies. His words recall the Funeral Speech of Pericles, especially II.37, evoking an image of the great statesman whose death was for Th. such a great loss to Athens and who would, surely, had he lived, have done everything in his power to prevent the Sicilian expedition from taking place.

**the name of his tribe:** tribes were the ten divisions that were the basis of military organization.

**VII.70. The Syracusans and their allies . . . about the same number of ships as before:** seventy-six; see VII.52.

**And hard fighting it was—more so than in any of the previous battles:** thus Th. will provide an account of it unique in its wealth of vivid detail and its emotional intensity.

**There were almost 200 of them:** some 186, in fact; see VII.72n.

**there were not so many attacks made with the ram amidships . . . the soldiers fought hand to hand, each trying to board the enemy:** the land battle at sea predicted by Nicias at VII.62.

**VII.71. great was the stress and great the conflict of soul among the two armies on the shore:** Th. turns his attention to the spectators, whose emotional involvement in the action is no less than that of those doing the fighting. After describing the Athenian defeat quite briefly, he returns to report the panic and desperation of the Athenians on the shore.

**they were now in much the same position as that into which they had forced their enemies at Pylos:** where, in 425, the Athenians defeated, isolated, and captured the Spartans (IV.2–23, 26–41). The reversal theme again; cf. VII.11n.

## VII.72–74. The Aftermath of the Battle

**VII.72. they never even thought of asking for permission to take up their dead:** an exceptional omission of a traditional postbattle ritual.

**for the Athenians had about sixty ships left, and their opponents had less than fifty:** from the Athenians' original 110 (VII.60) and the Syracusans' 76 (VII.70n.).

**VII.73. Hermocrates:** see IV.58n., VI.72.

**Heracles:** the demigod son of Zeus, considered by the Dorians to be the ancestor of their race; cf. I.12.

**people who brought news to Nicias about what was happening inside the city:** cf. VII.48–49 on the pro-Athenian faction in Syracuse.

## VII.75–87. The Retreat and Destruction of the Athenian Force

**VII.75. It was a terrible scene . . . :** one of a number of scenes of great pathos to be found in Th. (others include the plague at Athens and the slaughter at Mycalessus), who selected this war as his subject because of the extremes of suffering it brought about (I.23).

**they were like nothing so much as the fleeing population of a city:** cf. VI.23n.

**there was no longer any food in the camp:** see VII.60.

**They had come to enslave others, and now they were going away frightened of being enslaved themselves:** the reversal theme yet again, highlighted by Th. at the moment between defeat and retreat; cf. VII.11n. On "enslave" cf. I.98n., **lost its independence.**

**VII.76. Nicias . . . did the best he could:** defeat and the prospect of capture and death bring out the best in Nicias, but too late.

**VII.77. Athenians and allies, even now we must still hope on:** hope is now all Nicias can offer; cf. VII.61n. and later this chapter, "I have strong hope for the future."

**my illness:** a disease of the kidneys; see VII.15.

**you yourselves, wherever you settle down, are a city already . . . it is men who make the city:** cf. VI.23n., I.74n.

**VII.78. The army marched in a hollow square:** cf. VI.67.

**When they reached the crossing of the river Anapus:** i.e., they were marching in a westerly direction. After crossing the river they turned northwest up the valley of the Anapus toward **the Acraean cliff,** now called Monte Climiti, a huge plateau about eight miles northwest of Syracuse. At each side of it was **a rocky ravine.** The Athenians hoped to make their way through the bigger of these and thus escape to Catana.

**VII.79. Early in the morning:** of the fourth day of the retreat.

**they fell back more in the direction of the plain:** the valley of the Anapus. The next day, abandoning their attempt on the Acraean cliff (now Monte Climiti), they move further up the valley, keeping the cliff on their right.

**VII.80. During the night:** of the fifth/sixth days.

**they were now to go towards the sea:** in a southeasterly direction.

**something which happens in all armies, and most of all in the biggest ones:** panic is infectious, especially in a multitude; cf. II.65n., **as is the way with crowds.**

**especially when troops are marching by night:** cf. II.4n.

**the Helorine road:** the road from Syracuse southwest along the coast to Helorus.

**the river Cacyparis:** the modern Cassibile. The identity of **another river called the Erineus** is uncertain.

**VII.81. most of them accused Gylippus of having deliberately let them escape:** a sign of increasing tension between the allies as the pursuit drags out.

**VII.82. the islanders:** Athens' Aegean subjects. Most remained with the Athenians, but whether through fear or through loyalty is unclear.

**6,000 of them in all:** Demosthenes had had with him "rather more than half" (VII.80) of the more than forty thousand men who originally set out (VII.75). With the exception of a small proportion of slaves and the surrendered islanders, the rest of his troops must have perished on the journey.

**VII.83. Next day:** the seventh.

**VII.84. the river Assinarus:** variously identified with the Tellaro or the Fiumaro di Noto.

**VII.85. Nicias surrendered himself to Gylippus, whom he trusted more than he did the Syracusans:** in the following chapter Nicias is described as "Sparta's best friend."

**this had been a very great slaughter:** of the seven thousand or so soldiers finally captured by the Syracusans (VII.87), six thousand had been in Demosthenes' contingent (VII.82) and therefore only one thousand or a few more had been from Nicias' force of something under twenty thousand (VII.75, 80). Not all the rest had been killed, but Th. emphasizes the enormity of the slaughter, further evidence of the extremes of suffering caused by this war. Cf. VII.87.

**VII.86. the stone quarries:** located to the northeast of the theater of Syracuse.

**the campaign at Pylos and in the island:** Sphacteria; cf. VII.18n.

**by persuading the Athenians to make peace:** the Peace of Nicias in 421. See V.14ff.

**since he was rich:** cf. III.51n.

**a man who, of all the Hellenes in my time, least deserved to come to so miserable an end:** a generous tribute to a man who bore much of the responsibility for this disaster. Cf. the respect for him expressed at V.16.

**virtue:** Gk. *arete;* see IV.81n.

**VII.87. This was the greatest Hellenic action . . . the most brilliant of successes . . . the most calamitous of defeats . . . their sufferings were on an enormous scale:** Th. concludes his account of the expedition with a string of superlatives to leave the reader with a clear impression of the unique scale of this disaster. Cf. VII.85.

# Book Eight

The debacle in Sicily would have provided a fitting denouement to the tragedy of the Athenian empire, but the Athenians are determined to continue the fight, and the suffering is not over. The war enters a new phase; so does Th.'s history. The polish and artistry of bks. VI and VII are conspicuously absent from bk. VIII, a complex narrative, difficult to follow, even incoherent at times; much is unexplained, and the book is clearly incomplete (it even finishes midsentence). Moreover, bk. VIII contains no speeches or passages of authorial comment; the narrative, like much of bk. V, is uninterrupted by analysis of underlying themes or by discussion of issues raised by particular episodes. It is somehow unsatisfactory and unsatisfying, even disconcerting: as throughout his work, Th. is not easy on his reader.

## VIII.1. Reaction in Athens to the Disaster in Sicily

**people would not believe it:** on wishful thinking in Th. cf. I.121n.

**they turned against the public speakers . . . as though they themselves had not voted for it:** in fact there had been great enthusiasm for the venture; see VI.24, 31. Cf. II.65n., **as is the way with crowds.**

**prophets and soothsayers:** they tend to appear at great turning points or times of crisis; cf. II.8n.

**the loss of so many hoplites . . . the numbers of ships . . . were inadequate, as was the money:** vast resources had gone into the initial force sent to Sicily (VI.31) and the later reinforcements (VII.16, 20). On Athens' finances cf. VIII.15.

**men of military age who could not be replaced:** we are reminded of Pericles' words at I.143.

**it was decided that they must not give in:** the Athenians are down but not out. Th. admires Athenian resilience: cf. II.65, VII.28. For the revival of Athenian energy and decisiveness see, for instance, VIII.4, 15. For the enemy's underestimation of Athenian determination see VIII.24.

**getting the timber from wherever they could:** their main source was the Macedon/Thrace region; cf. II.14n., IV.108.

**Euboea:** cf. II.14n.

**measures of . . . reform:** the Gk. is a cognate of *sophrosyne;* see I.32n. Th. clearly approves.

**a body of older men to give their advice:** the Gk. is the verb from *probouloi,* "advisers"; cf. II.85n. There were ten according to *Ath. Pol.* 29, perhaps one from each tribe. We know of two of these men: one, Hagnon, had been general in 440 (I.117); the other, Sophocles the tragedian, was over eighty. No doubt older men were chosen to check youthful impetuosity, noted on a number of occasions by Th. (II.8n.), though in the case of the decision to go to Sicily the old had been as keen as the young (VI.24). This looks like a shift away from democracy in its radical form, though we do not know what powers the advisers had or how they were tied in with those of the boule, which continued in existence (VIII.66).

**like all democracies:** in fact the Gk. says that this is behavior typical of a *demos,* by which Th. means people in a mass. Cf. II.65n., **as is the way with crowds.**

## VIII.2–6. Preparations for the Renewal of War; the Beginning of Persian Intervention

**VIII.2. Next winter:** 413/2.

**the whole of Hellas:** it is clear from what follows that this is an exaggeration. Cf. text later in this chapter, **the subjects of Athens were all ready to revolt,** and see II.8n. Rebellions start at VIII.5.

**Those who had not been allied with either side:** in fact Th. records no intervention in the war by neutral states.

**allies of Sparta:** Boeotian enthusiasm for war is mentioned in VIII.5, but again Th. seems content to generalize without offering specific instances.

**they were incapable of taking a dispassionate view of things:** cf. I.121n. on wishful thinking.

**in the spring they would be joined by their allies from Sicily:** the first ships actually arrived late in the summer (VIII.26).

**they themselves would be left secure in the leadership of all Hellas:** a motive vastly different from the publicly proclaimed ambition with which Sparta entered the war (II.8).

**VIII.3. Agis:** his career had recovered since Mantinea. There is no sign here of the advisers imposed on him then (V.63). On his present powers see VIII.5.

**the Malian Gulf:** west of the northwestern tip of Euboea. The **Oetaeans**

lived inland to the west of the gulf, the **Achaeans of Phthiotis** to its north. For **the old quarrel** between the Oetaeans and Doris, Sparta's mother country, see III.92.

**the building of 100 ships:** much less ambitious than the fleet of five hundred planned at the beginning of the war (II.7).

**VIII.4. Sunium:** the headland at the southeastern tip of Attica.

**their cornships:** cf. I.2n., 89n.; VII.28.

**the fortified post in Laconia:** opposite Cythera; see VII.26.

**VIII.5. the Euboeans were the first:** precisely what Athens had feared (VIII.1).

**Alcamenes:** cf. VIII.10. **Sthenelaidas** was perhaps the ephor of 432/1 (I.85). **Melanthus** is otherwise unknown.

**freed helots:** Gk. *neodamodeis;* cf. I.101n.

**their claims were supported by the Boeotians:** Lesbians and Boeotians were both of the Aeolian race. According to tradition Lesbos had been founded from Boeotia; cf. III.2, VII.57, VIII.100.

**governor:** Gk. *harmostes,* a Spartan regional commander abroad. This is a unique instance of this term in Th., who, in the interests of making his history accessible to as wide as possible an audience, tends to avoid terminology peculiar to individual states; cf. II.2n.

**All this was done without consultation with the government in Sparta:** cf. V.60n.

**Decelea:** see VII.19ff.

**the Chians:** for evidence of earlier (suspected) disaffection on their part see IV.51. Since that time, 425/4, Chios had been loyal to Athens (e.g., V.84, VI.43, VII.20).

**Tissaphernes:** the successor (at an unknown date) of Pissuthnes, the satrap of Sardis (I.115n.). The Gk. is obscure and may mean that he had a special command in the west to fight Athens.

**Artaxerxes:** Th. mentioned his death at IV.50 but nowhere records that the Athenians concluded a treaty with his son, **Darius** (see *T.D.G.R.* 138), and that at some stage they broke it by supporting **Amorges** (though we do not know which came first—Persia's support of Sparta or Athens' support of Amorges).

**because of the Athenians:** the Greek cities on the eastern shore of the Aegean had been tributary to Athens, but at some recent date, perhaps when Athens supported Amorges, the Persians demanded tribute from them.

**Amorges:** Athenian support of him brought Athens into conflict with Persia, but Th. fails to explain the importance of this episode. See the Penguin translation, app. 4, p. 617.

**Pissuthnes:** formerly satrap (governor) at Sardis; see I.115, III.31–33.

**Caria:** the southwest corner of Asia Minor. For earlier Athenian attempts to exert influence there see III.19.

**VIII.6. Calligeitus . . . Timagoras:** otherwise unknown; see also VIII.8, 39.

**Pharnabazus, the son of Pharnaces:** satrap at Dascylium, on the southern shore of the Propontis. This satrapy seems to have been something of a family business: see I.129, II.67, V.I.

**Endius:** on his Athenian connections cf. V.44. Alcibiades' trickery (V.45) seems to have been forgotten.

**perioeci:** see I.101n.

**Melanchridas:** otherwise unknown. His successor as admiral is Astyochus (VIII.20).

**an earthquake:** a bad omen that would normally have resulted in the abandonment of the expedition (e.g., III.89, VI.95; cf. II.8n.). This campaign is too important to be aborted, though as a gesture to the gods some alterations are made in the arrangements.

**Chalcideus:** Spartan naval officer killed at VIII.24.

**they only equipped five:** see VIII.17n. for their employment in Chios.

## VIII.7–11. The Revolt of Chios; the Spartan Fleet Is Prevented from Leaving Greece

**VIII.7. to have the ships dragged . . . across the Isthmus:** along a stone slipway, known as the *diolkos,* that stretched from the Corinthian Gulf, across the Isthmus of Corinth at its southern end, to the Saronic Gulf. The same was done at the isthmus of Leucas (IV.8). Cf. Hdt. VII.24.

**VIII.8. another expedition:** in December; see VIII.39.

**on their own:** i.e., a separate expedition, which they financed.

**Ramphias:** cf. I.139, V.12.

**VIII.9. the date of the Isthmian festival:** late June or July. Cf. the **Isthmian truce** with the Olympic truce mentioned at V.49.

**Agis was quite prepared to make this expedition his own personal responsibility:** further evidence of his power and independence; cf. VIII.5.

**Aristocrates:** probably the same man who had sworn to the peace and the alliance of 421 (V.19, 24) and who is later prominent in both the coup of 411 and the dissolution of the extreme oligarchy (VIII.89, 92; *Ath. Pol.* 33) and in the following years (e.g., *T.D.G.R.* 154.35; Xenophon *Hellenica* I.4.21, 6.29).

**the people at Chios knew nothing of the negotiations:** Chios probably was governed by an oligarchy (cf. VIII.14), but the state had been loyal to Athens since 425/4 (see VIII.5n.), and the conspirators did not expect the support of the people.

**VIII.10. Cenchriae:** in the northwest corner of the Saronic Gulf.

**VIII.11. the Spartans were so discouraged:** it is characteristic of the Spartans to go on the defensive at the first sign of trouble. Cf. I.70.

**those that had already set out:** probably the five mentioned at VIII.6, but the reference is unclear—evidence, perhaps, of the incompleteness of this book.

## VIII.12. Alcibiades at Sparta; Alcibiades and Chalcideus Leave for Chios

**Alcibiades himself was not on good terms with Agis:** he is said to have had an affair with Agis' wife (Plut. *Alcibiades* 23), though Th. does not report the story.

## VIII.13. The Return of the Peloponnesian Ships from Sicily

**the sixteen Peloponnesian ships from Sicily:** there had in fact been seventeen in three batches (VI.104; VII.2, 7); one presumably had been lost.

**Leucadia:** the territory of Leucas.

## VIII.14–17. Events at Chios and Samos

**VIII.14. Corycus:** on the south of the Erythrae peninsula, opposite Chios.

**the Council:** clearly the decision-making body in the Chian government, but we have no details.

**Clazomenae:** east of Erythrae, situated partly on the mainland, partly on a nearby island.

**Polichna:** its location is unknown; see also VIII.23.

**all those who had now joined the revolt were busy in building fortifications:** a necessary precaution, of course. Cf. the earlier cases of Mytilene (III.2) and Chios (IV.51). According to Th. Ionia in general was unwalled (III.33n.).

**VIII.15. the greatest city among them:** see VIII.45, where the Chians are described as "the richest people in Hellas." Cf. VIII.24, 40.

**the 1,000 talents:** set aside in 431; see II.24.

**Strombichides:** an important Athenian general from this point.

**the blockading force at Spiraeum:** see VIII.10–11.

**The seven Chian ships:** see VIII.9.

**the slaves on board:** it is unclear whether they were members of the crew or personal servants of the officers; see I.55n.

**great energy was shown:** cf. VIII.1n. and contrast Sparta's poor morale at VIII.11.

**VIII.16. Teos:** south of Clazomenae, on the southern shore of the isthmus of Erythrae.

**the fortifications which the Athenians had built on the side of the city of Teos facing the mainland:** for protection against Persia. The demolition is completed by Tissaphernes at VIII.20.

**VIII.17. after arming the crews of the ships from the Peloponnese and leaving them at Chios:** these were the crews of the five ships of VIII.6, left to secure the loyalty of the Chians.

**Miletus:** a major Ionian town, on the coast southeast of Samos.

**as he had promised:** see VIII.12.

**Directly after the revolt of Miletus the first alliance between the King of Persia and the Spartans was concluded:** this is all Th. has to say on the background to this, the first of three agreements between Persia and Sparta; for the other two see VIII.37, 58.

## VIII.18. The First Agreement between Sparta and Persia

**All the territory and all the cities held now by the King or held in the past by the King's ancestors:** the Greek cities on the Asian mainland and, it would seem, those in Greece itself. See VIII.37 and Lichas' objections at VIII.43.

**preventing the Athenians from receiving the money:** cf. VIII.5.

**any people who revolt from the Spartans and their allies shall, in the same way, be regarded as enemies to the King:** such a revolt is an unlikely prospect and, in any case, the King would be able to offer little support. The agreement is weighted in Persia's favor and will be revised.

## VIII.19–36. The Spread of the Revolt in the Eastern Aegean; Athenian Countermeasures

**VIII.19. ten more ships:** in addition to the twenty mentioned at VIII.17.

**Anaia:** cf. III.19n.

**Amorges was coming up:** from his base at Iasus, to the south of Miletus.

**Diomedon:** a prominent Athenian general (VIII.54), one of those executed after Arginusae.

**even later than Thrasicles:** see VIII.15.

**Ephesus:** on the coast southeast of Notium. It appears to have joined Chios in revolt.

**Lebedus:** between Teos and Notium. **Erae** was west of Teos.

**VIII.20. the twenty Peloponnesian ships in Spiraeum:** see VIII.10.

**Astyochus:** successor to Melanchridas; see VIII.6.

**whatever was left of the fortifications at Teos:** see VIII.16.

**VIII.21. the rising of the people against the ruling class in Samos:** the standard form of stasis (I.2n.), with democrats (Gk. *demos*) opposed to oligarchs (Gk. *dynatoi* or *dynatotatoi,* "powerful men" or "most powerful men"; cf. VIII.47n.). Again Th.'s explanation of the background is inadequate. It is unclear whether democracy was reestablished in Samos after the revolt of 440/39 (I.115–17) or when this oligarchy came to power. Athens had been on good terms with the deposed government (VIII.16) but supported its replacement.

**independence:** Gk. *autonomia;* see I.67n.

**landowners:** wealthy nobles who had survived the revolution but who would not be allowed to participate in the new democracy or marry into newly powerful families.

**VIII.22. even without the Peloponnesians:** the Gk. as it stands denies the Peloponnesian contribution; the text may be at fault.

**the Peloponnesians who were there:** from Chalcideus' ships; see VIII.17n.

**the allies from that area:** the Clazomenaeans and Erythraeans of VIII.16.

**along the coast towards Clazomenae and Cumae:** i.e., from Erythrae. Cumae was northeast of Phocaea.

**not of the regular officer class:** one of the *perioeci;* see I.101n. Presumably such a command was unusual.

**Methymna . . . Mytilene:** see III.2n. Methymna had been loyal to Athens during and since the revolt of Lesbos in 428/7: see VI.85, VII.57.

**VIII.23. Astyochus set out according to plan:** see VIII.20.

**Leon:** a common name; this Leon reappears at VIII.54, 73.

**Pyrrha . . . Eresus . . . Antissa:** three of the five independent states that made up Lesbos, the other two being Methymna and Mytilene.

**The troops also which were on the ships:** this refers to the force mentioned in VIII.22, but there is a problem with the text, which ought, as it stands, to be translated "the land force from the ships," an inaccurate description of this force, even though the Peloponnesian element will have consisted of sailors armed by Chalcideus (VIII.17, 22).

**were to have gone to the Hellespont:** this destination was not mentioned earlier.

**Daphnus:** inland (VIII.31), but its site is unknown.

**VIII.24. twenty ships:** but nineteen at VIII.17.

**Panormus:** a harbor south of Miletus.

**Sidussa . . . Pteleum:** somewhere on the peninsula of Erythrae opposite Chios, but their exact sites are uncertain.

**hoplites who had been called up from the regular lists:** see VI.26n.

**marines:** normally Thetes (I.10n.), but there must have been a shortage of such men after the Sicilian disaster, with the result that hoplites (who were usually from the Zeugitae; see I.49n.) were now conscripted to take their place.

**Cardamyle . . . Bolissus . . . Phanae . . . Leuconium:** on the northeast, northwest, southwest, and east coasts of Chios, respectively.

**the time of the Persian wars:** Xerxes' invasion took place in 480/79. Th. may also have in mind the punishment of Chios by the Persians after the failure of the Ionian revolt in 493; see Hdt. VI.31.

**after the Spartans, the Chians are the only people I know of who have kept their heads in prosperity:** what Th. actually says is that the Chians exhibited *sophrosyne,* on which see I.32n. On Chian wealth see VIII.15n. On Spartan stability cf. I.18.

**incalculable as is the life of man:** cf. I.120n. on the role of chance in human affairs.

**many others who thought, like them, that Athens was on the point of collapse:** on Athenian resilience see VIII.1n.

### *VIII.25. The Battle of Miletus*

**transports:** triremes temporarily converted to carry troops.

**Phrynicus:** at this stage he was, as far as we can tell, a democratic leader, but he later turned to oligarchy and was prominent in the events of 411; see VIII.48ff.

**Onomacles . . . Scironides:** minor characters of whom little is known.

**in the confident belief that they had only Ionians to deal with:** on racial feeling between Ionians and Dorians see I.124n.

**VIII.26. the fifty-five ships from the Peloponnese and from Sicily:** Th. writes as if he has mentioned this number before; he has not, though he has referred to the prospect of Sicilian help in the Aegean (VIII.1–2).

**Hermocrates:** see IV.58n. He will command the Syracusan contingent: see VIII.29.

**Therimenes:** another obscure figure. He will soon be dead: see VIII.38.

**Leros, the island before Miletus:** it is in fact some forty miles to the southwest of Miletus. The **Gulf of Iasus** is south of the peninsula in which Miletus is situated. The site of **Teichiussa** is uncertain but is probably southeast of Miletus on the Gulf of Iasus.

**VIII.27. he said that . . . :** there are no direct speeches in this book, but Phrynicus is here accorded the next best thing, a full account of his advice, given in indirect form.

**intelligence:** see I.79n. Th. does not explain his judgment, and not all modern scholars agree with it, arguing that a valuable opportunity was wasted. It is later used against Phrynicus: see VIII.54. For further expression of approval of Phrynicus see VIII.48.

**VIII.28. Amorges:** cf. VIII.5n.

**for him [Tissaphernes] to take to the King . . . according to his instructions:** cf. VIII.5.

**one Doric stater:** "Doric" in the Penguin is an error and should be "Daric." This Persian gold coin, named after King Darius, equals twenty drachmae; see the Penguin translation, app. 2, pp. 612–13.

**Pedaritus, the son of Leon:** whether this is a Leon already introduced is unclear. Pedaritus figures in the subsequent narrative until his death at VIII.55.

**Philip:** not previously introduced and not referred to again (except perhaps at VIII.87).

**VIII.29. Next winter:** 412/11.

**as he had promised at Sparta:** see VIII.5 for the undertaking in principle, though no particular rate is mentioned.

**an Attic drachma a day for each man:** probably the going rate (but cf. V.47n.). See III.17n., VI.8, and the Penguin translation, app. 2, pp. 612–13.

**until he had consulted the King:** the issue remained in doubt for some time; see VIII.45, 58.

**For fifty-five ships Tissaphernes was paying thirty talents a month:** at the rate of three obols (half a drachma) per man (with two hundred men per ship) per day, this would pay for sixty ships but would be spread over fifty-five. But, as often, there is uncertainty over the figures in Th.'s text.

**VIII.30. Charminus:** his earlier history is unknown.

**Strombichides:** see VIII.17. We have not been told why he returned to Athens.

**Euctemon:** not mentioned before or after by Th.

**all their ships from Chios:** twenty-five; see VIII.23–24.

**thirty ships . . . seventy-four ships:** a total of 104 ships (plus an unknown number of transports taken to Chios). From the figures provided by Th. (VIII.16, 17, 19, 23, 25, 30) we would expect a total of 129. The discrepancy can perhaps be accounted for as follows: Strombichides had returned to Athens with at least one ship; Leon and Diomedon are later in Athens and may have taken more than one ship (VIII.54–55); 1,200 Argives returned to Greece, requiring at least ten ships (VIII.25, 27).

**the 1,000 hoplites:** presumably the Athenian one thousand of VIII.25.

**VIII.31. Astyochus, it will be remembered, was at Chios collecting hostages because of the conspiracy:** see VIII.24.

**ten Peloponnesian . . . ships:** the two batches, of four and six, from Cenchriae (VIII.23).

**Pteleum:** see VIII.24.

**Clazomenae . . . the pro-Athenian party there . . . Daphnus:** see VIII.23.

**Tamos . . . the King of Persia's officer in Ionia:** his precise rank and role are uncertain. In VIII.87 he is described as Tissaphernes' deputy.

**their city, which was unwalled:** see VIII.14n.

**VIII.32. another revolt . . . their previous failure:** see VIII.22–23.

**Pedaritus, who, as mentioned above:** see VIII.28.

**500 men . . . who had been left there from the five ships by Chalcideus:** see VIII.17. Five ships would have produced ca. one thousand men, but there could have been casualties, and Chalcideus could have brought some to Miletus (VIII.25).

**VIII.33. Miletus:** where the main fleet lay.

**he would most certainly not give them any:** cf. VIII.38, 40.

**The Athenians from Samos:** see VIII.30.

**VIII.34. Arginus:** the southwest corner of the Erythrae peninsula, where it is closest to Chios.

**the building of the fortifications:** Th. writes as if he has already referred to them, which he has not. Perhaps those at Delphinium in Chios (VIII.38) are meant.

**VIII.35. Hippocrates:** possibly the Spartiate mentioned in VIII.99, 107, but it was a common name.

**Dorieus:** the famous athlete, mentioned at III.8, who had migrated from Rhodes to Thurii in southern Italy.

**Cnidus . . . Triopium:** at the western end of the promontory on the mainland north of Rhodes.

**Egypt:** for ships trading between Greece and Egypt cf. IV.53.

**Cnidus . . . which was unwalled:** cf. VIII.14n.

**VIII.36. money looted from Iasus:** see VIII.28.

**the first agreement with Tissaphernes:** see VIII.18, with n.

**while Therimenes was still there:** he was sent to bring out the fleet (VIII.26) and, it seems, negotiate a new treaty (VIII.43, 52), and he departs after this agreement is concluded (VIII.38).

### VIII.37. The Second Agreement between Sparta and Persia

The first treaty (VIII.18) had the appearance of an informal working agreement and favored Persia. The content and the tone of the second, with its clear establishment of reciprocal obligations in the sort of language generally found in such documents, are more suggestive of an agreement between equals. Neither, it seems, was ratified at Sparta: see VIII.43n. Only the third (VIII.58) has all the formalities (notably the customary preamble) of a full, official treaty.

**and the sons of the King:** no such extension was included in the first agreement.

**the cities which now belong to King Darius or did belong to his father or to his ancestors:** as in the first agreement, Darius lays claim to the Greek cities of Asia Minor and the Spartans agree. But see Lichas' objections to its further implications at VIII.43.

**No tribute shall be taken from these cities . . . by the Spartans:** this privilege will belong to the Great King (Darius).

**All troops that are in the King's country, by the King's request, shall have their expenses paid by the King:** this assurance is now given formally, a concession to Sparta, though the rate is yet to be settled; see VIII.58n.

### VIII.38–44. Further Fighting; Discussions between Sparta and Persia

**VIII.38. Tydeus:** not previously mentioned.

**being pro-Athenian:** Gk. *attikismos,* "Atticizing"; see III.62n.

**the mercenaries of Pedaritus:** see VIII.28, 32.

**This he refused to do:** as he had warned them (VIII.33), but see VIII.40.

**VIII.39. the negotiations carried out by . . . Calligeitus and . . . Timagoras:** not mentioned since VIII.6, 8. Since the policy of supporting Chios had failed and relations with Tissaphernes had proved unsatisfactory, the Spartans now look to Pharnabazus and the Hellespont.

**the solstice:** 24 December.

**advisers:** Gk. *probouloi;* see II.85n.

**Lichas, the son of Arcesilaus:** clearly the chief member of this advisory commission. Cf. V.22n. and, on his later activities, VIII.43, 84.

**they were to dismiss Astyochus:** in fact this was not done.

**Malea:** the southeastern tip of the Peloponnese. **Melos,** due east, was now an Athenian possession (V.116).

**Caunus in Asia:** on the mainland, northeast of Rhodes. It is now inland but seems to have been on the coast in ancient times.

**VIII.40. There were many slaves in Chios—more, in fact, that in any other city except Sparta:** Th. must be thinking of the helots, who were not technically slaves (I.101n.). He must also be thinking not of numbers of slaves (for Chian slaves must have been outnumbered by Athenian) but of their proportion of the population. On the wealth of Chios cf. VIII.15n.

**Astyochus, after the threats he had made:** at VIII.33; cf. VIII.38.

**VIII.41. Meropid Cos:** better translated "Meropis on Cos." It was on the northeast corner of Cos, facing Halicarnassus, the chief city of Caria. On the unfortified state of the town see VIII.14n.

**Syme:** an island south of Cnidus.

**Chalce:** an island west of Rhodes.

**VIII.42. Teutlussa:** to the east of Chalce.

**VIII.43. all their ships:** originally seventy-four in number (VIII.30), but others may have come and gone and six had been lost at Syme (VIII.42).

**All the Peloponnesian ships:** so far (VIII.17, 23, 26, 33, 35, 39, 42) Th. has recorded the presence of some one hundred Peloponnesian and Sicilian ships, taking losses into account. In addition there were the twenty Chian vessels of VIII.17, but it is not clear whether they were with Astyochus at Cnidus. Astyochus also appears to have left a number of ships at Miletus when coming to Cnidus (VIII.61). There is some uncertainty, then, but we are told the size of the fleet that sailed from Cnidus to Rhodes: ninety-four ships (VIII.44).

**neither of the treaties could be regarded as valid:** this must mean that neither of these agreements (recorded at VIII.18, 37) had been confirmed by the Spartan government.

**that of Therimenes:** cf. VIII.36n.

**all the islands, Thessaly, Locris, and everything up to Boeotia:** those parts of Aegean and mainland Greece taken by Xerxes in his invasion of 480/79.

**Sparta was offering to the Hellenes not liberation:** see II.8n.

**VIII.44. some of the leading people:** Gk. *dynatotatoi* (VIII.47n.), oligarchs opposed to the ruling democracy.

**Camirus in Rhodian territory:** Rhodes was not yet unified but consisted of three cities, all democracies. **Camirus** was about halfway down the west coast of Rhodes. **Lindus** is a little below halfway down the east coast, while **Ialysus** is on the coast northeast of Camirus.

**thirty-two talents:** approximately equal to the annual tribute paid by the states of Rhodes to Athens.

**eighty days:** the figure is probably corrupt, since it would put Astyochus' return to Miletus and thus the end of Th.'s winter (VIII.60) in early April, whereas it is generally agreed to have been in early March (II.1n.).

**dragged their ships up on shore:** standard practice in such circumstances, to prevent the timbers from becoming waterlogged.

VIII.45–47. Alcibiades and Tissaphernes

**VIII.45. At this time, and even earlier:** a departure from Th.'s normal practice of dealing with events in strictly chronological order; see II.1n.

**After the death of Chalcideus and the battle at Miletus:** the former at an unknown date in the summer of 412 (VIII.24), the latter in late summer (VIII.25).

**He was a personal enemy of Agis:** cf. VIII.12n. Otherwise Th. fails to explain the growing rift between Alcibiades and the Peloponnesians.

**it was he who cut down the rate of pay so that, instead of an Attic drachma, only three obols a day were offered:** such a cut (or rather a cut to just over three obols) was discussed at VIII.29 (see n.) without reference to Alcibiades. It is tempting to assume that Th. is referring to the same event in both passages.

**leaving behind arrears of pay as a security for their proper conduct:** the withholding of part of sailors' pay for this reason was by no means unknown in Athens.

**the Chians . . . were the richest people in Hellas:** cf. VIII.15n. Chios is dealt with separately because it had not paid tribute to Athens; see I.19, II.9.

**the other cities:** the extent of the rebellion at this stage is not clear from Th.'s narrative.

**VIII.46. To Tissaphernes Alcibiades also gave the advice not to be in too much of a hurry to end the war:** on the grounds that the Persians would then find themselves in an expensive and dangerous conflict against the side that won.

**the Phoenician fleet which he was equipping:** not previously mentioned. Persian naval power in the Mediterranean was heavily dependent on the Phoenician fleet and Phoenician expertise. See also VIII.58, 87.

**to give the control of both land and sea to one Power:** i.e, to the Peloponnesians, of course. The uniting of the Phoenician and Peloponnesian fleet would give the Peloponnesians superiority over the Athenians on the seas, in addition to their traditional superiority on land. In fact Tissaphernes' agreements with the Peloponnesians show that he had no intention of allowing them any power on the Asian mainland.

**the Spartans . . . had come as liberators:** see II.8n.

**the morale and efficiency of their navy, which had been very great:** we have not been led to expect such a glowing judgment of Peloponnesian naval power. Th.'s source (it has been suggested that it was Alcibiades himself) was perhaps exaggerating. Cf. VIII.78.

**VIII.47. Alcibiades . . . gave them this advice . . . because he was looking for a way to be recalled to his own country:** as often, Th. seems privy to Alcibiades' private motives; cf. V.43, VI.15, VIII.17.

**leading men:** Gk. *dynatotatoi,* literally "most powerful men," a term often used to denote oligarchs.

**best people:** Gk. *beltistoi,* literally "best men," another term with oligarchic overtones. See Old Oligarch 3.10–11.

**that corrupt democracy which had exiled him:** see VI.61.

## VIII.48–51. The Beginning of the Oligarchic Movement at Samos; Phrynicus and Alcibiades

One of the primary themes of Th.'s work is the growth and devastating consequences of internal strife (Gk. *stasis;* see I.2n.) in Greek cities. In 411 stasis comes to Athens. Unusually for the history of the Peloponnesian War, we are well informed about this episode from other sources, among them Aristophanes, the orators, various documents, and, above all, Aristotle's *Ath. Pol.* Needless to say, the task of reconciling these various sources is complex, and a commentary on this scale can do no more than pick out some essential features. The reader who seeks greater detail and discussion is referred to the excursus in *H.C.T.* 5:184–256 and Rhodes 1981.

**VIII.48. the most powerful class of Athenians, who were also suffering most from the war:** the rich, who early in the war complained about the loss of their country estates (II.65) and had to pay extra taxes (the *eisphora;* see III.19) and who would have had to bear further burdens in the financial crisis following the disaster in Sicily (VIII.1). On "most powerful" (Gk. *dynatotatoi*) see VIII.47n.

**Phrynicus, who was still general:** he is about to lose office; see VIII.54. When Phrynicus turned to oligarchy (cf. VIII.25n.) is unclear. He had presumably done so by this point, when he attends a meeting of the conspirators, though he seems concerned here more with the activity of Alcibiades (an old enemy?) than with constitutional change, about which he is less than enthusiastic.

**He believed, quite correctly, that oligarchy and democracy were all one to Alcibiades:** by his aside, "quite correctly," Th. again claims knowledge of Alcibiades' innermost thoughts. The comment is in line with his approval of Phrynicus at VIII.27. This is the start of a second lengthy account of a speech of Phrynicus.

**internal revolution:** stasis, which had proved so destructive elsewhere in Greece; cf. I.2n.

**important cities in his empire:** e.g., Erythrae, Miletus, and Cnidus.

**who, no doubt, were promised oligarchical governments simply because Athens herself was no longer to be a democracy:** no such promise has been mentioned by Th. Any such undertaking would presumably be based on the principle generally (but not absolutely) followed by democratic Athens that states in the empire should be governed by democracies. Cf. V.29n.

**so-called upper classes:** Gk. *kaloi k'agathoi,* literally "brave and good" (the literal translation makes more sense of the "so-called"). The expression is used here (unlike in the case at IV.40) to denote political status, aristocracy.

**considering that when the democracy had committed crimes it had been at the instigation . . . and, usually, for the profit of these upper classes:** Th. omits to explain what these crimes were, how the upper classes prevailed on the democracy to commit them, and how they consequently benefited. This statement of Phrynicus (who as an oligarch himself is unlikely to be lying) runs counter to the general view that it was the masses who derived most benefit from the empire.

**the democracy offered security to the ordinary man:** one of the distinctive features of Athenian democracy, a benefit subjects as well as Athenians enjoyed, was its legal system, which ensured the right to a trial. As a general rule, a citizen of a city subject to Athens could not be executed without approval from Athens.

**VIII.49. Pisander:** we know nothing of his origins or family background. From numerous jokes about him in the works of comic poets, he seems to have formerly been a demagogue; but he is certainly an oligarch now. Cf. Phrynicus (VIII.25n.).

**VIII.50. He therefore adopted the following scheme:** the start of a lengthy account of some underhanded dealing on the part of Phrynicus, inadequately explained by Th. For a full discussion of this episode see Kagan 1987, 123–30.

**Magnesia:** on the river Maeander; once the domain of Themistocles (I.138).

**Samos being unfortified:** see VIII.14n., 51.

### VIII.52. Alcibiades and Tissaphernes Again

**the disagreement expressed by the Peloponnesians at Cnidus about the treaty of Therimenes:** see VIII.36.

**The quarrel about this had taken place already, since at this time the Peloponnesians were in Rhodes:** the Gk. is obscure, but Th. is perhaps saying that his narrative of the events of VIII.45–52 has reached the time when the Peloponnesians moved to Rhodes, which is where we left them at VIII.44.

**the argument used earlier by Alcibiades:** see VIII.46.

**the statement made by Lichas:** see VIII.43.

### VIII.53–56. Pisander at Athens, Then with Tissaphernes

**VIII.53. if they changed the democratic constitution:** Pisander knows there will be opposition and keeps his language vague.

**the enemies of Alcibiades:** see VI.28n., VIII.65n.

**being brought back from exile in a manner which involved breaking the law:** an alternative translation of the Gk., "returning from exile after having broken the law," should perhaps be preferred. Alcibiades had been accused (by unidentified enemies) of profaning the Eleusinian Mysteries but had never been tried (VI.28–29). When summoned back to Athens for his trial he had jumped ship and gone over to Sparta. He had then been condemned to death in his absence (VI.60–61).

**the Eumolpidae and the Ceryces:** the families from which were drawn the priests who conducted the mysteries.

**a more integrated form of government:** literally "government with greater *sophrosyne*" (I.32n.), again fairly moderate language, though *sophrosyne* can have oligarchic overtones.

**so that the King may trust us:** so Alcibiades claimed (VIII.48).

**VIII.54. ten others:** presumably one from each of the ten Attic tribes, a common arrangement.

**Phrynicus . . . Scironides:** for the former's opposition to the abolition of the democracy see VIII.48. The role of Scironides (cf. VIII.25) is unknown.

**Diomedon . . . Leon:** cf. VIII.19, 23. Th. has said nothing of their return to Athens.

**by claiming that he had betrayed Iasus and Amorges:** because he had persuaded the Athenians at Miletus not to fight; see VIII.27–28.

**clubs . . . for mutual support in lawsuits and in elections:** Athens had no formal political parties like those we are familiar with, but there were various types of organizations in Athens, both secret and open, whose members supported each other in political activity, as well as in social, commercial, and legal affairs.

**He urged them . . . to follow a common policy for getting rid of the democracy:** for some of their activities see VIII.65.

**VIII.55. Chalce . . . Cos:** see VIII.41n.

**the fortification protecting the Athenian ships:** see VIII.38, 40.

**VIII.56. Tissaphernes . . . was more afraid of the Peloponnesians than of the Athenians:** because the former had more ships there; see VIII.52.

**Alcibiades' . . . advice . . . to wear both sides out:** see VIII.46.

**the whole of Ionia:** i.e., the whole eastern shore of the Aegean.

**the claim that the King should be allowed to build ships and sail along his own coast:** it seems odd that the Athenians are prepared to grant the king the islands of the Aegean but not the right to sail in the vicinity of his new possessions. One suggested solution is that such a concession would contravene the Peace of Callias of 449 (I.112n.), which had forbidden the Persian fleet from entering the Aegean (*T.D.G.R.* 95). It may simply have been that the prospect of the king sailing in the eastern Aegean **wherever and with as large a fleet as he pleased** was seen as intolerable by the Athenians.

### VIII.57–59. The Third Agreement between Sparta and Persia

**VIII.57. Caunus:** see VIII.39n.

**Miletus:** closer to his base at Sardis.

**to supply them with pay:** the Peloponnesians would have been short of money. They had received thirty-two talents from Rhodes but had now been there nearly eighty days, during which time they had received nothing from Tissaphernes; see VIII.44.

**VIII.58. In the thirteenth year of the reign of Darius:** he came to the throne in March 423.

**in the plain of the Maeander:** this conflicts with the clear impression given in the previous chapter that the treaty was made at Caunus, which is well south of the Maeander. There may have been a gap between the initial negotiation of the treaty (at Caunus) and its final ratification (perhaps near Miletus, which is situated on the Maeander and to which the Peloponnesians return at VIII.60), but Th. says nothing of this.

**Hieramenes:** the representative of the Great King (Darius) on this occasion; possibly a relative of his. He is not mentioned again.

**the sons of Pharnaces:** we know of one, Pharnabazus, the satrap of the Hellespontine region; cf. VIII.6.

**The country of the King in Asia:** but no mention is made of former Persian possessions in Europe or Greece, as in the previous agreements (VIII.18, 37). Thus claims to these are renounced by Persia in accordance with the complaints of Lichas (VIII.43).

**Tissaphernes shall provide pay:** much needed by the Peloponnesians; see VIII.57n. On **the existing agreement** see VIII.29, 45, where the rate of pay is as yet undecided.

**the King's ships:** elsewhere called "the Phoenician ships" (I.16n.) and already referred to as being prepared by Tissaphernes (VIII.46). This fleet is now seen as the key to victory over the Athenians; but see VIII.59n.

**the Spartans and their allies are to repay to him the money which they shall have received:** i.e., the Spartans will receive not a grant but a loan. The Persians are not prepared to provide ships of their own and maintain those of the Peloponnesians simultaneously.

**VIII.59. making it appear:** the Phoenician fleet would not arrive; cf. VIII.87.

### VIII.60–63. Fighting in Greece, Chios, and the Hellespont

**VIII.60. Oropus:** on the coast north of Athens, close to the border of Attica and Boeotia. For Athenian occupation of Oropus see II.23, IV.96.

**Euboea:** cf. II.14n., VIII.5.

**the Eretrians went to Rhodes:** their previous application to Agis had been unsuccessful (VIII.5). Help will come eventually from Laconia (VIII.91).

**Chios in its distress:** see VIII.55–56.

**Triopium:** see VIII.35n.

**Chalce:** see VIII.41n.

**VIII.61. the next summer:** 411.

**Dercyllidas, a Spartan of the officer class:** i.e., a Spartiate. He achieved prominence after the war but is not mentioned again by Th. after this episode.

**Abydos:** on the Asian shore of the Hellespont, to the south and a little to the west of Sestos.

**the death of Pedaritus:** see VIII.55.

**a regular Spartan officer:** the Gk. is *epibates,* the normal word for a marine. Here it must mean something like "marine officer."

**Leon:** a Leon was the father of Pedaritus (VIII.28), but if this was the same man it is perhaps strange that Th. does not mention the relationship. A Spartan called Leon is also mentioned at III.92 and V.44. Whether any of these refer to the same man is unclear.

**five Thurian:** from Thurii in southern Italy; see VIII.35.

**four Syracusan:** see VIII.26, 35.

**Anaia:** see III.19n., VIII.19.

**VIII.62. Lampsacus:** on the Asian shore of the Hellespont, close to the point where it meets the Propontis. It was a wealthy state, well known for its wine: see I.138.

**Strombichides:** see VIII.30.

**Lampsacus, which was unfortified:** cf. VIII.14n.

**Sestos, the city in the Chersonese once occupied by the Persians:** see I.89. The Chersonese is the peninsula of Gallipoli.

### VIII.63–72. The Revolution of the Four Hundred at Athens

**VIII.63. the fleet:** presumably the twelve ships of VIII.61.

**or even earlier:** another flashback (cf. VIII.45n.), to an unspecified date, probably in early June. Th. goes back in time to explain the background of the events of VIII.67, the point at which Pisander arrives at Athens.

**After Pisander . . . had returned to Samos from Tissaphernes:** toward the end of March. For his discussions with Tissaphernes see VIII.54, 56.

**most important people:** Gk. *dynatotatoi;* see VIII.47n.

**the Samians had just had an antioligarchical revolution:** see VIII.21 and, for the progress of this coup, VIII.73.

**he did not want to join them (nor did he seem the proper person to come into an oligarchy anyway):** Alcibiades had not been supportive in the conference with Tissaphernes and had alienated the Athenian representatives (VIII.56). His behavior and well-known ambition would have suggested that he was incapable of cooperating on equal terms for a common end.

**VIII.64. Diitrephes:** probably the Diitrephes of VII.29, who was familiar with the Thracian area.

**the Thasians began to fortify their city:** cf. VIII.14n. Its walls had been destroyed after its subjection in 462 (I.101). For its links with mainland Thrace see I.100, IV.107.

**governments where the power was more concentrated:** the Gk. is in fact *sophrosyne,* here used, it seems, as a synonym for oligarchy; cf. I.32n. But Andrewes notes that *sophrosyne* must convey approval and suggests that, since that does not seem to be the case here, Th. is using it as "an ironical label for the sort of oligarchy that Thasos and the other cities would get from a reformed Athens" (*H.C.T.* 5:160).

**they went straight on to complete freedom:** cf. the remarks of Phrynicus at VIII.48.

**VIII.65. From some places they also took hoplites:** cf. VIII.69n.

**most of the work had already been done by members of their party:** according to instructions given by Pisander at VIII.54.

**Androcles:** clearly a prominent figure, perhaps the successor of Hyperbolus (VIII.73), but not mentioned elsewhere by Th. For his role in the case against Alcibiades see Andocides *On the Mysteries* 27 and Plut. *Alcibiades* 19; cf. also VI.28n.

**Alcibiades, who, they thought, was coming back from exile and bringing with him the friendship of Tissaphernes:** news of the failure of the negotiations with Tissaphernes (VIII.56) must have been kept from the conspirators in Athens in case it undermined their resolve.

**no-one should draw pay:** the Athenian democracy functioned through a large number of offices manned by Athenian citizens who were remunerated by the state.

**limited to 5,000:** the figure is a minimum in *Ath. Pol.* 29.

**the people best qualified to serve the State either in their own proper persons or financially:** men of hoplite status or above (cf. III.16n.), natural conservatives.

**VIII.66. This was merely a piece of propaganda . . . it was the revolutionaries themselves who were going to take over power:** Th. is claiming that the moderate program outlined in VIII.65 was a camouflage designed to conceal the true aims of the conspirators. But the program was genuine (cf. VIII.97), and there were moderates (e.g., Thrasybulus) among the oligarchs. Cf. Th.'s similar comment at VIII.89.

**the Council chosen by lot:** the boule, or Council of Five Hundred, established by Cleisthenes in 508, which prepared the business of the assembly. Under the radical democracy its members (fifty from each tribe), whose term of office was one year, were selected by ballot from lists of names advanced by the demes.

**some people whom no one could ever have imagined would have joined in an oligarchy:** in particular Phrynicus (VIII.25n.) and Pisander (VIII.49n.).

**VIII.67. they called a general assembly:** *Ath. Pol.* 29 gives a fuller account, with some divergences.

**a committee of ten:** *Ath. Pol.* 29 (and other sources: e.g., *T.D.G.R.* 148) says that it was a committee of thirty men, including the ten older and more moderate men already appointed as advisers (VIII.1n.)—who would give the new committee "an air of respectability," says Andrewes (*H.C.T.* 5:165)—and twenty men of more extreme views.

**full powers:** for what? The formulation of proposals would be in their hands, but such proposals were then to be submitted to the assembly. They may have been granted the right to bypass the boule and submit their proposals directly to the assembly.

**they held the assembly in a narrow space at Colonus:** it generally met on the Pnyx, a hill near the Acropolis, overlooking the agora. It occasionally met elsewhere, but this venue is unique and unexplained.

**one proposal and one only:** i.e., presumably, they could not agree on their ideas for **the best possible government.**

**any Athenian should be allowed to make whatever suggestions he liked with impunity:** there was a procedure in Athenian law whereby the maker of an illegal proposal could be indicted; this limitation is now removed, and anyone who attempts to bring such an indictment will be heavily punished (by death, according to *Ath. Pol.* 29).

**the holding of office and drawing of salaries . . . should now end:** for exceptions see VIII.65 ("members of the armed forces") and *Ath. Pol.* 29 (archons and prytaneis).

**100 men:** *Ath. Pol.* 29–31 disagrees, claiming instead that one hundred men, ten from each tribe, draw up a list of five thousand; when convened, the Five Thousand elect one hundred of their own number, who draw up a constitution for the future and propose the appointment of a Council of Four Hundred to meet the immediate crisis.

**convene the 5,000 whenever they chose:** in fact, they chose not to. The decree will have included details of the selection process for the appointment of the Five Thousand; this will have satisfied more moderate elements. But the extremists among the Four Hundred intended to rule themselves and did not even publish the names of the Five Thousand (cf. VIII.89, 92). There is serious disagreement here between Th. and *Ath. Pol.*, which claims that the Five Thousand did in fact exist (30–32).

**VIII.68. It was Pisander who proposed this resolution:** according to *Ath. Pol.* (30, opening sentence) it was the work of the committee of thirty, of which, however, Pisander was probably a member.

**Antiphon:** eminent politician, speechwriter, and orator, probably known personally to Th., who saw him as the brains behind the coup. It is uncertain whether he is to be identified with the Sophist of the same name.

**one of the ablest Athenians of his times:** i.e., he was second to none in *arete* (IV.81n.). Th. admires his intellect and oratorical ability but would not have approved of his extremism in politics; cf. Th.'s views at VIII.97.

**the people . . . mistrusted him because of his reputation for cleverness:** on overcleverness cf. Archidamus at I.84 and Cleon at III.37.

**the restoration of the democracy:** for the downfall of the Four Hundred see VIII.89ff. But it was replaced by the government of the Five Thousand, not a full democracy (VIII.97).

**up to my time:** 424, when Th. was exiled (V.26).

**Antiphon was himself on trial for his life:** he was in fact charged with treason, for negotiating with Sparta; see VIII.90. He was condemned and executed: see *T.D.G.R.* 151.

**He was afraid of Alcibiades . . . his intrigues with Astyochus:** see VIII.48, 50–51.

**Theramenes, the son of Hagnon:** the fourth member of this quartet of revolutionaries. Unlike the other three he survived until the end of the war, changing sides so many times that he got the nickname "the buskin," after a boot that can be worn on either foot. His father appears in Th. a number of times as a general and colleague of Pericles, as well as one of the ten advisers selected after the disaster in Sicily (VIII.1n.).

**about 100 years after the expulsion of the tyrants:** the Pisistratids, finally ousted in 510 (VI.59).

**VIII.69. the enemy at Decelea:** the fortress in Attica occupied by the Peloponnesians since 413; see VII.19ff.

**all Athenians were constantly either on the walls or . . . at the various posts:** cf. VII.28.

**some Andrians and Tenians, 300 Carystians:** enrolled by Pisander on his voyage to Athens; see VIII.65.

**some of the colonists from Aegina:** settled there in 431; see II.27.

**Hellenic youths:** the name of this group of thugs is inexplicable; the text may be corrupt.

**the Council chosen by lot:** cf. VIII.66n.

**VIII.70. When the Council had made way for them . . . the Four Hundred took their places:** *Ath. Pol.* 32 says that there was an interval of eight days between the expulsion of the democratic boule (on 9 June) and the inauguration of its replacement (on 17 June); Th.'s version suggests that the transition was effected without delay, though he may be compressing events.

**officers:** Gk. *prytaneis*, the name of the councillors under the democracy.

The use of the lot and the observation of formalities suggest that the oligarchs are keen to preserve, as far as possible, a sense of normality. Other democratic officers may also have been retained.

**VIII.71. the Long Walls:** the defensive system linking the city and the Piraeus, a distance of some four miles. The walls were completed in the 450s: see I.108.

**VIII.72. it was not only 400 but 5,000 who shared in the government:** propaganda for public consumption, as Th. has already noted (VIII.66), but the Athenians in Samos could perhaps be fooled for a while.

**as many as 5,000 Athenians had never yet assembled:** the Gk. (obscured in Warner's translation) says "never yet assembled to deliberate," implying a distinction between discussion and voting. In an ostracism, for instance, there was probably a quorum of six thousand (VIII.73n.). The comment should probably be taken with a grain of salt but must have had an approximate ring of truth to a contemporary.

**the men serving in the navy:** Gk. *nautikos ochlos,* "the naval mob," sometimes a term of contempt.

## VIII.73–77. The Counterrevolution at Samos

**VIII.73. The following events had taken place . . . when the Four Hundred were organizing their conspiracy:** another flashback, to the time of VIII.70, early June.

**as already mentioned:** see VIII.21.

**by Pisander, when he came there:** see VIII.63.

**Hyperbolus:** a demagogue in the mold of Cleon, attacked by Th. here and by Aristophanes in, e.g., *Acharnians* 846, *Knights* 1304, *Wasps* 1007, and *Clouds* 550–60. The invective to which Hyperbolus was subjected suggests that he was a prominent figure, but we know nothing of his policies. For the background to and date (418/17) of his ostracism see Plut. *Arist.* 7, *Nicias* 11, *Alcibiades* 13; *T.D.G.R.* 145.

**ostracized:** ostracism (the casting of *ostraka,* potsherds) was a device of the Athenian democracy for releasing political tension in the state through the expulsion of a citizen, possibly a party leader, whose presence was considered inimical to the welfare of the community. A quorum of six thousand met in the assembly; each of those present scratched the name of the man he wished to see expelled on a potsherd; the potsherds were counted and the man whose name came up most had to leave Attica for ten years, though his property was not confiscated. See *T.D.G.R.* 41.

**because he was a thoroughly bad lot and a disgrace to the city:** Th.'s own, highly colored interpretation of popular motives. The motive behind the ostracism was probably a wish to diffuse political rivalry.

**Thrasybulus:** soon to be appointed general (VIII.76) and later leader of the resistance against the Thirty Tyrants who reigned in Athens in 404/3. We know nothing of his previous career. His patronymic is given in VIII.75.

**Thrasylus:** his background is unknown; see also VIII.76.

**each man of which was a free-born Athenian citizen:** a large proportion of the sailors in the Athenian navy were foreign mercenaries; see I.121n. On the possible use of slaves in the Athenian navy see I.55n.

**VIII.74. Chaereas:** not an uncommon name; nothing else of him is known for certain.

**on patrol around Euboea:** cf. VIII.5, 60; on Euboea's importance to Athens see II.14n.

**a very exaggerated account of the terror in Athens:** Th. is no apologist for the Four Hundred (e.g., VIII.66) but will not allow outright lies to go unchallenged.

**VIII.75. All the Samians of military age joined them in swearing the same oath:** the Samians were loyal to Athens for the remainder of the war, and in 405 Athens rewarded them with a grant of Athenian citizenship; see *T.D.G.R.* 166.

**VIII.76. The army immediately held an assembly, at which they dismissed from office the existing generals:** the army thus takes on itself the role of government and control of Athens' armed forces.

**the war with Athens:** the revolt of Samos of 440–39; see I.115–17.

**the sea routes into Piraeus:** the Athenians in Athens depended to a large extent on imports of grain (I.2n.), and the Peloponnesian occupation of Decelea had increased this dependency.

**it would be easier for the army at Samos to deprive Athens of the use of the sea:** in fact, they did not have the ships to do this; they needed all they had to fight the Peloponnesians (cf. VIII.79).

**people who no longer had any money to send them:** in view of the importance attached to the financial aspect of warfare in the Archaeology (I.2–19) and elsewhere in bk. I, Th. gives fewer details than we might expect and no comprehensive survey of the matter. Athenian finances were last mentioned at VIII.15.

**Alcibiades:** still a key figure, whose influence with the Great King (Darius) is taken for granted.

**VIII.77. The delegates sent out to Samos:** see VIII.72.

VIII.78–88. Events at Miletus and Samos; the Recall of Alcibiades

**VIII.78. Astyochus had refused to fight a naval battle:** in VIII.46 this refusal is laid at the door of Tissaphernes, rather than Astyochus. See that chapter for Tissaphernes' failure to produce Phoenician ships and pay the men regularly.

**VIII.79. the disturbances at Samos:** the counterrevolution that began at VIII.73.

**112 ships:** the ninety-four ships of VIII.44 had been reinforced by others from Chios (VIII.63n.), though we are not in a position to account for the exact figure of 112.

**eighty-two ships:** another inexplicable figure, higher than expected. Th. does not attempt to keep track of the movements of all ships.

**the ships that had gone from Chios to Abydos:** see VIII.62, where Strombichides' base is said to be Sestos.

**the ships from the Hellespont:** these numbered twenty-four (VIII.62), which should give a total of 106, rather than 108.

**VIII.80. Clearchus . . . Pharnabazus . . . the original instructions from the Peloponnese:** see VIII.6, 8, 39.

**Byzantium:** modern Istanbul. It had revolted with Samos in 440 (I.115–17).

**the Megarian Helixus:** not mentioned elsewhere. Byzantium had been a Megarian foundation.

**VIII.81. He gave a very exaggerated idea:** cf. VIII.82, 88, 108.

**political clubs:** see VIII.54n.

**Aspendus:** on the river Eurymedon, a few miles north of its mouth, within striking distance of the Aegean. See also VIII.87.

**VIII.82. the previous ones:** see VIII.76.

**VIII.83. when the Athenians had sailed up to Miletus:** see VIII.79.

**some place where they could be sure of supplies:** Pharnabazus had offered to support the fleet; see VIII.80.

**VIII.84. Most of the Syracusan and Thurian crews were free men:** i.e., some were slaves; see I.55n.

**the Syracusan . . . crews:** cf. VIII.78 on their outspokenness.

**Dorieus:** leader of the Thurian detachment; see VIII.35.

**When the general mass of the men saw this happening they lost all**

**control, as sailors do:** Th. has little respect for the self-discipline of large gatherings; cf. II.65n., **as is the way with crowds.**

**took refuge at an altar:** cf. I.24n.

**the fort built in Miletus by Tissaphernes:** not previously mentioned by Th.

**Lichas:** cf. VIII.39, 43.

**their dependence:** the Gk. is from *douleia,* "slavery"; see I.98n.

**until the war was satisfactorily concluded:** a surprising addition. The treaty contained no such qualification (VIII.58).

**VIII.85. Hermocrates:** the Syracusan commander; see IV.58n., VIII.26. Th. offers neither a date (merely an enigmatic "finally") nor an explanation for his exile, which followed a period of civil strife at Syracuse. Xenophon (*Hellenica* I.1.27–31) put these events in the following year, but there is much confusion in his narrative at this point.

**VIII.86. delegates from the Four Hundred:** see VIII.72, 77.

**nor was it in order to surrender Athens to the enemy:** untrue, of course; see VIII.70.

**when the enemy made their invasion:** possibly a reference to the Peloponnesian movements described at VIII.71, though they hardly merit the name of invasion.

**the slanderous report of Chaereas:** see VIII.74.

**There was not another man in existence . . . :** Th., who has mixed feelings about Alcibiades (cf. VI.15), now acknowledges the force of his character and the power of his oratory.

**the original Council of the Five Hundred should be reinstated:** the boule; see VIII.66, with n.

**Argos:** not mentioned since VIII.27, when the Argive contingent returned home after some heavy losses. Argos, a democracy, was a rival and often an enemy of Sparta and would have been worried by the Athenian oligarchs and their plans for peace.

**with instructions to sail round Euboea:** see VIII.74.

**Laespodias, Aristophon, and Melesius:** their identities are uncertain. It seems extraordinary that they should have been entrusted to democrats, but Th. makes no comment along these lines.

**VIII.87. Aspendus:** see VIII.81n.

**his deputy Tamos:** see VIII.31.

**Different explanations are given . . . various conjectures have been made . . . According to one view . . . Others say . . . Another theory . . . I myself feel quite sure:** Th.'s normal practice is to weigh the evidence privately and then present us with his judgment. It is very rare for him to offer a variety of possible interpretations (though it is less uncommon for him to acknowledge the difficulty of sorting out his facts: see I.22, II.5, VII.144). In addition to Th.'s various explanations, a possible revolt in Egypt (presumably unknown to Th. at the time of writing: our evidence, which is less than secure, is Aramaic, with Diodorus XIII.46) may have been a further factor in the decision to send back the ships to Phoenicia. But given Tissaphernes' keenness to wear out both sides, it seems unlikely that he would have brought up the Phoenician fleet in support of the Peloponnesians: Th. would seem to be right. Any trouble in Egypt would have provided Tissaphernes with a useful excuse.

**his original plan of wearing down the Peloponnesian forces:** cf. VIII.46, 56–57.

**fewer ships had been collected than the King had ordered:** Diodorus (XIII.36.5) gives a figure of three hundred for the king's requirements.

**a Spartan called Philip:** probably the man put in charge at Miletus in late 412; see VIII.28.

**VIII.88. he would bring the Phoenician fleet to the Athenians himself:** an unlikely prospect since the breakdown in negotiations between Athens and Tissaphernes in VIII.56, but Alcibiades must maintain the impression that he has influence with the satrap; cf. VIII.81–82.

### VIII.89–93. The Fall of the Four Hundred

**VIII.89. the representatives who had been sent out by the Four Hundred:** see VIII.72, 77, 86. See VIII.86 also for Alcibiades' message.

**Theramenes:** see VIII.68n.

**Aristocrates:** see VIII.9n. Note that he is not mentioned in the list of leaders at VIII.68.

**the Five Thousand should be appointed . . . should exist in real fact rather than as a mere name:** see VIII.67n.

**This, in fact, was mere political propaganda:** Th. made a similar judgment at VIII.66; see n. there.

**personal ambition:** an important element in Th.'s analysis of Athenian failure at II.65. Personal rivalry is destructive in oligarchy, as it is in democracy. Cf. text later in this chapter, **Each one of them . . . tried to get in first as leader and champion of the people.**

**For no sooner is the change made than . . . :** we do not have the evidence to assess Th.'s generalizations on splits in oligarchies, but there is little to support them.

**not content with being the equal of others:** in fact the Gk. says "not content with not being . . . ," i.e., with being a cut above the masses.

**In a democracy . . . someone who fails to get elected to office can always console himself with the thought that there was something not quite fair about it:** Th.'s meaning is far from clear, particularly the phrase translated as "something not quite fair about it." He is drawing a distinction between an oligarchy (especially one recently established), in which each man, considering himself the equal of his peers, strives for the supreme position and is aggrieved if he fails, and a democracy, where a man seeks power through election, in which the candidates are unlikely to be starting from the same position; this makes defeat more bearable.

**VIII.90. Phrynicus . . . who had quarrelled with Alcibiades:** see VIII.48, 50–51.

**Aristarchus:** we do not know his background; see also VIII.92, 98.

**Pisander, Antiphon:** see VIII.68.

**Eetionia:** a short promontory on the northwestern side of the main harbor, jutting into the harbor and dominating its entrance. It was already defended against attack from outside by walls to the north and west, with a tower at its southern end. Modern authorities cannot agree on where the oligarchs were building, but their purpose is clearly stated by Th.

**a warehouse:** in fact a stoa or colonnade used for storing grain, the so-called *makra stoa* on the northeastern shore of the harbor.

**the corn that was brought in by sea:** cf. VIII.76n.

**VIII.91. Tarentum and Locri:** both pro-Peloponnesian; see VI.44, 104; VII.1.

**the Euboeans:** they had been keen to revolt for some time; see VIII.5, 60.

**Las in Laconia:** southwest of Sparta's naval base at Gytheum.

**keep control over the allies as well:** thus the oligarchs clearly wished to retain the empire. The idea of abandoning the empire surfaces occasionally in Th.: see I.75n.

**VIII.92. the militia:** translated elsewhere (IV.67n.) as "home guard," but we have no certain knowledge of who they were.

**Phrynichus:** for further (and conflicting) details of his death see Lysias XIII.70–72 and Plut. *Alcibiades* 25. In 409 the assassins were publicly honored and rewarded for services to the Athenian democracy: see *T.D.G.R.* 155.

**the man who had struck the blow:** Thrasybulus of Calydon, according to Lysias; thus he receives particular honor, including citizenship, in the preceding decree.

**political clubs:** see VIII.54n.

**Hermon:** otherwise unknown.

**Munychia:** the third of Athens' harbors, at the western end of the bay of Phalerum (I.107n.).

**their action met with the approval of . . . the hoplites:** the army now turns against the extremists; its support in what follows is vital.

**The elder men did what they could:** on the contrast between young and old in Th. see II.8n.

**Thucydides the Pharsalian:** not otherwise known. The Gk. for **representative** is *proxenos;* see II.29n.

**avoided saying straight out "whoever wants the people to govern":** if the subject is the hoplites these words suggest that they wanted a return to full democracy. Given recent events it seems unlikely that the hoplites would have been quite so reticent.

**VIII.93. the theater of Dionysus near Munychia:** Munychia is the high point of Piraeus; the theater of Dionysus was on its northwestern slope.

**the Anaceum:** the precinct of the temple of the Dioscuri, on the north slope of the Acropolis; it was used as a parade ground.

**they said that they would publish the names of the Five Thousand:** probably a delaying tactic rather than a genuine offer.

## VIII.94–95. The Battle of Eretria

**VIII.94. from Megara:** the last we heard of these Peloponnesian ships was that they were at Epidaurus (VIII.92).

**VIII.95. Sunium:** the southeastern tip of Attica.

**Thoricus and Prasiae:** on the east coast of Attica, the former some six miles north of Sunium.

**Oropus:** on the north coast of Attica, opposite Eretria in Euboea. It had been occupied by the Boeotians late in the winter of 411: see VIII.60. On its importance to Athens see VII.28.

**now that they were cut off from Attica:** because of the Spartan occupation of Decelea.

**Euboea was everything to them:** cf. II.14n., VIII.96.

**Thymochares:** otherwise unknown.

**the ships already in Euboea:** not previously mentioned, apart from a troop carrier sent out to patrol Euboea at VIII.74.

**Oreus:** or Hestiaea, at the northern end of Euboea. It had been in Athenian hands since the rebellion of 446; see I.114 with n.

## VIII.96–98. The Establishment of the Five Thousand

**VIII.96. the very greatest panic that had ever been known there:** Th. uses similar language of the abortive Peloponnesian attempt on Piraeus in 429 (II.94).

**there was every reason for despondency:** whereas they had quickly recovered from the shock of the news from Sicily and immediately took remedial action (VIII.1). On this occasion too, according to the next chapter, their spirits soon recover.

**they had no more ships:** though twenty are mentioned in the next chapter.

**as on many others:** Th. perhaps has in mind, among other examples, the earlier attack on the Piraeus. He may also be thinking of Spartan apathy during the period of the Pentecontaetia, which allowed Athens to grow strong (cf. I.68ff.).

**the very great difference in the national characters:** cf. the words of the Corinthians at I.70, with n.

**the Syracusans, who were most like the Athenians in character and fought best against them:** a rather sweeping generalization; it is not clear what aspect of the Syracusans Th. has in mind. Like the Athenians they were democratic and imperialist and could show a quality akin to the enterprise and ambition of the Athenians (see, e.g., Th.'s comments at VII.56), though their success against Athens in Sicily had depended on Spartan support. Or perhaps Th. was thinking of Syracusan participation in more recent events and in particular of the strength of character exhibited by Hermocrates (VIII.26, 45; cf. VI.72).

**VIII.97. the Pnyx:** a gently sloping hill overlooking the Athenian agora.

**where they used to meet before:** i.e., in the days of the democracy.

**it was voted that power should be handed over to the Five Thousand:** by "power" (Gk. *ta pragmata,* literally "affairs") Th. must mean control of the state's affairs via the franchise and other political rights; he does not expand on the nature and extent of this control. Our meager sources suggest that in its institutions the new constitution resembled the old democracy: the assembly met; elections were held to fill the democratic offices (e.g., during the archonship of Theopompus; see *Ath. Pol.* 33), though without payment; the generals at Samos continued to serve; there was a boule based on prytanies; and the courts still functioned (Plut. *Moralia* 833e–f). Th. has nothing to say on the duration of the Five Thousand and the transition back to democracy; only the *Ath. Pol.* (34) remarks on this, saying no more than it happened "quickly." The issue is controversial, but it appears from a decree against the overthrow of democracy, dated summer 410, that democracy had been restored by then (Andocides *On the Mysteries* 96–98).

**the Five Thousand, who were to include all who could provide themselves with a hoplite's equipment:** i.e., all classes except Thetes (III.16n.), who would include the sailors in the fleet, now debarred from the franchise. The figure of five thousand is meaningless in this new context; actual numbers were probably double that.

**no-one . . . was to receive any remuneration for the holding of any office:** to save money for the war effort, of course. A decision to this effect was originally taken at the Colonus assembly: see VIII.67.

**legal advisers:** Gk. *nomothetae,* "lawgivers," not a feature of the democracy. We are left to guess at their precise function.

**during the first period of this new regime . . . at least in my time:** the Gk. is difficult to interpret and its meaning is another area of controversy; in particular what Th. means by "the first period" (out of some nine months) is quite unclear. An alternative translation is "Indeed, for the first time, at least in my life, the Athenians appear to have been well governed." This translation avoids the distinction between different phases of the rule of the Five Thousand but seems to ignore Th.'s earlier commendation of the administration of Pericles (II.65).

**the Athenians appear to have had a better government than ever before:** it is unclear whether the Gk. for "better government" (literally "was governed well") means that the form of government was good or the government's conduct of affairs was good. The next sentence (which should start "For there was . . . ") suggests the former, though perhaps both are implied. Whatever the exact meaning, this is high praise from Th.

**a reasonable and moderate blending of the few and the many:** once again the precise meaning of the Gk. is unclear and much disputed. It is tempting to see this as a comment on the constitution of the Five Thousand, but the exclusion of the Thetes ("the many") from the Five Thousand seems to argue against this. Yet it is not obvious to what else it could refer. Perhaps the expression is Th.'s way of describing a broadly based oligarchy or a mixed constitution. What is clear is that the avoidance of extremes particularly meets with his approval. His attitude says a great deal about his own political preferences.

**They also voted for the recall of Alcibiades:** in fact, he did not return until 407 (Xenophon *Hellenica* I.4); the restored democracy may have been less keen on the idea.

**and of others:** a full list of those who fled into exile following the affairs of the herms and the mysteries of 415 (VI.27ff.) is given in *H.C.T.* 4:277–82; the effect of this recall is unknown.

**VIII.98. Pisander and . . . all the most extreme leaders of the oligarchical party . . . got away to Decelea:** the absence of the name of Antiphon from this chapter has puzzled commentators, especially as he stayed in Athens and was later tried; see VIII.68.

**some of the least Hellenized of the archers:** the city maintained a contingent of Scythian archers who acted as a police force.

**Oenoe:** cf. II.18.

## VIII.99–109. The Peloponnesians Move to the Hellespont; the Battle of Cynossema

**VIII.99. the position of the Peloponnesians at Miletus was as follows:** Th. summarizes events recounted at VIII.87.

**the officers:** it was Tamos who had been charged with the responsibility for paying the Peloponnesians at VIII.87, but the discrepancy is probably not significant. At VIII.87 the pay had got worse; it has now shrunk to nothing.

**Hippocrates:** see VIII.35.

**Pharnabazus continued to ask for their assistance:** cf. VIII.80.

**he, too, like Tissaphernes, wanted to bring about the revolt:** on their rivalry cf. VIII.6.

**the cities in his province that were still subject to Athens:** in fact, Th. has told us of only one Athenian loss, Abydos (VIII.62), but there were probably others, as is implied here.

**seventy-three ships:** there were 112 at VIII.79. Taking into account the movements described in VIII.80 and in the sentence following this one, we have a total of eighty-six. Diodorus (XIII.38) reports that thirteen ships were sent off by Mindarus to deal with a threatened revolution in Rhodes: this would account for the discrepancy.

**Icarus:** an island west of Samos.

**VIII.100. fifty-five ships:** there were 108 at VIII.79. There had been some movements since, but Th. does not account for the whereabouts of all the ships.

**the Lesbian city of Eresus:** its second revolt; see VIII.23.

**the racial connection between Lesbos and Thebes:** they were both Aeolian; cf. VIII.5n.

**VIII.101. Carteria, in the Phocaeid:** its exact location is unknown, but it was an island off the coast of Phocaea, which is on the mainland southeast of Lesbos.

**Harmatus:** otherwise unknown.

**Lectum, Larissa, Hamaxitus:** these seem to be in reverse order. Hamaxitus is on the mainland, approximately north of Methymna; Larissa is north of Hamaxitus; Lectum is on the Troad, south of the entrance to the Hellespont.

**Rhoeteum . . . Sigeum:** on the southern shore of the Hellespont, just inside its mouth. Mindarus had thus sailed over one hundred miles in less than twenty-four hours.

**VIII.102. Elaeus:** on the northern shore of the Hellespont, close to its mouth.

**Protesilaus:** a Greek hero who fought and died in the Trojan War. Herodotus (IX.116) also refers to this shrine.

**VIII.103. eighty-six ships:** sixteen came from Abydos, and Mindarus had seventy-three, of which he lost two (mentioned later in this chapter). They total eighty-seven; one remains unaccounted for.

**VIII.104. the Athenians, with seventy-six ships:** sixty-two ships at Eresus (VIII.100; I assume the Methymnians were left behind), plus the fourteen that survived from the squadron at Sestos (VIII.102).

**Idacus . . . Arrhiani:** both were down the coast from Sestos, near Cynossema, but their exact locations are unknown.

**Dardanus:** on the southern shore of the Hellespont, roughly south of Cynossema.

**VIII.106. river Midius:** its identity is uncertain, but it is generally identified with a river east of Cynossema.

**failures in some minor actions:** at Syme (VIII.42), at Eretria (VIII.95), and at Elaeus (VIII.102).

**final victory:** not quite what the Gk. says; see II.13n.

**VIII.107. the Athenians in Sestos:** they presumably went there after the battle, but Th. has not informed us.

**Cyzicus:** on the southern shore of the Propontis, where the Arctonnesus joins the mainland. Its revolt has not been mentioned before.

**Harpagium . . . Priapus:** also on the southern shore of the Propontis, west of Cyzicus, near the mouth of the Granicus.

**which was unfortified:** see VIII.14n.

**Epicles:** otherwise unknown.

**VIII.108. Alcibiades with his thirteen ships returned from Caunus and Phaselis:** see VIII.88.

**Halicarnassus:** the chief city of Caria, where Charminus sought refuge at VIII.42. On **Cos** cf. VIII.41n.

**Tissaphernes . . . hurried back from Aspendus:** see VIII.87.

**the Antandrians . . . Mount Ida:** cf. IV.52, with n.

**Atramyttium:** at the eastern end of the Gulf of Atramyttium, which faces the northeastern side of Lesbos.

**(after having been removed from their homes by the Athenians because of the purification of Delos):** in 422; see V.1, 32.

**VIII.109. Miletus:** see VIII.84.

**Cnidus:** Tissaphernes had organized its revolt in the of winter 412/11 (VIII.35). Th. has made no mention of its garrison being driven out.

**He was also upset by the idea of Pharnabazus receiving their help:** cf. VIII.99.

# Glossary

Brief definitions of the following terms can be found at the references given.

admiral: I.48
agora: I.67
arbitration: I.28
archon: I.93
assembly: I.31
boule: IV.118
cleruch, cleruchy: III.50
colonization: I.12
deme: II.19
drachma: I.27
ephor: I.18
general: I.48
governor: I.115
helot: I.101
hoplite: I.49
knight: III.16
metic: II.13
ostracism: VIII.73
peltast: II.29
Pentacosiomedimni: III.16
perioeci: I.101
phalanx: I.49
polis: I.2
proxenia, proxenos: II.29
prytaneis, prytany: IV.118
Sophist: I.32
Spartiate: IV.8
stasis: I.2
synoecism: I.10
Thetes: III.16
tribe: II.34
tribute: I.96, II.13
trireme: I.14
trophy: I.30
tyrant: I.13
Zeugitae: III.16

# Select Bibliography


Thucydidean Studies

Adcock, F. *Thucydides and His History.* Cambridge: Cambridge University Press, 1963.

Cogan, M. *The Human Thing: The Speeches and Principles of Thucydides' History.* Chicago: University of Chicago Press, 1981.

de Romilly, J. *Histoire et raison chez Thucydide.* Paris: Les Belles Lettres, 1956.

Dover, K.J. *Thucydides.* Greece and Rome: New Surveys in the Classics, no. 7. Oxford: Oxford University Press, 1973.

Finley, J.H. *Thucydides.* Cambridge: Harvard University Press, 1942. Reprint, Ann Arbor: University of Michigan Press, 1963.

———. *Three Essays on Thucydides.* Cambridge: Harvard University Press, 1967.

Hunter, V. *Thucydides the Artful Reporter.* Toronto: Hakkert, 1973.

———. *Past and Process in Herodotus and Thucydides.* Princeton: Princeton University Press, 1982.

Pouncey, P. *The Necessities of War: A Study of Thucydides' Pessimism.* New York: Columbia University Press, 1980.

Rawlings, H.H. *The Structure of Thucydides' History.* Princeton: Princeton University Press, 1981.

Stadter, P.A., ed. *The Speeches in Thucydides.* Chapel Hill: University of North Carolina, 1973.

Westlake, H.D. *Individuals in Thucydides.* Cambridge: Cambridge University Press, 1968.

Woodhead, A.G. *Thucydides on the Nature of Power.* Cambridge: Harvard University Press, 1970.

Thucydidean Commentaries

Dover, K.J. *Thucydides Book VI.* Oxford: Oxford University Press, 1975.

———. *Thucydides Book VII.* Oxford: Oxford University Press, 1978.

Rhodes, P.J. *Thucydides History III.* Warminster: Aris and Phillips, 1994.

Rusten, J.S. *Thucydides Book II.* Cambridge: Cambridge University Press, 1989.

Rutter, N.K. *Thucydides Books VI and VII.* Bristol: Bristol Classical Press, 1989 (now London: Duckworth).

Wiedemann, T. *Thucydides I–II.65.* Bristol: Bristol Classical Press, 1985 (now London: Duckworth).

## General Historical Works

Davies, J.K. *Democracy and Classical Greece.* London: Fontana, 1978.

Hammond, N.G.L. *A History of Greece to 322 B.C.* 3d ed. Oxford: Oxford University Press, 1986.

Hornblower, S. *The Greek World, 479–323 B.C.* London: Methuen, 1983.

Kagan, D. *The Archidamian War.* Ithaca: Cornell University Press, 1974.

———. *The Peace of Nicias and the Sicilian Expedition.* Ithaca: Cornell University Press, 1981.

Sealey, R. *A History of the Greek City States, ca. 700–338 B.C.* Berkeley: University of California Press, 1976.

# Index of Places and People

Reference to a place-name should be taken to cover also the inhabitants of that place.


Abdera, 105
Abronichus, 53
Abydos, 289, 295, 302, 303
Acanthus, 187, 188, 193–95, 204
Acarnania, 14, 70, 94, 95, 106, 123, 124, 130, 163, 165, 166, 169, 185, 258
Acesines, R., 174
Achaea (Peloponnese), 68, 70, 73, 96, 127, 162, 174, 228, 259
Achaea Phthiotis. *See* Phthiotis
Acharnae, 102, 103
Achelous, R., 166
Acheron, R., 34
Achilles, 14
Acrae, 229
Acragas (Agrigentum), 229, 235, 259, 261, 265
Acropolis, 81, 101, 291, 299
Acte, 187, 210
Adeimantus, 37
Adriatic, 26
Aegaleus, Mt., 102
Aegean, 2, 11, 13–15, 17, 20, 21, 36, 37, 56, 58, 69, 70, 77, 85, 129, 165, 175, 187, 193, 222, 225, 264, 273, 276, 279, 283, 287, 295
Aegina, 19, 32, 39, 40, 42, 52, 65, 68, 69, 73, 76, 87, 105, 153, 156, 180, 214, 218, 246, 256, 264, 292
Aegospotami, 122
Aenus, 129, 175
Aeolia, 246
Aeolus, 13
Aeolus, islands,161
Aeschylus, 44, 63
Aetolia, 14, 129, 163, 166, 167, 169, 264
Agamemnon, 15
Agariste, 82
Agesippidas, 215
Agis, 216, 217, 272, 274, 283, 288
Agraeans, 185
Agrigentum. *See* Acragas
Albania, 26
Alcamenes, 273
Alcibiades (i), 212
Alcibiades (ii), 6, 42, 45, 79, 81, 95, 105, 120, 122, 143, 203, 211, 212, 214, 216, 218, 219, 222, 223, 226, 227, 231–34, 237, 239, 243, 248, 249, 256, 266, 274, 275, 283–87, 289, 290, 292, 294–98, 301, 303
Alcidas, 137, 139, 140, 155, 156, 162, 187
Alcinous, 155
Alcmaeon, 131
Alcmaeonids, 81, 243, 249
Alicyae, 259
Alpheios, R., 210, 214
Alyzia, 258

Ambracia, 27, 97, 123, 126, 165, 177, 185, 251
Ambracian Gulf, 166, 258
Ameinocles, 18
Amorges, 273, 276, 279, 287
Amphiaraus, 123, 131
Amphilocia, 123
Amphipolis, 36, 37, 58, 61, 84, 115, 190–92, 199, 200, 204, 208, 232, 254, 256
Amphissa, 164
Amyclae, 205, 207
Amyrtaeus, 70, 71
Anaceum, 299
Anactorium, 35, 97, 106, 178, 209, 258
Anaia, 139, 141, 184, 276, 289
Anapus, R., 244, 251, 268
Andocides, 35
Andocides (orator), 243, 290, 300
Androcles, 143, 237, 290
Androcrates, 139
Andros, 292
Antandrus,179, 184, 303
Antiochus of Syracuse, 228
Antiphon, 187, 291, 292, 298
Antissa, 138, 140, 277
Aphrodisia, 180
Aphrodite, 241
Aphytis, 38
Apollo, 15, 18, 19, 27, 57, 79, 81, 83, 89, 101, 134, 162, 165, 189, 194, 204, 206, 228, 242, 246, 250
Apollonia, 27
Arcadia, 203, 216, 235
Arcesilaus, 282
Archelaus, 130
Archias, 174
Archidamus, 9, 12, 22, 38, 39, 46–48, 50, 78, 80, 88, 93, 95–99, 102, 103, 127, 136, 144, 151, 173, 187, 188, 202, 292
Archonidas, 253
Arctonnesus, 303
Areopagus, 81
Argilus, 84, 191, 204
Arginus, 280
Arginusae, 36, 119, 277
Argolid, Argolis, 63, 65, 105, 115
Argos (Amphilocia), 123, 165, 166
Argos (Peloponnese), 10, 15, 43, 63, 67, 71, 84, 92, 96, 123, 130, 177, 197, 202, 206, 209, 211, 213, 215–19, 222, 226, 230, 233, 235, 237, 243, 249–51, 264, 280, 296
Aristagoras, 190
Aristarchus, 298
Aristeus, 37, 123
Aristides, 53, 54, 57, 204
Aristocrates, 274, 297
Aristogiton, 23, 242
Aristophanes, 25, 30, 40, 45, 60, 62, 66, 87, 94, 103, 121, 134, 139, 143, 159, 160, 177, 231, 284, 293
Aristophon, 296
Aristotle, 166
Aristotle (writer), 22, 25, 68, 284
Arnae, 101
Arne, 17
Arrhaebaeus, 196
Arrhiani, 303
Artaphernes, 178
Artas, 259
Artaxerxes, 64, 85, 178, 273
Artemis, 19, 165
Artemisium, 24, 150
Asia, 14, 58, 60, 75, 82, 83, 86, 123, 274, 281, 282, 288
Asine, 172, 249
Asopius, 134
Asopus, R., 94
Aspasia, 139
Aspendus, 295, 296, 303
Assinarus, R., 269
Astacus, 106, 130
Astyochus, 274, 277, 280, 282, 292, 295
Atalanta, 105, 161, 205
Athena, 23, 56, 70, 75, 82, 100
Athenagoras, 12, 95, 143, 227, 234, 236, 239, 240
Athens: passim
Athos, Mt., 193, 210
Atramyttium, 179, 303
Atreus, 15

Attica, 12, 13, 16, 21, 31, 41, 64, 66, 72, 80, 86, 88, 89, 92, 97, 99, 100–102, 104, 113, 114, 124, 125, 133, 137, 141, 159, 161, 163, 169, 170, 189, 192, 204, 206, 249, 257, 261, 273, 288, 292, 293, 299

Benghazi, 262
Beroea, 37
Bisaltia, 193
Black Sea, 17, 52, 54, 109, 129, 133, 184, 235
Boeotarchs, 129, 185, 189, 211
Boeotia, 68, 70, 74, 92, 96, 133, 136, 152, 153, 163, 164, 183–85, 189, 190, 193, 197, 204–7, 209, 211, 214, 215, 232, 257, 258, 261
Bolbe, Lake, 37
Bolissus, 278
Bomians, 163
Bon, Cape, 262
Bottiaea, 37, 126, 130, 170, 186
Brasidas,14, 36, 43, 46, 58, 78, 96, 104, 127, 128, 155, 156, 162, 164, 172, 183, 185–88, 190–97, 199–203, 208–10, 212, 219, 225
Brilessus, Mt., 104
Bromiscus, 191
Bulgaria, 129
Buphras, 194
Byzantium, 54, 60, 75, 85, 95, 295

Cacyparis, R., 268
Caeadas, 84
Callians, 163
Callias, 31, 37, 51, 60, 71, 74, 141, 287
Callicles, 220
Calligeitus, 274, 282
Calydon, 164, 298
Camarina, 43, 54, 174, 182, 200, 222, 229, 235, 241, 245, 259
Cambyses, 18
Camirus, 283
Canastraeum, 194
Cantharus, 53
Cappadocia, 122
Cardamyle, 278
Caria, 14, 60, 124, 274, 282, 303
Carteria, 302
Carthage, 10, 19, 228, 233, 238, 248, 249
Carystus, 59, 72, 292
Casmenae, 229
Castor, 156, 193
Catana, 182, 200, 228, 235, 241, 244, 245, 250, 259, 260, 265, 268
Caulonia, 257
Caunus, 282, 287, 288, 303
Cecrops, 101
Cecryphalia, 65
Cenchriae, 177, 275
Centoripa, 250, 259
Cephallenia, 34, 89, 94, 95, 106, 126, 175, 210, 215, 240, 248
Ceramicus, 108, 242
Ceryces, 286
Chaereas, 294, 296
Chaeronea, 185
Chalce, 282, 287, 288
Chalcedon, 184
Chalcideus, 274, 275, 277, 278, 280, 283
Chalcidice, 37, 38, 115, 126, 130, 170, 182, 186, 193, 209, 210, 219, 230, 232
Chalcis (Corinthian Gulf), 69
Chalcis (Euboea), 20, 73, 160, 229, 232, 246, 258
Chaonia, 126
Charicles, 257
Charminus, 280, 303
Charoeades, 161
Chersonese, 52, 177, 289
Chimerium, 28
Chios, 13, 22, 35, 55, 74, 75, 97, 115, 135, 136, 141, 165, 172, 179, 196, 222, 240, 248, 256, 264, 273–78, 280, 282, 283, 288, 295
Chrysis, 93, 197
Cilicia, 71
Cimon, 1, 34, 54, 58, 61–64, 66–68, 71, 98
Cithaeron, Mt., 92, 139
Clazomenae, 141, 275–77, 280
Cleaenetus, 173

Cleandridas, 251
Clearchus, 295
Clearidas, 206
Cleisthenes, 102, 107
Cleobulus, 231
Cleombrotus, 125
Cleomenes (i), 81
Cleomenes (ii), 139
Cleon, 18, 24, 46, 48, 49, 108–11, 116, 117, 119–21, 135, 136, 139, 142–49, 151, 153, 159, 173–78, 195, 199–202, 207, 212, 221, 234, 238, 239, 292, 293
Cleonae, 250
Cleone, 217
Cleopompus, 115
Clinias, 212
Cnemus, 122, 126
Cnidus, 141, 281, 282, 285, 286, 304
Colonae, 83
Colonus, 291, 301
Colophon, 141
Conon, 258
Copais, Lake, 189
Corcyra, 18, 19, 25–38, 41, 47, 76, 81, 84, 93–95, 104, 110, 112, 114, 121, 126, 134, 137, 155–57, 159, 163, 167, 178, 237, 238, 240, 247, 257–59, 264
Corfu, 26
Corinth, 18, 27, 28, 30–36, 38, 39, 41, 42, 45, 47, 48, 60, 64, 65, 68, 72–74, 76–78, 86, 95, 111, 117, 127, 134, 135, 137, 177, 178, 180, 182, 204, 206, 213, 218, 219, 232, 238, 245, 247, 251, 259, 264, 274, 300
Corinth, Isthmus of, 18, 64, 65, 102, 177, 183, 205, 274
Coronea, 152, 153, 189, 212
Corycus, 275
Coryphasium, 194, 205, 264
Cos, 282, 287, 303
Cotyrta, 180
Cranii, 215
Crestonia, 193
Crete, 13, 14, 127, 128
Crissaean Gulf, 67, 124, 127
Crocylium, 163
Croesus, 18, 20
Crommyon, 177
Cropia, 102
Ctesias, 69
Cumae (Aeolis), 277
Cumae (Italy), 229
Cyclades, 14
Cyclopes, 228
Cyllene, 28
Cylon, 81
Cynossema, 303
Cynuria, 105, 202
Cyprus, 54, 56, 64, 65, 71
Cyrene, 70, 262
Cyrus (Persian king), 18, 20
Cyrus (satrap), 122
Cythera, 179, 180, 194, 196, 202, 205, 210, 219, 256, 264, 273
Cyzicus, 141

Danube, R., 129
Daphnus, 278, 280
Dardanelles, 52
Dardanus, 303
Darius (son of Artaxerxes), 74, 178, 273, 281, 287, 288, 294
Darius (son of Hystaspes), 19, 20, 190, 243, 279
Dascon, 244
Dascylium, 274
Decelea, 79, 88, 114, 160, 206, 249, 256, 257, 261, 273, 292, 294, 299, 301
Delium, 120, 185, 188–90, 202
Delos, 15, 18, 21, 22, 55, 57, 69, 96, 113, 165, 199, 209, 242, 303
Delphi, 27, 67, 71, 72, 76, 78, 79, 81, 83, 86, 89, 101, 151, 162, 164, 194, 204
Delphinium, 280
Demeter, 101, 237
Demosthenes (general), 95, 119, 161–66, 169–71, 175, 184, 245, 255, 256, 258–60, 268, 269
Demosthenes (orator), 44
Dercyllidas, 288
Derdas, 37
Deucalion, 13

Diacritus, 98
Diitrephes, 289
Diodorus, 41, 51, 54, 55, 60, 65, 68, 69, 72, 75, 118, 124, 162, 297, 302
Diodotus, 24, 46, 74, 78, 116, 119, 144–48, 151, 157, 224
Diomedon, 277, 280, 287
Dionysius of Halicarnassus, 53
Dionysus, 101, 205, 242, 299
Dioscuri, 156, 193, 299
Dium, 210, 219
Dolopia, 59
Dorians, 17, 21, 52, 79, 114, 162, 177, 181, 201, 230, 246, 254, 267, 278
Dorieus, 134, 281, 295
Doris, 66
Doriscus, 58, 60
Doros, 13
Drabescus, 61, 190
Durres, 26
Dyrrachium, 26

Edonians, 193
Eetionia, 298
Egesta, 33, 69, 228–30, 232, 234, 235, 238, 241, 259, 265
Egypt, 65, 69, 70, 71, 109, 281, 297
Eion, 170
Eion (Strymon), 58, 60, 61, 178, 190–92, 200
Elaeus, 302, 303
Eleusis, 73, 101, 102, 237
Elis, 15, 28, 78, 204, 206, 209, 210, 213, 215, 232, 233
Elymi, 232
Endius, 212, 274
Enipeus, R., 186
Ephesus, 165, 277
Ephialtes, 62, 67, 108
Epicles, 303
Epidamnus, 26, 28, 31, 92, 95, 155
Epidaurus, 34, 65, 72, 89, 114, 135, 177, 214, 215, 218, 219, 237, 256, 299
Epipolae, 246, 250, 253, 260, 261
Epirus, 12, 27, 28
Erae, 277
Erectheus, 101
Eresus, 138, 140, 141, 277, 302, 303
Eretria, 73, 82
Erineus, R., 259, 268
Erythrae (Boeotia), 139
Erythrae (Ionia), 108
Eryx, Mt., 228, 241
Eteocles, 123
Etna, Mt., 167, 250
Etruria, 19, 193, 248, 251, 263
Euboea, 17, 25, 50, 58, 59, 72, 73, 92, 100, 104–6, 134, 137, 160, 160–62, 229, 257, 258, 264, 272, 273, 288, 294, 296, 298, 299
Eucles, 191
Euctemon, 280
Euesperitae, 262
Eumenides, 81
Eumolpidae, 286
Eumolpus, 101
Eupalium, 164
Euphemus, 42–45, 54, 79, 221, 222, 248
Eupolis, 87
Euripus, 258
Europe, 288
Eurotas, 210, 216
Euryelus, 250, 253, 260
Eurylochus, 165
Eurymedon, 119, 156, 157, 167, 169, 178, 227, 255, 258–60, 262
Eurymedon, R., 60, 65
Eurystheus, 15
Euthydemus, 255, 266
Euxine Sea, 129
Evarchus, 106, 130

Fiumaro di Noto, 269

Galepsus, 192, 200
Gallipoli, 52
Gela, 200, 229, 235
Gelon, 19, 229, 234
Geraestus, 134
Geraneia, Mt., 64, 67
Gongylus, 82
Graecia, 12

Granicus, R., 303
Gylippus, 251, 253, 262, 266, 268, 269
Gytheum, 69, 269

Hagnon, 75, 115, 129, 190, 201, 237, 272, 292
Haliae, 65
Halicarnassus, 282, 303
Hamaxitus, 302
Harmatus, 302
Harmodius, 23, 242
Harpagium, 303
Harpina, 214
Hebrus, R., 129
Helen, 15
Helixus, 295
Hellanicus, 23, 57, 92
Hellas, 10, 12–14, 18, 29, 30, 42, 46, 47, 56, 60, 69, 79, 80, 86–88, 96, 98, 123, 135, 141, 150–52, 228, 246, 248, 260, 263, 265, 266, 269, 272, 276, 283
Hellen, 12, 13
Hellenic Sea, 14
Hellespont, 52, 58, 60, 77, 83, 122, 179, 242, 278, 282, 288, 289, 302, 303
Helorus, 244
Hephaestus, 161
Hera, 27, 93, 197
Heraclea (Black Sea), 184
Heraclea (Trachis), 27, 162, 164, 185, 201, 214
Heracles, 17, 203, 267
Heraclids, 17, 27, 130, 228
Heraea, 217
Hermes, 236
Hermione, 34
Hermocrates, 12, 42, 46, 56, 78, 79, 85, 151, 160, 209, 238–40, 245–47, 267, 279, 296, 300
Hermon, 298
Herodotus (Hdt.), 2–5, 9, 12, 13, 16–21, 26, 32, 44, 52–55, 57, 58, 60, 63, 65, 66, 74, 77, 80, 81, 83, 85, 92, 93, 96, 129, 130, 150, 152, 157, 162, 176, 190, 193, 211, 229, 234, 242, 247, 274, 278, 303
Hesiod, 163
Hestiaea, 73, 246, 264, 299
Hetoimaridas, 54
Hieramenes, 288
Hieron, 19
Hierophon, 166
Himera, 167, 229, 234, 244
Hipparchus, 23, 242
Hippias, 242, 249
Hippobotae, 73
Hippocles, 243
Hippocrates (Athenian), 104, 185
Hippocrates (Geloan), 229
Hippocrates (Spartan), 280, 302
Hippocrates of Cos, 112
Homer, 2, 13, 14, 16, 24, 93, 111, 155, 165, 203, 228
Hyacinthus, 207
Hybla, 250
Hyccara, 255
Hyperbolus, 120, 142, 290, 293
Hysiae (Argos), 219
Hysiae (Boeotia), 139

Ialysus, 283
Iapygia, 237, 259
Iasus, 276, 279, 281, 287
Icarus, 302
Ida, Mt., 303
Idacus, 303
Illyria, 14, 27, 196
Imbros, 134, 175, 201, 264
Inessa, 165, 250
Ion, 13, 57
Ionia, 2, 13, 14, 17, 19, 24, 43, 52, 54, 57, 67, 79, 96, 101, 140, 141, 162, 165, 190, 201, 229, 246, 247, 254, 275, 278, 287
Ionian/Ionic Gulf, 26, 129, 251, 259
Ionian Sea, 233, 237, 239
Ischagoras, 206
Istanbul, 83, 295
Istone, Mt., 159
Italy, 10, 17, 31, 33, 109, 193, 200, 227, 235, 237, 240, 243, 249, 251, 259, 264

Itamenes, 141
Ithome, Mt., 61, 62, 66

Labdalum, 250, 253
Lacedaimonius, 34, 98
Laches, 159, 161, 167, 212, 227, 230, 241, 246, 249
Laconia, 16, 61, 68, 105, 172, 180, 209, 210, 273, 288, 298
Laespodias, 296
Laestrygonians, 228
Lamachus, 184, 231, 241, 251, 254, 260
Lampsacus, 141, 243, 289
Larissa, 186, 302
Las, 298
Laurium, 114, 249
Lebedus, 277
Lectum, 302
Leda, 156, 193
Lelantine Plain, 20
Lemnos, 74, 134, 175, 201, 264
Leocorium, 243
Leon (Athenian), 277, 280, 287
Leon (Spartan), 279, 289
Leon (in Syracuse), 250
Leonidas, 83
Leontini, 31, 33, 69, 160, 200, 228–32, 235, 238
Leos, 243
Leotychides, 52
Lepreum, 209, 210, 214, 216
Leros, 279
Lesbos, 22, 41, 55, 57, 74, 75, 83, 97, 115, 133, 148, 179, 199, 222, 240, 246, 273, 277, 302, 303
Leucadia, 177, 275
Leucas, 27, 28, 97, 134, 137, 162, 170, 251, 253, 258, 274, 275
Leuconium, 278
Leuctra, 215
Libya, 70
Lichas, 96, 206, 214, 218, 276, 281, 282, 286, 296
Lindus, 283
Lipara, islands, 161
Locri (Epizephyrian), 97, 160, 164, 169, 174, 240, 253, 257, 259, 298
Locri (Opuntian), 97, 160, 283
Locri (Ozolian), 14, 64, 68, 97, 160, 163
Lycaeum, Mt., 203
Lycia, 60, 124
Lycurgus, 21
Lydia, 18, 20, 122, 140
Lyncestians, 186
Lyncus, 197
Lysander, 122
Lysias, 298
Lysicles, 139
Lysimeleia, 263

Macarius, 166
Macedon(ia), 12, 27, 36, 37, 77, 94, 129, 130, 196
Maeander, R., 86, 286, 288
Maenalia, 216–18
Magnesia, 86
Malea (Laconia), 282
Malian Gulf, 190
Mantinea, 197, 208, 213, 215–19, 230, 233, 235, 237, 243, 244, 249, 272
Marathon, 12, 21, 43, 58, 108, 150
Marcellinus, 1, 2, 142, 207, 208
Mardonius, 100
Marea, 64
Marseilles, 19
Massalia, 19
Mecyberna, 204
Medes, 18, 152
Mediterranean, 14, 20
Megacles, 82
Megara, 20, 25, 32, 39, 40, 42, 63–65, 67, 72, 73, 76, 96, 99, 102, 106, 128, 177, 183, 185, 188, 193, 204, 206, 209, 232, 264, 299
Megara (Sicily), 229, 240, 241, 250, 257, 265
Megarid, 64, 66, 68, 92, 99, 106, 177, 183
Melanchridas, 274, 277
Melanthus, 273

Melesias, 75, 119
Melesippus, 98
Melesius, 296
Melitia, 186
Melos, 15, 43, 44, 89, 97, 125, 135, 136, 141, 145, 150, 151, 153, 155, 161, 162, 200, 209, 220–26, 245–47, 265, 266, 282
Memphis, 65
Menander, 255
Mende, 195, 197, 200
Mendes, 70
Menedaius, 166
Menelaus, 15, 203
Meropis, 282
Messenia, 16, 61, 62, 97, 156, 166, 170, 216, 248, 264
Messenian Gulf, 172
Messina, 161, 169, 174, 200
Metapontum, 259
Methana, 177, 205, 210
Methone, 37, 77, 196, 230
Methymna, 133, 148, 222, 240, 248, 264, 277, 302, 303
Midius, R., 303
Miletus, 74, 179, 276, 278, 279, 280, 282, 283, 285, 287, 288, 295–97, 302, 303
Miltiades, 58
Mindarus, 302, 303
Minoa, 149, 183, 194
Minoans, 14
Minos, 11, 14
Minyae, 185
Molycrium, 164
Monte Climiti, 268
Morgantina, 182
Motya, 228
Munychia, 53, 298, 299
Mycale, 21, 24, 52, 70, 135
Mycalessus, 258, 267
Mycenae, 15
Mygdonia, 37
Myrcinus, 192
Myronides, 66, 68, 189, 218
Mytilene, 78, 110, 117, 123, 128, 133–36, 138–42, 173, 179, 184, 231, 242, 246, 275, 277

Nabeul, 262
Naupactus, 64, 68, 69, 73, 94, 97, 124, 128, 134, 155, 156, 164, 175, 214, 248, 255, 258, 259, 260, 264
Naxos (Aegean), 55, 59, 75, 85, 159
Naxos (Sicily), 160, 174
Neapolis, 262
Nemea, 163, 215
Nepos, 44, 75
Nestus, R., 129
Niceratus, 149
Nicias, 9, 12, 13, 42, 44, 57, 85, 91, 95, 96, 105, 109, 116, 119, 120, 122, 127, 149, 161, 175–77, 179–81, 187, 194, 196, 199, 200, 202, 203, 206, 207, 212, 219, 225, 227, 230–32, 234–37, 239–41, 244, 245, 249, 251, 254–56, 260–67, 269
Nicostratus, 196
Nile, R., 64, 65, 70
Nisaea, 64, 72, 73, 106, 174, 183, 184, 188, 190, 194, 204
Nisus, 194
Notium, 141, 277

Odrysia, 129
Oedipus, 123
Oeniadae, 70, 126, 130, 134, 155, 163, 185
Oeneon, 163, 164
Oenoe (Argolid), 63, 65
Oenoe (Attica), 102, 301
Oenophyta, 68, 163, 189
Oesime, 192
Oetaeans, 272, 273
Oinous, R., 210
Old Oligarch, 45, 68, 74, 77, 109, 116, 119, 236, 284
Olorus (i), 1, 191
Olorus (ii), 1
Olpae, 95, 164, 166
Olympia, 15, 56, 67, 78, 86, 89, 135, 143, 173, 205, 209, 213, 214

Olympieium, 244, 260
Olynthus, 37, 204
Oneion, Mt., 177
Onomacles, 278
Opicia, 228, 229
Orchomenus (Arcadia), 216, 218
Orchomenus (Boeotia), 185
Orestheum, 216
Oreus, 299
Orneae, 217, 230
Oropus, 104, 161, 257, 288, 299
Ortygia, 253, 257, 263
Oscius, R., 129

Pagondas, 20
Pallene, 36, 38, 194
Pamphylia, 60
Panactum, 200, 205, 210, 211
Panormus (Asia), 278
Panormus (Sicily), 228
Pantacyas, R., 228
Paris, 15
Parnes, Mt., 104
Parrhasians, 210
Parthenon, 99, 100
Patrae, 214, 259
Pausanias (king of Sparta), 97, 139
Pausanias (Macedonian), 37
Pausanias (Spartan), 44, 54, 80–85, 125, 150, 153
Pausanias (writer), 63, 67, 86, 134, 208
Paxos, 28
Pedaritus, 279–81, 289
Pegae, 64, 67, 70, 72, 73, 174, 183
Peithias, 105
Pelasgians, 13, 193
Pella, 37
Pellene, 195
Peloponnese: passim
Pelops, 15
Pentelicon, Mt., 104
Perdiccas, 36, 94, 105, 126, 129, 186, 192, 196, 197, 200, 219, 230, 254
Pericles, 6, 12, 15, 18, 20, 22, 24, 32, 42, 44–49, 70–72, 75, 76, 78, 79, 81, 82, 85–88, 90, 98–103, 106–11, 114–21, 125, 127, 137, 139, 141–44, 146, 147, 158, 160, 170, 175, 178, 181, 182, 203, 211, 221, 231–33, 237, 239, 240, 257, 266, 271, 292, 301
Perrhaebia, 186
Persephone, 101, 237
Perseus, 15
Persia, 3, 10, 17–21, 42, 44, 46, 48, 49, 52–54, 56, 60, 61, 63–65, 69, 71, 90, 94, 96, 100, 122, 123, 125, 135, 141, 150, 152, 153, 162, 178, 190, 229, 234, 238, 246, 247, 257, 273, 276, 278, 280, 284, 287–89
Phacius, 186
Phaeacia, 27
Phaedon, 59
Phalerum, 53, 66, 100, 298
Phanae, 278
Pharnabazus, 123, 274, 282, 288, 295, 302, 304
Pharnaces, 123, 199, 274, 288
Pharos, 64
Pharsalus, 70, 185
Phaselis, 303
Philip (Macedon), 37, 129
Philip (Spartan), 279, 297
Philocharidas, 206, 212
Philoctetes, 16, 19
Phlius, 215
Phocaea, Phocaeid, 19, 277, 302
Phocis, 66, 68, 70, 71, 97, 163, 228
Phoenicia, 20, 61, 65, 71, 228, 241
Phormio, 35, 37, 75, 88, 95, 106, 123, 126, 127, 130, 131, 134, 155
Phrygia, 104, 122
Phrynicus, 46, 278, 279, 285–87, 290, 298
Phthiotis, 14, 186, 273
Phyrcus, 214
Piraeus, 19, 53, 65, 66, 100, 128, 130, 149, 292, 294, 299, 300
Pisander, 286, 289–93, 298, 301
Pisistratids, 46, 187, 242, 243, 292
Pisistratus, 18, 20, 21, 57, 101, 165, 241, 242, 249
Pissuthnes, 71, 74, 75, 140, 141, 273

Plataea, 21, 24, 49, 80, 91–94, 102, 108, 125, 139, 146, 149–54, 156, 183, 187, 188, 190, 206, 209, 220, 223, 256, 264
Pleistarchus, 54, 83
Pleistoanax, 67, 72, 97, 103, 139, 203
Plemmyrium, 253, 256, 257
Pleuron, 164
Plutarch (Plut.), 1, 32, 33, 40, 53–56, 58–63, 66–68, 71–73, 75, 81, 84, 85, 87, 96–98, 109, 116, 118, 119, 143, 160, 212, 226, 236, 251, 275, 290, 293, 298, 300
Pnyx, 291, 300
Polichna, 275
Pollis, 123
Pollux, 156, 193
Polycrates, 18, 165
Polydeuces, 156
Pontus, 133, 184
Poseidon, 82, 127, 194
Potidaea, 25, 27, 36–38, 41, 75–77, 81, 87, 92, 100, 106, 115, 119, 123, 124, 126, 135, 138, 197, 209, 237, 246
Potidania, 163
Prasiae (Attica), 299
Prasiae (Laconia), 256
Priam, 15
Priapus, 303
Priene, 74
Procne, 105
Propontis, 129, 274, 289, 303
Propylaea, 99
Proschium, 164
Proteas, 104
Protesilaus, 303
Psammethicus, 71
Pteleum, 278, 280
Ptelium, 205
Ptychia, 178
Pydna, 37, 230
Pylos, 79, 88, 96, 120, 170, 172, 174–76, 179, 186, 197, 201, 202, 205, 208, 212, 215, 219, 226, 232, 249, 251, 256, 257, 264, 267, 269
Pyrrha, 138–41, 277
Pythia, 101, 205
Pythion, 72
Pythium, 242
Pythodorus, 93, 119, 167, 169

Ramphias, 201, 274
Rhegium, 31, 33, 69, 160, 169, 229, 241
Rheitus, 177
Rhium (Achaea), 214
Rhium (Molycrium), 214
Rhodes, 281–83, 286, 287, 288, 302
Rhodope, Mt., 129
Rhoeteum, 179

Sadocus, 105
Salaethus, 141
Salamis, 19, 24, 37, 44, 52, 53, 80, 90, 247
Salynthius, 185
Saminthus, 215
Samos, 18, 32, 41, 55, 57, 62, 70, 72, 74, 75, 95, 124, 139, 141, 144, 145, 148, 165, 179, 229, 246, 275–77, 280, 286, 289, 292, 294, 295, 302
Sane, 205
Santa Panagia, 250
Sardis, 74, 273
Saronic Gulf, 19, 64, 65, 105, 137, 156, 177, 188, 214, 274
Scione, 195, 197, 200, 205–7, 209, 221, 226
Sciritis, 217
Scironides, 278, 287
Scolus, 204
Scyros, 58
Scythia, 14
Segesta. *See* Egesta
Selinus, 229, 235, 241, 249, 254, 265
Sermyle, 205
Sestos, 52, 289, 295, 303
Sicanus, 262
Sicels, 161, 165, 174, 238, 240, 251, 253, 259, 265
Sicilian Sea, 174, 233
Sicily, 10, 17, 19, 20, 26, 31, 33, 44, 47, 77, 78, 89, 95, 96, 109, 110, 120, 122, 135, 160, 161, 165, 167, 169, 174, 178,

180, 181, 183, 200, 209, 212, 227–33, 235, 236, 238–41, 245, 247, 249–51, 253, 254, 258, 259, 261, 264, 266, 271, 272, 275, 279, 285, 300
Sicyon, 65, 70, 72, 219
Sidussa, 278
Sigeum, 242, 243
Simonides, 170
Singaeaens, 204
Sisyphus, 177
Sitalces, 94, 105, 114, 123, 129, 130, 190
Sithonia, 193
Sollium, 106, 163, 209
Soloeis, 228
Solon, 100, 112, 137, 240
Solygia, 177
Sophists, 3, 24, 29, 30, 143, 144, 246
Sophocles (general), 119, 167, 169, 190
Sophocles (tragedian), 272
Sparta: passim
Spartolus, 126, 204
Sphacteria, 96, 170, 172, 174, 180, 201, 202, 207, 210, 212, 218, 256, 269
Spiraeum, 276, 277
Sthenelaidas, 6, 24, 39, 48–50, 137, 144, 153, 234, 273
Streams, The, 102
Strombichides, 275, 280, 289, 298
Strymon, R., 58, 129, 170, 178, 190, 193, 200
Sunium, 114, 257, 273, 200
Sybota, 33, 34, 156
Symaethus, R., 244
Syme, 282, 303
Syracuse, 15, 19, 31, 35, 45, 161, 182, 228, 229, 234, 235, 238, 239, 241, 243–46, 248, 250, 253, 254, 256, 257, 260–63, 266–69, 296, 300

Taenarus, 82, 84, 256
Tamos, 280, 296, 302 .
Tanagra, 67, 68, 185, 187, 218
Tarentum, 239, 240, 251, 298
Tegea, 197, 209, 211, 216, 217, 219
Teichussa, 279
Tellaro, R., 269
Temenids, 130
Temenitis, 253
Tenedos, 141
Tenos, 292
Teos, 276, 277
Tereus, 105
Terias, R., 241, 250
Terinean Gulf, 251
Teutiaplus, 140
Teutlussa, 282
Thapsus, 229, 250, 262
Thasos, 41, 55, 61–63, 65, 67, 85, 105, 129, 144, 148, 191, 289, 290
Thebes, 53, 80, 91–93, 125, 145, 150–53, 185, 187, 256, 261
Themistocles, 19, 21, 42, 44, 46, 52–54, 59, 80–86, 117, 286
Theopompus, 67, 71, 300
Thera, 97, 262
Theramenes, 292, 297
Therimenes, 279, 281, 283, 286
Thermaic Gulf, 37, 130, 230
Therme, 37, 106
Thermopylae, 24, 83, 162, 176
Theseus, 46, 58, 101
Thespiae, 150, 197, 250, 257, 261
Thesprotis, 28
Thessalonica, 37
Thessalus, 242
Thessaly, 14, 17, 59, 63, 67, 68, 70, 104, 164, 185, 186, 188, 192, 201, 283
Thoricus, 299
Thrace, 1, 14, 37, 58, 60, 84, 94, 105, 126, 129, 162, 185, 209, 230, 232, 272, 289
Thrasicles, 277
Thrasybulus, 290, 294, 298
Thrasylus, 294
Thrasymachus, 220
Thria, 73
Thronium, 105
Thucydides (Th.) (author): passim
Thucydides (Athenian), 75
Thucydides (Pharsalian), 229
Thucydides (son of Melesias), 119

Thurii, 33, 36, 69, 243, 248, 251, 259, 265, 281, 289
Thymochares, 299
Thyrea, 105, 211, 250
Tichium, 163
Timagoras, 274, 282
Tissaphernes, 273, 276, 279–84, 286–90, 295–97, 302–4
Tolmides, 68, 70, 72
Tomeus, 194
Torone, 153, 193–95, 199, 200, 205, 209, 226, 266
Trachis, 162, 185, 201
Triopium, 281, 288
Troad, 83, 179, 302
Troezen, 34, 52, 73, 174, 177, 195
Trogilus, 250, 253
Trotilus, 228
Troy, 15, 16, 44, 83, 228
Tunisia, 262
Tydeus, 281
Tyndareus, 15
Tyrrhenians, 193
Tyrrhenian Sea, 174, 243

Xanthippus, 70, 82
Xenares, 213, 231
Xenophon (general), 124
Xenophon (historian), 36, 54, 105, 119, 162, 207, 226, 233, 274, 296, 301
Xerxes, 19, 21, 64, 85, 100, 152, 178, 193, 278, 283
Xuthos, 113

Zacynthus, 94, 95, 122, 126, 170–72, 175, 248
Zancle, 229
Zea, 53
Zeus, 15, 16, 78, 89, 156, 193, 203, 209, 214, 242, 267
Zeuxidamus, 102